No, Not Bloomsbury

No, Not Bloomsbury

MALCOLM BRADBURY

New York   Columbia University Press   1988

823.912
BRA

c. 1

Printed in Great Britain by
St Edmundsbury Press, Bury St Edmunds, Suffolk

Library of Congress Cataloging-in-Publication Data

Bradbury, Malcolm, 1932-
 No, not Bloomsbury.

 1. English fiction — 20th century — History and
criticism.   I. Title.
PR883.B64   1988   823'.912'09   87-23845
ISBN 0-231-0672 6-7

For Rachel Temperley with love

CONTENTS

PART FOUR: Celebrating the Occasion

INTRODUCTION

The essays here, the first of two collections, all have to do in one way or another with the busy and creative period in British writing, and especially in the novel, that came after the Second World War and, as far as I know, still thrives about us. The pieces have all been restudied and rewritten, but they come from some twenty-five years of writing, reviewing, teaching, lecturing, travelling, fiction-making and having the occasional rest. They are the essays of a writer who is also a critic, a critic who is also a writer, and though quite a number of them deal in part with the theoretical adventures of recent literary criticism they are also very much concerned with the practicalities of writing and are decidedly intended to be readable.

As I explain in my starting essay, the co-habitation between the writer and the teacher-critic has been common enough over recent years, but it creates its tensions and poses its problems. I am critic enough to believe passionately that there is good literature only when there is a serious critical debate alive, surrounding and stimulating artistic activity and judgement. I am writer enough to believe that it is not history, culture or language that is the sole source of literature, but hard-working, creatively vital writers themselves, and that much theory comes from too little understanding of actual practice. So some of these essays, particularly in the back end of the book, have a strong practical cast, and they basically derive from the working occasions of writing – from the novelist entering television, growing involved in prize-giving, and attending to and keeping abreast of the creative achievements of one's own contemporaries and successors.

The essays here fall into four sections – "Writer and Critic", largely about my own experience as a writer in an age of challenged humanism; "Decades and Seasons", an exploration of our literary culture since the 1940s; "Contemporary Writers", large essays about the novelists and critics of our time I consider most important; and "Celebrating the Occasion", essays or extended reviews which concern the current state of writing and the work of some of the most important newer authors.

If I were asked to distinguish the main themes here, I would say there were three. One is the belief that we have been through and are still in an extremely vital period in British writing. The criticism of British fiction in recent years has often been thin and patronising. Indeed it is sometimes supposed that the British, as they sink giggling into the sea, may produce the odd splendid artefact, but it will almost certainly be of a traditional kind, literature's variant on Cooper's Oxford Marmalade or a Laura Ashley fabric. I see a time of great literary power and considerable innovation and experiment, and at the moment an exciting revival of serious fiction that I trust will go on. Another concern is the way in which our modern ideas, our modern sense of history and of the nature of the person, have pressed on our humanism, and affected the spirit of our writing. And a third theme is the belief that literature is an international form, the novel a serious and developing mode of enquiry, and that an awareness of our most powerful fictions is as profound an insight into our lives and condition as there is.

Many people have helped these essays and this book into existence. I must particularly thank Tom Rosenthal, who has stimulated many of the thoughts of this book as well as the book itself. Another is Anthony Thwaite, who not only edited this text but, in previous editorial incarnations, commissioned the original form of a fair number of the pieces that make it up. I am equally indebted to many other editors, perhaps particularly Brian Cox and Tony Dyson, who stirred me to action. Another important debt is to Catherine Carver, who edited a previous collection of my essays, *Possibilities*, from which some of these pieces (now much updated) are drawn. I am also grateful to Chris Bigsby, David Lodge, Angus Wilson, Ihab Hassan, Harriet Harvey Wood, Lorna Sage, and many colleagues at the University of East Anglia, where, I am happy to say, the study of contemporary literature is a thriving affair. And of course I am endlessly grateful to Elizabeth, my wife, who stops me writing when I have done too much of it, and makes sure it ends up with its true destination, the reader.

PART ONE

Writer and Critic

WRITER AND CRITIC

"We laymen have always been intensely curious to know ... from what sources that strange being, the creative writer, draws his material ... Our interest is only heightened the more by the fact that, if we ask him, the writer himself gives us no explanation, or none that is satisfactory ... "
> *Sigmund Freud, "Creative Writers and Day-dreaming" (1908)*

"I begin to hate criticism. Nothing can come of it."
> *Sir Walter Raleigh (1906)*

"Rather than occasional criticism by amateurs, I should think the whole enterprise might be seriously taken in hand by professionals. Perhaps I use a distasteful figure, but I have the idea that what we need is Criticism, Inc., or Criticism, Ltd."
> *John Crowe Ransom, "Criticism, Inc." (1938)*

1 From time to time, forsaking all else, I go out into the world and give lectures, finding myself on platforms in distant rooms in foreign countries, where someone introduces me as a speaker who needs absolutely no introduction. This is generally followed by a long one, usually – according to the rules of the genre – a little inaccurate. So I am regularly announced as the notable science-fiction author whose great novel about book-burning, *Fahrenheit 451*, will never be forgotten, unless of course they burn it; or else as the author of the great masterwork of modernity and Mexico, *Under the Volcano* – which, it was once explained, I published exactly ten years before my death from excess in 1957. But more often introductions are truer without quite being truth. At the Institute of Contemporary Arts in London (where momentous aesthetic issues are regularly discussed virtually within earshot of the Queen), I was welcomed as the well-known author of *Skipping Westward*, presumably one of my more lighthearted and carefree books, and of *The History of Man*, presumably one of my most complete and compendious. I do not say this to criticise introducers, for to them I have long been grateful. Theirs is a

difficult and boring job, generally unappreciated; I have a colleague
who usually finds it so hard and tiring he thereafter falls asleep on the
platform, lolling his head against the arm of the speaker. I am
dreadful at the task myself – I once introduced a very well-known
writer as a so-called novelist of the Angry Young Man school, instead
of a novelist of the so-called Angry Young Man school – and I have an
enormous regard for those who take on this thankless duty and get it
right, which of course is usually the case.

I mention all this to explain that the figure who sits shivering on
the platform, waiting for the applause to die down and the dreadful
realisation to sink in that I am neither Ray Bradbury nor Malcolm
Lowry but some bodged-up compound of the two, not even David
Lodge, is a sentient being like everyone else. And when one is not
worrying about people getting it wrong, one is thinking about those
who are getting it right. Recently I have found myself reflecting on a
phrase that does come up regularly in such introductions: I am, I find,
usually described as "the writer and the critic". The description is
perfectly true, and I use it of myself. I am a writer of works of fiction
and books of literary criticism. But lately I have started to speculate
rather more about this twosome. Aren't they a rather odd couple?
What kind of marriage or live-in relationship do they have? Is it happy
or sad? Who cooks and who sews? Who does what, and to whom?

There was a time when the marriage of writer and critic was
extremely close – or, as we say nowadays, symbiotic. It was often *so*
symbiotic that the writer and critic were exactly the same person, one
common and unified flesh. The great critics – Sidney and Ben
Jonson, Dryden and Samuel Johnson, Wordsworth and Coleridge
and Hazlitt – were the great writers too. Those who speculated on art
and guided taste and judgement were the creators of the art in the
first place, and their criticism not only assessed the past, judged the
present and pointed to the future but also, as Wordsworth said,
established the taste by which they might be understood. Literature's
great truths were, as Dr Johnson said, universal, and specialist cadres
working on optative counterfactuals in elegiac works were not then
deemed necessary. The critic who was not a creator was, said
Coleridge, rightly to be suspected: "Reviewers are usually people who
would have been poets, historians, biographers if they could: they
have tried their talents at one or the other, and have failed; therefore
they turn critics." There were major philosopher-critics like Lessing,
but even they were frequently willing to defer to practice, or what they
called "genius". As Lessing said in *The Laocoon*: "How many things
would prove incontestable in theory, had not genius succeeded in
proving the contrary in fact!"

And well into our own century a similar state of affairs continued.

When the great movement of modernism developed, declaring itself as *the* twentieth-century art and overturning the art and tradition of the past, there was a major supporting movement in criticism. Again, though, the great critics were largely the great writers: Valèry and Mallarmé, Eliot and Pound. Indeed, said the writers, the age needed criticism, to reconstruct the tradition and to establish the new paideuma – Pound's term for the structure of culture and thought. And, with a confidence that some might later have come to regret, many of the great moderns called for the professionalisation of the critical task. This is why Henry James wrote the prefaces to his novels, intended, he said, as "a sort of comprehensive manual or *vademecum* for aspirants in our arduous profession", but also a stimulus to critical activity. "They are, in general," he told William Dean Howells, "a sort of plea for Criticism, for Discrimination, for Appreciation and other than infantile lines – as against the so almost universal Anglo-Saxon absence of these things, which tends so, in our general trade, it seems to me, to break the heart." Indeed the cry for more and better criticism was pervasive throughout the modern movement. "Nothing will persuade the Englishman to adopt a critical attitude," complained Ford Madox Ford: he set about the task with great goodwill, and eventually, of course, ended up in France. So did Ezra Pound, who also summoned the critics to teach us *How to Read*, and how to master the new paideuma. The critical moment had come, he said, though he did add that, its work done, "criticism shd. consume itself and disappear."

Of two things we may be certain. The summons was answered, and critics appeared, celebrating Donne, displacing Milton, chasing the dissociation of sensibility, going where none had gone before to find strange deposits of wit, irony and ambiguity. Texts that had once seemed innocent objects took on strange complexions; reading a poem was no longer the same as *really* reading a poem. The other certainty is that, if criticism did to some degree consume itself (indeed that is mostly what it does), it did not then disappear. If you care to examine the pages of the trade journal called *Publications of the Modern Language Association*, or *PMLA*, you will find the literary critical profession's equivalent of the charts, the scholar's Top Ten. Here you will discover that in the United States 95 doctoral dissertations in English literature were in progress in 1945, 727 by 1965, and by 1970 there were 1,237. In 1973, when there were 1,032 theses in English, the top scorer was Shakespeare (276 theses), rather distantly followed by Faulkner (105 theses), with hard on his heels Chaucer (103 theses). Next came Milton and Henry James, who each got 99 theses on other than infantile lines, and were actually trotting ahead of Charles Dickens, who only got 97, but was way out ahead of

Melville and Spenser, trailing with only 79 apiece. Clearly God heard James's prayer for more criticism, and answered it, though as with so many prayers perhaps not quite in the way that was meant. Criticism indeed came, in ever-increasing quantities.

Just the other day I was examining another professional journal I attend to, and my eye was caught by the following advertisement: "Forthcoming," it said, "Unofficial, Unauthorized Sexual Behaviour and Its Consequences." Being over twenty-one and a serious student of art, I naturally checked where to send away for this item in plain brown cover. It proved to be an announcement for volume IX, no. 3, of *Eighteenth Century Life* (Individuals $12.50, Institutions $17.50), a learned journal which was advertising with a great many other learned journals in a special issue of my own learned journal, *The Times Literary Supplement*, or *TLS*.

I realised then that the paper was running a special supplement on the subject of learned journals, to coincide with a major conference, which was on the subject of, of course, learned journals. With mounting amazement I turned the pages, confronting my intellectual ignorance; page after page of outlets were there for contemporary critical practice – or, as they say in *West Coast Marxist Hermeneutics*, praxis. "Trenchant Sharp Vigorous Provocative", said another advertisement: "If these are among the adjectives that describe how you want your literary scholarship, you want *Critical Inquiry (CI)* and *Modern Philology (MP)*." Yet more striking still was an advertisement for another learned activity that showed that criticism was not dead, but alive, and well, and living in the New York Hilton. "You should have been there! More than a footnote to literary history. Jorge Luis Borges was there; so was Ralph Ellison. And Joyce Carol Oates, David Ignatow . . ., Kurt Vonnegut and Cynthia Ozick. Cleanth and Peter Brooks were there, not to mention Northrop Frye . . ., Wayne Booth . . ., Jonathan Culler, Stanley Fish, Terry Eagleton . . . and ten thousand other people who know and appreciate good reading and good writing. They talked about . . . androgyny, archetypes, . . . Erich Auerbach, Jane Austen, and almost seven hundred other subjects. Hilton Kramer found enough outstanding Marxists, feminists, and poststructuralist critics to fill out most of three days, and that was only a fraction of what went on at the 1983 MLA convention. If you missed it, don't worry: it happens once a year, and *you* can be there next time." As David Lodge says, it's a small world; but it sounds like a pretty big small world to me.

I think we can all agree that a certain changing of places has occurred. For, as we know, poetry is exhausted, the drama dying, and the novel already dead. The word is in crisis, the signifier has lost its signified, and the battlefield is strewn with the corpses of creation. No wonder writers go to the MLA conference to talk to Hilton Kramer, and find out how it is all done.

For criticism . . . no, criticism is not dead, or not in the sense that we usually call "dead" dead. Its written word, as it considers the collapse of language or the death of the novel, has never looked more stable or more secure. It was surely never more alive, and its practitioners wander the world in numbers never before dreamed of: at least ten thousand of them, plus Stanley Fish, Terry Eagleton, and Hilton Kramer. Its products multiply in an ever expanding labyrinth of words, part of a larger web of reading lists and set texts, footnotes and *curriculi vitarum* and conference grants, protected by complex systems of tenure and promotion. We have only to enter the bookstores to see its plenitude, and how it is jostling the works of actual creation, unless they are, of course, set texts, off the shelves. Theory abounds, enough of it to detain Hilton Kramer for very nearly all of three days. Modern scientific methods of analysis have been established. Linguistics and philosophy and anthropology, psychology and sociology and narratology, Marxism and feminism and structuralism and deconstruction have proved the great theorem, the revised new syllabus, the complete and total picture. For criticism has left the *ateliers* and the bohemian cafés or the pages of the avant garde reviews, and moved into the groves of academe. There, with its own institutional momentum and its own institutional funding, it has become what we now see it to be: independent, professionalised, an educational function, an academic subject, a tenured enterprise. Once criticism used to be called the handmaiden of writing. Today we know what happens to handmaidens; they claim their entitled liberation and go into business on their own account.

This should not surprise us. The idea of criticism's professionalisation has been an important twentiety-century aim. In 1938, John Crowe Ransom, who needs no introduction, the excellent writer and critic, proponent of irony, wrote an essay called "Criticsm, Inc." in which some of that commodity seems present. Here he suggested that criticism should leave the hands of amateurs and be taken on by professionals: "Perhaps I use a distasteful figure, but I have the idea that what we need is Criticism, Inc., or Criticism, Ltd.". Criticism, Inc., or *CRINC*, is now, as we know, an international multi-million dollar corporation, and its executives fly Club Class to conduct its business. The offices in the rue des Ecoles are in constant telex communication with the offices of Harvard, Yale and Princeton. CRINC-sponsored fellows attend CRINC-run conferences on a worldwide basis. CRINC passwords, words like *aporia* and *mis-en-abyme*, are all that is needed to gain entrance to the many CRINC conventions, their delegates readily distinguishable by both their

CRINCian lapel-badges and the large pile of inspection book copies they carry, given them by publishers specialising in CRINC-related texts.

What happened, then, to the writers? As you may see, some came too, though perhaps not quite in the star role they might once have held. Here is, as they say, a quote from the French critic Pierre Macherey (it is well known by modern students that writers write only quotes), who makes the point very clearly. "Between the writer and the critic, an irreducible difference must be posited right from the beginning . . .," Macherey, or the text bearing his name, writes. "The work that the author wrote is not precisely the work that is explicated by the critic. Let us say, provisionally, that the critic, employing a new language, brings out a *difference* within the work by demonstrating that it is *other than it is*." Today, he emphasises, the critic is no longer an understudy. He is "a prototype, a guide, a prophet of new signs".

If we give this a moment's thought, or, as we say, deconstruct it, then it is clear what is being said. Significance has moved, from writer to reader; and in the end not just to any reader, but to the critic as reader. Yet the term "reader" is too passive a term, for the critic, far from simply reading the text, rewrites it. Indeed what keeps criticism going – as opposed to reaching a dead stop because the correct reading has now been agreed – is precisely the endless rewritability of literary texts, the inexhaustible plurality of interpretation. A literary text – if, provisionally, we were to agree that there can be such a privileged entity as a "literary" text, or even a literary "text" – is thus an infinitely permutable item or commodity, a socio-psycho-culturo-linguistico-ideological discursive event constructed from the paradigmatic and syntagmatic aspects of language, the permutables of narratological discourse, the paradoxes of ontology and the sociological and ideological constraints of the episteme. In a discursive object which creates an illusion of complexity, an implied author tries to construct a delusory paradigm seeking to signify to an implied reader, in an endless circle of mutuality. Luckily there is always nowadays a critic, waiting to deconstruct this. Or, in short, criticism, freed of its old bondage to the real writer or the stable text, is now well set on the path toward becoming definitive: a system, a methodology, a new science, a meta-language. Meanwhile, back there in small wooden sheds, you may, if you care to look, discover over their writing machines the small solitary producers whose odd task it is to produce these contestable and deconstructable goods. These persons are, or used to be, called "writers".

2 What must be clear from all this is that in the age of *Critical Inquiry* and *Glyph* it is not quite the same thing as it once was to be both a writer and a critic. Today writers are lonely and humble figures, probably living, if they are British, in some country rectory, sadly fantasising about unusual sexual couplings, or else in Islington, doing much the same sort of thing. The critic, on the other hand, is almost certainly a member of a critical salariat, living on a campus or at a congress in a community of what he or she likes to call his or her peers. Writing, in short, is the trade, and criticism the profession, and the balance of power has changed quite remarkably. This is an international phenomenon, but especially true in Britain, where the new situation simply confirms an old prejudice. For in Britain the phrase "living author" has long been regarded as a contradiction in terms. The British have always thought of their writers just as the US cavalry thought about Indians: the only good one is a dead one. And to pass from simply writing writing to writing literature a passport in the form of an obituary has always been required. Literature courses in British universities are normally about the dead or the foreign. "I have been slung out of all the Senior Common rooms where his name & mine were linked," wrote a friend the other day from Oxford, where he has been writing on a British living writer who like most living British writers does his actual living in France. "Truth to tell, X [an American modernist he is also working on] earns a few boos and sneers too. But at least he's dead and a CLASSIC." There was the tragic period a few years back when – due to industrial action, which like so many British terms means its opposite – the London *Times*, which prints our best obituaries, did not appear for ten months, and any writer unfortunate or unwise enough to die in that period probably lost all hope of becoming an object of literary study. In general most British academic critics do not enjoy mixing with writers, and certainly not reading their works. And the disregard, it seems, is mutual.

Yet it used to be that critics needed writers, for it was, after all, about writers that they wrote. Nowadays, when literary theory can be practised without any reference to an author or a text, this is no longer the case. It used to be that writers needed critics, to understand and interpret what they wrote, and guide the taste by which they might be understood; today, when criticism preserves its hermetic impenetrability like some hard-won prize, not even writers can understand it. It also used to be the case that critical thought and creative speculation were virtually parts of the same process, cut, so to speak, from the same roll of cloth, so that the mind that could do the one was intimately related to the mind that could do the other. But in the modern division of functions this is increasingly unlikely, though the odd amazing example – Umberto Eco, Italo Calvino – does arise. Writers and critics still *appear* to have much in common: both are seemingly devoted to literature, and both produce written fictions. But the communities are not identical, the underlying interests not the same. And two strange worlds circle endlessly round each other, forming not so much a literary community as a literary misalliance.

So writers talk best – if they have no lover available – to other writers, for whom they are humam, and not merely items of purely scientific interest, and with whom they can discuss serious and mystical matters: the trauma of waking up in the morning with not much of anything to say, the comparative effects of coffee and tea on the compositional process, the improvements in artistic technique generated by the word processor, the track records of literary agents, the malpractices of publishers, and so on. So, in due course, late in the evening, they end up discussing the one fundamental literary question – which is, of course, the relationship between the bare, base solitude in front of the daily blank sheet of paper, and the amount of money it takes to keep you there. On the whole, in my experience, matters of high aesthetic concern tend only to get the most modest airing. Sometimes disputes of a highly technical kind do arise – is it best to write lying down, or standing up, like Hemingway, or naked, like Victor Hugo, or late at night, or in a swimming pool, or under the influence of drugs or alcohol, or outside marriage, or in a hotel in New Orleans; and should one use a pen, or an IBM computer, or write in the dust with a stick. In the United States there are creative writing courses and literary summer schools entirely devoted to such questions. But key issues, like whether to live in an age of the *scriptible* or the *lisible*, or whether Propp's thirty-one plot functions are or are not reducible to seven, or whether Paul de Man's approach bears or does not bear the mark of a lingering Sartrean influence, are only rarely engaged in.

Perhaps deep in their own skulls writers are thinking about these matters all the time, but in public they tend toward an aesthetic of silence. Today writers tend to be the pragmatists of writing, leaving critics to look after the theory. And this is why literary interviews, like those in *Paris Review*, where some hotshot young critic confronts a famous writer, often lying drunk on his back in bed, tend to be disappointing. There are exceptional writers who can spin you a fine theory at the drop of a lunch, but often they are not the best writers. Many writers do reflect somewhat on aesthetic matters, but it must be said that a good deal of their achievement, and much of the impulse of their style, arises instinctively, as a kind of intuitive bodily gesture, like walking. This is why they so frequently enrage critics when they meet them, and why critics will constantly tell you that this author or that simply does not know how good he or she is.

And that is why, just as writers talk best to other writers, critics talk best to other critics – who understand what they mean, and why they think it important. Critics can discuss with critics – but not with writers – Propp's thirty-one functions, and *lisible* and *scriptible*, and the Derridean difference, and *aporia*, and *mis en abyme*, and many other things of a similar kind which, to be honest, writers are rarely to be heard discussing at all. So these days it is the critics who make all the aesthetic running, and align the historical and linguistic imperatives under which writing must work, and invent names for movements, like postmodernism and meta-fiction, and fit writers into them. Writers once did this for themselves ("I don't care any more than you do about the word 'Naturalism'," wrote Zola. "However, I repeat it over and over again because things need to be baptized, so that the public will regard them as new"), but under the new union rules this is critical activity. Today writers seem to have little time for such things, but critics thrive on them, and many of the most profound difficulties of contemporary writing – the Plight, the Crisis of the Word, the Collapse of Signification – have been invented very largely by them.

Sometimes they find it necessary to use writers, dead or living, as examples, though, as Macherey says, mainly to make them different from what they are. For the judgements are made according to the plots and fictions the critics themselves are weaving, and this can be bewildering to writers, who believe that they plot others and are not plotted themselves. Yet criticism is, as we have seen, not a way of reading and explaining literature, but a way of rewriting it. This confuses writers, who tend to think that critics are people competent to give credible and sensible interpretations of the content and intention of their work. Content and intention! This is not what university teachers are employed for; they are there to contest the prevailing paradigmatic hegemonies, to prove the absence of the author, the death of the subject, the incongruity of the reader, and also to invigilate examinations when required.

So conflict is inevitable. Each group has different interests to serve, a different goal to reach. It is critics who talk about money in literature, in Jane Austen's novels, for example, as a "symbolic rate of exchange"; writers normally have a strong sense of the tactility of the stuff. It is critics who talk about "implied authors"; I never met an author yet who did not consider that he or she was real and not implied – even if he or she thought nothing else was. So in general writers and critics move in different ambiances, have different mistresses, go to different parties, have different patterns of speech. But they do meet on occasion, at carefully pre-planned parties, or international congresses like MLA. Yet frequently evasion and disguise is rife. The business of the writer is quite clear, to improve, or at any rate not diminish, his or her credit rating with the critical management. For today critics, whether they realise it or not, are the writer's true posterity. Once a writer was gratified by a tomb in Westminster Abbey, if, that is, the news ever got through to him. Now the important thing is to be a set text. So on these occasions the writer should always take William Faulkner's advice, and lie as convincingly as possible. Many a writer is learning the complex dimensions of this art, appearing from time to time on university campuses, or dealing with the many students who are writing a thesis on his work, and who appear on the doorstep to ask what he has written, what his ontology is, and then for a fiver for the train home. But the truth behind all these encounters is simple. Writers do not really want to be analysed, interpreted and put on record. They simply want to be totally and entirely *understood*, wordlessly valued for their irreduceable perfection. In this, of course, they are just like the rest of us.

So, far from there being a natural kinship between the writer and the critic, there is a sharp boundary. The writer must achieve literature in constant existential anxiety, wakes up each morning to the task, and never knows finally whether the result is literature or not. The critic, the apparent keeper of the gate of literary institution, is expected to make that decision, but is just as likely to suggest that there is no such gate and that the institution behind it closed down some time ago. The quarrel continues. But writers do possess one strange understanding that many critics seem not to share; they know that whatever writing is conditioned by, one of the most important is by its actual creator. They know what they did write and what they didn't write, and what they might have written and how different it all might have been. They know in short that writing is finally the product of their own existence, whatever else the critic might care to say. For critics reify writers, and writers, who are as touchy as anyone else in this liberation-hungry and self-regarding world, are inclined to resent it. So, like men and women, writers and critics often have complementary characteristics and complementary needs, which bring them into quite intimate contact on certain occasions. And, also like men and women, they have their own distinctive interests to pursue, and their own becoming to ensure. At times the boundary between them seems ridiculous. After all, every writer *is* a critic, and amends, qualifies and rewrites the works of others. And every critic is a writer, producing those distinctive plots and structures that

Jonathan Raban has nicely called "crictions". Some of our writing, our "metafiction", or "surfiction", is almost criticism. Some of our criticism is almost literature, answering metafiction with "metacriticism". The boundary is permeable, the link trembles within reach, the promise of re-merger is just before us. Yet the difference remains, and seems quite real.

3 So, in these circumstances, what sort of creature is "the writer and critic"? Well, as I have been suggesting, there are in our time many people who walk this difficult boundary, frequently wondering whether it is there at all, and even pass back and forth through the wire and into the other territory. And I, I suppose, am one of them: a critic and teacher by day, a writer by night and during the holidays, when everyone else has finished and is off in Tenerife or the Dordogne. How, then, do *I* manage the transaction? There are many versions of it, from that start of perfect equilibrium where the "creative" work intersects with the "critical", to the opposite state, where the "critical" instinct seems to be the natural adversary and destroyer of the imaginative processes.

And what kind of critic am I, what kind of writer? For many years I have been pondering these questions, but I cannot offer an easy answer. But the technical term for my own state is probably schizophrenia, or certainly divided personality. That is to say, I have this critic, a rather powerful, troublesome superego; and this writer, a sweet, passive and elusive id. My critic is a noisy fellow, obsessive with his theories of fictionality and his folklore of plot and form and topoi. He bullies and cajoles; you can hear him at it all day and most of the night. There is something to be said for him, for he works hard and reads a lot; I depend a good deal on his training, his background, and his library. Nonetheless, if I am to write fiction at all, which is what I wish most to do, then all I can do is sneak away, in the small hours, when he is quiet, and run away to America. It is a long trip, but very necessary. For there, in upper New York State, among fir trees, there is a home for battered writers, an artists' colony, where they switch off the phones all day, and where critics, if they stumble into the place, are sent right back down the path up which they came. I sit there in a studio, in a high room overlooking wet trees and a classical statue or two, where, they say, Saul Bellow wrote *Herzog* and Philip Roth *Portnoy's Complaint*: the room, it must be said, explains a lot about both books. Outside the window, one sees squirrels, and one or two other writers – poets mostly, with time to spare – jogging in shorts to keep their weight down. Roland Barthes does not come here.

Jacques Derrida is absent, or not present. No-one says *langue* or
parole or *aporia* or Cartesian ego. It is very quiet. I put paper in some
rented typewriter. And, lifting two fingers, I write.

It is, of course, classic pastoral. There is a colourful American fall.
The colonists, as they call us, have their bodily wants attended.
Lunch comes to the door in a luncheon pail, with milk in a flask, to be
consumed over the typewriter; I think Beckett worked here too. For
no-one disturbs anyone else until six; indeed the only person to
disturb you, day after day, is you yourself. As long as the book keeps
moving, the creative process functioning, it is splendid to be a writer,
writing. Naturally there are a few literary casualties; notes are found
on beds saying "Can't stand it any longer; have run away." But I can
recommend it. The eyes shine brighter, the mind in its plotting
freshens, and old assigned roles drop away in favour of the new one:
one feels entirely a writer. And other writers are nicer to you than
other critics are to you when you are a critic. This year they are largely
discussing diet, which, along with sueing doctors, has replaced sex as
the prime American cultural interest. Writing writing, undisturbed,
from morning till six, no interruptions, is an infinitely pleasing mode
of being. It has its dark days, its ugly phases of the manic cycle, when
the writing sticks or the psychic flow crosses through strange barriers.
But the self grows and spreads into the book and back again. *People*
are nicer to writers than to critics.Waiters are sometimes impressed;
personable companions pick out writers at art openings and want to
know about their work and their desires. Nothing of this kind ever
happens to critics. Pastoral is exactly what it is, but writers need it.
However, as all critics know, pastoral is an interlude, to be interrupted. And so was mine. I thought for a time I had lost him, my
critic, but I discovered he was there, indeed had never been away. For
I found him hidden, inevitably enough, in the one place I forgot to
look – right there in the pages of the book I was writing.

4 Now here, if I were introducing myself, I would need to explain
that, in the course of a busy and generally well-spent lifetime devoted
to reading and writing, editing and reviewing, teaching and examining, serving on committees and going to faculty parties, I have
industriously produced ten or so works of literary criticism and a
smaller number of novels. I have a meticulous nature in literary
matters, and I revise everything excessively; so each novel takes me
about a decade to write and for me is something like a reflection on
the decade in which it is written. In my writing lifetime, I have
published only four novels, one for each of my adult decades – a novel

apiece for the Serious Fifties, the Swinging Sixties, the Sagging Seventies and the Economic Eighties. I feel guilty for this slow rate of production, and sometimes feel it is I who is making history move forward so slowly; but given all the other things I do you will see the reason why. What is more, each one of those novels has been accompanied by a work or several works of criticism, sitting there in the next typewriter. And, like the novels, the critical books have reflected the different preoccupations of the different decades. If over those decades the novel has changed very considerably, the spirit of criticism has changed even more. Thus our marriage, this marriage of the writer and the critic, has quite a history to it, and like most old marriages it has been through many vicissitudes. Indeed, as Howard Kirk would put it, ours hasn't just been one marriage, it's been several.

I began my first novel, as a brylcreemed youth, in the early Fifties, and for a good reason; my experience at the time had been that of some portable identikit anti-hero from everybody's Fifties novel. I grew up down in the lower middle class and in the provinces, a kind of compound of Jim Dixon, Joe Lampton, Arthur Seaton and Billy Liar. I went in 1944 to grammar school, a product of the Butler Education Act, a Richard Hoggart scholarship boy. From there I went as first generation student to a redbrick university, one of the reddest, an institution which started life as the local lunatic asylum and sat across from the local cemetery; Philip Larkin was a librarian, Kingsley Amis was said to be writing some novel about it. Naturally, since I seemed to be living the Fifties novel, I started writing it. Fifties novels were all set either in provincial redbrick universities or around a rugby club in Bradford, and I chose the first, knowing little about rugby. I wrote it about liberal anxieties, and in the prevailing spirit of moral seriousness. Indeed the book radiated morality in its very title, for it was called *Eating People Is Wrong*, an opinion I changed subsequently. My critic, whom I got to know very well at the same time, was likewise a severe and virtuous fellow, deeply into F.R. Leavis and Lionel Trilling, the great tradition and the liberal imagination, a devotee of moral scruple and critical responsibility and the best that was known and thought in the world. It was true that he also believed, with Leavis, that because of the debasement of the culture and the domination of the Bloomsbury-oriented upper-middle-class metropolitan socio-literary elite no good art could now be produced. Nonetheless we got on well, and he tolerated mine, and common puritan seriousness drew us closer together. We wore homespun clothing and an air of aesthetic solemnity, and in life-enchancing Lawrentian fashion we felt part of one ebb-and-flow, members of the same moral church, signers of the same literary pledge. As you know, the plots of Fifties novels start in alienation and end in acceptance of responsibility: marriage, money and work. And so did ours. Reader, I married him.

But after the Fifties there came, as if inevitably, the Sixties, and we soon found we had to renegotiate our relationship. It was all very understandable. The atmosphere was changing everywhere, we were all into spontaneous bop prosody, and all the talk was of liberation and improvisation. Writers loosened their clauses and let their modifiers dangle, and it was time to get out of the study and onto the road. Radical America was the great good place, the land of therapeutic selfhood, and the old culture of puritan seriousness and British provincialism began to look very bleak and limiting. So we got on the boat, my critic and I, and sailed westward, our typewriters under our arms, ready to start all over again. The American university seemed an ideal place for our combination; writers on campus were in vogue, seducing the faculty wives and writing books in one seminar room so that they could be taught in Contemporary Literature 305 in the classroom next door. We set off together for the groves of academe, teaching freshman courses in how to find the library in middlewestern universities. Here, amid the cornstalks, I wrote my second novel, *Stepping Westward*, Henry James in reverse, British puritan innocence seeking American experience. If I had changed a lot, so had my critic. He had put down his Leavis, and put on his levis. His desk was stacked with McLuhan, Norman O. Brown, Marcuse, Wilhelm Reich. Soon, in our jeans and our tee-shirts, we were into all kinds of new practices. In bed at night, he'd murmur about how Roland Barthes said text was *plaisir* and art was *jouissance*. Where, in the Fifties, we had agreed Eating People Is Wrong, we were doing it all the time. Even Aristotle was summoned to justify our, I'm afraid, somewhat louche behaviour. If you look at *Stepping Westward* you'll find the epigraph from Aristotle reads: "The flute is not a moral instrument; it is too exciting." And exciting it all was, perhaps too exciting. For I can't help thinking it was now our troubles started.

By the end of the 1960s it was clear something had changed between us. I think the first real sign was the Fictiveness. We had acquired a lot of postmodern friends who used to come over and drink a bottle of Robbe-Grillet with us, and it was then his behaviour really began to alter. Now the books that began to fill his shelves were all by authors whose very names sounded fictional to start with: Barthes and Barth and Barthelme, Burroughs and Burgess and Borges and Beckett and Butor, Saussure and Sapir, Schlovsky and Scholes, Sollers and Simon. He even explained that the fact all their names began with B or S was a modern alphabetical plot. In fact he began to see plots everywhere; he even started distrusting our nice mailman, Mr Tristero. His habits grew secretive; he'd read all day, then go out at night; when I had him followed I discovered he was attending meetings of Absurdists Anonymous. When he came back he'd pour himself a drink and say I didn't realise the world was constructed to an inhuman code; and writers who thought reality was just friendly old nice reality now bored him, he'd cry, looking hard at me. I reminded him of the old days, when he too had believed in moral realism and deep seriousness. Leavis is dis-Kermoded, he'd say, if not entirely dis-Lodged; now we're working with structuralism. I recalled our earlier moment of liberation, when we put on our jeans and went to America; you're stuck, he told me, with the wrong Levi-Strauss. And when I mentioned Marcuse to him, he just said Foucault.

And it was now I realised that our days of blissful contact were over, that, dear reader, our signifiers were coming apart from our signifieds. He began telling me that literature was exhausted, and that when I served up my hegemonic paradigms he could hardly touch them any more. Fiction is finished, he'd say, so write. What do I write? I'd ask. Metafiction, surfiction, intertext, he'd say. What about? I'd cry. There is no about about to write about, just write, he'd shout, with a new and unpleasant note of impatience. I am not a difficult person, and I try to please, but I have to confess all this worried me a little. I wrote a book, *The History Man*, that was all a parody of realism, a mockery of history, a book about plots and plotters, an abstractified novel, all very textual, reversing background and foreground, displacing character from that trap of sympathy in which, my critic said, only a fallacious liberal realism had placed it. It was a hard, object-ridden book, with figures brutally set in harsh cityscapes: multistorey carparks, concrete shopping precincts, cement new universities. I showed it to him, and could see at once he was disappointed. Not postmodern enough, he said, I can understand it. That night in bed he came and murmured in my ear: I want you to go to the zero degree of meaning. You're telling me I don't exist, I said. You do in a sense, he said, there has to be a something we can deconstruct.

Do you wonder, dear reader, that I thought of leaving him? Or that, while he goes to MLA to talk to Hilton Kramer about Kristeva, and Kristeva about Hilton Kramer, I sneak off to my writers' colony to work on my books – books which nonetheless show me I haven't escaped him? For the book I started there in the Portnoy Room in my Arcadia was about, well, an imaginary country, and about a character who is really not a character caught in the labyrinth of an imaginary language which changes about him as he tries to learn its nonexistent messages. There is a storyteller who does not complete her stories, though she does believe in stories as magic; and there is an ending that has no closure, though I like to think it does have significance.

Who put these things there? Was it I, with my belief in the wonder of fictions; or was it he, with his deep dark deconstructive habits? Finishing the book, I called it *Rates of Exchange*, and I am still not sure whether it was my title, or his, or ours. Perhaps one of the epigraphs really expressed my message; I took it from the story "The Purloined Letter", which I say is by Edgar Allan Poe, and he says is by Jacques Lacan. The passage reads: " 'You have a quarrel on hand, I see,' said I, 'with some of the algebraists of Paris; but proceed.' " Well, I have; and I did; and I just hope he deconstructs it.

Well, my tale draws to a close; that is our story, or most of it. But old-fashioned readers, I am told, are coming back, in their Laura Ashley dresses, asking "What happened?" and "How did it end?" Well, one word respecting my experience of married life, and one brief glance at the fortunes of those who have most frequently recurred in this narrative, and I have done. Alas, it is not like the end of *Jane Eyre*; I do not hold myself supremely blest, beyond what language can express; endings these days are bound to be less conclusive. We hang together, after a fashion, for I still remember our good old days, when he read Lawrence and not Lyotard, liked people, and believed art was moral knowledge. Story is magic, I still sometimes murmur to him; discourse is dead, he shouts back from the bathroom. Yet things are changing with him. He talks from time to time about something called postpostmodernism and de-de-de-de-deconstruction, and if he says Derrida again I think I shall scream; but his heart isn't in it. The packets of theory he used to have smuggled in from Paris seem not to come quite as often, and I gather that some of his old suppliers have closed down altogether. He tells me that from a contemporary narratological viewpoint plots have inevitable dialectics arising from their codified variables; and I suppose it is quite clear what our plot is likely to be. We've been having marriage therapy, but it doesn't do much good; when he comes into the house, I tend to go out of it. He tells me I will not write well unless I get free of him; when I offer to leave he says he cannot exist without me. He starts me and he stops me; when one of us wants the other, the other doesn't want the one. Yet I go on living in the hope that he will contrive his literature; he goes on living in the hope that I will one day contrive mine. So there, dear reader, you have it; or do you? For what I have given is just one side of a story, a confessional text, a gender-based discourse, a playful lexical flow.

Or, as my critic prefers to describe it, just another fiction.

A DOG ENGULFED IN SAND
Character and abstraction in contemporary writing and painting

---

"On or about December 1910 human nature changed . . . . "
Virginia Woolf, "Mr Bennett and Mrs Brown" (1924)

"A generation that had gone to school on a horse-drawn streetcar now stood [during World War One] under the open sky in a countryside in which nothing remained unchanged but the clouds, and beneath these clouds, in a field of force of destructive torrents and explosions, was the tiny, fragile human body."
Walter Benjamin, "The Storyteller" (1936)

"What is obsolescent in today's novel is not the novelistic, it is the character; what can no longer be written is the Proper Name."
Roland Barthes, S/Z (1970)

1 "A Dog Engulfed by Sand" is the title of a painting by Goya – one of the famous "black paintings" which he painted from private need and despair onto the walls of his country house sometime between 1814 and 1819, and which were later removed and displayed in a single room in the Prado Museum in Madrid, which also supplied the title of the work. It is a painting which for some reason has long fascinated me; and it came frequently to mind when I was writing my novel *The History Man*. When that book was published in hardback in 1975 I asked to have the painting on the cover of the British edition. This, when it appeared, attracted the attention of Michael Levey, director of the National Gallery, who was running a series of lectures about the relation between works of fiction and works of art. He asked me to speak about the connection, and what follows is my explanation. It is, as it happens, an oblique and indirect one. The painting is never referred to in the book; the subject of the book – radical opportunism and the way we use history as fashion – is in no sense the subject of the painting. But the problems posed by the style and subject of a painting can provide, and for me did provide, a figure or mnemonic, for the stylistic questions and methods of perception a novel is trying to explore. Writing a novel is like painting a painting in that one must

construct a style, a grammar of perception. Pursuing a subject, one is also pursuing a form, and the book searches for itself somewhere between the realistic and aesthetic, the figurative and the abstract. Above all, Goya's strangely abstract painting, which I try to describe later, seemed to raise a problem that, in the writing, concerned me greatly, as it has other modern writers and painters. The best way to explain this is to say that it is the problem, in a modern work, of putting in the person.

Anxiety about the representation of the human figure in art is in no way new. Islamic art still retains a good deal of the traditional prohibition against the representation of human subjects. In the European arts it was only in the era of humanism that the representation of the human figure began to move near art's centre, and then usually only in some form of idealisation. But humanism developed toward realism, and portraits of human figures and common life became an essential artistic concern. However, by the beginning of our century the anxiety had resumed. Direct portraiture no longer satisfied either the aesthetic curiosities and experiments of artists themselves, nor, in a psychologising age, our notion of a person or his or her "reality". Modern painting stepped away from portraiture and the depiction of the exteriorised human subject; something similar can be perceived in the literary arts too. "You mustn't look in my novel for the old stable *ego* – of the character," wrote D.H. Lawrence about *The Rainbow* (1915). "This difference we make so much of, this identity we so feverishly cherish, was overcome," Virginia Woolf writes triumphantly at the end of *The Waves* (1931). "No more psychology," Kafka declared in his programme for modern fiction; Sartre demanded an art of situations and not of characters. Into the novel, apparently the most representational and person-centred of all the artistic forms, had come a new questioning of the figurative, what José Ortega y Gasset called a "dehumanization of art". Modern theories of behaviour and consciousness, the troubled history of humanism in our times, the sense that language itself writes the falsehood of the Subject, the distinctive human person, into existence, have intensified the issue, and it persists powerfully in the contemporary arts, as in contemporary thought. "I began writing fiction on the assumption that the true enemies of the novel were plot, character, setting and theme," the American novelist John Hawkes has said, "and having once abandoned these familiar ways of thinking about fiction, totality of vision or structure was really all that remained." The old realistic and linear poetics of fiction, which Hawkes is here dispensing with, have had a hard time in our age. And in particular, just as in painting there has been a lasting anxiety about the human figure, so modern fiction has displayed a deeply troubled relation to what used, once, to be called the "character".

So, explaining the *nouveau roman* in his essay "New Novel, New Man" (1961), Alain Robbe-Grillet remarked that "the construction of our books is only confusing to those who insist on looking for elements which have, in fact, over the last twenty, thirty or forty years, disappeared from every living novel, or which have at least become singularly debilitated: characters, chronology, sociological studies, etc.". "The novel of characters belongs entirely in the past," he also commented. "It describes a period: that which marked the apogee of the individual." Robbe-Grillet's comments are very consonant with the body of ideas that had developed philosophically in the movements of thought we call structuralism and deconstruction, where the Death of the Author and the Death of the Subject have been theoretically pursued. Roland Barthes tells us that "what can no longer be written is the Proper Name"; Derrida has proposed that all concepts of "identity" and "presence" have been decentred. In his influential *Writing Degree Zero* (1953), which closely coincided with the formulation of the *nouveau roman*, Barthes explained that we have left the high bourgeois age when the novel could have a name, proclaim itself, and come to a time when "reality becomes slighter and more familiar, it fits within a style, it does not outrun language". Language, he suggests, is given to the writer as a compromising instrument, "inherited from a previous and different History". So today we have no common reality to read together, no sure text to share, and we can read only the process of writing. Neither the author nor the character can be united in fiction; in Barthes, Foucault and Derrida they become a kind of lexical misadventure, a false signifier, or, as it has been said, "the basis of a false rapport" protecting the reader against the full anxiety of discourse.

Our modern complexities of form are thus webbed in with a dark contemporary sense of broken connections, between sign and subject, individual and society, person and nature, the fictions of the imagination and those potent and powerful ones which pass for history and political necessity. In the course of our century we have grown far more anxious about the way from the imagination to the facts and realities of the world. This is often expressed as a loss – social, moral, philosophical, linguistic, aesthetic. The old language of art goes because the old language of truth goes. For obvious reasons reality has been a matter of anxiety right through our anxious century, as our age has deprived us of the familiarities that make the familiar world real to us. If some of our critics are to be believed, we have passed through an historical fracture in our capacity to depict the real, moved, as Roland Barthes argues, from the age of the *lisible* to the *scriptible* through a breakdown of language. Uneasy dealings with mimesis have become our convention. "Men have learned to live with a black burden, a huge aching hump; the supposition that 'reality' may be only a 'dream',", one of our greatest modern writers, Vladimir Nabokov, writes in *The Real Life of Sebastian Knight* (1941). "How much more dreadful it would be if the very awareness of your being aware of reality's dream-like nature were also to be a dream, a built-in hallucination." This narcissistic circle, image turning back on image, has released a good deal of our best art, and we now have many works that play with or upset those elements of the real they gesture toward representing – as we have some that, drawing on fiction's essential ambiguity, tell us they represent nothing whatsoever. A literary criticism that has been much influenced by the arguments of structuralism and deconstruction has given these works a central place in the canon; and the self-begetting novel, the narcissistic narrative, the fictionalist fiction are felt to be the most expressive examples of our serious modern art. Nabokov tells us that the heroes of his fiction are methods of composition, and we know many such works now which force us beyond mimesis to the stuff of which art is made. The same self-questioning occurs in the supposedly "factual" forms: history-writing, travel-writing, biography, journalism. And of course in painting we are driven to look to the canvas, the composition, the colour. The art-object moves into the foreground, the represented object to the background, or is not there at all.

This questioning of realism is intimately related to the dissolution of character, or the bounded representation of the human figure; we no longer think it easy to pose an identifiable human figure in a world or landscape that can be considered substantive and realistic. "The contemporary writer who is acutely in touch with the life of which he is a part – is forced to start from scratch: Reality doesn't exist, time doesn't exist, personality doesn't exist . . .," claims the "postmodern" American writer Ronald Sukenick in his aptly titled *The Death of the Novel and Other Stories* (1969). No doubt artists have always claimed much the same, but Sukenick is adding to the traditional assumption a peculiarly modern dimension, a very contemporary notion of the loss of signification and the exhaustion of all traditional artistic forms, and speaks to a contemporary situation where the creative process is put in the foreground and the represented object passes back into the realm of speculation. The linear representation of story, the detailed description of a milieu, the authority of the author, the stability of the text, the representation of the discrete human personage, all come into question. In our art and our fiction, in our film and our drama, we now have many works of art where object, scene and figure are clouded, and we look behind and beyond to the discourse of the composition, which is itself seen not as fixed but provisional, if not still to be constructed. This is often associated with that break in the tradition, that fracture in signification, in which, as Barthes suggests, the old bourgeois sense of reality loses its transcendent support, and fails. The old language of art has faded not merely because we have found new techniques of expression, but because the old language of truth has gone; and modern art can be made only from broken relations, between discourse and its subject, consciousness and society. Above all the problem of broken signification attaches to the idea of the disappearance of the distinctive individual; "what can no longer be written is the Proper Name".

As Saul Bellow once observed, we do not necessarily have to accept this. "Undeniably the human being is not what he was commonly thought a century ago," he says. "The question nevertheless remains. He is something, what is he?" In fact it has been a notable feature of some American and much British writing that the notion of character has, by compensation, not so much weakened as strengthened, as if to face that question. When John Fowles seeks to grant existential freedom to his characters at the close of *The French Lieutenant's Woman*, or when Iris Murdoch insists on the novel's function as "a fit house for free characters to live in", we may sense a conscious revolt against such de-centering and deconstructive philosophies. Murdoch, who has much of importance to say on the matter, argued in a television programme that divergences from realism in art have a strange power to create unease; art does speak to our desire to have a commonsense reality, and remains a repository for our sense of the real and the true. The novel in particular goes along with our moral wish that the contingencies of life be apprehended, ordered, assessed. There is human desire for the world of rounded social selves we find in fiction; and divergence from this – in fictions that become predominantly textual, or pattern or deface the person – disturbs us humanly. "Against the crystalline work, the simplified fantasy myth, we must pit the destructive power of the now unfashionable naturalistic idea of character," Murdoch says in her essay "Against Dryness" (1961), seeing this as the way art works against simplified formal consolations in the direction of a transcendental good. Yet she acknowledges herself that the empirical and representational aspects of art, while crucial to its meaning and use, have always raised Platonic anxieties. In our great writers and painters, realism has never been simply innocent, of an agreed and fixed nature, or exterior to artistic scepticism and enquiry.

Yet no-one can read through the major works of modern literature without recognising that the traditional figure of the character as hero, the image of the discretely bounded individual shaping out an intelligent life in a comprehensible and substantial material world, has been challenged. "Character" is a less than adequate word to describe the new webs of human and inhuman relations that populate, or depopulate, our fiction, a word from an old poetics that itself no longer quite serves. Yet we read this fiction with unease, pitting our readerly desires against the text, sustaining what Fredric Jameson has called "the stubbornly anthropomorphic nature of our present categories of character". Indeed all this poses a special problem for the novel – of all the artistic forms the one most committed to using the human figure to familiarise and give access to its world. It is through the character that we generally enter its world of story; our faces meet theirs, we use their company to take us through the meaning of the events we encounter, and enter the art-work through them, as the very history of titles suggests. Don Quixote, Robinson Crusoe, Pamela, Tom Jones, Tristram Shandy, Emma and Emma Bovary, Jane Eyre and David Copperfield, Daniel Deronda, Tess of the D'Urbervilles and the obscure Jude all give their names to the books in which they are represented, and these novels are the story of the building of their lives.

But in modern fiction this dimension has much diminished. "For a writer or critic to show delight in a character would seem today rather naive, an old-fashioned response from the days of Dickens or Surtees," John Bayley says in *The Characters of Love* (1960). "Characters, it seems, are no longer objects of affection. The literary personality has gone down in the world." As Bayley – whose comments also illuminate the work of his wife, Iris Murdoch – says, in this matter writers and critics have run parallel. Today the writer rarely seeks from the novel that creative stimulus that comes from the imaginative power won from composition through character. "From the intense and curious apprehension of a separate being," the old-fashioned idea of character has, he says, "sunk into the vast middle depths of fiction, where it survives in a diminished and mechanical form and where the conventional character is observed rather than loved. In what indisputable masterpiece of to-day could we expect to find a character of such vitality that he established his right to existence – even to the domination of his *milieu* – in the very teeth of the author's purpose?"

In contemporary fiction, then, the boundaries of what used to be called "character" are regularly transgressed, to allow access to a world beyond identity, beyond personality, a world of tropisms, images and, above all, discourse. In the *nouveau roman*, Robbe-Grillet tells us, there are no "characters" in the traditional sense – however, man is present on every line, narrating man, "*always* engaged in a passionate adventure of the most obsessive type – so obsessive that it often distorts his vision and subjects him to fantasies bordering on delirium". This can be represented as a freedom, where the new arts of consciousness have triumphed over the old conventions of representation and story, allowing the subject of the book to become the artist or writer, or indeed, as in much modern theory, the composing reader. So, forsaking its dependence on character, the novel is returned to its freedom as a form of narrative speculation. Yet the freedom makes disquiet, for the idea of character relates to a humanism with which the novel has long been intimate, but has been thrown in our century into a kind of despair. So the fading of character is part of a dismaying loss in the credibility of the individual. "There are almost no characters in this story . . .," says Kurt Vonnegut in *Slaughterhouse-Five* (1969). "One of the main effects of war, after all, is that people are discouraged from being characters."

Thus an art made grotesque, abstract, ironic and robbed of human attachments seems an appropriate art for the crisis in our times. Robert Musil's *The Man Without Qualities* presents a man with, quite simply, no qualities, only a contingent existence. In Kafka, as Milan Kundera has said, "it's never the richness of [K's] soul that dazzles us. K's reasoning is strictly defined by the authoritarian and tyrannical situation in which he is completely absorbed. The novel as written by Prague authors does not ask: What is the hidden treasure of the human psyche? But rather: What are the possibilities for humanity in the trap that the world has become?" In Beckett's great trilogy the human figure is constantly diminished in attributes, losing society, chronology, dense material life, and becoming finally nameless, the unnamable. In the black humour novels of the 1960s existence is comically random or absurd, life a meaningless joke. In American novelists such as William Gaddis, William Burroughs or Thomas Pynchon, characters are pasteboard and the world is composed of enormous outward plots and codes dissolving inner life and producing entropy. In the *nouveau roman* the novel is purposefully placed beyond tragedy or humanism, its subject the smooth, meaningless, amoral face of the world, with no transcendent appeal beyond it. In Peter Handke or Italo Calvino, the inheritance left after absurdity is clear; the world cannot be reconciled with consciousness, and threatens or nihilises the self.

So the displacement of the person may produce an intensification of form, a new pre-eminence for the text as discourse. But it may also produce an ironic realism, making the systems and processes dwarfing individual life the centre of our attention. If our modern art has grown more compositional and abstract, this is not simply because it has grown free, as Henry James promised, to be more itself. It is of a piece with our historical experience and many of our modern

theories, sociological, psychological, philosophical, which point toward the waning of signification and the "death of the subject". And
its anxieties about the human figure, its move toward compositional
abstraction, are usefully illuminated by considering the painterly
analogy, the striking and persistent parallelism between modern
writing and modern art.

2 Here it is well to begin with the familiar warning: writing and
painting are not the same sort of thing at all. Painters paint, or draw,
or sketch, and today do many other things, with buckets, bricks and
bicycle-pumps, but they practice in an eminently visual and spatial
medium, and their main instruments of expression are design, form,
colour, perspective or flatness, light or shade. They create objects of
and for perception, exploring one of the more crucial of human
boundaries, that between seer and seen. Their sign is complete, and
they make unspeaking and – in the strict sense of the term –
unspeakable objects, which can be taken in as a unity (and anyone
watching a reviewer at an art-opening will know how quickly this may
be done). There is no inherent reason why their work should be
representational, or realistic. Writers, on the other hand, write, using
language, an ostensibly agreed community of signs, names and
grammars, a set of public structures for ordering and discoursing,
which is difficult to privatise. Writing is not only referential but serial,
discursive rather than iconographic, and is normally assimilated in
sequences, though some forms, like the lyric poem, čan aspire to
imagistic or a-chronological form. There is a classical analogy, *ut
pictura poesis*, a poem is like a picture; but, as Lessing argues in the
Laokoon (1766), it is false, since we need to distinguish between
spatial and temporal arts. The comparison that is weak with poems is
weaker still with novels, which depend on narrative and seriality, and
which are committed by definition to length.

    In modern times Jean-Paul Sartre has argued that the depend-
ence on prose and the discursive length of fiction made the language
of fiction transparent, and hence required of the writer a necessary
engagement, a commitment to freedom. We do not need to agree to
all his distinctions between poetry and prose to acknowledge that the
novel works by the rules of extended narration and has kinship with
expository forms like history, biography, travel-writing, or philosophy,
on which it frequently draws for its manners and structures. And it
comes in that complex system of infolded packaging we call a book,
demanding unwrapping, interleaving, and hence a sequential mode of
readerly attention. Its contract is between author and single reader,

and it depends on certain customary habits of association and intimacy. All this helps explain why we look to paintings for style and form and to novels for narrative and plot, why we commonsensically suppose that paintings are a window on the world whereby we examine the window, novels one whereby we examine the world. The distinction, though not fully true, contains a truth; though most novelists, even the most realistic, have constantly insisted on the ambiguity of fictional representation, and most of us know that a fiction is also a lie, the novel has deep empirical as well as narrative roots. But because the distinction is not entirely true, and the fictive aspect of fiction constantly needs emphasis, novelists have turned regularly to the painterly analogy to express and clarify the formal or aesthetic nature of their enterprise. Certainly the habit goes back in Britain to the origins of that new genre that was called the "novel".

A new form can only be explained as a mutant of old codes, and when such major innovators as Fielding and Sterne sought to describe, in neo-classical terms, their generic innovation, they had four main points of reference to turn to: history-writing, drama, poetry and painting. Fielding's famous preface to *The History of the Adventures of Joseph Andrews* (1742) drew on all four to explain the new species, which, using the neo-classical poetics of Aristotle, he called "the comic epic poem in prose". But then he turned to painterly practice and to Hogarth to consider the problem of the comic depiction of human figures. The crucial distinction made here, between "character" and "caricature", was then illustrated by Hogarth in several cartoons, one of which hangs on my wall as I write. "Writers of my stamp have one principle in common with painters. – When an exact copying makes our picture less striking, we choose the less evil, deeming it even more pardonable to trespass against truth, than beauty," comments Tristram Shandy/Laurence Sterne, that great user of the book as visual object. Indeed in the age of Reynolds and a great painterly tradition the fictional writer was often perceived as a verbal painter:

> I will not so much as take pains to bestow the strip of a gauze wrapper on it [Truth], but paint situations as they actually arose to me in nature, careless of violating those laws of decency that were never made for such unreserved intimacies as ours . . . .

says another, very seductive eighteenth-century narrator of a book who has difficult problems of pictorial representation. Her name is Fanny Hill, otherwise John Cleland, whose difficulty was that of reproducing in prose the post facto, indeed post coital, details of erotic sensation. Could a novel be as kinetic as a painting? And how does one depict in prose "the most interesting moving picture in nature"? The difficulty here is somewhat specialised, since the subject in question is the erect male organ. But we must acknowledge that even Cleland was devoted to the general eighteenth-century speculation about how a visual image became a form of discourse.

This somewhat envious relation persisted into romanticism. As aesthetics changed, to emphasise the radiating inward power of the imagination and the subjective nature of perception, while seeking the transformation of history, the writer envied the painter his scenic power, the painter envied the writer his historical sweep. But both were romantic heroes, carriers of vision, seeking to regulate the powers of imagination to those of a dramatic new history. Painters grew discursive, posing their figures in an historically moving world. Storytellers sought a painterly stasis, hungered for the picturesque, and Washington Irving took, like many of his contemporaries, a painterly persona, calling himself "Geoffrey Crayon, Gent.". The great romantic novelists, such as Scott and Cooper, created their fictions through a sequence of painterly historical poses – settings are held still, figures are posed in the landscape, words report on scenes as if they were already painted, and novels acquire the static indurance of myth, and enriched sensibility of romance. Dickens depended heavily on the pictorial analogy, beginning as "Boz", a verbal illustrator working with a visual one, and his novels possess a visionary sense of scene, place and person, an artistic sense of "character".

Indeed the novel in the middle of the nineteenth century acquired a capacious sense of character. In the expansive stage of bourgeois society, it became the book of the individual in a progressive and complex social world, and, exploring the discursive strangeness of relations, the massing of new fact and detail, freely noting the slow passing days of individual lives, it could become an apparent form of truth itself. This was the spirit of realism, in which the imaginary seemed to fall within the domain of the real, and the aesthetic gave way to the moral. In *Middlemarch*, when Dorothea Brooke goes to Rome and finds herself at odds with the bohemian, aestheticising world of artists there, she returns both to the moral world of provincial life and an art of the middle ground. Yet if it sometimes seemed in dispute with an aesthetic idea of art, realism was itself the great art-movement of the middle nineteenth century, the avant gardeism of the times. And, after 1848 in Paris, its cumulative achievements were formulated as a movement that united painters and writers: Degas, Courbet, Flaubert, the Goncourts, Champfleury. The underlying analogue of the realist novel – whether it was Dickens's satirically abundant kind, Balzac's form of human comedy, Flaubert's ironic distancing, or George Eliot's compassionate humanism – was the realist painting. Hence George Eliot's famous pronouncement in *Adam Bede* (1859):

> All honour and reverence to the divine beauty of form! Let us cultivate it to the utmost in men, women, and children – in our gardens and in our houses. But let us love the other beauty too, which lies in no secret of proportion, but in the secret of deep human sympathy. Paint us an angel, if you can, with floating violet robe. . . .; paint us yet oftener a Madonna . . .; but do not impose on us any aesthetic rules which shall banish from the region of Art those old women scraping carrots with their work-worn hands, those heavy clowns taking holiday in a dingy pothouse, those rounded backs and stupid weather-beaten faces that have bent over a spade and done the rough work of the world . . . .

Thus she is painting not large historical canvases nor pietas, but "faithful pictures of monotonous homely existence" in the manner of the Dutch genre paintings. Realism is a kind of painting, and the writers and painters of the time acknowledge it not as a transparent form of truth but as a style; as Champfleury put it, realism was "only a transitional term which will last no longer than thirty years". It was compositional rather than innocent; Flaubert's writings, works from the realist studio, embody painters, canvases, frames, and enact their compositional process. In fact it is realism's formal self-consciousness that allows Barthes to see it as the fragmentation leading toward our anxious modernism.

But it is of course in the great coming together, the general synaesthesia, of the arts at the end of the nineteenth century, when, it seemed, all arts commonly aspired to the condition of all others, and art was for art's sake, that the link between fiction and painting came to its most intense. As the Victorian world-picture began to disintegrate, and a bleaker lore from Darwin and positivism put the landscape into a new perspective and shrank the image of the human figure, the sense of historical optimism evident in much early realism gave way to darker pictures, of process, indifference, and victimisation. The path onward from realism divided: one part, which followed Zola in regarding the study of reality as an experimental science, became naturalism; another, following realism's emphasis on the intensification of awareness, and emphasising the act of consciousness, became impressionism. Both involved some displacement of the realist notion of character. In naturalism, the free-standing character is displaced, ironised, set against or engulfed by the world of processes and systems, made less the subject of a plot than its victim. In impressionism, Pater's art of arts, not the moral form of experience but experience itself becomes the end, and the experiencing individual is the artist himself, heightening his sensations, stylising his

pose. Consciousness meanwhile dissipates into contingency or randomness – but, by the magical rescue of the imagination, form is
distilled. Beyond lies chaos or naturalist waste. These dissolving
landscapes and cityscapes – in late Turner, Whistler, the French
impressionists – take the age of steam and city, but divest it of
Courbet's narrative, Frith's abundance, obscuring the image but
hinting at mass and force beyond. Insisting on the moment of
perception, the position of the perceiver, it centralises the role of the
artist, seeking in contingent reality his instant of pure form.

In both parts of this double movement away from realism –
toward naturalism, toward impressionism – we may find a basis for
modern abstraction in the arts. The social communion and the vision
of a liberal relation to history diminish. Process operates against man;
consciousness is elevated. The human subject of art is reduced, while
art itself grows more formal. In naturalism the social or determining
process is stressed, in impressionism the structure of consciousness.
Often we see the two tendencies merge, as in Stephen Crane's *The
Red Badge of Courage* (1895). Crane, like many of the time's writers,
had trained with painters, and written the fashionable "city-
sketches". His short, mannered novel joins a naturalistic view of the
universe as hostile and indifferent with an impressionist view of
consciousness as a flickering, momentary mode of apprehension. War
and aggression are fundamental metaphors, heroism can only arise
ironically, and the almost unnamed central character colludes with
the artist-author in seeing the world as a sequence of instantaneous
impressions. This collusion between artist and character, this method
of framing images of consciousness, becomes characteristic of many
works of the late nineteenth-century "decadence". The very titles
explain this: *The Portrait of a Lady*, *The Picture of Dorian Gray*, *A
Portrait of the Artist as a Young Man*.

No writer makes this new alliance of artist and novelist clearer
than Henry James, for whom the art that makes life is supported by
granting to most of his major characters an intensely artistic nature.
From Roderick Hudson on, many of his characters are artists,
painters or sculptors, or else possess the painter's need to see, to take
an impression. Not only does this allow the characters to act as direct
surrogates for the writer himself, and experience his concern with the
right relation between image and truth, art and reality; it also allows
him to explore how the moral pursuit of the real germinates not just
story but a larger process, "form", and to consider the ambiguous and
solipsistic processes of perception. James's early, realist work considers how we negotiate with the materiality of a solid, social world about
us, acquiring as moral awareness a sense of the real and true. But as
the problem of generating perception as moral knowledge grew more

difficult, his writing turned toward a complex grammar of abstraction. The famous opening of *The Wings of the Dove* (1902) shows his later manner, with its displaced grammars, strange mirrored refractions and hazardous subject-object relations:

> She waited, Kate Croy, for her father to come in, but he kept her unconscionably, and there were moments at which she showed herself, in the glass over the mantel, a face positively pale with the irritation that brought her to the point of going away without sight of him. It was at this point, however, that she remained; changing her place, moving from the shabby sofa to the armchair upholstered in a glazed cloth that gave at once – she had tried it – the sense of the slippery and of the sticky . . . .

James has become the anxious seer, caught amid the complex synaesthesic problems of the time. Material goods are positioned strangely in relation to consciousness; the person is an aesthetic receptor, open to multiplied points of reference, angles of vision. *The Ambassadors* (1903), James said, was the story of a man who learns to *see* – to become, in effect, an impressionist painter. James too became one, with symbolist leanings. As the century turned he wrote a famous essay on the future of fiction, claiming that, freed of the moral constraints of the early Victorian era, it was free to become more itself. But if his own case was a guide – and for many major writers of the early twentieth century it would be – then that freedom came in the form of a new abstraction, and it was guided by the painterly analogy.

3 Thus, whatever the differences between them, novelists and painters have long considered themselves kin. And one important way this is apparent is that they generally share common views about the stylistic direction and development of art. So the times when the painterly analogy is likely to be most important are times of radical stylistic change, which itself of course reflects deep-seated perceptual, political and philosophical change in society. No change could have been greater than the enormous shift in social perception and in artistic sensibility that happened at the beginning of our own century, which we call "modernism". Its scale was amazing; in painting, Herbert Read declared in *Art Now* (1933), "the aim of five centuries of European effort is openly abandoned." Painting was just one, though the most visible, witness to the perceptual change that spread through every form – reflecting not just a risingly confident avant garde, but the new views of consciousness and perception, the new apocalyptic awareness of modernity and universal change, that was brought by an age massing technology, new social conflict, increasing urbanisation, and the growing systematisation of life. But if the arts reflected such social changes, they were also assertively *artistic*, declaring their own independent radical awareness, their wisdom as a modern mode of vision. They had their own country, bohemia, and their own independent aesthetic authority. The painter became the exemplary visionary radical, and the spectacular exhibitions of the arts of the new movements – post-impressionism, fauvism, cubism, futurism – not only provoked general outrage and excitement but forced writers into a profound reappraisal of their own work.

In the novel there came a deep transformation, a movement away from nineteenth-century realism and moralism – not a total over-throw, but a steady questioning and undermining of the dominant conventions. Indeed it was a bifurcation, and a new avant gardeism grew up side by side with an adaptive continuity developing out of realism and naturalism, so that it was long possible to dispute, as Georg Lukacs did, whether the new experiment was anything more than a tangental deviation from social (or socialist) realism. Today it is clear that the modernist revolution in fiction was a major change, even for those writers who sought to deny the transformation. But it was those writers who most explored the change, and sought to free themselves from the moral and social practices of popular and conventional fiction, who found the greatest kinship with painters. It had great impact on many we do *not* regard as "modernists" (Somerset Maugham, Arnold Bennett, John Cowper Powys, Joyce Cary, for example); but for those who took the path toward the self-questioning novel the new painting was crucial. Joseph Frank's famous essay on "Spatial Form in Modern Literature" (1963) suggests how modern writers who aimed to define themselves as explorers of art and consciousness broke with the representational by emphasising space over time, aesthetic transcendence over narrative drive. Aiming to realise the novel spatially rather than discursively, as a form rather than a discourse about a subject, writers declared themselves artists, with the same problems as the artist. This is the enterprise of James Joyce's exemplary modernist *Portrait of the Artist as a Young Man* (1915), in which Stephen Dedalus seeks to elaborate a philosophy of art as a "luminous silent stasis" affording aesthetic pleasure, and aims himself to become its exemplary artist. Out of the contingency of narrative metonymy comes the "epiphany", giving clarity and coherence to an otherwise discursive artistic object.

Throughout the many phases of modernism, from the turn of the century to the end of the 1930s, the novelist and painter met and re-met – in different mixes, different capitals, through different movements with different names and aesthetics. Some novelists were painters, like D.H. Lawrence; some painters were novelists, like Wyndham Lewis. Often the link was directly acknowledged: "I learn as much from painters about how to write as from writers," said Ernest Hemingway. One crucial and illustrative connection was that betwen Leo and Gertrude Stein, and the cubist painters. The Steins came to Paris as art-collectors, settled on the Left Bank, and became involved with the post-impressionists, including Cezanne, the fauves, and the movement into cubism. Stein's *Three Lives* (1909), a trans-formation of Flaubert's *Trois Contes*, was completed under a portrait by Cezanne of his wife which gave Stein, she said, "a new feeling about composition". Picasso, who painted her portrait, had much to do with her next venture, *The Making of Americans*, mostly written between 1906 and 1908, the crucial years of cubism. It was an attempt at an "abstract" novel, rejecting conventional principles of remembering and the realist noun. Despite its great length, of more than a thousand pages, it hungers for the synchronicity of a painting. As a result Stein came, like many at the time, to doubt the novel entirely. She turned next to short prose portraits, collages, abstracts: in short, to word painting. And when the post-impressionist and cubist canvases were displayed for the first time in America at the Armory Show of 1913, the "literary wing" was none other than Stein. Indeed her influence passed readily to most of the major American writers of the 1920s – Anderson, Hemingway, Fitzgerald, Faulkner.

Joyce, Proust and Stein were part of the great artistic coming together, the formal synaesthesia, of the years just before 1914. It was also striking that the new spirit mattered greatly in Britain. When Roger Fry organised the London post-impressionist Exhibition at the Grafton Galleries in 1910, even Arnold Bennett, thought to be the arch-materialist of fiction, reflected that were he a young novelist he might have to begin again. It was around the implications of this show that Fry elaborated those concepts of Significant Form that were to link modernism with Bloomsbury. And Virginia Woolf surely had the show in mind when she said that it was on or about December 1910 that human nature changed, and with it the entire nature of the modern arts, which had somehow lost their old materialism and become arts of consciousness: "All human relations shifted – those between masters and servants, husbands and wives, parents and children. And when human relations change there is at the same time a change in religion, conduct, politics and literature." Like Stein, she felt this transformed the nature of the novel, which needed to pursue a more "abstract" reality. As she suggested in her 1924 essay "Mr Bennett and Mrs Brown", this meant a new conception of the human figure in art; it must be dematerialised, consciousness must enfold it, it must be made as fragmentary as the atoms of experience of which it was the sum. The novel was an aesthetic object resembling a painting, and capable of a similar impressionist abstraction. Indeed *To the Lighthouse* (1927) is an elegant, abstract triptych, and it is completed when Lily Briscoe, who has been working on her canvas, finishes her painting, giving the form to the human absences of the fictional world.

If, then, there was a word that helped explain this movement away from the representational and the mimetic in fiction as in other arts, that word was "abstraction". "The primal artistic impulse has nothing to do with the rendering of nature," wrote the German art-historian Wilhelm Worringer in his *Abstraction and Empathy* (1908), the influential aesthetic work that coincided almost exactly with the opening strike of cubism, and the writing of *The Making of Americans*: "It seeks after pure abstraction as the only possibility of repose within the confusions and obscurity of the world-picture . . . ". Worringer's view of abstraction as repose resembled Stein's and Woolf's idea of an art freed of material or historical constraints. It was a notion similar to that being elaborated by the Russian formalist critics, who spoke of "defamiliarisation", the great "making strange" through which art, instead of consoling us that it is just a mirror to life, forces us into its own complexity and making, separating us from obsession with its human contents. But darker implications of the idea were also apparent, for the decentering of the human figure, what Ortega y Gasset would call "the dehumanisation of art", had, in the wake of naturalism, a more ironic and disturbing meaning. Joseph Conrad's *The Secret Agent* (1907) is a novel of strange post-naturalist resonance, a novel without a hero, only the idiot Stevie attracting our ambiguous sympathy. But the overriding tone is irony, and Stevie is a victim, like all those who try to act in the world of pervasive anarchy that lies behind the facades of apparent civilisation. Irony is the dominant spirit throughout, emptying away traditional significance. It gives abstraction to the book, not to express a new freedom of art but to disclose an absurd world and a destructive, nihilistic age of random political violence and social rage. This kind of abstraction was to become an essential strand of modernism, its source lying not in the aesthetic refinement of the work but in the interpretation of modern society and the way it undermined significant existence and stable meaning. It was not the refinement of art but the force of history that was driving the figure from the landscape and giving to much modern fiction a profound irony of form.

As war came closer this kind of abstraction, harder and more violent, became more evident – in expressionism, futurism and vorticism. "As far as one can see, the new 'tendency toward abstraction' will culminate, not so much in the simple geometrical forms found in archaic art, but in more complicated ones associated in our minds with the idea of machinery," said T.E. Hulme in his 1914 lecture on "Modern Art", which looked in the direction of futurism. When in 1918 Wyndham Lewis, essentially a painter who turned to fiction and brought to it the ideas of vorticism and futurism, published his "vorticist" novel *Tarr* it was a comedy of machines, where the characters are automata, human mechanisms seen in absurd performance. Tarr's mind is full of "sinister piston-rods, organ-like shapes, heavy drills", and this rendering of the human figure produces a Bergsonian comedy, the method of "the Great Without". Lewis was determinedly rejecting "fiction from the in-side", the interiorised novel of consciousness such as Virginia Woolf would write, on the grounds that it romanticised consciousness. Such views from futurism had great impact, even on the apparently romantic modernism of D.H. Lawrence. "It is the inhuman will, call it physiology, or like Marinetti – physiology of matter, that fascinates me," he wrote in the famous letter of 1914 to Edward Garnett about his intentions for *Women in Love* (1915), which was to dispense with the "old-fashioned human element". "I don't so much care about what the woman *feels* .... I only care about what the woman *is* .... You mustn't look in my novel for the old stable *ego* – of the character ...". If Lawrence was attacking those powers of the mechanical arrayed *against* consciousness, he also saw the kinetic energy needed for a new novel of will and consciousness. This turning point in his work also coincided with his sense of a sharp break in history brought about by the war (it was, he said, in 1915 that the old world ended). Thus "abstraction" was increasingly being seen both as an artistic innovation consequent on new psychology *and* as a response to a dark historical circumstance: the process of mechanisa-tion that displaced the human being, and much of the humanist lore supporting him, from the centre of the world, and now victimised and destroyed him on the modern battlefield.

So *two* conceptions of abstraction had grown in the pre-war climate, and war brought them closer together. One saw the new forms as opportunity for deeper penetration of consciousness and the human subject; the other saw the displacement of the human figure as an anarchic historical victimisation. It took the calamitous war of 1914–18, which destroyed much of the content and hope of tradit-ional culture, questioned all affirmative rhetorics, disoriented moral-ity and faith, and challenged the view that man was master of the machine or historical process, to ensure the more ironic view grew more dominant. The art of the 1920s became an art of loss, with romantic hopes of significance and heroism defeated, the naturalist

lesson of victimisation true. It was, said Lawrence, a tragic age that
could not express itself tragically, and turned to irony. The modernism of the 1920s bears the marks of this, with its displacements of
story, its sense of culture in fragments, its wounded, battered and
broken image of the human figure. The violence and nihilism of the
battlefield had, suggests Frederick J. Hoffman in his fascinating book
The Mortal No: Death and the Modern Imagination (1964), become
components of modern style. "One important description of violence
is that it serves to threaten the balance of forms," he notes. "Since
forms are a result of the mental and imaginative functions, violence
frequently comes from a distortion of one or the other, which throws
the formal economy into imbalance." Like Walter Benjamin in his
essay "The Storyteller", Hoffman sees the penetration of war's
violence as the violence of modern change itself, becoming assailant
to the "tiny, fragile human body". Thus comes a changed concept of
art, dealing with force from the outside, and generating a sense of
insignificance and nihilism. The human figure lies wounded in a
world of violent and tragic absurdity – as do Ford's Tietjens,
Hemingway's Jake Barnes, several of the early heroes of Faulkner
and, more ambiguously, Lawrence's Clifford Chatterley.

In the painting and writing of the 1920s, we are thus aware of
abstraction not as a matter of purified form but a matter of history.
Often a tone of hard comic irony administers the sense of human
belittlement, as do the many characterless characters – Evelyn
Waugh's Paul Pennyfeather, Musil's "man without qualities" who
feels like "a human something floating about in a univeral culture-
medium", Svevo's self-ironising figures, or, of course, Kafka's
identityless heroes – who become the qualified, virtually absent
centre of an essential form of modernist fiction. "The one constant in
them all [Joyce, Woolf, Hemingway, Faulkner, Waugh and Huxley] is
the virtual disappearance of that focal character of the classical novel,
the conceptual Hero," says Sean O'Faolain in his book on the novel
of the 1920s, called *The Vanishing Hero* (1956). The destruction of
war, the defeat of significant values, the sense of historical decline,
the diminishing of human security, the new laws of uncertainty made
the notion of sympathetic fictional humanism implausible. As Waugh
puts it in *Decline and Fall* (1929), "the whole of this book is really an
account of the mysterious disappearance of Paul Pennyfeather, so
that readers must not complain if the shadow which took his name
does not amply fill out the important part of hero for which he was
originally cast."

This image of man as a weak, defeated actor on a dark and
dangerous historical stage, filled with racing history and an aggressive
external futility, moves on into the novels of the more political 1930s,

where the methods of surrealism and new preoccupations with psychological extremity intensify the sense of a simultaneous political and psychic displacement. Unstable and unfixed figures move through mysterious and darkly hostile landscapes – as they do in the still underestimated novels of Edward Upward and Rex Warner – toward some kind of destruction by the obscure but organised powers of force. There were now a number of different kinds of "dehumanisation" apparent in fiction, as in painting too. There is a sense of the pluralisation of the meanings of reality, which is at once totalistic and relativising; a sense too that the human self is a passive ego or patient-like id invaded by language. There is a sense of cultural emptiness and social dehumanisation, a vision of the process of modern society as inherently destructive to the individual. The "dehumanising" aspect of art now seemed increasingly to express an awareness of the exposure of the artist himself or herself. In interwar art there is often a strange duplicity, as we confront the work of fiction or the surrealist painting unsure whether its deformities are meant as positive acts of formal innovation or images of suffering. Surrealism frequently depends on the ambiguity; Francis Bacon's painting sustains it still. Thus abstraction might manifest new content but also loss of content, and it might be a willed anti-realism, or a new realism. Often it seems to fall between the poles, in a paradox of style. But in general it drives us to a dark conclusion. As Wylie Sypher puts it in his notable study of these things, *Loss of the Self in Modern Art and Literature* (1962), what much modern art surely discloses to us is that "the romantic-liberal tradition created an idea of the self we have not only rejected but destroyed".

4 Today, of course, we no longer consider ourselves under the regimen of modernism. What came after still seems somewhat obscure; the period since World War Two has been one of wide and varied creativity but a great range of stylistic manners, and it has been hard to propose a coherent concept of contemporary style, though many attempts have been made, some very partial if not *parti pris*. But Christopher Butler's *After the Wake: An Essay on the Contemporary Avant Garde* (1980) seems to me a well-judged and well-illustrated attempt, notable in drawing less on contemporary literary theory, which has its own preoccupations, and more on the aesthetic arguments of artists and writers themselves. The book moves freely through fiction and painting, as also through contemporary music, drama and film, to discern the "common, though not necessarily explicit, aesthetic principles underlying much recent art". Butler

concludes that we indeed live "after the wake", that is, in a time stylistically successor to Joyce's *Finnegans Wake* (1939), the last great example of modernism. Following on not only from Joyce but the existentialist movement, he sees a distinctive stylistic phase emerging during the 1950s, variously expressed in the music of Boulez, Henze and Stockhausen, the painterly movements of abstract expressionism and pop art, the new cinema of Chabrol, Truffaut and Godard, and the *nouveau roman*: "For better or worse, this is the age of Beckett and Robbe-Grillet, of Cage, Messiaen, Boulez, of Pollock, Rothko, Stella, and Rauschenberg." He also sees two primary trends, apparently antithetical, yet often interlinked, in these new arts: a line of works dominated "by a theory of their own rule-dominated means of creation" (such as the novels of the *nouveaux romanciers*) and another shaped by theories and methods "irrationalist, indeterminate or aleatory" (the novels of Burroughs, the action paintings of Pollock).

We have tried to draw much of this together under the term "postmodernism", on which I reflect in another of the essays here. If it is useful, it seems to me best to apply it capaciously, to an international range of trends and tendencies some of which, like those of modernism, appear profoundly contradictory and in contest. Above all it seems useful to consider it in relation to the steady oscillation between realistic and abstract impulses which seem to me to have dominated aesthetically since the war – a period which has seen both the existentialist-influenced realistic revival of the 1950s and the much more playful and abstractified experiments of the 1960s and since. As modern painting has shifted between abstract expressionism and hyper-realism, op art and pop art, so the fiction has shifted freely between the non-fiction novel and the new journalism and the self-begetting, self-questioning novel of the new fictionalists. The novelist, as David Lodge put it, seems to stand at the crossroads, disenchanted by median realism but also by the modernist inheritance: "the pressure of scepticism on the aesthetic and epistemological premises of literary realism is now so intense that many novelists, instead of marching confidently straight ahead, are at least considering the two routes that branch off in opposite directions from the crossroads. One of these routes leads to the non-fiction novel, and the other to what [Robert] Scholes calls 'fabulation'." Yet often, he points out, the roads meet further on, realism being now full of fictionalist scepticism and the fictionalist novel seeking to make its return to history in a time when, as Philip Roth once observed, contemporary reality sickens, infuriates, and outruns the imagination of any novelist.

What does seem clear in current painting and writing is that one of the great desires of modernism – to create a transcendent form that would stand outside history and reality in a great freeing of art – is hardly possible. Art is presented as subjective creation or a challenge to the reader or spectator, and it breaks and ironises its own frame in a latter-day scepticism. Painting and writing acknowledge the exhaustion of signs, the compromising of languages, the loss of transcendent signification, the need for quotation, parody and irony. Our painting and our writing switches between reduction and minimalism and fluent excess, high redundancy, challenging any wholeness of form, any clear epiphany. Abstraction challenges fixity. As Jackson Pollock put it: "Abstract painting is abstract. It confronts you. There was a reviewer a while back who wrote that my pictures didn't have a beginning, middle or end. He didn't mean it as a compliment, but it was." Fiction too refuses completion. "Endings are elusive, middles are nowhere to be found, but worst of all is to begin, to begin, to begin," writes Donald Barthelme, the American author who has persistently written by benefit of the painterly analogy, indeed often pictorialising his stories. We have an art in which realism itself feels like a quotation, an art that insists on its own lexical character while insistently questioning any lexical truth. "In all fictions of the future," writes the Franco-American novelist Raymond Federman, "all distinctions between the real and the imaginary, between the conscious and the unconscious, between the past and the present, between truth and untruth, will be abolished." Fictions both over-assert the presence of reality to the point of parody, or insist on their own process of making, produce their own *mis-en-abyme*.

From the moderns the tradition we seem to take most is the tradition of historical irony and anxiety, less that of Proust, Joyce, Woolf or Faulkner than that of Dostoevsky, Musil, Kafka. Our fiction is largely that of the lost subject, of waning humanism, disorienting history, unfixed and transient identity. Thus Manfred Pütz in his *The Story of Identity: American Fiction of the Sixties* (1979) proposes that in the American new fiction "subject matter and thematic concerns are transposed from problems of fictional characters to problems of the character of fiction . . . ". The collapse of the traditional "identities" of fiction not only involves a fading of the character, but of author, and reader. In an age when the general sense of human identity grows both flamboyant and parodic, when our presentation of self in everyday life becomes what Erving Goffman calls simply "a dramaturgical effect", an art in every sense without character seems an appropriate form. I have observed the demotion of the literary personality in fiction, and it might be said that even those writers who have used the novel to challenge this "loss of self in fiction" have felt the pressure of modern form. Bellow's novels are burdened with the existential loss of self, one essential topic of Herzog's maddened epistolary quarrel with the bearers of modern thought. Murdoch's "fit house for free characters" often has a strangely gothic facade. Fowles's desire to "free" characters from the prison of his own plot is set against the acknowledgement that he lives in the world of Barthes and Robbe-Grillet.

Our fiction bears our paradox, and of it we can again offer two accounts. One is that this art is enraged by and assaults our contemporary dehumanisation in the world of onerous realities, organisation men, the exterior plots of society and system. The other is that it is a post-humanist art, of a piece with the new indifference. Again, as in some modernism, much of the work seems itself ambiguous – the paintings of Warhol, the "cybernetic" novels of Pynchon, the so-called satires of Burroughs. But what is clear is that our technetronic age has its own art of vacancies and absences, where the human figure exists as cardboard cutout, parody performer, or clear absence. Ralph Ellison's *Invisible Man* is a portrait, as Philip Roth says, of a figure "as alone as a man may be". Jacob Horner, in John Barth's *The End of the Road*, exists "only in a sense". Thomas Pynchon's character V. is literally, as it were, deconstructed. Yet the disappearing figure is constantly seen in the light of history, as part of a vision of an increasingly characterless world. We could say that, in some kind of creative hope, the idea of character has been displaced, deferred, given a potential promise. Or we might say that the contemporary novel is witness to a disappearance that, no longer tragic, becomes simply a fact, that much fiction today is reaching the demise of the Proper Noun.

5 By this long path I return to Goya's painting on the walls of the Prado, and its importance to me. Goya, of course, worked long before most of the events and aesthetic attitudes on which I have been reflecting, and his work belongs to the turn from neo-classicism to romanticism. So, visiting the Prado, one sees many Goyas – the neo-classical and the dark romantic, the painter of court portraits and sensuous nudes, of formal events and the horrors of war, the artist of reason and the artist of unreason who gave to his early Caprichos the ambiguous motto "The sleep of reason begets monsters." But the monsters came to Goya, especially in the black paintings, surreal and terrible fantasies done in his darkest period, over a time of political disenchantment and withdrawal, serious illness, growing deafness and rising despair and nihilism. Anguish, horror and reason's sleep are manifest in these grotesque, surreal works – studies in pain, portraits of suffering and cruelty, desperate images drawn up both

from the imagination and the facts of a war-torn and violent world. The colour-range is narrow and sombre, the faces in the figure paintings contorted, the subjects horrifying: Saturn, or Time, devouring his own children; a battlefield seen as a terrible witches' sabbath. The paintings form a sequence; but "A Dog Engulfed in Sand" stands out from the others, and this is mainly because of its element of abstraction.

Indeed on first sight it appears not to be a figure painting at all. There are two dominant blocks of colour, distinct but intersecting; a fainter third panel rises on the right. But on the line where the two main panels meet, a flurried blob of grey paint reveals a figurative subject, hard to identify. It is one of Goya's anguished heads, the head of a dog protruding up from the lower colour plane. The body is absent, and we could think of it as hidden from us by the contours of rolling sand, or (as the museum title of the painting suggests) being engulfed or swallowed in quicksand. The recognition transforms, humanises and makes terrible the painting, removes it from abstraction. Like a character in a novel, it generates empathy, produces realism. The sandy shade becomes the sand, the greens, browns and blues a pitiless sky. The construction remains abstract but loses its nature as pure form; the abstraction surrounds, threatens and ironises the living figure. "Abstraction" is a modern word, outside Goya's aesthetics. And since the painting underwent restoration in the move from Goya's house to the museum, some of its abstraction may come from loss of detail. But the composition seems clear; three large blocks of colour form the fundamentals, and emphasise the smallness and bodilessness of the figure. So the painting allegorises the problem it poses. Its abstraction *emphasises* its fantastic realism. Form *and* the pitiless world engulf the central figure, asserting and denying the pure composition. The painting opens two divergent dimensions of art; one toward an intense and agonised realism, the other toward a greater formalism and a purer abstraction.

Probably Picasso knew the painting, and drew on it for his own abstraction. So too, I expect, did Ortega y Gasset, who gave us one of the most thoughtful reflections we have on the matter I am concerned with, in his essay "The Dehumanization of Art" (1948), which deals with modern art, and especially with its tendency to "dehumanize" itself by rejecting familiar identifications and sympathies, and removing itself into the realm of aesthetic speculation. The impulses of modernist art, he says, are striking precisely because they are "not of a generically human kind", since the modern artist feels the need to violate normal perception in order to establish art's true subject; which is art itself. "Before, reality was overlaid with metaphors by way of ornament; now the tendency is to eliminate the extra-poetical, or

real, prop and to 'realize' the metaphor, to make it the *res poetica*."
Ortega's proposals closely resemble those of the Russian formalist
critic Viktor Shlovsky, whose essay of 1917, "Art as Technique",
offered the concept of "defamiliarisation" or "making strange" that
has been fundamental in modern aesthetics: "The technique of art is
to make things 'unfamiliar', to make form obscure, so as to increase
the difficulty and duration of perception," he observed. Ortega had a
similar view, though where Shlovsky is seeking a theory of form from
this, Ortega is specifically interested in what happens to the human
figure. "For the modern artist," he says, "aesthetic pleasure derives
from . . . triumph over human matter. That is why he has to drive
home his victory by presenting in each case the body of the strangled
victim." The "strangled victim", of course, is the trace of the human
figure, or the humanist and realist outlook, that remains a marker in
much modern art.

This, Ortega emphasises, is not at all new. Indeed "All great
periods of art have been careful not to let the work of art revolve
around human contents." But during the nineteenth century the arts
had moved toward realism, "a maximum aberration in the history of
taste", humanising art and laying it open to our identification and
feeling of direct involvement. It is by the "defamiliarization of the
familiar", he explains, that the artist establishes his appropriate
subject, art itself, but in the nineteenth century realism and humanism consorted, and men, houses and mountains in art became "our
good old friends". This went with the flourishing of narrative and the
novel, and in another essay, "Notes on the Novel", he goes on to
argue that this is the form where "imaginary personages appear like
living beings", a metaphor becoming a reality. So the modern arts of
abstraction have serious consequences for the form, turning its
direction away from being an art of adventures to an art of figures. As
I have said, this is a familiar view of the novel; as Iris Murdoch
observes, people have long read novels to know the world and share
its human contents. Others, including E.M. Forster in *Aspects of the
Novel* (1927), have made a similar point; Forster speaks of "round-
ness of character" as one of the novel's great achievements: "Since
the novelist is a human being there is an affinity between him and his
[human] subject-matter which is absent in many other forms of art."

What Ortega argues is that because of this companionship
between the novel and humanism the arts of abstraction, dehumanisation, function in a special way, as a kind of irony. In the novel,
perhaps more than in any other form, we are aware of Ortega's
"strangled victim", and responsive to his appeal. Ortega emphasises
that this is the aesthetic effect of many great modern fictions, and
certainly in many of our most experimental modern works – *Ulysses*,

As I Lay Dying or *The Unnamable* might be examples – realism and form tug painfully at each other, creating an art somewhere between metonymy and metaphor, an art where what Forster calls those "wordmasses . . ., [the novelist's] characters" lie ambiguously somewhere on and beyond the page. Ortega emphasises the power of this frequent irony, suggesting that modern readers cannot read a work without it. But, as I have been arguing, this irony is not solely an aesthetic effect; it has something to do with our vision of our condition, and in many of our best writers, from Conrad to Kafka, Camus to Beckett, it carries a sense of human victimisation. "It would be senseless for author to try to convince readers that his characters had actually lived," Milan Kundera writes in *The Unbearable Lightness of Being* (1984). "They were not born of a mother's womb; they were born of a stimulating phrase or two or from a basic situation." Yet this does not prevent them from carrying a burden of existence. "The characters in my novels are my own unrealized possibilities," Kundera writes: "The novel is not the author's confession; it is an investigation of human life in the trap the world has become."

It is because of this irony that Goya's painting exercises its extraordinary impression. Neither a work of pure abstraction nor of definite intent to abstraction, it is a comment on the painter's own psychological state and his view of history. If anything, Goya was prefiguring nineteenth-century romantic realism rather than twentieth-century abstraction. But it was its sense of the "strangled victim" that made it directly significant for the novel I was writing. I had begun writing fiction in a time of humanistic realism, and I did not mean to reject realism and all its works. *The History Man* is about history, about the way we construct it as a fiction, in the presence of reality, much as we do a novel. It is history, as reality, that my central character, Howard Kirk, believes he can summon to do his work. Where others see contingency, accident, or moral ambiguity he sees process, and in a plotless world he has the will and some of the power to plot it, transforming the present into a promise for the future, the fashionable into an ultimate form of truth. It is also a novel of dehumanisation, and not solely because it seeks to abstractify form. That arises from other fictions we have constructed with the same sense of history, from the modern cityscape, the blank world of multistorey carparks, cement shopping centres, treeless spaces, dead underpasses, even in the paradisal place itself, the new university, where the architecture is filled with postmodern conceits, and the graffiti and revolts of modern irritability show everywhere. The abstraction of this world is hardly my own. It is a collective product of our behaviourist thinking and our blank-faced social order, our massing and our materialism, our endless displays of egotism and indifference, our community of hard abstraction where it is indeed difficult to find a way of putting in the person.

In one sense my book is almost over-insistently realistic, filled with material history; goods and chattels, designer objects and brand-labels, the fads and fashions by which we hope to construct the year of 1972 or whatever, and put it in history. In another sense it is abstract, separated from sympathy and warm feeling, certainly a large step away from the affectionate, familiarising realism of my first two novels. It vacates a space at the centre, the space filled by that realism that makes the world our good old friend. No doubt my view of things had darkened, my sense that the struggle for humane values was put in doubt as much by the utopian desires of radicalism as by the materialism of modern society much increased, for the values of humanism – scepticism, tolerance, gentleness – seemed rejected on all sides in a world more and more given to totalistic ideas and millennial and coercive visions. For a hard world hard ironic methods seemed in order, and these had to do with my own sense of truth. Irony seems to me to be an art of troubled displacements, and in her novel *The Black Prince* Iris Murdoch has some fascinating passing thoughts on this topic, suggesting that irony is our way of coping with our lack of a more direct access to beauty and truth. Yet, as Ortega says, we seem curiously to need it to withdraw from the sentimental, the romantic and the utopian, to inject the sense of indirection, obscurity and pain. As comedy so often deals with the gap between our ideals and our practice, irony more bitterly creates distance, difficulty, estrangement, makes us aware of the pain that lies in the body of the strangled victim.

Few writers know the sum of their style, and novelists can do little to explain their novels, especially in the age of the death of the author. But they can reflect a little on what they have deliberately chosen to do. I meant *The History Man* to be a book read from a distance, without directly engaging sympathy or intimacy, without offering an easy entrance. Thus I chose not to enter the psychology or conscious-ness of the characters, but to present them from outside by their speech, their signs, their actions, having them reveal themselves by their words and their historical behaviour. Even their dialogue, presented as just another phenomenon in paragraphs, all about the same length, which mixed speech with event, is intended to hold them inside the text. The narrative tense is largely the present tense, emphasising the instantaneous and the phenomenal, and reducing causality and explanation. The narrative is circular, and words and phrases that start the book with variation end it. It is manifestly not a story the author would have happen. The one apparently sympathetic character, Anne Callendar, cannot sustain her values in this world, and is compelled to sacrifice them to the one character who can, Howard Kirk. Kirk, the radical sociologist who, four years after the apocalyptic moment of 1968, is, after all, the one figure of will and energy in this passive world, and you might say he was post-humanism about its business; for, in a world without actors, he acts, and this gives him a virtue. Otherwise, in a time where goodwill cannot attach itself to any action, passivity is the norm. Life seems contingent, made of accidents or happenings; in a plotless world, Howard is the only one who plots, meaning everyone's good, his success however being at the price of a tragic victimisation of another character whose story is not fully told. The mode is irony, and neither the world nor the people in it feel like our good old friends.

It is this mood of tragic irony that I associate with Goya's painting, and made me relate it to the book. In the painting's anxious duplicity, as abstraction and as pained realism, I found, I suppose, a reminder that style is never pure theory nor solely an answer to aesthetic preoccupations. It is a negotiation with one's sense of experience in history, a grammar for trying to apprehend our world in its significances and insignificances, connections and disconnections, through the complex instrument of fiction and form. The novelist's form is language, our particular means for attempting to construct through that problematic and now much-questioned instrument, our relation to the world we call real. Realism is a form of artistic expression, and already it is implicitly abstract. But it treats its abstraction as more than an aesthetic convention, and it has come to be one crucial way with which in art we may deal with our world. If our arts – fiction and painting, drama and film – offer us a new and hard modern topography, an eviscerated significance, a displacement and a sense of dehumanisation, there is good reason. Indeed it provokes identification and recognition, as somehow in the hardened acrylic realism of Hockney, the contingent world of Calvino, the detached landscape of Handke we encounter the sign of a world that is ours. The weakened characters, the uncertain plots, the hard edges, the troubled images, are forms of abstraction, but they are in our arts because they are also present outside them. In a process-centred and depersonalising world that displaces and shrinks the human figure, and which is fed by philosophies that justify the process, art can too easily acquiesce in all this; it also has a power of engrained resistance. The power of Goya's painting for me is that it enacts abstraction as tension, pain, unease, horror. The novel can never have its immediacy, but standing, as such a painting does, somewhere between realism and abstraction, form and history, it possesses a similar power of irony – the power, in the conflict between subject and form, to bring into being a sense of the suffering of the strangled victim.

AN AGE OF PARODY
Style in the modern arts

"We are backward-looking explorers and parody is the central expression of our times."

Dwight Macdonald, Parodies: An Anthology (1916)

"We have defined literary discourse as parody, as a contestation of language rather than a representation of reality. It distorts rather than imitates. Moreover the idea of imitation, correctly understood, implies distortion . . . . In this sense, all literature is ultimately baroque in inspiration."

Pierre Macherey, A Theory of Literary Production (1966)

"So This Is Dyoublong?
Hush! Caution! Echoland!"

James Joyce, Finnegans Wake (1939)

1 Now and then it is my way to go off to conferences, strange and unnatural occasions where the devotees of some important intellectual thought or other gather with lectures in their briefcases and plastic nametags on their lapels to discuss crucial matters, often in some distant place where the sun beats distractingly down outside and the surf bangs noisily against the nearby beach. Ignoring all this, the devotees explore their devotion and then return home, to explain to their loved ones that they have seen neither sign nor sight of the place to which they have jetted so far. More strangely, they frequently come back totally reinforced in the opinions they went with, and explain the congress as a complete confirmation of them. Hence there are times when people – especially those who do not go to conferences – wonder whether and why others go to them at all. But the price of contemporary intellectual life is high, so despite all this I occasionally agree to attend such events, and a few years back I went to an international symposium of writers and critics who gathered on a group of Pacific rocks which Captain Cook had named the Sandwich Islands but the modern natives call Hawaii. The venue was for once appropriate, because this was an occasion when writers and

critics from the United States and Europe were meeting with writers and critics from the countries of South East Asia and the Pacific, for the purpose of discussing the global nature of modern culture and the general internationalisation and cross-cultural fertilisation of the arts. Conferences often gather together to agree on the obvious, and I went assuming that the internationality of the modern arts was one of those matters that, like goodness and virtue, all those present would profess themselves in favour of. In the event, it turned out when we gathered that I was quite wrong.

In the Western arts, the notion of the international republic of letters, the Arnoldian view of culture as the best that is known and thought in the world, is a deeply rooted value. It goes back to the cosmopolitan history of intellectual relations that derive from the Graeco-Roman world, develops through the wandering scholar and the notion of a common European intellectual heritage, and has spread through the invention of printing and publishing and the general growth of literacy. If we assume that our arts owe much to the local and the regional, to homely and domestic sources, we also assume that they have much to do with travel and emigration, wandering and exile. Our artists – not all, but many of them – assume that they belong to the frontierless world of the arts which has its capitals and provinces on a different map from that of conventional geography, and whether driven by artistic need or the taxman they frequently settle elsewhere. The Dedalus voyage of the artist leaving home and country in order to forge the uncreated conscience of the race is for us a source of a major quality of our arts, its transnationality, its polyglottism, its hunger for globalism. The great movements in our arts, from neo-classicism to modernism, have developed on international foundations, the flow of style and thought, and this has been particularly true of modernism. As George Steiner has pointed out, many of our major modern arts have been "extra-territorial", the work of writers unhoused, displaced not only geographically but linguistically, sometimes by the disorders, wars and revolutions, or the intellectual persecutions, of our states in an age of power and totalitarianism, but sometimes by their own artistic need. From Joyce and Conrad to Mann and Brecht and Nabokov and Beckett, our arts have an expatriate or émigré quality, a strong sense of translatability, a global reach. They have grown from friction along cultural borders, from bohemian interchange, from the pressure of language on language, the superimposition of styles and forms on other forms, from the intersection of worldviews and mannerisms.

In all of this achievement, this creation of a major phase of art, we can read out a price. Modernism itself seems to be a condition of modernisation, the great historical disorientation that has moved us

from the older world of the *gemeinschaft* into that of the *gesellschaft*. It
belongs not just to an age of avant garde bohemianism and generative
new forms, but to the workings of new technologies, new systems of
communication, new economic spread and aggression. Its arts are
often fed by a rage against this world, and shaped by a haunting sense
of fragmentation and loss, of waste land exposure and alienation. The
writings of modernism and those arts that have followed on from it,
and that we now have come to call postmodernism, are thus, as our
critics point out, troubled by silences and absences, a consciousness
of lost meanings and lost coherences, feelings of absurdity and
nothingness. The sign will not signify, the real will not reveal itself,
and humanism feels like a trace. (So, says Pierre Macherey in his book
A Theory of Literary Production, "You will understand why, in this
book, the word 'creation' is suppressed, and systematically replaced
by 'production'.") Our arts bear the burden of revolt against the
technological and material world that seems to have displaced them,
and speak of codes and structures that defamiliarise their materials,
drives the subject into system, and the self into silence. They are arts
both of complex and self-generating form and historical vacancy, of a
resounding and exotic fullness and a striking emptiness, arts that have
vacated the middle space of culture, arts that, as Kurt Vonnegut puts
it, seek to be reasonable all the time in a universe that was not meant
to be reasonable.

To many of the writers from South East Asia and the Pacific at
our conference, it is not the arts of such flamboyant complexity and
alienation which matter. Belonging to cultures where the arts are
closer to the habitual and the customary, where the oral tradition
often dominates over the written, and the artist is closer to a speaking
voice and a living memory in a local or regional community, to them
the very idea of global culture seemed a form of oppression, an aspect
of a general new imperialism. They did not acknowledge the
standards of originality and artistic individuality; they were less
concerned with the mannerist arts of modernism or postmodernism
than the pressure of the general cultural system out of which they
arise, the spread of Western commerce and technologies, the dominant power of mechanical mass-culture. The world culture that is
spreading from the West and penetrating everywhere now is modern
Superculture, in a sense everyone's culture and in another sense
no-one's at all. The new technologies may be assimilated and
developed, but the technology secretes its content. In Sony lies
Dallas, beyond the avant garde lies the endless mass-media serial that
encompasses alike *Ulysses* and *Starsky and Hutch*, in the world market
lies the collapse of habitual and rooted cultures. Superculture speaks
to a certain kind of human universality, and a certain kind of

emptiness. It disrupts old and customary uses for art, generates economic and linguistic generation, fragments culture, and leaves the artist as a commercial expert in fragile phenomena. Art becomes assimilated into the overwhelming production systems which package and distribute it. There is a great multiplicity of goods, a general universalising of signs, but there is also a want of significance. And it is not surprising, several of these writers suggested, that art becomes detached, rootless, pure style, or perhaps pure anti-style.

These were the debates of our conference, perhaps itself an image of the issues it raised, as writers from the Pacific, South East Asia and Japan gathered in a Westernised Pacific centre and spoke the *lingua franca* of English. But conferences often do take breaks, and one afternoon we were persuaded to stop talking and visit nearby downtown Honolulu, which was reputed to be attractive. And indeed there was sun, surf, beach and iced-drinks, but the object of pilgrimage chosen for our quest turned out to be a shopping centre, the Aloa Moana, said to be the largest in the world. And no doubt that week or that year it was; now, somewhere, in Tokyo or Toronto, Munich or Manchester, Hong Kong or Dusseldorf, there must be a bigger biggest. Its form was familiar, a great conglomerate of stores and boutiques with massive capital outlay and accumulation of commodities, laid out on many levels, covering many acres, brightened by trees and musak, umbrellas and fire-eaters, a great *souk* of carefully displayed offerings in elegant seductive orifices which tempted desire, entry and even purchase. And since this was Hawaii, where the main utterance is *aloha*, and East and West do indeed meet together, the mixture was richer and more polyglot than usual. You could walk through galleries and terraces, up elevators and down escalators, past palm-trees and tropical flowers, screeching birds and screeching stereos, benches for the exhausted and the excluded, and here was a Japanese teahouse, an Hawaiian mummu store, a Parisian boutique, a Belgian chocolate shop, there an English pub, an American burgerhouse, a Finnish textile-store, a Thai tie-shop. If appetite struck, there were food areas sacred to Colonel Sanders and Arthur Treacher, but you could also eat Polynesian, Korean, Chinese, Japanese, Jewish, Turkish, Polish, Armenian, Indian, Filipino, English, Australian and junk. Nothing seemed absent, everything seemed present, and nothing seemed there.

Perhaps because the shopping centre offered useful commentary on our discussion, perhaps for more venial reasons, we manged to detain ourselves there for most of an afternoon, wandering in and out of the fancy boutiques that, with their designer Band-Aids and left-handed mugs, offered us the new redundant necessities of life. For what, of course, was on display were not simply things as things, but a variety of styles and identities, ways of being, images, facades. Each temping orifice therefore promised not simply a commercial encounter with life's drab cash-register but a transforming cultural experience, an abbreviated course of style. You could be yuppie and guppie, hippie and faddie, upmarket or downmarket, young or ageing, a gourmet or a glutton, a health-freak or a surf-bum, and as Korean or Japanese or French or Italian or Californian as you liked. Buying the signs, you could take them home and let them radiate through your kitchen and your dinette, your living room and your bedroom, your life-style and your love-life. No identity was denied you, except possibly the one you probably thought you brought with you when you arrived in the first place. It was, often at knockdown prices, a sale of culture without consequences, or just as many consequences as you wished to have. It was a playful modern theatre of international commodity existence, with all the pleasure of theatre and all its anxiety, as facades crumble, experiences dissolve, the scene changes, the actors recostume. The actors are us, and we have learned, and learn increasingly, to live in a display of multiple and random styles which are the stuff of our present often self-doubting existence.

So today it is possible to pass through an international airport anywhere in the world and have this same sense of theatricality, as we find it impossible to identify the nationality of the faces, the bodies, the clothes, the styles that pass in front of us – not just because the same goods from the same world stores with the same logos are universal, but so are the same facial expressions and ways of asserting presence, conviction, resentment, desire. The polyglot semiotics may hide many faiths, rages, different means, the sensuous surface of modern commercialism overlaying a turbulent process of global renegotiation of power and a fundamental process of historical change. But style itself has become our means of negotiating with history, consuming, displaying, spending, discovering, asserting, desiring. And it is style as collage, produced from cultural inter-penetration and the acceleration of human expectations, and creating a post-culture of rapid and instant identities made for an age that consumes them, constantly presents and performs, lives by signs and images, and has broken with the older and continuous imagery of a coherent culture.

We should not sentimentalise the certitude of the past, which often derived from oppressive authority, but we have entered an age of historical theatre different from that of the past. Modern man, as Karl Mannheim once observed, tells by the clock of history what the time is, and the signs of the times provide us with our auguries. "The self, then, as a performed character," Erving Goffman tells us in *The Presentation of Self in Everyday Life* (1959), "is not an organic thing that has a specific location, whose fundamental fate is to be born, to mature, and to die; it is a dramatic effect arising diffusely from a scene that is presented, and the characteristic issue, the crucial concern, is whether it will be credited or discredited." Goffman's "dramaturgical analogy" is of a piece with the newest philosophies of the Death of the Subject and the randomness of signs, the endless sense that style and self have become collage, that nothing has a single and unicultural meaning. Culture is seen as synchronic, history as change, and both become part of a politics of performance, self-knowing and ironic, by which we enact as much substance as we care to have, and reserve the right to invest ourselves differently tomorrow.

And this is of a piece with the "postmodern" condition in which our arts say they reside. André Malraux once suggested that, thanks to worldwide access and modern systems of retrieval and storage, we now live in an "imaginary museum" in which all styles from the present and the past exist simultaneously, and freely intersect. No one style or single mannerism is ours, to express our cultural unity or reality. Yet all are available. Our postmodern buildings declare themselves as constructs of random, eclectic quotation, where any reference can be relevant, form not following function but building fancy into it. We hear the same messages from our philosophers, exploring the gap between sign and signification, exploring the gap and slippage between stimulant and desire. Our painters work by collage and *objet trouvée*, our writers exploit random reference and chance. John Barth has announced "the literature of exhaustion": "Suppose you are a writer by vocation . . .," he observes, "and you feel, for example, that the novel, if not narrative literature generally, if not the printed word altogether, has by this hour of the world just about shot its bolt . . . [I]f you were the author of this paper you'd have written . . . novels which imitate the form of the Novel, by an author who imitates the role of Author." Like the manners of our lives, the arts suggest the present as a playful mood of carnival, and Barth speaks also of the "literature of replenishment", reinvigorated by random freedoms; fullness and emptiness seem much the same thing, circling round a vacated centre. Yet the suspect currency of our performances haunts us; surrounded by images, fed by the serial news of the times, reflected and refracted, we no longer believe we are in an era of reality.

The story of Narcissus is an old story, of a special relevance to the arts, always a repository of the mirrored and the mannered, the stylised, the ornamental and the decadent. For the arts that story has always been a guiding myth, since they are founded on the paradoxes of representation and the refraction of images. Art has always exposed its false-seeming and its transience, displayed its self-begetting. But it certainly does so the more today, as Linda Hutcheon emphasises in her book *Narcissistic Narrative: The Metafictional Paradox* (1980); it is the mirroring myth of Narcissus that best explains our modern writing. In his brilliant study of the contemporary American character *The Culture of Narcissism* (1978), Christopher Lasch suggests some interesting connections between the rising mannerism of our arts and the temper of the times. He sees the narcissistic temperament, the "banality of pseudo-self-awareness", as the guiding temper of a period when a traditional sense of historical realities has died, and an old way of life is coming to its end – "the culture of competitive individualism, which in its decadence has carried the logic of individualism to the extreme of a war of all against all, the pursuit of happiness to the dead end of a narcissistic preoccupation with the self". Lasch's book is a powerful study of the American "me decade", an era of political withdrawal, obsession with therapies, the time of Eric Berne's "intimacy, spontaneity and awareness" and Wayne Dyer's "Live . . . Be You . . . Enjoy . . . Love". He is particularly concerned with the break with an older politics and the emergence, in the 1960s, of a new radicalism of performance, a self-oriented revolt of styles, and of a politics of display, when, as in the Nixon presidency, pseudo-events and misinformation dominate, and statements are no longer true or untrue but operative or inoperative. The spirit of narcissism, a half-ironic pleasure in one's own performance, a hunger for recognition and celebrity, a desire to obliterate the identity of others through the mirrored acts of the self, the tendency to consume one's person as style, prevails. And in "postmodern" art he sees this same "irony of an increasing self-consciousness", expressing itself as a weariness. He quotes Donald Barthelme's wry reflection: 'Another story about writing a story! Another regressus in infinitum! Who doesn't prefer an art that at least overly imitates something other than its own processes?" But what art most mirrors is the mirror of narcissistic life. It is not alone in art but in life itself, increasingly fictionalised, that we live in an age of parody.

2 Certainly, whether because of the nature of the culture that surrounds us, the direction of our literary theory, or the practices and refractions of much of our major art, the notion that we do live today in an age of parody, and indeed an age of *modern* parody, has taken on powerful force in contemporary literary thought. "We are backward-looking explorers and parody is the central expression of our times," Dwight Macdonald tells us in the preface to his fine anthology *Parodies* (1961), suggesting that we live in an elderly culture that has been dependent on the artistic forms of the past. Others would explain modern parody as a distinctive and radical mode of break with the past, and assertion of the present. But Macdonald's own anthology, which takes us back as far as Chaucer and could have taken us much further, is enough to remind us that parody itself is nothing new. The term itself returns us to the Greeks, when it was associated with an inner commentary or ironic counterpoint in drama, and became seen as part of the repertoire of comic forms, a mode of imitative mockery. Certainly ours is by no means the only age to consider itself an Age of Parody, and several in the past have claimed the same. And many of what we see as central features of our own art and having to do with the parodic impulse have a similarly long history. If "self-reflexiveness" and "self-begetting" are part of it, then the arts have long been commentaries on themselves. If "mis-en-abyme", the self-mirroring, repeated reduplication, and entry into the apertures or labyrinths of the work's existence is required, then this too takes us far back through the history of art. If "intertextuality" is important, then the arts have long been concerned with imitation with variation. As Harold Bloom suggests, artists have always lived under the "anxiety of influence" and art has always proceeded by radical and creative misreading. Nearly all periods of artistic innovation have had a strong parodic impulse, advancing generic change. As the Russian formalist Boris Eichenbaum once put it: "In the evolution of each genre, there are times when its use for entirely serious or elevated objectives degenerates and produces a comic or parodic form . . . . And thus is produced the regeneration of the genre; it finds new possibilities and new forms."

Indeed the notion that all writing is a rewriting, all discourse an allusion to other discourse, is intellectually pervasive now, though that too is not new. Pierre Macherey suggests that *all* literary writing imitates the real use of language in an endless tease and questioning, and is therefore parody: "We have defined literary discourse as parody, as a contestation of language rather than a representation of reality. It distorts rather than imitates." Nonetheless the notion that the persistence and prevalence of parody in our own time has been so great as to change not only our aesthetic situation but our very ways of understanding the nature of literary and nearly all other writing has been strongly urged; the term "parody" has taken on an importance in literary theory it has never really had before. Indeed historically critics have normally relegated the parodic to the basement of low-grade literary activity, along with other base tactics like satire, travesty, burlesque and pastiche, all of which are themselves in the parodic repertoire. Now larger accounts are in vogue, and the intimacy between the parodic impulse and the major processes of modern art have been seen. So the term has taken on a critical and crucial function in our understanding of modernism and what has followed, those arts that are now called postmodern and, according to viewpoint, either dominate or represent one strand of the aesthetic developments of the latter half of our century. The arguments about whether the term is useful or the identification appropriate continue; "postmodernism" may be considered as no more than a local phenomenon largely confined to the United States in a limited period, or as a dominant concept as powerful as romanticism or baroque. But it is clear enough that we do have major arts which both allude to and transfigure those of modernism, and exist in an intertextual, or we could indeed say a parodic, relationship to it.

In fact, in taking the earlier term inside the later one, we directly propose by it an anxiety of influence, an historical condition – an art that in some fashion knows and reads modernism and acknowledges its centrality. Indeed that allusion shows on our painting and emerges from a significant part of our writing. Beyond that there is the further allusion or anxiety that has been imprinted on modernism itself, its own debate with and partial rejection of what in turn went before it, the era of realism. That double haunting does seem a familiar feature of quite a lot of our writing, seeking its new relation both with the fracturing spirit of modernism and the ways of nineteenth-century *vraisemblance*. And it seems therefore reasonable to claim, as a good many modern theoreticians have, a special closeness between the parodic impulse and this condition. Haunted alike by sense of alienation from coherent languages, forms and types, shaped by a high stylistic self-consciousness in an age when style seems to manifest both overfullness and emptiness, intensely aware of the fictionality of experience and the weary irony of narcissism, our arts seem especially disposed this way. We live, as Nathalie Sarraute once told us, in an "era of suspicion", when fictions of the real no longer satify; and it is not surprising that the modern writer thinks he shares a situation with those who feel their search for the "real" is beset by knowledge of its fictionality. This might drive art back into its own ambiguous paradoxes, which is that it is simultaneously allusive and self-referential; hence all art might seem a form of parody. If parody is a form of writing which seeks to allude without making fully real, if it persistently and mockingly hints at its own inauthenticity, if it implies that its themes and stories are already exhausted, this does not of itself make it new. But it does seem a culturally insistent tone, a feature of our age of glut and excess, our multiplying systems and structures of narrative and our ever-extending technological machinery for presenting them, our refractive culture constantly pluralised by travel, technology and cultural inter-penetration. It can indeed be argued that parody has moved from the margins to the centre, even as the centre, in the form of unified culture or authenticated and firmly authored facts, departs.

Certainly it has been commonplace over the last two or three decades for writers and critics to argue that we have reached a point of narrative exhaustion, though also to argue, as John Barth has done, that we have also found an oblique means of replenishment. Perhaps, as I have said, the two are not distinguishable. We are rich in abundance of invention, and our endless supply of fictions, films, dramas, novels, happenings offer a rich bazaar of styles and manners. But we are drawn again and again to manifesting this as incompleteness, irony, self-commentary, self-mockery; in film we have the mock western and the pastiche detective story and a massive inward system of allusion and commentary. Our paintings constantly allude to older paintings, our fictions to past fictions, either through formal self-mockery or what Antonia Byatt nicely has called "reader's greed", an uneasily engaged existence in the afterlife of past great texts. Parody is, I take it, an ironic renegotiation of the relationship between style and substance, so that the stylistic presentation passes into the foreground and the content is minimalised to the background, this often having comic effect. And at all cultural levels parodic forms of such a kind surround us, playing games with memory, nostalgia, recreation, conventional type. If we entrust to art the quest for authenticity, then that has been minimalised. Perhaps the notion of parody does help us cross the bridge between the nature of our modern historical situation and the direction of modern art. Many recent critics seem to have thought so, and taken the idea as a centre. Indeed this is the implication of two fascinating recent books – Margaret A. Rose's *Parody/Metafiction* (1979) and Linda Hutcheon's *A Theory of Parody* (1985), which in different ways and with a certain protective caution explore the literature and arts of modernism and postmodernism and make the case for a "modern parody".

3 As Margaret Rose emphasises, most of our great writers seem to have possessed the knowledge that in some sense all literature is a parodic imitation, all writing a *re*writing. Literature is the name for a monument that is both solid and evanescent: parody accepts the truth of the monument but also questions and tests the artifice used in its construction. It perpetuates and destroys, becomes a form of mysterious translation, exploring the mystery of institutionalisation and the paradox of the existence of any art-object. It exaggerates the process present in all art, the oscillation between mimesis and artifice, and emphasises both the present force and the redundant emptiness of some preceding aesthetic case. Thus it is a form of criticism, and most great writers have practised it. Sometimes what is parodied is a single writer, monumentally in the way, sometimes an entire phase of style or a genre, sometimes it is the work presently being constructed, a self-parody. Apparently defacing a classic text, parody can become one. Chaucer parodied the old romances, and Shakespeare Petrarch; the list is endless. Cervantes's *Don Quixote* parodied both the old romances and their reader in the text, and we take the work as an exemplary work of formal change. As Michel Foucault puts it in *The Order of Things* (1966):

> *Don Quixote* is the first modern work of literature, because in it we see the cruel reason of identities and difference making endless sport of signs and similitudes; because in it language breaks off its old kinship with things and enters into that lonely sovereignty from which it will reappear in its separated state, only as literature . . . .

Cervantes's great work, according to Foucault, represents the beginning of the modern *episteme* in literature – though, paradoxically, it also represents that move toward realism which many have seen as the prisonhouse of modern literature.

But *Don Quixote* is indeed a classic example of parody as generic innovation, just as were those radical works in Britain in the eighteenth century that evolved the genre we appropriately call "the novel". Henry Fielding, in his Preface to *Joseph Andrews*, tries to define the new genre, making it clear that it exists in mock-relation to the classic universals; it is "an epic poem in prose". It was also a parody of Richardson's fiction, itself a mixture of mock high-life romance and sentimental realism. Twenty years later Laurence Sterne parodied the emergent novel-form itself, with its tendency to tell the story of a hero's life from birth to maturity, proceeding by chronological sequence and the laws of cause and effect. Sterne starts his *Tristram Shandy* not with a birth but a botched conception; Tristram cannot maintain the order of logic, being drawn by random association; the linear plot cannot be maintained; and the story cannot be completed by anything other than the death of the author. As in Spain with *Don Quixote*, the novel and anti-novel in Britain start more or less side by side, and it is indeed the totality of the parodic purpose that makes these books what they became – not only the prototypes of fiction but the prototypes of modern parody.

The nineteenth century was another age of parody, from Jane Austen at the beginning of it to Henry James at the end. But *Northanger Abbey, Madame Bovary* or *Washington Square* are parodies of the sentimental romance, and their move is toward scepticism and realism. They familiarise the commonplace rather than defamiliarise the text, intensifying the sense of literature's authenticity, creating new styles conceived of as addressing both social and moral reality and realism. It was the antithetical impulse, that which emphasised fiction's nature as self-making, fiction, forgery that the twentieth century has released, making this kind of parody an essential part of modernism, and of modern literary theoretics.

4 We may certainly claim that in that massive change of forms and sensibility that came around the turning of the century and which we call modernism the arts of parody took on a far more central role. Perhaps all major new movements are a rewriting, of the forms of art, of the function of artists, of the notion of tradition and of the literary institution, and modernism was an overwhelming one. Its particular challenge was to realism, out of the self-challenges of which it was born. And realism was itself a self-conscious art, often investing its sensibility in parody. But it was also an investment, in some fundamental sense, in cultural substance; proposing, with whatever self-questioning, that the world is out there, and that words, sentences and fictional orders may evoke a sense of what is communally known to *be* out there and what the artist might record. If it plays with forgery and falsehood, if its art is made manifestly self-aware, then it does this in the interests of transmitting the sense of a greater truth, or conveying a fuller impression. It is a localised and familiarising art, asserting culture's determining wholeness and energy. In proportion as it grows more aestheticised and cosmopolitanised, it begins to lose something of its substantive realism. Thus Henry James's later work, deeply conscious of the presence of the artist and the cosmopolitanism of art, grows increasing derealised, emphasising the gap between aesthetic perception and the material world. It was just this that Gertrude Stein, that understanding admirer of the late James, was to read in his novels, recognising that they were potential works of modernism.

For indeed modernism proposed the disintegration of social substance, of first-order references, secure narrative traditions. It defamiliarised, derealised, made fragments the essence, aestheticised, abstractified, conceptualised. It shared with the new thought of the age the notion of man as the product of his own conceptual activities; as Ernst Cassirer put it in the 1920s, cognition was to be seen not as "a mere mirror, simply reflecting images in inward or outward data", but as "the well-springs of all formation". In the modernist arts the concept of the art and the manifest presence of the artist become aspects of the text, and the work is usually seen in the light of its own begetting, becoming not what is written but what is in the writing. This is what Robert Alter calls the self-aware novel, which is "a consistent effort to convey to us a sense of the fictional world as an authorial construct set up against a background of literary tradition and convention". And, aware of its own composition, its own textual relation with the realism that had gone before, its own fiction or forgery, it came to move toward the parodic. Recapitulating older predecessors with a new sense of tradition, quoting past forms to make new ones, the art of Proust, Joyce, Woolf, Mann, Gide, Faulkner, Beckett and Nabokov was novel and often deeply invested with the parodic. The parody, deeply rooted in such works as *Ulysses*, *The Waste Land*, or *The Counterfeiters*, could indeed seem of a new kind. Certainly many of our greatest moderns in writing and painting – from Joyce and Beckett to Picasso, Duchamp, Matisse, Magritte, Escher – have not only been parodists but have inhabited some of the central paradoxes *of* parody. We can take them as great modern stylists, while acknowledging that in their concept of style there is a profound undermining, an awareness that there is no stylistic certainty, no ultimate assertion that words and forms can convey as a totality. Indeed in their work we can see parody moving toward the centre of modern forms, becoming a constitutive mode of art.

Thus James Joyce, rewriting *The Odyssey*, set it in modern Dublin, as seen from the distance of Paris, looking back from an international distance at his provincial city, lovingly accumulating its naturalistic material, but enacting his distance as a style. The borrowed plot of the novel is of course the tale of a hero's wandering, testing and homecoming, the myth of the wanderer who returns in disguise to his native shore and discovers his world anew. Joyce engages a good deal of the myth, as he had earlier engaged the myth of Icarus, but he also parodies it, compressing its epic size into a narrowed space and subjecting it to the pressures of realism and specificity. Yet the realism is disputed too, and *Ulysses* is a narrative of many voices, each alluding to more stories and modes of storytelling. Above all there is a story of stories, about the wily hero narrating himself into his wife's bed, but the controlling storyteller proliferates modes of telling, a multiplicity of cultural voices and registers. The correspondences with old stories are both true and false: "not that the cases were identical or the reverse". At times the parodies, in the traditional fashion, mock verbal or artistic excess; more commonly they generate it, functioning more radically to exhibit the articulated flexibility of language and hence to generate a new form.

This is the enterprise that extends vastly further in *Finnegans Wake*, about which Samuel Beckett said: "Here form is content,

content is form .... His writing is not about something, it is something itself." The book – which Christopher Butler, in his *After the Wake* (1980), calls "the supreme example of self-conscious 'ecriture' ", and rightly takes as the source of much subsequent writing – is a multiple accumulation of crossed languages and language systems, a multicultural system of references and mythic typologies. Joyce's project for a supra-language for the novel generates a collaged discourse which, as Clive Hart advises, is also best read as an unbroken series of parodies. Some parts travesty previous tropes of expression, some mock specific works, including Joyce's own. But the self-parody works more fundamentally, to encompass the whole text it creates. As Jacob Korg puts it, the aim is multivalency of language, so that "no meaning is ever fixed, no word ever achieves a stable form, no location is final". *Finnegans Wake* accumulates pastiche to digest it, becoming a great work of linguistic pluralism, a totalistic parody, anti-imitative and standing only for itself. We could call it parody transcendent, or in Margaret Rose's term "parody/meta-fiction".

It is this that has given that hard and in some ways hostile text, produced just as the Second World War began, its central role in recent literary history, and indeed in recent literary theory. Christopher Butler suggests in *After the Wake* that its subversive parody opens out into new traditions, those we consider as postmodernism, and that what followed were two main heritages – a line of works dominated by "a theory of their own rule-dominated means of creation", self-begetting works like the novels of Beckett, Nabokov and Robbe-Grillet, and works of willing randomness, "irrationalist, indeterminate or aleatory", like the novels of William Burroughs or the paintings of Jackson Pollock. Indeed Joyce's "meta-fictional mirror to fiction" has itself been monumentalised. The works that follow frequently follow its way of being both a writing and a dissipation of writing, to the point where the text becomes a task for the reader to constitute (the quest offered to the reader/readers in and outside Italo Calvino's *If on a Winter's Night a Traveller* ... (1979), for example, which initiates, parodies and forecloses on ten different types of fictional opening). As Robert Scholes has put it, the modern multiplicity of styles is a function of a Joycean awareness of the problem of notation: "If each aspect of reality requires a different language, then Joyce would counter by generating an astonishing variety of codes." Yet, he adds, the postmodern writer cannot even accept Joyce's faith "in the transcribability of things. It is because reality cannot be recorded that reality is dead .... There is no mimesis, only poesis. No recording, only constructing." All manners are available, none are overtly referential, all stories are used up, and all are usable. The author is there, but does not affirm. The text itself reads, and misreads, a prior text. This puts parody at the centre of our fiction, a polyglot and cultureless form, an open knowledge of the ways of literature's making that refuses to conclude, to settle on the single narrative code, but tests and teases the mutability of literature's many different rates of exchange.

5 So it seems clear that in our century parodic activity has vastly increased, moved, in art and literature, in practice and theory, from the margins to the centre, and become a primary level of textual or painterly representation. An essential part of our art is an art of mirrorings and quotations, inward self-reference and mock-mimesis, of figural violation and aesthetic self-presence, which has displaced and estranged the naive-mimetic prototypes we associate with much nineteenth-century writing and challenged its habits of direct *vraisemblance*, orderly narrative, and dominant authorial control. Parody has made our disquiet with realism, and our foregrounding of writing, not a dispute with form but a new form – confirming the belief that somewhere a great fracture in writing occurred, some-where toward the end of the nineteenth century, shifting it, as Roland Barthes puts it, from the condition of the *lisible* to the condition of the *scriptible*, or self-conscious writerliness. And in this sense the centra-lisation of literary parody is closely twinned with the philosophical theories of an age, when, our leading philosophers tell us, we have done with the metaphysics of presence, with the controlling subject, and when we ourselves are written by writing like texts themselves, and are equally fragmentary, finding ourselves in a time when the real can only be quoted, or misquoted – indeed an age of parody. As Julia Kristeva puts it, "every text takes shape as a mosaic of citations, every text is the absorption and transformation of other texts. The notion of intertextuality comes to take the place of the notion of intersubjectiv-ity." Thus, interpreter and deconstructor, the parodic writer becomes a sufficient analogue of the contemporary philosopher, a bearer of the modern *episteme*.

And it is this that has reinforced the notion of a distinctively *modern* spirit of parody, and the view that parody not only accounts for the condition of writing in our time but its historical condition generally. As Margaret Rose puts it, not without some irony of her own:

> parody not only represents the rejection of an older concept of imitation, but comes to stand for a new idea of what "really

happens" – for, that is, the "deformation" of reality which is necessary to its reconstruction of the literary work. It is hence also important to note that such "deforming" imitation has now also come to describe parody, and to equate it with "mimesis"!

Indeed this is much the view Pierre Macherey takes, when he suggests that *all* literature is distorted imitation and is therefore parody. In other theory, however, parody has an historical evolution, relating those novels of the Enlightenment that can be seen as what Rose calls a "meta-fictional mirror to fiction" to the arts of modernity. Certainly it is not surprising that Cervantes, Rabelais and Sterne should not only have influenced modern writers, from Joyce and Woolf to Beckett and Borges and Nabokov and Grass, but become essential prototypes for modern literary theoreticians, from the Russian formalists of the earlier part of the century, like Shklovsky and Eichenbaum, to more recent theorists of the modern and the postmodern like Bakhtin, Macherey, Foucault, Iser and Derrida. Shklovsky found in *Tristram Shandy* a clear "laying bare of the literary device" that made it what we might now call a primary case of *écriture*. And the critical perception of literature as an art of "defamiliarization" and "deformation", of "ludic action" and "carnivalization", of "deconstruction" and "intertextuality", owes much both to the identification of these as the classic texts, and to an interpretation of the arts which identifies them with parody.

The issue whether there is a distinctive *modern* parody, different in kind from that of the past, is thus a problem important to contemporary theory, and in fact it is much considered in the two books by Rose and Hutcheon. Hutcheon acknowledges not difference in kind but in degree, while Rose suggests that there is, in effect, a modern form of meta-parody which is largely congruent with the meta-theory of the deconstructive enterprise of modern philosophy. Thus, says Rose,

> Parody in the work of modernists like Magritte (whose combination of images and signs can sometimes be compared with the game of "cross-reading") appears as a symptom of a new episteme – one in which not only the standard forms of representation and communication are questioned, but meta-criticism itself is ironized.

Indeed we know that Magritte suggested that Foucault's comment on the fracture between words and things fitted his own work, or the work to which he signs or sometimes does not sign the name "Magritte"; Foucault in turn wrote a commentary on Magritte. In this sense parody seems aware of the same crisis of nomination as is apparent in contemporary structuralist and deconstructionist theory. Everything is a writing or a semiotic, coded from the start, and the unmaking or deconstructing of codes becomes an activity in which the parodic writer and the philosopher become co-conspirators. Just this notion of the modern writer found in the position of modern deconstructive philosopher is advanced by J.-F. Lyotard in an essay in Ihab and Sally Hassan's collection *Innovation/Renovation* (1983):

> The postmodern would be that which, in the modern, puts forward the unpresentable in presentation itself; that which denies itself the solace of good forms, the consensus of a taste which would make it possible to share collectively the nostalgia for the unobtainable; that which searches for new presentations, not in order to enjoy them but in order to impart a stronger sense of the unpresentable. A postmodern artist or writer is in the position of a philosopher; the text he writes, the work he produces, are not in principle governed by pre-established rules, and they cannot be judged according to a determining judgment, by applying familiar categories to the text or to the work.

The connection is thus not hard to see. The parodic is the deferring indeterminacy, the opening of spaces and fractures, that is the mark alike of a modern writing and a modern post-essentialist philosophy. It belongs with the floating free of the signifier and the crisis of nomination; it claims the ludic freedom of a writing beyond nomination.

And no doubt there is a common condition that relates the practice of twentieth-century parody to those philosophies so much concerned with the disappearance of transcendence, the death of the author, the absence of the subject, and the foregrounding of language and the already coded and written. For many features of parody are analogous: its undermining of originality and the original, its insistence both on the dominant presence and the vacant absence of the prior text, and the making of the present text not as a report but as a writing. Existentially bereft, our modern arts do persistently incline to treat codes of sincerity and authenticity in ways which produce their collapse, to set habitual and received codes and aesthetic conventions in motion only that variation, combination and deviation can occur. Referential elements are absurdly highlighted or subverted, so that "character", "setting", "plot" and "theme" are no longer elemental but allusive. Narrative, grammatical and referential systems cross, and genres are intermingled. Fictions become labyrinths or enigmas, leading us back into the circular ruins of their own forged plots: "The heroes of the book are what can be loosely called methods of composition," says Vladimir Nabokov of one of his novels. As Raymond Federman puts it, the primary purpose of fiction becomes "to unmask its own fraudulence, and not to pretend any longer to pass for reality, for truth, or for beauty". Borges's own Don Parodi sees all structures as concepts of the mind, of types of fiction, open to the combinations of chances, a great garden of forking paths. Instances of the different *types* of parody occur widely through our arts and our writing, and all deserve their different kinds of analysis.

But we are left with a larger question. In Roland Barthes, Foucault, Derrida and others the decadence of writing is proposed. In this is an historiography of a certain kind, what Derrida describes as "a catastrophic consciousness, simultaneously destroyed and destructive". The present is seen as necessarily an era of disintegrative enterprises, and hence the parodic expresses loss, or at the least deferral. It is, as it were, ideological. In meta-fictional texts like the novels of Thomas Pynchon, with the abundant multiplication of narratives and registers without full signification, we have not only a parodic text but a parodic self, a world in which animate has become inanimate and we are simply writerly Stencils or yo-yoing Profanes. The intimacy between the parodic and the sense of literary exhaustion and writerly disintegration has been much canvassed. We can thus read in our times an art of accelerated parody congruent with our cultural pluralism, our sense of collapsed signification, or loss of subject and of sign. Yet this needs to be viewed with care. Fictions in literature and art have always sought to live within the self-governing and self-questioning mechanisms of their own making. The parodic frequently arises from the sense of the buoyancy and plurality of creation, out of the examination of stabilised or elevated models of artistic action. Artists and writers have long felt the need to deface the monumental, to open the door to the museum, to rewrite the written, to construct the premise of a new originality.

To create literature is to hunger for style and mannerism, and yet to seek to evade the rule of the already written. All writing is in some form what Raymond Queneau calls "exercises in style". Certainly in a growing spirit of experimental variety parodic and self-questioning modes multiply in our arts, and they parody not simply some prior text but the form of writing, the author, the reader, the book. Books come, like B.S. Johnson's *The Unfortunates*, in boxes for the pages to be shuffled, with many endings, like Fowles's *The French Lieutenant's Woman* or Brautigan's *A Confederate General at Big Sur*, as fictions for tape and live voice, as in Barth's *Lost in the Funhouse*. Imitation grows closer and closer to full knowledge of its own absurdity, and pastiche stories, borrowed characters and mimed styles fill our arts, in fiction, for example, in the work of Beckett and Borges, Calvino and Barth, Nabokov and Fowles. Parody, which is at once imitation and forgery, enters deep into many of these texts, and skates buoyantly along its surfaces. Yet, as Donald Barthelme suggests, in the spaces there is often a sadness. "Nothing is real. All is fiction," says the central character of John Fowles's *The Enigma*; but a sense that at the heart of the story there *is* an enigma still survives. No doubt our parody is an historical and a cultural as well as a formal event, relating to the pervasive fictions of the world, the vacancies and deadened codes of our system-ridden and material social order. The penetration and interpretation of parody, and our sense of it as a major artistic premise, probably best helps if we do not see it solely either as a trivialising or as a totally deconstructing enterprise, but as a form of enquiry for disorienting but also innovative times. And parody is not simply a crisis of language, but a major form of creative play and artistic self-discovery which can give us a joyously experimental and comic art.

PART TWO

Decades and Seasons

"CLOSING TIME IN THE GARDENS"
Or, what happened to writing in the 1940s

"But from now onwards the all-important fact for the creative writer is going to be that this is not a writer's world. That does not mean he cannot help to bring the new society into being, but he can take no part in the process *as a writer*. For *as a writer* he is a liberal, and what is happening is the destruction of liberalism. It seems likely, therefore, that in the remaining years of free speech any novel worth reading will follow more or less along the lines that [Henry] Miller has followed .... The passive attitude will come back, and it will be more consciously passive than before. Progress and reaction have both turned out to be swindles. Seemingly there is nothing left but quietism – robbing reality of its terrors by simply submitting to it. Get inside the whale – or rather, admit that you are inside the whale (for you *are*, of course). Give yourself over to the world-process .... "

George Orwell, "Inside the Whale" (1940)

" 'Nothing dreadful is ever done with, no bad thing gets any better; you can't be too serious.' This is the message of the Forties from which, alas, there seems no escape, for it is closing time in the gardens of the West and from now on an artist will be judged only by the resonance of his solitude or the quality of his despair."

Cyril Connolly, "Editorial", Horizon, December 1949/January 1950

1 The historians tell us that the decade is far too brief a time-span to reveal an historical trend or manifest any significant process of change or evolution. In artistic and cultural history it has a good deal more importance, for it is about the time it takes for a particular artistic generation to coalesce, or a particular style or mannerism to become central. Those large units we use to define the styles, intellectual directions and cultural values of whole eras – neo-classicism, romanticism, modernism – themselves dissolve into smaller processes of oscillation and variation. In our own historically accelerated century, when, as Karl Mannheim put it, we have learned "to tell by the clock of history what the time is,", and historicity has

become one of our most stimulating drugs, the cycle of decades has been an important part of our inheritance of thought and artistic experience. The massive historical events of the century – its scientific, technological and political revolutions, its two World Wars – have intensified the process. Today we have behind us decades that have taken on great intellectual and artistic character *as* decades. The fragile, decadent and transitional 1890s, the gay, materialistic lost generation of the 1920s, touched by the wound of war and the boredom of peace, are distinctive in this way. Usually they have been intimate with some large historical change. The 1890s was heavy with apocalyptic intimations of the new century to come. The 1920s began as the war ended, and closed in October 1929 with the Great Crash. The 1930s, which attempted to substitute politics for aesthetics, bolshevism for bohemia, began with the Depression, and ended with the outbreak of a new World War.

The immediately postwar decades now have acquired a somewhat similar clarity. The war marked a sharp break in cultural continuity, especially in those countries which were occupied or finally defeated, and in France, Germany and Italy the fracture was large. Previous styles and tendencies were tainted with accusations of intellectual betrayal and irresponsibility, and even in the victorious nations there was a sense of a break with the past, as if the directions of the first forty years of the century had been largely erroneous. This was the mood caught by existentialism, which, said Albert Camus in *The Rebel* (1951), was a reaction against the rise of those great historical nihilists Hitler and Mussolini, an endeavour, "in the face of murder and rebellion, to pursue a train of thought which began in suicide and the idea of the absurd", but led to a new "revolt of moderation". The revolt of moderation was the flavour of the Fifties, a time dominated by images of Auschwitz and Buchenwald, Hiroshima and Nagasaki, the post-nuclear anxiety and the revival of cold war. The mood of the Fifties was that of the cautious reassertion of humanism, of distrust of the political gods of the Thirties and the extremities of avant gardeism in art. The mood of the Sixties, liberationist, radical and provisional-ised, was a revolt against the moralism and apoliticism, and the aesthetic caution, of the previous decade. Since then tendencies have grown less clear, perhaps partly because we are closer to them, partly because the historical markers of our own age – the oscillations and the economic world order, the vagaries of detente, the cycles of growth and depression that mark the uncertainties of the two dominant political systems, capitalism and communism – are them-selves less well defined. The dialogue and dispute between the Fifties and the Sixties still seems to dominate the directions of our art and culture, as we move toward a new and crucial marker, the end not only of a century but a millennium. But in this evolution one decade still seems obscure – the 1940s, the decade in which in fact the fundamental directions of art in the twentieth century seemed to change.

2 The 1940s, in Britain and elsewhere, seems to mark a vacancy in recent cultural history. They threw up few major new artists and writers, and the movements that were active in the decade – from hyper-reportage to surrealism and the New Apocalypse – never attained strong influence in the tradition. At first sight this seems hardly surprising. Artists in wartime are focused more on action than art, and more concerned with their own rather than the word's mortality. Even in societies that were not occupied and retained many of their liberal institutions, the facilities for artistic activity diminished. Though fewer artists and writers were killed in the Second World War than in the First, many were engaged in some form of active or national service. Lasting artistic production came to matter less, and, as George Orwell put it, "only the mentally dead are capable of sitting down and writing novels while this nightmare is going on." The relative artistic silence of the period from 1939 till toward the end of the 1940s seems very comprehensible, until we recall that the First World War, quite as terrible, and with equal restrictions on artistic activity, was a major seedbed of modern artistic innovation.

This is worth consideration, for it suggests a fundamental difference of reaction among artists to the First World War and the Second. We usually date the development of the modern movement from the 1890s, when the Victorian synthesis began to disintegrate, the impact of the new sciences and psychologies widely reshaped aesthetic values, and the intimations of the massive modernising changes of the twentieth century fragmented and restructured the direction of the arts in the West. The modern movement was active and vital long before 1914, yet in many ways the First World War seemed its validation. Its prophetic nihilisms and ironies, its consciousness of the dominating power of mechanism, the militaristic imagery that served its avant garde, conducting their campaigns and forays against bourgeois culture, the explosions and the blasts, its sense of lost signification, came to match the experience of chaos, nullity and the collapse of the whole era of cultural confidence. Georgian poetry famously died on the Somme, and the new Imagist anthologies appearing in London, with their hard and ironic verse, stripped of sentimental and natural imagery, became a newly

appropriate voice. The dislocations of experimental fiction caught the
new spirit, and many of the great modernist novels were written over
the bridge of the war, or in the years following it, a number of them
taking war as their theme. The crisis all this implied for the direction
of Western culture was, said Henry James, "too tragic for any words",
but the words came, fed by the apocalyptic implications of modernist
art. The sense that an era was over was universal – "It was in 1915 the
old world ended," said D.H. Lawrence – but so was the implication
that a new one, perhaps more terrible, was being born in the phoenix
rebirth. That sense of rebirth was justified in the experiments of the
1920s, one of the great eras of artistic revolution and reformation,
which still has its impact upon us today.

The mood as the Western nations embarked on the century's
Second World War was greatly different. Recording the event in his
autobiography *World Within World* (1951), Stephen Spender emphasises the sense of emotional and aesthetic passivity, of voicelessness,
taking a telling image from his diary: "Peter Watson travelled from
Paris to Calais a few days ago in a troop train. The compartment was
crowded with soldiers. They sat all the way in absolute silence, no one
saying a word." The passivity resembled the sense of art being
swamped by events that had been growing through the terrible
disorders of the Thirties, as in Christopher Isherwood's Berlin
stories, where the writer's eye becomes a flatly recording camera. For
an age of historical outrage and enormity, reportage, journalism, diary
and memoir, the arts of the provisional and transitional seemed the
right instruments. Art was forced to engage with "actuality", its sense
of the real deriving from an alert historical awareness and a physical
presence at the battlefields of the age; art yielded to action. Where the
First World War provoked new arts of minimalism, new vortices of
artistic energy, the Second apparently dulled expression. Perhaps the
two things were connected; Keith Douglas, one of the few important
poets to emerge from the wartime experience, observed that the same
horror cannot be written of twice; perhaps the literature of the
Second World War had already been written during and after the
First. Important writing did emerge, of course, often from writers
well established. The fragility and indirection of Elizabeth Bowen and
Henry Green seemed to encompass the chaos and fragmentation of
war as a natural subject, and once the war was over notable war novels
– Waugh's *Sword of Honour* trilogy, Olivia Manning's *Balkan Trilogy*
and *Levant Trilogy*, and so on – did appear, while the theme of war has
dominated much subsequent writing. But closer to the prevailing
mood was the spirit of Waugh's *Work Suspended* (1941), the novel he
was writing as war broke out. He left it unfinished, with a title
appropriate to the season: " . . . all our lives, as we have constructed

them, quietly came to an end," the narrator comments. "Our story, like my novel, remained unfinished – a heap of neglected foolscap at the back of a drawer."

The war, indeed, seemed to mark the end of the whole direction of recent writing. "Periods end when we are not looking . . .," wrote Cyril Connolly, that tireless promoter of the new arts, in his magazine *Horizon* for August 1941. "The last two years have been a turning point; an epidemic of dying has ended many movements." The deaths on which he was reflecting were those of Freud, Sir James Frazer, Sir Hugh Walpole, Virginia Woolf and James Joyce; he might have added a number more, including those of Yeats, Scott Fitzgerald and Nathanael West. What might have been expected was that a successor generation would emerge, and magazines like *Horizon* and John Lehmann's *New Writing* and *Penguin New Writing* existed to stir it into existence. But, by 1942, Lehmann was complaining that "this war has still found no writer in prose or verse to interpret it with anything like . . . depth and power." By the issue of *Horizon* for December 1947 Connolly was even more emphatic, declaring "such a thing as avant garde in literature has ceased to exist." The war had not produced the significant new talents, and the peace that followed, sombre and cautious, was not producing them either. The revelations of 1945, of the holocaust and the atomic bombings of Japan, seemed to prolong the silence. "We come *after*," George Steiner explained in his book *Language and Silence* (1967), "and that is the nerve of our condition. After the unprecedented ruin of humane values and hopes by the political bestiality of our age." "No poetry after Auschwitz," said Adorno; it was not surprising that the arts that did emerge postwar were marked by minimalism and muteness.

Perhaps the most telling prophecy of this state of affairs had come in an essay written by George Orwell as the war started, "Inside the Whale" (1940), where he argued that the rise of totalitarianism and the military state had finished bourgeois literature, and shown "the impossibility of any major literature until the world has shaken itself into its new shape". Orwell proposed that the new literature would be neither democratic nor humane, but something new altogether. The prophecies, happily, were to prove imperfect, but they still have considerable meaning for us. The notion that our arts have grown bereft of their humane and moral content, that we suffer great difficulty in constructing an art of humanistic power in the technetronic, politically massed and materialistic age in which we live, still affects us. Much of our postwar writing has felt the force of the crisis of an age in which, as Philip Roth once wrote, the actuality continually outdoes our talents, and the horrors and deceptions of the time outrun any inventions of the imagination. The sense of fracture marked by the 1940s has shaped literary and artistic directions ever since, and our arts have regularly alluded to it. We now have the tendency that is perhaps gracelessly called "postmodernism", its name an expression both of break and continuity; the gap it speaks of seems to lie somewhere in the silences of the 1940s.

That sense of fracture appears as the great mark of writing in the 1940s. The "epidemic of dying" Connolly refers to seemed to go with the close of an era. Famously, Auden and Isherwood went to the United States, their symbolic departure a sign of fundamental change, to be followed by Auden's famous "change of heart" and the rewriting of his poems. We can trace similar changes in the careers of most of the dominant writers who continued their work onward from the 1920s and the 1930s. The pylon poets of the left withdrew from their political allegiances, and in the 1950s began to speak of the great political gods which had failed. Evelyn Waugh's work changed deeply over the wartime period, becoming a dark record of the failure of the just war to bring justice, and of the age of collectivism and the common man. War and the seediness of postwar austerity naturalised Graham Greene's novels of psychic crisis and spiritual betrayal; the ersatz world of George Orwell's fiction of the 1930s acquired the character of modern parable in the later novels that dominated the end of the 1940s, *Animal Farm* (1945) and *Nineteen Eighty-Four* (1949). Only one writer, Ivy Compton-Burnett, seemed able to take the historical world as eternal and untransformed, but by retaining the world that was she was able to maintain a conceit so powerful that it gave an extraordinary and radical convention to her work. So strong was this sense of break or fracture that most writers and intellectuals from the pre-war period seemed to challenge their forms and recant their allegiances in the postwar world. The 1940s was a period less of major arts than of fundamental redirections, redirections of enormous and powerful impact on our arts through to the present.

3 Literary history as written by writers is something of a personal matter, an endeavour to account for their own sense of direction and development. I started writing in the 1950s, and with a strong consciousness of a recent change of climate; it seemed to me that in the decade before some fundamental artistic and cultural transaction had been completed, altering the conditions and assumptions of writing. Over the 1940s, the direction of modern writing had indeed altered radically, and in that change of direction many of the tendencies of postwar writing were forged. The complex and varied achievement of the arts of the first forty years of the century had clearly been historicised and to some degree tainted by the historical events with which it had consorted, been moved back into the usable or maybe even the unusable past. Both the great era of modernism, the movement that still dominates the arts of our century, and the counter-movement against it that had grown up in the Thirties and assaulted its apoliticism, seemed no longer available, one reason why so many writers of the rising generation of the 1950s began to look back beyond and behind the creative directions of this century to the realism of the Victorian novel or the relative clarity and formalism of Victorian and earlier verse.

The "Modern Movement" that transformed the arts of the early twentieth century is a complex phenomenon, one we are still continuing to explore. But its roots lay in the collapse of the Victorian world-picture, the growing apprehension of a world of modern change and relativity, and in a fundamental redefinition of the role of the arts and the artist so profound that it seemed to many that the past had been abandoned. Modernism was indeed an art of modernity, of modern conditions and modern psychologies, and it shocked, outraged and transformed. But if many of its finest achievements lay in the period before the First World War, its peak undoubtedly came just after the war, and especially in what Harry Levin has identified as the "anni mirabili" of 1922 to 1925. Over these years appeared many of the key works of modernist literature; some had been long in the making, but they made their appearance at a moment of maximum concentration. Thus over those years there came out the middle volumes of Proust's *A la recherche du temps perdu*, Joyce's *Ulysses* (1922), Yeats's *Later Poems* (1922), Eliot's *The Waste Land* (1922), Svevo's *The Confessions of Zeno* (1923), Rilke's *Duino Elegies* (1923), Forster's *A Passage to India* (1924), Mann's *The Magic Mountain* (1924), Hemingway's *In Our Time* (1924), Lawrence's *England, My England* (1924), Woolf's *Mrs Dalloway* (1924), Kafka's *The Trial* (1925), Dos Passos's *Manhattan Transfer* (1925), Fitzgerald's *The Great Gatsby* (1925), Stein's *The Making of Americans* (1925) – and, far from incidentally, Spengler's *The Decline of the West* (1922), followed three years later by Hitler's *Mein Kampf* (1925).

Most of the younger writers who came to notice in the interwar years went in some fashion or another to school with all this. They assimilated many of its essential attitudes and ideas, took many of its principles and forms for granted, and generally shared its urgent sense of the pressure of the modern. What many – like Fitzgerald, Faulkner, Huxley or Waugh – added to this was a sense of their own war-formed modernity, a feeling of membership in a wounded generation which shared provisional sensibilities and fragile and threatened personal values, always at risk. In a society fascinated by the collapse of the cultural tradition, the loss of discourse and moral direction, and a Spenglerian sense of crisis, the modern mannerism in art acquired increased public acceptance and made many of these writers popular successes. Modernism was no longer the work of a remote avant garde; it was linked with contemporary sensibility and the flamboyant styles of the time, bearing the signature of a dominant cynicism and a darkened Waste Land sensibility that seemed to go with the feeling that this was a crisis age. The style of art came to match the style of life, the revolution of the word now seemed parallel to the revolution of the world. History seemed chaotic and contingent, but there was the redemption of form and style, style hard and yet fragile, ironic and indifferent, the telling voice of a disorderly age.

But by the 1930s, as economic depression raged, political crises deepened and fascism rose in Europe, a counter-movement rose. As Martin Green observes in his study of modern British intellectual culture, *Children of the Sun*, the decadents of the 1920s began to be replaced by the radicals of the 1930s, but they were much the same sort of people, with similar public school and university educations and related tastes. Modernism did not die in the 1930s, for the counter-movement acknowledged many of its implications, but sought to ally the modernist spirit to progressive and revolutionary functions. They asserted the claims of history and the relevance of politics, and challenged the "aesthetic" emphasis of the 1920s. Some of the modernists of the 1920s, especially in the United States, followed this new direction, but others deeply disputed it, generating a quarrel that was to be sustained right through the decade.

The fate of modernism and the successor tendency of the 1930s can be usefully read through the pages of the literary magazines. As modernism peaked in the early 1920s, T.S. Eliot started his review *The Criterion*, its first issue in 1922 containing his own "The Waste Land". "A review should be an organ of documentation . . .," he explained, "the bound volumes of a decade should represent the development of the keenest sensibility and the clearest thought of ten years." *The Criterion* performed this task sturdily, publishing Pound, Yeats, Hart Crane, Mann, Hesse, Pirandello and Cavafy, and announcing in 1929 that it had been the first British periodical to print Proust, Valéry, Cocteau, Jacques Riviere, Jacques Maritain, Charles Maurras, Wilhelm Worringer and Ernst Robert Curtius. In the 1930s it was to print Auden's "Paid on Both Sides" and Hugh McDiarmid's "Hymn to Lenin", but its broad alliances were not with the Left. Eliot had announced himself as a classicist, an Anglo-Catholic and a Royalist; his editorials insisted on the need to "maintain the autonomy and disinterestedness of literature", and to preserve cultural standards. Newer reviews, from *New Verse* to *The*

Left Review, grew up to offer a Left-wing literary standpoint, and
bitter arguments rose. By the end of the 1930s *The Criterion* was in
difficulties, and in January 1939 Eliot closed it with a set of depressed
reflections:

> For the immediate future, perhaps for a long way ahead, the
> continuity of culture may have to be maintained by a very small
> number of people indeed – and these not necessarily the best
> equipped with worldly advantages. It will not be the large organs of
> opinion, or the old periodicals, it must be the small and obscure
> papers and reviews, those who are hardly read by anyone but their
> own contributors, that will keep critical thought alive, and encour-
> age authors of original talent.

When magazines fail, editors understandably feel depressed, but
Eliot's instinct that a period was ending was valid enough. For Eliot
this was the cultural autarky that followed on political and economic
autarky, but there were others of very different disposition who saw
the paths of art being blocked. Virginia Woolf who, representing
Bloomsbury, was in retrospect to be seen as perhaps the most central
of British modernist novelists, found an even deeper despair. Her
novels of the Twenties have come to be regarded as exemplary
aesthetic objects, and her literary commentaries put at its best the
literary case for an art of modern fragments and apprehensions.
During the Thirties she maintained a close relation with the spirit of
what came to be called "new writing": indeed her Hogarth Press
printed those two key volumes of verse edited by Michael Roberts,
New Signatures (1932) and *New Country* (1933), which established the
Auden generation. Nonetheless her work was criticised for its
aesthetic rather than political emphasis, an accusation she confronted
in an essay, "The Leaning Tower", published in John Lehmann's
Folios of New Writing in 1940. If she acknowledged her own doubts,
she also looked with some irony at the public school radical writer
who "sits on a tower raised above the rest of us; a tower built first of
his parent's station, then upon his parent's gold", and who, when the
tower begins to lean, turns on society. The essay caused resentment,
and Edward Upward, B.L. Coombes and Louis MacNeice variously
attacked it in the next issue. Yet Woolf was essentially acknowledging
the precariousness of her own position, and by the time the replies
appeared she was dead by suicide, driven to despair by the bombing
of London and a sense of that dark modern flux that also haunted her
fiction. Her death, with that of Yeats and Joyce, marked the end of a
whole era of modernism, and to a considerable degree of the aesthetic
domination of Bloomsbury over British writing.
 The crisis that Woolf referred to in "The Leaning Tower" was a

complex one; what was dying, she felt, was not modernism but the
1930s spirit of bourgeois radicalism in writing. The writers who had
seen modernism as a "distortion" and history as the great experimen-
ter had been powerful for a decade, moving toward a new realism and
surrealism, a writing that was drawn to a new psychology and
sociology to explore the ersatz, surburbanised, troubled Thirties
world. The writer, Edward Upward declared in *The Mind in Chains*
(1937), now had to perceive through the eyes of the class that cannot
solve the problems confronting it, finding "reality" by moving to the
progressive side of the conflict, and only then will "it be possible for
his writing to give a true picture of the world". Thirties writers, said
John Lehmann, summing up the wave of "new writing" in his
Penguin book *New Writing in Europe* (1940), had become conscious of
"the great social, political and moral changes going on around them",
and had resolved to "communicate their vision of this process, not
merely to the so-called highbrow intellectual public to which their
predecessors had addressed themselves, but to the widest possible
circles of ordinary people engaged in the daily struggle of their
existence". But Lehmann's book, written in wartime, acknowledged
that much of this enterprise was over. His study tried, he said, to show

> how the seed which lay at the heart of the whole movement, – to put
> it shortly, the idea of *public* writing, of speaking to the people and
> with the people in their struggle for a better world, – reached its full
> flowering during the early period of the Spanish [Civil] War. I have
> also tried to show that contradictions were beginning to appear even
> while the movement was at its height. The real disintegration
> started before the War was over . . . .

Thus, by the end of the 1930s, this tendency too was in disarray,
and Marxist reality was proving as fictional as any other. The Moscow
Show Trials, the Soviet manipulations of the Republican cause
during the Spanish Civil War, and the Nazi-Soviet Pact intensified
disillusionment, and by the time of war's outbreak the mood of the
writers of the Left had changed. As J.A. Morris has pointed out, the
collapse of proletarian realism encouraged the release of many of the
under-movements of the 1930s – satire, allegory, parable, fable.
Modern history was less a crisis of real forces than a mass psychosis,
and the immediately pre-war years saw the publication of a striking
group of literary works concerned with socio-psychotic disorder:
Auden's and Isherwood's *On the Frontier* (1938), Spender's *Trial of a
Judge* (1938), Rex Warner's *The Wild Goose Chase* (1937), *The
Professor* (1938) and *The Aerodrome* (1941), Edward Upward's *Journey
to the Border* (1938), Graham Greene's *The Power and the Glory*
(1940), and Arthur Koestler's portrait of the Moscow purges,

Darkness at Noon (1940). As Lehmann explained it in *The Whispering Gallery* (1955), the hangover had set in, and the best books became "those which illuminated, not the cruelties of fascism and the perversions of fascist thinking, but the equally menacing evils that fanatical left-wing idealism could lead to". And a writing that had been dominated for some time by images of the marauding raid, the barbed frontier, the flights of bombers, crashed aircraft, damaged factories, fumbling wasteland lusts and uniformed encounters, ersatz foods, queues and ration books, as well as the stench of betrayal and the aroma of suspicion, now found this the stuff of direct reality, as the barbed wire and sandbags went up in London and the raids began.

All this was the background to George Orwell's essay "Inside the Whale", which he printed in an essay-collection of that title in 1940. Orwell's argument assessed the entire direction of writing since the First World War, discerning three possible postures for the writer. One was the posture of irony and despair he associated with modernism, and found "reactionary". Another was the commitment of the Thirties writers, lost bourgeois searching for new faiths and institutions by turning to communism. And the third was quietism, the response of the writer who, knowing he was trapped in the womb of modern history, caught inside the whale, then displayed his anarchistic and obscene protest as an individual – a writer like Henry Miller, who was, he said, "a passive accepter of evil, a sort of Whitman among the corpses". Orwell's own essay marked a turning point, for some an apostasy. Orwell went on to offer a dire warning to those who saw writing as cognate with liberalism and humanism, forewarning all such writers that they faced "the age of totalitarian dictatorships – an age in which freedom of thought will be at first a deadly sin and then a meaningless abstraction". Literature would suffer a necessary death and then a drastic rebirth:

> The literature of liberalism is coming to an end and the literature of totalitarianism has not yet appeared and is barely imaginable. As for the writer, he is sitting on a melting iceberg: he is merely an anachronism, a hangover from the bourgeois age, as surely doomed as the hippopotamus.

To a degree the literature of liberalism *has* survived, and Orwell's bleak prospect has not yet fulfilled itself, though it still remains as a lasting fear; Orwell's question about whether the "natural" liberalism of the arts can survive will not entirely go away. What is clear is that Orwell, writing at a time when war had come and thought was being organised, individual consciousness being summoned into the massing of ranks and the building of armies, was setting down a convincing question that was to persist into the writing of the 1950s, when his own late novels returned to the same question. Extreme or apocalyptic as his attitude can seem, Orwell and his note of authentic and critical commonsense was to sound like one of the few sound remaining voices in British writing.

4 The gloomy prophecies and the general sense of collapse of the literary tradition around 1940 did not offer great hopes for the writing of the coming wartime decade. There were practical problems to add to the dismay. Theatres closed, and there was severe paper rationing and control over book publication, so that the number of novels published dropped by three-quarters between 1939 and 1945. A good number of the literary magazines of the 1920s and 1930s collapsed either from artistic and intellectual difficulties in the months before the war, or in the production problems that arose once it started; *New Verse* and *Left Review* went the way of *The Criterion*. Several struggled on (*The Adelphi, Life and Letters Today*, and F.R. Leavis's *Scrutiny*), and a few new ones started, including Julian Symons's and George Woodcock's anarchist *Now* (1940–47) and Tambimuttu's eccentric and wonderfully lively *Poetry London*. But two magazines conspicuously dominated the decade, and set its tone with considerable clarity. One was Cyril Connolly's flamboyant "review of art and literature", *Horizon*, which produced its first issue in January 1940 and appeared monthly throughout the decade, dying with a double number for December 1949/1950 just as things seemed to be looking brighter. *Horizon* found its rival in John Lehmann's striking venture *Penguin New Writing*, which had a roughly parallel history, coming out in December 1941, publishing monthly through 1942, and then appearing quarterly through to its fortieth and final issue in 1950. These two magazines spanned the decade, and between them they displayed much of its flavour, directions and uncertainties. They also carried forward the issues left over from the 1930s, for Connolly may fairly be called a bellelettristic descendant of modernism and Bloomsbury, and John Lehmann was, of course, a central organising figure of the "new writing" movement of the 1930s.

Connolly, it appears, had planned to start an avant garde magazine in Paris during the 1930s, and he had trained on *Life and Letters*, admired the bellelettristic tradition represented by Desmond Mac-Carthy, and had an intense but mannered appreciation of "the Modern Movement" in literature and art. The cause for which Connolly spoke was "culture", and "When I hear the word gun I reach for my culture," he said in an *Horizon* editorial in a memorable phrase. In another, in the second issue, he declared his aestheticism and indifference to the practicalities of war: literature is "an end in itself as well as a means to an end, and . . . good writing, like all art, is capable of producing a deep and satisfying emotion in the reader whether it is about Mozart, the fate of Austria or the habits of bees". Julian Symons, attacking *Horizon* from the Left, was to complain that the paper was "keeping a flag flying for a social as well as a cultural elite", and he noted that the general editorial tone combined "the voice of the circus barker and the arty-tart". *Scrutiny* complained, too, of its bellelettrism and its failure to define any clear critical standards, observing Connolly's way of putting "an emphasis on personality which personality alone cannot bear". In the end, *Horizon* was largely to represent the continued spirit of Bloosmbury, and to some degree it explains the attacks on Bloomsbury modernism that preoccupied many during the 1950s, not least of them the growingly influential critics of *Scrutiny*.

There could equally be no doubt about the roots of *Penguin New Writing*. In 1936 Lehmann, with the aid of Isherwood, Spender, Ralph Fox and Lehmann's sisters Beatrix and Rosamond, had founded an expensively made, twice yearly book-magazine called *New Writing*, which ran until Christmas 1939. Its main concern was young writers, prose, and work of unorthodox length, and it was determinedly anti-fascist in spirit, if in a mildly contorted way: the magazine was "first and foremost interested in literature, and though it does not intend to open its pages to writers of reactionary or fascist sentiments, it is independent of any political party", said the initial announcement. One crucial feature was Lehmann's strong European orientation and his good contacts with anti-fascist writers on the continent, and this enabled the magazine to convey the implications of Hitler's rise, record the interwar writers' congresses, reflect the trips to Europe taken by the editors and central contributors, and display the divided allegiances in the Left during the Spanish Civil War. Some very notable work appeared – Isherwood's *The Novaks*, Upward's *The Border-Line*, Warner's *The Wild-Goose Chase*, Orwell's *Shooting an Elephant* – and there were important new working-class writers like James Hanley, George Garrett, B.L. Coombes and Sid Chaplin, mixed with major work from European authors, including Pasternak, Brecht, Malraux, Silone, Giono, and Sartre. These would prove valuable funds when *Penguin New Writing* started, for in the early days it was largely concerned with reprinting from the more highly priced book-magazines Lehmann also edited. *New Writing* itself collapsed at the end of 1939, but in 1940 Lehmann resumed with a similar venture, *Folios of New Writing*, rather different in political tone and directed to new circumstances; its aim was, it said, "to create a laboratory where the writers of the future may experiment and where a literary movement will find itself". This merged after four issues with another venture, *Daylight*, which concentrated on the wartime reactions of European writers, and the joint *New Writing and Daylight* continued through to 1946.

All this was the seedbed for *Penguin New Writing*, which came out of the alliance forged between Lehmann and John Lane's innovatory paperback publishing house, which had been transforming the pattern of book publishing since 1935. Lane was quick to see the potential of paperback publishing for the armed forces, generating a new series which mixed a sense of cultural heritage with a concern with contemporary issues. Lehmann's ventures matched the Penguin spirit, and Allen Lane committed himself to the series, which satisfied Lehmann's desire to make the concerned and contemporary writing he had supported more widely available ("I believed that *New Writing* could and should appeal to a far wider public than that which a book costing 6s or 7s 6d reaches," he explained). As the venture moved away from reprinting important work from the 1930s, Lehmann explained its wartime purpose, announcing that he hoped for "a regular flow of stories, poems and sketches to be submitted to me, . . . many of them . . . by soldiers, sailors, airmen and other directly involved in the operations of the war, and about their own experience." Major contemporary writers – Auden, Spender, Isherwood, Orwell, Greene, Laurie Lee, George Barker, Roy Fuller and major European figures from Malraux to Silone – appeared beside the topical series of articles ("The Way We Live Now", "Shaving Through the Blitz", "Books and the War") for which the paper is still remembered. Some new writers did appear from the war-zones: Denton Welch, Alun Lewis, J. Maclaren-Ross, Henry Reed, F.T. Prince. And the venture, allowed five tons of paper per volume, reached sales of over 75,000 at its height, many of them to readers in the services, creating, as Lehmann said in the final issue, "a story, we believe we can say without vainglory, that forms part of the history of our time".

With the cheap *Penguin New Writing* and the more elegantly and expensively produced *Horizon* on offer throughout the decade, literature seemed well-represented, and so it was. The immediate conditions of war created an active and topical writing, and a large and interested readership, and both papers appealed to the cultural community of wartime, with its mood of common cause, shared experience of disaster, and the collapsing of old political and cultural barriers. The differences between them diminished. Connolly had Peter Watson as art editor, and Stephen Spender, through to 1941, as co-editor. "The strength of *Horizon* lay not in its having any defined cultural or political policy, but in the vitality and idiosyncracy of its editor . . .," Spender later explained in *World Within World*. "I, who started out with concern for planning post-war Britain, defending democracy, encouraging young writers, and so forth, was disconcerted to find myself with an editor who showed little sense of responsibility about these things." Connolly worked, he said, by carrying on "a kind of editorial flirtation with his readers so that they were all in some way admitted to his moods, his tastes, his fantasies, his generous giving of himself, combined with his temperamental coyness". *Horizon* may have been, as Julian Symons said, "a neo-Georgian literary paper with modernist overtones", putting Auden and MacNeice beside Walter de la Mare and Hugh Kingsmill. But it printed many of the same contributors as *Penguin New Writing*, and its interpretation of the decade was in the end to prove very close to John Lehmann's own.

5 "A magazine should be a reflection of its time, and one that ceases to reflect this should come to an end," Connolly wrote in the first issue of *Horizon*, and he went on to explain how he interpreted the time his magazine sought to reflect. "Our standards are aesthetic, our politics in abeyance," he declared, and went on:

> The moment we live in is archaistic, conservative and irresponsible, for the war is separating culture from life and driving it back on itself, the impetus given by Left-wing politics is for the time exhausted, and however much we should like to have a paper that was revolutionary in opinions or original in technique, it is impossible to do so when there is a certain suspension of judgment and creative activity.

Ten years later, in the final issue, Connolly summed up the paper's achievement as he saw it. It had effectively related literature to art, fiction and poetry to literary criticism, and emphasised the importance of major foreign writers. The starting phase had been "tentative and eclectic . . ., apt to combine the better Georgian writers with the official school of the Thirties". It had then entered on a "more definite war footing, fulfilling a double purpose – that of conserving the heritage of Western humanism in times of danger and that of bringing out the young war writers and that particular kind of serious reporting that grew up round the war". But the curve of the whole decade was clear: "We can see, looking through . . . old *Horizons*, a Left-wing and sometimes revolutionary political attitude among writers ... boiling up to a certain aggressive optimism in the war years, gradually declining after D-day and soon after the victorious general election [the 1945 Labour victory] despondently fizzing out ... ". In fact, like Eliot in *The Criterion*, Connolly closed the magazine on a sense of depression, reading into the cultural situation a general process of decline.

Connolly's tone had always been one inclined to world-weary despair, inclined to emphasise the will to failure and the defeat of cultural promise, as he displayed in his role of "Palinurus" in *The Unquiet Grave* (1944). His theme was closure, and through much of the life of the paper he presented it as teetering on the edge of failure. Yet, faced with the difficulties of all literary magazines (he listed them in an editorial as apathy of the great; collapse of contributors; decay of the reading public; and technical difficulties), the paper survived remarkably for 120 issues, and was, he explained, no ordinary failure: "there were several years when solvency reared its ugly head, and we sank, gracefully, by the stern with the band playing to a circulation of nearly nine thousand." When it ended, readers were left with Connolly's explanation that, though more subscribers, brilliant writers, and rich patronage might have saved things, "they could not, perhaps, have made a great difference to the fatigue of the mind, the disabusedness with the contemporary world, the increasing apathy to creeds and governments", felt by its editor.

Throughout Connolly had been conducting a central campaign, to create an "English literary renaissance". By June 1941 he was proposing to stimulate this by ferrying over from the United States "about a hundred representative American writers, painters, photographers, editors and artistic directors", chosen by a committee chaired by "a great English writer who is also an American", T.S. Eliot. Renaissance could happen, he said in the next issue, only when "there is a common attitude toward life, a new and universal movement. The English mistrust of the intellectual ... must go." His subsequent editorials observed the ending of the century's major movement and the failure of a new one to start. In 1944 he was asking what had been gained intellectually by four years of war; in 1946, asking the new government for state aid for literature, to overcome the national philistinism, he noted "Literature has been robbed of Joyce, Yeats, Virginia Woolf, Valéry, Freud, Frazer, to name but a few, and their places are not being filled. This is not because of a decline in talent, but on account of the gradual dissolution of the environment in which it ripens." In the postwar years the review had many distinguished pieces and discovered a few major writers, the most notable being Angus Wilson. But in July 1947 Connolly was declaring that the English Renaissance, "whose false dawn we have so enthusiastically greeted, is further away than ever". The postwar years were displaying the demise of the Left-wing movement in literature, the end of Europe's golden age, and the defeat of all expectations of a "merry and aesthetically-minded Socialist state". In April 1947 he was writing:

> It is disheartening to think that twenty years ago saw the first novels of Hemingway, Faulkner, Elizabeth Bowen, Rosamond Lehmann, Evelyn Waugh, Henry Green, Graham Greene . . ., but no new crop of novelists has risen commensurate with them. Viewing the scene of 1947 moreover, one is conscious of a certain set of names, the literary "Best People", who somewhat resemble a galaxy of impotent prima donnas, while around them rotate tired business men, publishers, broadcasters and Civil Servants who were once poets, novelists and revolutionary thinkers.

Art was insufficiently supported and financed, the cultivated bourgeoisie were disappearing, and "such a thing as *avant garde* in literature has ceased to exist . . . . There is an intimate connection between the Twilight of the Arts and the twilight of a civilization."

Connolly's despair was so legendary that it could well have seemed personal, but a similar mood was also radiating from *Penguin New Writing*. As the war ended, its cover was redesigned and presentational quality improved, and Lehmann declared that it now emerges "from its wartime chrysalis, and spreads its wings into the thundery post-war day". But its attempt to summon up the new postwar mood was noticeably unsuccessful, in part perhaps because its wartime circulation was dropping away. Lehmann was now warning of the dangers of a literature too overtly committed, while V.S. Pritchett called the novel back from the political and religious ideologising of the 1930s to serious moral reflection. But the paper's hope of summoning up a new generation of British writers was not succeeding. The paper began to falter in publication, and it began to change its orientation away from Europe and toward the new American writers, printing Lionel Trilling, J.F. Powers, Eudora Welty, Paul Bowles, Tennessee Williams and Saul Bellow. This important transformation was also evident in *Horizon*. Connolly visited the USA after the war and came back to note a Britain where "the ego is at half-pressure". *Horizon* began to print an English edition of the excellent American journal *Partisan Review*, and the double American number of October 1947 was, he claimed later, "probably the solidest of all editorial attempts to convey a present atmosphere with truthful alertness". The issue contained Marianne Moore, e.e. cummings, and Wallace Stevens; another issue was devoted to the book which won the magazine's prize for a short novel,

Mary MacCarthy's admirable satire of a radical utopian community, *The Oasis* (titled in the English book version *A Source of Embarrassment*).

When *Horizon* came to its end over the New Year of 1949/50, Connolly attempted to sum up "the inscrutable Forties" as he saw them:

> One can perceive the inner trend of the Forties as maintaining this desperate struggle of the modern movement, the struggle between man, betrayed by science, bereft of religion, deserted by the pleasant imaginings of humanism, and the blind fate of which he is now so expertly conscious .... "Nothing dreadful is ever done with, no bad thing gets any better; you can't be too serious." This is the message of the Forties from which, alas, there seems no escape, for it is closing time in the gardens of the West and from now on an artist will be judged only by the resonance of his solitude or the quality of his despair.

The pessimistic tone can indeed be read as part of Connolly's *fin du monde* disposition, but it conveyed more, transmitting the mood in which the writing that did of course follow the war largely began. The mood was fearful, unsure, forged in the assumption that an era of Western culture was over and that cultural power and influence were shifting elsewhere. Though not a defeated nation, postwar Britain was a depleted nation, touched by the feelings of historical ruination that were running through battletorn, seedy, economically troubled and politically fearful Europe. Even in the United States something of the same note was being sounded. Malcolm Cowley, surveying the American scene in *The Literary Situation* (1954), contrasted the post-World War Two mood with that after World War One, depressedly reflecting that where what had burgeoned then was a great age of experiment in poetry, fiction and drama, what was burgeoning now was institutional literary criticism. John Aldridge, in *After the Lost Generation* (1954), made a similar point, finding his literary contemporaries in a sterile situation, too empty of moral community and mythological vision to allow a major art to develop. Intellectual life itself seemed timid and fearful, intellectuals conformist, swamped now not by hot war but by cold.

5 The obsequies were, of course, to prove premature. But the sense of defeat following victory was strong, especially in Europe, dependent on Marshall Aid, while inBritain the glow of victory was soon dissipated by the continuing austerity and the dismantling of imperial

power. American writers like Edmund Wilson, visiting Britain after the war, felt it had the look of a damaged nation, and many British intellectuals agreed. "England as a great power is done for . . .," Waugh noted in his diary of 1946, "the loss of possessions, the claim of the English proletariat to be a privileged race, sloth and envy, must produce an increasing poverty . . . until only a proletariat and a bureaucracy survive." Others of different political views welcomed the world of the Beveridge Report and the Butler Education Act, and the dominant mood was a liberal one, but it was liberalism with the fearful overtones of Orwell's vision. Rationing continued, travel was restricted, totalitarianism from without or within still seemed a threat, and England looked gloomily in on itself. Intellectuals also felt incapacitated by the illusions and apostacies left behind from the Thirties, that "low, dishonest decade", and the general mood of austerity seemed to reinforce the anti-intellectualism and philistinism of the British, so that the avant garde showed small signs of being renewed. (Waugh commented sourly on this too, suggesting that the new writers who were emerging were simply state-trained production-line specimens.) The new statism did not seem to favour the arts, except in official forms of public celebration like the Festival of Britain, which to the cynical was planned joy, culture on the cheap day return. Curiously it now seemed to be the wartime age just gone that seemed the better time, a time of common purpose when writing had mattered, the international perspective reigned, horizons had grown broader.

What, then, was postwar British writing going to be like? Many of the older writers indeed continued to dominate: Waugh and Greene, Powell and Henry Green, Compton-Burnett and others. The later years of the war brought a spurt of new magazines (*Poetry Quarterly*, *Outposts*), and then there came Peter Russell's *Nine* and the Marxist-oriented *Arena*, which published international writing, from Camus to Malcolm Lowry. But the postwar magazines seemed largely to derive from Oxford and Cambridge, offering glimpses of modest unknowns like Philip Larkin, Kingsley Amis, John Wain, Kenneth Tynan, Anthony Thwaite and George MacBeth, and showing an increasing bias toward serious literary criticism. This mood was picked up elsewhere in more polemical journals like *The Critic* and *Politics and Letters*, led by names like Raymond Williams and D.J. Enright. And above all there was *Scrutiny*, challenging the metropolitan intellectuo-literary scene from the standpoint of a strict critical rigour. A new seriousness which to many looked strangely hairshirted and bespectacled was becoming a primary voice in culture, and moving literary activity toward the academy and the provinces, and away from the metropolitan literary world with all its Bloomsbury shadings. When

John Lehmann started a new magazine, *The London Magazine*, in 1954 – the year when in fact the presence of what was called "the Movement" was declared, and there was a new explosion of writing – he began by complaining that for the first time since the 1870s there was in Britain no real avant garde. A solemn lower-middle-class severity seemed the new tone, and in many of the magazines a modest quarrel erupted between the older writers and the new, who became identified as ink-spotted grammar school boys complaining about cultural life, and, in Somerset Maugham's word, "scum".

But most of the new magazines did not last long, as printing costs rose and readerships did not, and even the influential *Scrutiny* was not to outlast the 1950s. For a period at least the best literary magazines in Britain were American ventures like *The Kenyon Review* and *The Partisan Review*, circulated by the Ford Foundation. The sense of pessimism dragged on, and Connolly and Leavis seemed to agree on at least one thing, that the prevailing conditions of British culture simply did not favour major art. When by the mid-1950s it was apparent that a new generation and tendency had emerged, it was marked, it seemed, by a going back, to purity of diction, to strict forms, anti-romantic and ironic sensibility, commonsensical liberal and moral realism. Its adversaries were the new romanticism and apocalypticism of the 1940s and the spirit of Dylan Thomas, the political commitments of the 1930s, and, it seemed, much of modernism. Certainly the new writers seemed severe, lacking the flamboyance of the avant garde and the style of Bloomsbury, inclined to emphasise the commonplace and commonsensical, the provincial and the regional, their heroes the likes of George Orwell and E.M. Forster rather than Joyce or Woolf. Sometimes claiming Anger, they appeared liberal in politics and conservative in subject and technique. The "good brave causes", John Osborne announced, had been discredited, and the totalising and to some potentially totalitarian forms of modernism were no longer desired. The broad waves of international thought, the great "mind of Europe" to which Eliot and the writers of the Left in the 1930s had so variously alluded, guided them little, except perhaps in the matter of existentialism; they sometimes drew some influence from the United States. A new writing was indeed being forged, but with little direct continuity from the work of the 1920s and the 1930s. In time this was to prove not only a powerful but a very varied generation, but it was decidedly slow-burning. The gardens were not closed, but they were slowly being re-landscaped, and like all new planting the process took some time. But that is another story.

THE NOVEL NO LONGER NOVEL
Writing fiction after World War Two

"It may happen in the next hundred years that the English novelists of the present day will come to be valued as we now value the artists and craftsmen of the late eighteenth century. The originators, the exuberant men, are extinct and in their place subsists and modestly flourishes a generation notable for elegance and variety of contrivance. It may well happen that there are lean years ahead in which our posterity will look back hungrily to this period, when there was so much will and so much ability to please."

Evelyn Waugh, The Ordeal of Gilbert Pinfold (1957)

"The situation of the Western novel during the past forty years has been precisely one in which a large amount of local movement has been evident, but no overall development since the achievement of Proust and Joyce and the other major innovators of the early twentieth century . . . . If the novel is truly no longer novel, then many of our critical procedures for discussing it will need revision; perhaps, even, we shall do well to think of another name for it."

Bernard Bergonzi, The Situation of the Novel (1970)

1 Current anniversaries tell us that it is forty years since the end of World War Two, and for all that time we have been living with the Postwar Novel. This is a long period in writing, indeed roughly the time it took the major literary and artistic movement of this century, modernism, to emerge, develop, peak, change and die. It was in 1897 that James, after a period of disillusion, returned to the novel with *What Maisie Knew*, that pioneering work of fiction as enquiring aesthetic and philosophical consciousness, and in the next decade, the opening decade of the century, it was clear that his prophecies for a new novel were fulfilling themselves. In Ortega y Gasset's phrase, the novel shifted from being an Art of Adventures to an Art of Figures, and the old "burgher epic" of the nineteenth century – with its individualised and very material characters, its social specificity, its moral assertion, and above all its realism – began to die. A new art of fictional expression, an art that knew very well that it *was* modern,

shaped by twentieth-century ideas of relativity, the unconscious, and contemporary social relations, an art that perceived anarchy within culture and the fading of old moral and religious certainties and teleologies, emerged, in Conrad, Lawrence, Joyce, Ford Madox Ford, Virginia Woolf, and their European and American contemporaries. It was a modernity the First World War seemed to confirm, and through the 1920s its achievement multiplied, and also darkened, as the vision of cultural chaos intensified. Some forty years on from James's return to the novel, James Joyce published *Finnegans Wake*, seventeen years in the writing, and needing, Joyce said modestly, as long to read. The Wake, in a way, was modernism's own; the book's spirit both of completion and exhaustion made it seem the culmination of an entire process. It appeared in 1939, the year of another World War; Joyce, forced out of the modernist's capital, Paris, died a year later in Zurich, one of several literary deaths in quick succession that seemed to mark the end of the modern movement. In the same year, 1940, Scott Fitzgerald and Nathanael West died in Hollywood; in 1941 Virginia Woolf and Sherwood Anderson died; in 1946, Gertrude Stein, still asking, as she always had, "What is the answer?" and then "What is the question?"

Of these first forty years of the century we have acquired a sense of artistic clarity, and a feeling for the range of its achievement. But of the forty years that followed the war we have no such clear picture. Our critical records are slight, and our sense of the major directions at work uncertain. We are not yet sure who the major novelists and writers have been, nor what they represent, and though the period is filled with currents and counter-currents we do not really have a firm idea of how to map them. This is to a point understandable; the classic assumption that only time and history clarify artistic significance has some truth. Our arts have proved elusive in part because of their plurality and stylistic variety, and they have lacked the certain and self-asserting movements that made up the spirit of modernism. The writers whose achievements dominate the period are mostly still living, and they lack the distancing, respectful attention we give to the dead.

Nonetheless it is surely true that our ignorance constitutes a kind of neglect and perhaps a form of disappointment, for the period, both in artistic achievement and in critical assessment, has remained very largely dominated by the radiation that still comes from the writers of the earlier part of the century, the writers we still go on calling modern. This domination takes perhaps two forms. One is that those writers who continue to regard the arts experimentally and seek to transform and advance its directions in a radical or avant garde way are still called "postmodern", a term that acknowledges both a fracture and an inevitable succession. And the other is that those writers who revolted against modernism by seeking to go before and behind it, reconstructing elements from the previous tradition, have been seen as limited and self-qualifying, writers, as Evelyn Waugh suggested, of a Silver Age, "a generation notable for elegance and variety of contrivance", but not for radical innovation.

Over the history of the novel of the last forty years, the shadow of modernism has been particularly strongly cast. For what the extraordinary achievement of that international and compelling tendency has seemed to imply was nothing less than the Death of the Novel – the death, that is, of the novel in its traditional form as the burgher epic, the novel of social reality, moral assessment, direct representation of life and history. The Death of the Novel was a kind of rebirth too, the coming into being of a fiction that challenged its own history and its own reality, and it culminated in a number of major texts – the most remarkable and conclusive is James Joyce's *Finnegans Wake* – of such massive self-questioning that it challenged all possibility of development and continuity. Since then we have had a continuation, which has also been a qualification, of that experiment – in the French *nouveau roman* from the late 1950s, in the American "metafiction" of the 1960s, in the "magical realism" of Latin America, which had such a strong radiation in the 1970s. Yet this "postmodern" writing, displaying the exhaustion of the Western metaphysic, the defeat of signification, the novel as a post-humanist form, has itself often appeared no more than a pale shadow of the modernism it both alludes to and deconstructs, an act of belated avant gardeism in an era when avant garde revolt came to seem tame and conventional. It was, said one American practitioner, John Barth, "a literature of exhaustion", a fiction made of the "used-upedness" of stories: though it led, he suggested, to a new plenitude. "Postmodernism" has been one latter-day answer, but we have also had a significant revolt in the other direction, away from the modernist line, and from the notion of the novel as, fundamentally, an experimental discourse. There has been, amongst many writers in a number of countries, a willed return to the manners of realism, the reconstruction of convention, the tradition and past practice of the novel as an habitual and agreed public convention.

Yet, in the wake of modernism, neither direction has quite seemed to satisfy our hopes of a great late-twentieth-century era of fiction. To the gloomiest of our critics, the post-modern situation has suggested that the contemporary novel – the "postwar novel" – has been doubly disenfranchised, cut off alike from the traditional novel and the new. Modernism detached us from the traditional novel, but also in effect wrote the appropriate novel of our century; this left subsequent writers with little to go forward from, and little of modern relevance to go back to. Bernard Bergonzi, in his interesting *The Situation of the Novel* (1970), suggests this very plainly, proposing that the novel today is simply "no longer novel", and has settled for predictable pleasures: of conventional genre fiction, or a pallid experimentalism in no way capable of outrunning what our early twentieth-century predecessors already achieved. Bergonzi was writing from the position of some time back, and he was probably very conscious of the strictures of George Orwell's "Inside the Whale" (1940), that key essay in which Orwell proposed that the decline of modernism represented the end of the tradition of liberalism in literature. Certainly his book suggests that postwar writers were faced with a choice, differently resolved in different countries, between holding on to the traditional "liberal" novel of social and moral realism, and creating what he calls "a fiction of the Human Condition" that, reacting to the conditions of modern history and politics, pointed toward a totalistic if not totalitarian view of form and of life. Bergonzi's impressions are important and interesting, though I think they are limited in their view of the tendencies and the complexities of the forms of fiction that have grown up since 1945 in a period of major fictional developments.

My own conviction is indeed that the last forty years are a major creative period in the novel, a period, still very ill-defined, when the form has not only changed and significantly transformed itself in Britain, Europe, and the United States but has received new and striking injections from world-wide sources: from African writing, New Commonwealth writing, Latin American writing, Indian writing, Japanese writing, Eastern European writing. Its tendencies and counter-tendencies have been many, and it has produced figures who will, I believe, seem as major in their way as those who now have our credit as the central voices of the early twentieth century. Their achievement lacks, perhaps, that feeling of clear development that we can now attach to the modernist movement, though much of that sense of clarity is a latter-day canonisation of what at the time seemed multi-directional and chaotic. It has also been with us long enough for us to see that there is not one single flavour of postwar fiction, but in fact a variety of directions in a variety of phases. We are still not quite sure who the major figures are, where the major tendencies lie, and how the novel has changed.

But one way to understand it is to go back to the fragile and difficult time when the political, intellectual and artistic life of the West began to reforge itself in the years immediately after 1945, the broad vague period we characterise now as the 1950s. It was a time when, for most of those who attempted to write, the climate had changed so fundamentally and in so many respects that the entire task of fiction needed to be reconstructed, just as did the lives and the values, the war-torn cities and collapsed economies, of all those who woke up to find themselves in the cold, chaotic clarity of the new postwar world.

2 That the Second World War and the consequences that followed it marked a major fracture in human experience can scarcely be denied. The sudden disclosure of the horrors of the Holocaust, the terrifying impact of the dropping of atomic bombs on Japan, and the realisation that the ending of the hot war of 1939–45 was to lead not to a peaceful and stable future but to a new cold war between two hostile superpowers and two competing systems of social organisation, the individualistic and the communitarian, the capitalist and the communist, meant that the mood after the World War Two was very different from that after World War One. "The Age of Anxiety", W.H. Auden christened the new period in an influential long poem, and though the Age of Anxiety was also, in the West, to become in time what the sociologist David Riesman called the Age of Abundance, a period of consumer mass-society with substantial rewards in the material realm, the disorientations as well as the pleasures of an age of commodities were in due course to become increasingly apparent. It was also, Riesman suggested, an Age of Conformity, and he and other social commentators argued that in the Western nations we had come to the End of Ideology, the great internal disputes and ideological divisions which had split Western thought during the earlier part of the century have died in the era of Cold War realignment and consumer satisfaction. In the ruins of Europe, and in the fading of those grand imperial systems which had set European life at the centre of the world, the task of reconstruction seemed terrible, and the errors of the past overwhelming. Certainly Western intellectuals now seemed chastened and cautious, and most of their pre-war allegiances shattered. Some had colluded directly with the totalitarian regimes now defeated, and the taint stood over at least a part of modernism itself; Ezra Pound was in a mental hospital in Washington, DC, unfit to plead on a charge of treason. Many of the writers and intellectuals who had been on the liberal and revolutionary Left repented their pre-war allegiances, and communism, which now appeared to be threatening postwar world security, was the God that had Failed. But above all in extreme times the arts

of extremity seemed hardly what was needed, and the general mood was in favour of a return to the liberal centre, to the mediatory intellectual role.

France, which had suffered the humiliation of occupation and to some degreee the taint of collaboration, the treason of the intellectuals, now seemed in the forefront of intellectual recovery, and it was the movement of existentialism which exemplified this, exerting enormous influence on intellectuals and writers throughout the West. The postwar writers, Jean-Paul Sartre suggested in his key study *What Is Literature?* (1947), faced an unprecedented task of redefining artistic and philosophical responsibility. They were, he said, the writers of the century's "third generation", preceded by two generations of bourgeios modernism which both in its spirit of aesthetic detachment and its sometimes collusory relation with totalitarian force had effectively discredited or displaced itself. Sartre acknowledged the force of the artistic achievements that had gone before, but also the striking dehistoricisation that seemed part of modernism. War had changed all this, demanding writers to state their allegiances and move from imagination into action, forcing them to face what André Malraux called "the human condition", the necessity to choose. This required a new view of the role of the word itself. "The war of 1914 precipitated a crisis of language," Sartre wrote. "I would say the war of 1940 has revalorized it." This called for a perhaps gratuitous or assumed act of faith in history, reality and action, a "commitment". It derived from an existential paradox, for it sought moral authenticity and "signification" in a world it also defined as contingent or absurd, but the act of faith required a new realism and specificity of art, and above all from work in prose: "The empire of signs is prose," said Sartre.

Existentialism derived as much from the ethical conflicts and specific experiences of wartime and its sense of human risk and victimisation as it did from the philosophical tradition to which Sartre attached it. It was also deeply reinforced by the achievement in fiction of Sartre himself, and that of Albert Camus, whose own critical and philosophical writings took a related path. In *The Myth of Sisyphus* (1942), written in wartime, he had asserted the need for moral struggle in a world robbed of all familiarity; he took the theme further in *The Rebel* (1951), the book where he considers the impact of Hitler's "nihilist revolution" and the question of whether there is a path beyond. Camus's answer was that mankind was left with the need to rebel against history as chaos, and was compelled to reconstruct it by producing out of absurdity a revolution of humanism. The difficulties of that revolt had already been constructed by Sartre in his pre-war novel *La Nausée* (1938), about alienation and the modern sense of inauthenticity. The book can be read in a modernist tradition that goes back to Musil, Svevo or Kafka, a novel of "the man without qualities" in a meaningless world. Antoine Roquentin lives in a world where signification fails: "The word remains on my lips; it refuses to go and rest upon the thing." Only in things themselves does essence occur ("Existence had lost the offensive air of an abstract category; it was the very stuff of things"), but toward the end of the book he breaks from his boredom to write a book – a novel, which, like music, seems to offer the solution that writing about history cannot: "history talks about what has existed – an existant can never justify the existence of another existant."

La Nausée, like Samuel Beckett's *Murphy* of the same year, was to come to seem a novel of the modern absurd; but Sartre himself repudiated the path it implied. Indeed history, in the making, became the stuff of his fiction, and his novel-sequence *The Roads to Freedom* (*The Age of Reason*, 1945; *The Reprieve*, 1945; and *Iron in the Soul*, 1949), directly carries his hero Matthieu from the year of his previous novel, and of Munich, through to the fall of France, until, gun in hand, he finds a communitarian obligation: "Freedom is exile and I am condemned to be free." Sartre's book *What Is Literature?* took much the same path, calling for fiction to deal "with significations", and insisting that prose, unlike poetry, was an art of representation and moral and political action (as Iris Murdoch put it in her brilliant little book on Sartre, what he requires from art "is analysis, the setting of the world in order, the reduction to the intelligible, where the intelligible is something smooth and balanced").

Camus's fiction, in more complicated fashion, seemed to take the same path. His wartime *The Outsider* (1942) is the other classic novel of existential alienation, the story of Meurseult, the young clerk from Algiers who lives on the instant, without affect or feeling. Sartre himself pointed to the modern force of the book; in it, he said, Camus creates a passive or decausalised form of discourse to present a world of immediate presences and moral absences. When Meurseult in a "meaningless" act kills an Arab, and later passively consents to his own execution, our sense of the absurd is strong, though Camus presents the book less as a story of tragic loss than a story of "the benign indifference of the universe", and said himself that "Everything which exalts life adds at the same time to its absurdity." But the problems of ethical decision enlarge in his later work; *The Plague* (1947), a parable about the German occupation in France, deals with an epidemic of bubonic plague in Oran, but Dr Rieux, its central character, while knowing that he too suffers from "the present sickness", confronts meaninglessness with humanism. Camus explained of his later work that the absurd was the starting point, not the conclusion, of his enquiry; humanism might be hard to derive philosophically from the modern sense of nihilism and exposure, but it was the ethically necessary revolt of the times.

The return to signification in French fiction was subsequently to have powerful implications later on, and the French *nouveau roman* can surely trace its roots here. For if, as Nathalie Sarraute said, the novelist now lived in "an era of suspicion", when his witness to reality was in doubt, then the anthropological humanism derived by Sartre and Camus was an artistic illogicality. It presented, said Alain Robbe-Grillet in his *For a New Novel* (1963), as tragedy what was a normal state of affairs, that we live with "the smooth, meaningless, mindless, amoral surface of the world". If the empire of signs was prose, the signs carried no certain signification. For, said Roland Barthes, the syntax of humanism could not reconcile literature with history: "Literature is openly reduced to the problematics of language; and indeed that is all it can now be" (*Writing Degree Zero*, 1953). In the *nouveau roman* of Sarraute, Robbe-Grillet, Michel Butor and others, emerging from around 1953 onward, this seemed acknowledged. As Robbe-Grillet suggested in his essay "From Realism to Reality", writers can construct the pursuit of reality only as an enquiry, and not as a conclusion. "No true creator starts off with an idea of his 'meaning'; the writer's project is more or less a project of form," he said. "A novel must *be* something, before it can begin to *mean* anything." The arguments in existentialism about "essence" and "authenticity" became intellectually qualified and challenged, as much in structuralist philosophies as in the new forms of fiction, with its challenge to the "Sartrean novel", which, said Barthes, "gives the novel the ambiguity of a testimony which may well be false".

In the other crucial Western literatures we may see something of the same course tracked. Germany was a defeated and divided country, where writers had been forced into collusion, silence and exile; the tradition of the past seemed overthrown, and language drained of all meaning. Nonetheless there was a need to reconstitute it within and on behalf of contemporary history. In 1947 Hans Werner Richter convened the gathering of German writers who came to be known as Gruppe 47, to begin a process of intellectual and literary renewal: the group contained Günter Grass, Heinrich Böll, Peter Weiss and Alfred Andersch, all to play a great part in the spirit of postwar German writing. Inevitably, they urged the need for writing to have a political and moral function. Grass tells the story by parable in his *The Meeting at Telgte* (1979), dedicted to Richter, which imagines the literary debates that took place exactly three hundred years before 1947, at the end of the Thirty Years' War, when the land was again ravaged, intellectuals and artists were defeated, and the need for a literature of moral intervention, a writing that would "bring back the long war as a word-butchery", was felt. Böll's novels, too, deal with the self-limitation, the misuse, and the propagandistic use of language, and the need to recover the facts. But this realist aim is, as Böll makes clear in his novel of wartime, *Group Portrait With Lady* (1971), touched with a chilling irony, for realism is also the language of the police report: "Everything – everything – has been done to obtain the kind of information on Leni that is known to be factual . . ., and the following report may be termed accurate with a probability bordering on certainty."

Böll and Grass both represent the search for realism in historical extremity, and this of course is the theme of the most compelling of the postwar German novels, Grass's *The Tin Drum* (1959), where Grass turns to the gross psychology of the Hitler years and constructs a fantastic creativity which might both report it and revolt against it. By making his dwarf Oskar into an arrested identity, banging his apparently childish tin drum of anarchy and nonsense in the presence of ideology, Grass creates him as a multivalent and extraordinary presence, making a strange and grotesque art that can mirror and protest against the time. For propaganda, and now the political and linguistic division of Germany, left the postwar writer with a difficult problem of representation. The *two* German languages, with their two different stories of Germany, became the theme of the novels of Uwe Johnson (*Speculations About Jacob*, 1959; *The Third Book About Achim*, 1961), books in which official languages meant that novels written with public meanings in mind could only begin to fracture. The writer who tried to bring this sense of fracture home was Peter Handke, the much younger Austrian writer who, at a reconvening of Gruppe 47 in 1966, argued: "People fail to recognise that literature is made with language and not with the things that are described in language . . . . The words for the objects are taken from the objects themselves." And like so much German, Austrian and Swiss writing (Max Frisch's *I'm Not Stiller*, the novels of Durrenmatt or Thomas Bernhardt), Handke's writing has carried on into the postwar world and its materialistic, morally flattened landscape the sense that self and existence are identityless, signs random, and actions arbitrary, though the quest for the moment of true feeling still compels us.

In Italy, another defeated nation where intellectual life had been tainted by fascism, we can find the major writers following a somewhat similar path. Here, with Ignazio Silone, Alberto Moravia, and Cesare Pavese, a link could however be found with the anti-fascist Left of the 1930s. Silone was an exile in Zurich during the war, returning back through the battlefields as the fascists collapsed, and his work was invigorated by his commitment to the poor and the peasants. Moravia, forced into a greater surrealism by political control (his allegorical *The Fancy Dress Party* (1941), a cryptic satire of fascism, was personally censored by Mussolini), also returned to realism and naturalism after the war; indeed this was an era of "neo-realism", an attempt to capture the pain, poverty and tragedy of ordinary Italian people; and Pavese's work, while drawing on American modernist influences, followed a similar path. Yet the neo-realism was itself qualified; Moravia, for example, insisted that his work always came from a sense of "the absurdity of a reality insufficient to persuade one of its real existence". For the whole of the postwar period Italian writers have felt a strong pressure toward political commitment, but it has not finally produced a literature we feel to be predominantly realistic. For example, surely the best of the postwar Italian writers, Italo Calvino, began in the spirit of neo-realism, writing fiction of the resistance and the ordinary postwar world. But his fictional modes multiplied, into science-fiction, folktale, travel-tale; the task of reconciling the fictionalist imagination with the hard indurant fact became his fundamental theme, constantly restated; he may be claimed as one of the strongest voices of contemporary experiment, and in a way the exemplary postmodern writer.

And much of the same spirit was to be echoed in the literature of the United States. America had been internationalised by war, thrown into the conditions of modern history; it had reached, said one critic, Leslie Fiedler, the final end of innocence. Fiction was marked by much of the same absurdist awareness, the sense of evil, the appeal of humanism, that passed through contemporary European writing. The newer American novelists looked less to their own tradition than to European sources to capture the new state of affairs, and many of the most important of them were now those who could speak for the new acquaintance with a darkened modern history. Of particular importance, in the United States as indeed as in France and Italy, were the writers of Jewish background, like Saul Bellow, Bernard Malamud and Norman Mailer, who were conscious of their own role as survivors of a racial disaster. The militarisation of society and the sense of the power of modern totalitarianism drove their work toward the absurd, but the great issue was moral recovery, the need for a humanism that worked toward a sense of common obligation. Saul Bellow, to my mind the greatest of the postwar American novelists, led the way with *Dangling Man* (1944), his story of a man from the 1930s who, in the abeyance of wartime, loses his politics and his sense of reality, and becomes, indeed, an absurdist anti-hero. Yet he is hungry for humanism ("He asked himself a question I still would like answered, namely: 'How should a good man live; what ought he to do?' "), and finally, in a strange Bellovian contract, he accepts the cancellation of his freedom and the regimentation of military service. Bellow's book was a work of existential crisis, with clear allusions to *La Nausée* and *The Outsider*, and the general mood of amended modernism; his later novels were to be much concerned with the human contract and its transcendental implications. Bellow's fiction was a desperate attempt to discover a justification for the self in a time of abstractifying and disorienting pressures which, as he said, drove the self into hiding; other writers had darker visions, as did Mailer. Yet the moral and the humanistic theme runs through the American writing of the 1950s, giving it a note of troubled realism. In other writers, including the Southern gothic novelists, a sense of confrontation with moral evil and extremity was strong; J.D. Salinger presented a world divided dangerously between love and squalor, moving toward breakdown. Black writing too expressed a sense of victimisation and absurdity, and indeed some black writers like Richard Wright and James Baldwin turned for a time to Paris and existentialism.

But though the sense of evil, the awareness of grotesque powers struggling for the human soul, and the feeling for the absurd was powerfully expressed in much of this fiction, its direction pointed toward a recovered humanism. By the early 1960s the mood was to change. In the fictionalist novel, in the non-fiction novel, and the black humour novel of the new decade we may see a process compensating for, to some degree reversing, that of the 1950s, while at the same time everywhere bearing its imprint. The "black humour" novel presented a nihilistic and absurdist world, and the new fictionalism that followed on from the powerful impact of Jorge Luis Borges and Vladimir Nabokov, two survivors of modernism who reconstructed the implications of that tendency in the 1950s, challenged the resort to realism and humanism. Humanism became displaced from the text and directed toward it as a missing implication; after all, as Kurt Vonnegut said in *Slaughterhouse–5*, there is nothing to say after a massacre. Behind these "postmodern" fictions is a strong image of a world haunted and disoriented by the unreality of war itself, deculturating, victimising, abstractifying, generating awareness of senselessness and evil. The fiction of realism seemed insufficient to the case, and a new experimentalism and linguistic scepticism grew in American as in much European fiction.

3 What, then, was happening in the British novel? For people in Britain as in other countries, the war was a fundamental watershed, destroying the familiar map of nations, altering the balance of global power, and shifting the ideological drift of the century. Britain remained uninvaded during the war, though the threat came close; it emerged from the war a victor, but a depleted one, its economy drained and close to collapse, its imperial role waning rapidly. The British had not known the experience of occupation, collaboration or the direct treason of the intellectuals; indeed the wartime experience had increased rather than split social cohesion. But large internal social changes had taken place, amounting to a modest but real social revolution. The world of the 1930s was no more, and the Beveridge Plan which opened the way to the welfare state, the Butler Education Act which opened the door to a new meritocracy, and the landslide election of a Labour government in 1945 all deeply changed the flavour of society. But rationing, austerity and the wartime economy continued, travel was restricted, and there was deep dependence on American Marshall Aid. The country was not only losing its imperial role but many of its historical world functions, undergoing a crisis of national psychology still not fully resolved. An old way of life and an old class which had administered it was dying, and the attempt to create a postwar culture was a matter of serious internal anxiety. The old intellectual allegiances were fading. If some writers, like Evelyn Waugh, expressed a fertile social rage with the new Britain, and some on the Left held to their Marxist allegiances, the general mood was one of a broad, cohesive liberalism and anti-totalitarianism. Extreme attitudes, whether of the Left or the Right, now were in distrust, along with irrationalist and romantic philosophies. The two writers most influential on the postwar scene were E.M. Forster, who had not published a novel since 1924 but represented an essential spirit of liberal humanism, and George Orwell, whose honest English tone seemed to turn that liberalism toward a rooted national revolt against the rising powers of world totalitarianism released not only by the pre-war political spectrum but the disarray and territorial aggression that marked the postwar period. As in the United States, as in another way in France and Germany, an anxious liberal mood prevailed.

Perhaps because there had apparently been no fundamental split of the generations in Britain, the "third generation" feeling in Britain seemed slower to emerge. Major figures from the 1920s and 1930s – Ivy Compton-Burnett, Evelyn Waugh, Aldous Huxley, Graham Greene, Christopher Isherwood, Anthony Powell, C.P. Snow, Lawrence Durrell, Henry Green and others – continued to write, some markedly changing in style, subject and social attitude, others not. There was a sense of break with the movement of modernism and with the committed Left-wing realism of the 1930s, but great uncertainty about how the postwar novel would be constructed.

"Flaubert, Henry James, Proust, Joyce and Virginia Woolf have finished off the novel," declared Cyril Connolly in *The Unquiet Grave* (1944), "Now all will have to be re-invented from the beginning." For a time it seemed as if no new body of talent, no "third generation" to compare with developments in France, Germany or the United States, was emerging, and not until the middle 1950s was the feeling that there had been a "new movement" strongly felt. But important first novels had come out, in quick succession, from a number of new writers – Angus Wilson, William Cooper, John Wain, Kingsley Amis, Iris Murdoch, Doris Lessing, William Golding, Muriel Spark – and there was, indeed, an evident new generation, many of whom form the senior generation of our letters today. Their work made it clear that a break had occurred, and that postwar writing was significantly different in temper from what went before. Whether, however, the change represented anything like a radical development seemed to many critics more doubtful. Apart from reflecting the sharp social changes that had taken place in Britain since the war, and displaying in its heroes or anti-heroes a spirit of "anger", a mixture of social protest and existential alienation, the new novel seemed cautious and tentative.

The conventional account in the critical folklore was soon to become something like this. From the beginning of the century to the end of the 1930s there was a high season of British fiction, dominated by major and innovative figures. The war broke the sequence, and British fiction drew away not only from the modernist experiment but from the significant developments in fiction taking place elsewhere, looking instead back to nineteenth- or eighteenth-century sources, returning to the novel of Bennett and Galsworthy, Dickens and George Eliot, seeking to reconstruct a pre-modern tradition. In the process the traditional preoccupations of British fiction, with class and morality, reasserted themselves, in part as a mode of documentation in a changing Britain, in part as a return to native and provincial artistic sources. The tone, suggested Frederick R. Karl in an interesting study, *A Reader's Guide to the Contemporary English Novel* (1959: revised edition, 1963), was that "the experimental novel . . . is no longer viable and retreat is perhaps expedient," and he conveyed the general feeling he felt was in the air:

> We have been reminded with alarming frequency that the English novel of the last thirty years has diminished in scale: that no writer has the moral urgency of a Conrad, the verbal gifts and wit of a Joyce, the vitality and all-consuming obsession of a Lawrence; furthermore, that the novel has forsaken its traditional role of delineating manners and morals, and, finally, that the novel is in a decline from which rescue is impossible.

Karl is partly reflecting the period mood, displayed in the doubts of Cyril Connolly, the complaints of F.R. Leavis, but he comes to familiar conclusions. Postwar British fiction has decided to be "restrictive rather than extensive, to bring back traditional character and plot rather than to seek the inexpressible; in brief, to return to a more self-contained matter while retaining, however, many of the technical developments of the major modern. The contemporary novel is clearly no longer 'modern'."

This broad impression has been reinforced frequently since. It has come from the assumption that in the wake of modernism and the death of the novel a new climate was emerging, post-mortem and postmodern, manifest in the philosophical anxiety of new French fiction, the retreat into the self of American fiction, the political urgency of new German fiction. Thus, suggested Bernard Bergonzi in his *The Situation of the Novel* (1970), a study with the benefit of a broader perspective and a later date, a "fiction of the Human Condition", philosophical and in some of its implications aesthetically totalitarian, had developed in other countries, challenging the traditional liberal view of character as a free and independent agent, the coherent and progressive plot as a view of experience, and realism as a natural mode of fictional address to a world that could be approached by direct representation. British fiction was far less shaken by the horrors of modern history, and far less concerned to clarify a contemporary philosophy or establish a radical new discourse. Writers had settled for "the ideology of being English", and insisted on seeing "the nineteenth century as a going concern". This reflected a basic difference in cultural situation, which meant that the absence of radical vigour had its compensating advantages: "If England is still a country less dominated by totalitarian structures – whether of the state or of capitalism – than others, where liberal values are still more alive and the individual worth more, and where novels still contain characters, this is something on the credit side."

Indeed it came to seem that if postwar fiction was a fiction of anxious realism and troubled humanism, responding to the depersonalisation of the modern self and the disordered nature of modern reality, the newer British novelists were adopting a particularly nasty subterfuge, responding as if there were no crisis at all. A new conventionality became the tone; there was, suggested another critic, Rubin Rabinowitz, a dominant "reaction against experiment", and writers turned to the tradition of the British novel of the past, which appeared readily available, finding, beyond and behind Conrad, Woolf and Joyce, Wells and Bennett, Dickens and George Eliot, Jane Austen and Henry Fielding. The novel was less a mode of formal or aesthetic enquiry than a practical and workaday instrument of social expression. The characteristic British novel seemed to become a contemplation of a working-class or lower-middle-class scholarship boy wandering, in a condition of solemn but remediable social anguish, along a canal bank near Wakefield or Nottingham. There was a cult of formal modesty and provincialism, a process of withdrawal into native themes and social preoccupations which went along with the decline of British power and prestige, a subject itself to grow dominant in postwar British writing – from Waugh's *Sword of Honour* trilogy (1952, 1955, 1961) to Paul Scott's *Raj Quartet* (*The Jewel in the Crown* (1966), *The Day of the Scorpion* (1968), *The Towers of Silence* (1971), *A Division of the Spoils* (1975)) and J.G. Farrell's *End of Empire* trilogy (*Troubles* (1970), *The Siege of Krishnapur* (1973), *The Singapore Grip* (1978)). The title of Kingsley Amis's *I Like It Here* (1958), which mocked expatriatism and abroad, and celebrated the regional present, seemed to sum up the mood. It was a fiction of strong talents, but it lacked ambitious intentions and did little to advance the novel as a self-aware form, instead committing itself to that gravitational tug of realism which so much great modern writing had already tested and challenged.

That image of British fiction has been long-lasting; indeed it still forms the basis of many conventional accounts of the current British novel. It contains an element of truth, but also a good deal of neglect. Such maps were always highly provisional, and even at the time British fiction was developing in a significant variety of directions. The careers of many of the writers who began to write at that time, and now form the senior generation of British letters, tell, however, a much more complicated story. The cultural mood of the 1950s was made up of a great many contradictory strands, and the trouble with such accounts is not that they are false but far too narrow, and do almost nothing to suggest the potential that was actually coming alive in British fiction, and would shape a good many of its directions, debates and oscillations over the next forty years.

4 It was somewhere between the war's end and about 1956, when, with the Royal Court production of John Osborne's *Look Back in Anger*, a new spirit in theatre began paralleling the change in poetry and fiction, and attention started to move more toward drama, that the postwar generation in British fiction was born. It was a time of damaged cultural confidence and of a considerable change in intellectual directions, marked in part by a declining connection with Europe and a growing one with the ever more influential United States. The British, though losing a physical empire, were conscious

of retaining a moral one, and in political life the moral and liberal attitude was powerful. Thus, as in the United States at the same time, there was a strong feeling of the need for intellectuals to represent Western liberal and democratic values, rather than the independent attitudes of a radical and rootless avant garde, against the forces of totalitarianism that had been so powerful in recent history. With the publication of Orwell's late novels and the early fiction of a writer like Angus Wilson, who expressed the sense of liberal ambiguity as well as the sharp social changes the postwar world had brought to Britain, a new mood began to grow. A significant number of new talents began to emerge, both in poetry and more gradually in fiction, and a number of the new writers were working in both genres – like Philip Larkin, whose novel *Jill* (1946) has some claim to representing the start of a new mood in fiction much as his *The Less Deceived* (1955) did in verse. The new mood was assertively severe and anti-romantic, but it did not appear to express a strong aesthetic, and it did not take on greater character until around 1950. But publication of William Cooper's *Scenes from Provincial Life* and Doris Lessing's *The Grass Is Singing* in 1950, and then of Angus Wilson's *Hemlock and After* in 1951, began a general change that accelerated toward the middle of the decade. John Wain's *Hurry On Down* (1953), Kingsley Amis's *Lucky Jim* (1954), Iris Murdoch's *Under the Net* (1954), William Golding's *Lord of the Flies* (1954), and several other significant debuts – Dan Jacobson in 1955, Anthony Burgess in 1956 – brought forward a new generation of writers who won much attention, and many of them were to become major figures. Another important round of new authors presented themselves in the decade's second half: Muriel Spark brought out *The Comforters* in 1957, the same year as John Braine won attention with *Room at the Top*; in 1958 came Alan Sillitoe's *Saturday Night and Sunday Morning*, in 1959 V.S. Naipaul's *Miguel Street* and Andrew Sinclair's *The Breaking of Bumbo*, and in 1960 David Storey's *This Sporting Life*.

The literary journalists and reviewers attempted to characterise and categorise all this, identifying a spirit in fiction akin to that in the new poetry, where a generally anti-romantic, anti-experimental and liberal rationalist tone prevailed. In 1954 *The Spectator* announced the "New Movement", identified rather less by its forms than its subjects and its tone, and the mid-1950s saw a strong attempt to interpret this. It was held that there was a movement of "Angry Young Men", of "outsider" heroes (the term then popularised by Colin Wilson in a 1956 book of that title, an imbibing of French existentialism), at odds with the social system; the term was to bag many fish decidedly too big to fit in or under the net. In various magazines a kind of dispute of the generations developed, as a number of older writers castigated their successors for their puritanical critical and aesthetic attitudes and their meritocratic sensibility.

The issue of political commitment was active, and in a volume called *Declaration* in 1957 a number of writers (several of them now on the Right) declared themselves politically on the Left. It was undoubtedly the case that class factors were important; and if there was an international reaction away from modernism, this social preoccupation distinguished the British version, in characteristic fashion, from parallel reactions in other countries. Angus Wilson was later to observe that this tended to obscure far more important issues, and that the anti-experimental mood was infected with "reasons which are really extraneous to the novel but which are something to do with the social battle inside England, and which should never have played a part in deciding the form". The revolt against modernism was thus somewhat selective, a reaction against "Bloomsbury", the upper-middle-class aesthetic intelligentsia who had not only appropriated the direction of early twentiety-century fiction but control of the contemporary literary scene. They had given to British culture a mannered and metropolitan aesthetic tone that does much to explain the substitution of more commonplace and familiar voices in the poetry and prose of the late 1940s and early 1950s; and the theme of who should or would inherit England took on a new substance in British fiction. Wilson's own fiction presented the "darling dodos", now in process of dispossession, and books like *Jill* or *Scenes from Provincial Life* had in them the sound of new classes and world-views claiming their fictional rights.

This social preoccupation indeed explains part of the character of the "revolt against experiment" that concerned the 1950s. "During the last years of the war a literary comrade-in-arms and I, not prepared to wait for Time's ever-rolling stream to bear Experimental Writing away, made our own private plans to run it out of town as soon as we picked up our pens again – if you look at the work of the next generation of English novelists to come up after us, you'll observe we didn't entirely lack success for our efforts," declared William Cooper in an essay of 1959, "Reflections on Some Aspects of the Experimental Novel". The "literary comrade-in-arms" was C.P. Snow; and Cooper, Snow, Pamela Hansford Johnson and some others became influential voices in a campaign against what Cooper called "the Thirties novel, the Experimental Novel", which had to be swept out of the way before the new writers could get a hearing. The aim was a new fiction of society: "the Experimental Novel was about Man-Alone; we meant to write novels about Man-in-Society as well," Cooper said. The characterisation of what had gone before is obviously slapdash, and Snow himself was in many ways a Thirties novelist, whose major enterprise, the *roman fleuve Strangers and Brothers* (1940–70), was begun before the war, takes the social changes of the 1930s as a central subject, and deals with many of the main moral and political crises of wartime, including the involvement of politicians and scientists in the development of the atomic bomb. But it was also a long tale, open to historical fortune, of the rise of the "new men", the meritocratic young men of British society who, entering science, the professions and political life, hoped to make a more rational social order for the new age. Snow's spirit was in fact very Wellsian, but his liberal scientific moralism and his progressive rationalism consorted well with the postwar mood. Cooper's influential and very pleasing *Scenes from Provincial Life* (1950) was also set very suitably at the end of the 1930s, under the shadow of Munich and the coming of war. But it was a transitional novel, a story in retrospect, celebrating in a classic comic spirit the commonplace virtues of life in a provincial British town, contrasting ordinary lives with great political events and ideological attitudes. Like Orwell's postwar novels, *Animal Farm* (1945) and *Nineteen Eighty-Four* (1949), Cooper in particular called up a note of liberal honest Englishness that could be set against the irrational and the totalitarian, and this plainspeaking realism and commonsense affection for the stuff of familiar and ordinary life had a lot to do with the voice of at least one part of British fiction throughout the 1950s.

Cooper and Snow had good reason for claiming that they had an influential effect on the writing of the 1950s in Britain, Cooper in particular affecting the work of several young writers. However, the season threw up other strong influences. One, unquestionably, was F.R. Leavis, whose important critical study of the English novel *The Great Tradition* (1948) argued that there was a fundamental line of evolution running through the English novel from Jane Austen, Charles Dickens, George Eliot, Conrad and D.H. Lawrence which was essentially social and moral in character, a tradition of adult moral seriousness which had been compromised by aesthetic trivialities. In the United States Lionel Trilling's also very influential, and more explicitly political, book *The Liberal Imagination* (1950) reinforced the point, urging that the novel at its best was an expression of moral realism, "a perpetual quest for reality, the field of its research being always the social world, the material of its analysis being always manners as the direction of man's soul". And if the novel of society, morals and manners had often been scanted in the American tradition, it was deeply alive in the British. Trilling, like Leavis, presented a contemporary situation in which the liberal imagination, challenged by the political errors of the 1930s, had to renew itself by encountering the forces arrayed against it – the power of human evil, the temptations of ideological self-deception, the complex mixture of communal and anarchic motives that made up human behaviour and demanded subtle assessment. Fiction was the field of liberalism's highest awareness, the awareness of complexity, and the visions of chaos and anarchy that had displaced the control of reason and judgement in much modernist writing now had to be overcome. The recovery of the novel as a moral and a humanist form was one presiding theme of fiction in the 1950s, in the United States and Britain; but Britain in particular seemed a repository of social reality in literature, affording a hope for the reconstruction of the novel as the good book of life.

In due course this came to be identified as the dominant mood of British fiction in the 1950s, and seen as a new form of traditionalism. Arguing, as Angus Wilson did, that "No sharpening of the visual image, no increased sensibility, no deeper penetration of individual consciousness . . . could fully atone for the frivolity of ignoring man as a social being," writers seemed ready to react against modernism by reacquainting themselves with the long tradition of the British novel, incorporating it by allusion and direct imitation into their fiction. William Cooper's title, *Scenes from Provincial Life*, quietly acknowledges the subtitle of George Eliot's *Middlemarch*. Angus Wilson's fictions of the 1950s acknowledge a complex of traditional influences, from George Eliot to Charles Dickens, on whom he wrote a brilliant book. Kingsley Amis's *I Like It Here* (1958) salvages the unhappy disaster of a literary voyage to Portugal by finding there the grave of Henry Fielding, and so a tradition of comic empiricism that can be set against expatriate experimentalism. The line of modern realism that reached back to H.G. Wells and Arnold Bennett went through a period of recovery; John Wain, from the Potteries, acknowledged Bennett's influence, and Margaret Drabble, whose first book *A Summer Birdcage* came out in 1963, wrote a good book on him. It seemed that British novelists were reconstructing a native tradition that led back to a conviction of the power of a stable realism, and this matched the dominant tendency in poetry, which, bypassing much of modernism, was looking back to Hardy and the Victorians, and to the eighteenth century, and the orderly pleasures of rhyme, metre and purity of diction. This, as Bergonzi suggests, appeared to have the effect of protecting the tradition of the liberal novel, the novel of character, and distinguished British fiction from "the fiction of the Human Condition, of existential isolation and alienation, of efforts at self-definition and vain sisyphean struggles, that for good historical reasons has the most direct appeal throughout the world today".

All this made the British novel of the 1950s seem easily characterised, and more for its social contents rather than its literary form or its contemporary intellectual vigour. It was anti-romantic and anti-experimental, anti-ideological and eminently realistic. It was devoted to the commonplace and the ordinary, conventionalised according to the traditional fictional types, much concerned with characters, manners, and social practices. It was a fiction of the provincial and the commonplace, its stories often told from the point of view of the lower middle classes and the working classes whose experience seemed under-recorded in British fiction. Novels like *Under the Net* and *Lucky Jim* represented its earlier stage, showing the tone of an angry social rebellion which directed its indignation less against commonplace and ordinary contemporary life in the welfare state than against the still influential darling dodos – the madrigal-singing academics of *Lucky Jim*, still celebrating life in medieval England, the experimental painters and romantic poets, the new opportunists. These were less the radical philosophical alienations of existentialist fiction than tales of a social displacement which, very often, was amended by the plots of the novels themselves. In the later 1950s the note of social protest came from working-class heroes, like Alan Sillitoe's Arthur Seaton in *Saturday Night and Sunday Morning*, the anarchic but now well-paid worker in the bicycle factory who means to cheat the world before it cheats him, but who finally becomes the caught fish, readjusted to society by marriage. The old preoccupations of British fiction – with class and custom, manners and morality – had reasserted themselves, and the novel was now less a formal or metaphysical enquiry than a practical and popular form of narrative expression. The trouble with the view was not its inappropriateness – it still holds a truth about one aspect of postwar British fiction – but its incompleteness. For many of the most interesting writers were not really of this kind at all, and there was a much broader array of artistic attitudes and contradictions, many of them having a great deal of importance for the subsequent development of the British novel.

5   This, largely, is what has gone into the critical record. But we can surely see that it excludes many writers and many tendencies just as, or even more, important, tendencies which became part of the dialogue of fiction, and made the British novel part of a much larger debate, thanks to which we can lay claim to a fiction of more than predominantly sociological interest which still concerns us artistically and philosophically, as well as morally, today. For one thing, the experimental and international tradition left behind by modernism was far from dead, though, characteristically, its major voices were expatriate figures who had forged much of their careers out of Britain

(like, of course, many of the great modernists themselves). Malcolm Lowry, Samuel Beckett and Lawrence Durrell, all of whom had been linked in different ways with the modern movement in the 1930s, produced some of their finest work in the 1940s and 1950s. Malcolm Lowry, who had published one youthful novel, *Ultramarine*, in 1933, before going up to Cambridge, had educated himself with various of the modern masters, ranging fron Conrad Aiken to Joyce. During the 1930s he had travelled to the United States and Mexico, settling during the war in a squatter's shack on the Canadian Pacific coast. Here he worked on the book which, set in Mexico in the 1930s, on the Day of the Dead, 1938, right after the signing of the Munich agreement, was to be published in 1947 as *Under the Volcano*, arguably the best novel to appear in Britain in the immediate postwar period. Its Joycean overtones are apparent – the novel of a single day, capturing in its events and its complex management of consciousness a massive weight of mythical and cabbalistic materials, and functioning through a multiplicity of styles – but so too is its contemporary urgency. In the famous letter of 1946 Lowry wrote to the publishers Jonathan Cape, nervous about the complex structure of the book, he explained that it was also a contemporary parable, about "the universal drunkenness of mankind during the war, or during the years immediately preceding it, which is almost the same thing".

It was also part of a vast and ambitious scheme, *The Voyage That Never Ends*, where it would be the inferno, to be followed by a purgatorio and a paradiso. The story of Geoffrey Firmin, the dipsomaniac British consul who spirals downward toward his death in the *barranca* in an atmosphere of historical crisis, political corruption, state brutality, sexual despair and romantic self-destruction, clearly had an explicit historical meaning as well as a multi-layered and symbolist method; and this, at the time, was largely how it was read. But, as Lowry's letter also explained, it was also a work of complex codes and mythic ambition, "so designed, counterdesigned and interwelded that it could be read an indefinite number of times and still not have yielded all its meanings or its drama or its poetry." It was meant as an antiphonal novel, a kind of opera, a work of complex laws of series, "a prophecy, a political warning, a cryptogram, a preposterous movie, and a writing on the wall". Lowry's mythic and experimental intentions, his expressionist and romantic bias, did not entirely endear him to his time, and the prodigious task he set himself was dogged with misfortune and interruption, so he did not produce another major book in the remaining ten years of his life. His expatriate internationalism made him appear to lie outside the British tradition, and to this day he is also identified as a Canadian or non-British writer. But his importance and his influence were to be recovered; today he can be seen as a writer of major contemporary importance, a great if imperfect author whose ambitions very properly quarrelled with the prevailing cult of formal modesty and sustained the idea of a major modern fiction.

But clearly the major figure who was to advance fiction onward from modernism was Samuel Beckett, equally angular to the British tradition, but of enormous long term importance to it. He had taken the more conventional expatriate path from Ireland to Paris and modernism, producing a major book on Proust in the 1930s, and helping James Joyce to copy out *Finnegans Wake* and translate it into French. Two important words of fiction, *More Pricks Than Kicks* (1934) and *Murphy* (1938), came out in London in the 1930s; the seedy world of the latter, with its witty Cartesian anxieties about the split between mind and body and its Irish black humour, passed fairly directly on to a number of the young British writers of the 1950s. During the war Beckett remained in Paris, involved in the Resistance, on the run from the Gestapo, and he wrote, in English, a novel called *Watt*, its main character a question constantly finding a philosophically negative answer, which was not to appear until 1953, in Paris.

By this time Beckett had become closely associated with the French postwar scene, become thought of as a major absurdist writer, and was writing his books initially in French. At the beginning of the 1950s there appeared in Paris his major trilogy, *Molloy* (1951), *Malone Dies* (1952) and *The Unnamable* (1953), which were no longer spectacular Joycean comedy of ideas but a vision of minimalism and comic and cosmic absurdity. Throughout the trilogy the landscape thins, the material world is reduced to a small number of permutable objects ("To restore silence is the role of objects"), and human motion slows to a kind of mental imprisonment or a late life arrest. In *Malone Dies*, the act of writing becomes ambiguous, and in *The Unnamable* it begins to lose its representational or signifying powers. As writing moves toward silence, character toward figure or author-surrogate, the identityless agent producing text without certainty or clear purpose, language toward babble or gabble, and fact takes on the nature of an obscure memory incapable of being exactly evoked, a sense of modern tragedy arises. Beckett's characters became lost ones, caught in an obscure and parodic quest, "a veritable calvary, with no limits to its stations and no hope of crucifixion", painfully struggling toward motion in a world of travail without result which is the human condition. The great Cartesian anxieties of mind and body are concentrated on questions as to whether thought constitutes existence, the mind seeks meaning through its own quandaries and arrests, the body perpetuating itself beyond clear purpose or desire; the result is an agonised comedy that returns us to fundamental questions of fictional enquiry. Beckett's fiction, with its absurdist aspects, was consonant with existentialism. But his work went further, into the world of lost signification explored by the structuralists. "There could no things but nameless things, no names but thingless names," we are told in *Molloy*; Beckett's work was visibly part of the mood of Roland Barthes's "Literature is openly reduced to the problematics of language."

For British writers it was perhaps Beckett's modern irony, his pained vestigial humanism, that mattered most, but for many of them he became the writer who most suggested the potential of an experimental postwar tradition, moving artistically and philosophically forward from modernism. His radical form was the antithesis of the novel of social representation favoured by British novelists – a reminder that the realism is not a secure and stable entity, but a construct made by a fictionalising imagination out of a language the basic grammatical and perceptual proposals of which are always in change, and that the novel is not a set matrix, but a form of narrative invention endlessly reconstituting itself. After *Waiting for Godot* was staged and the trilogy translated into English in the late 1950s, Beckett became perhaps the strongest example of the modern avant garde for younger British writers, and had a continuing if oblique influence on them.

But Beckett's philosophical and perhaps decidedly French experimental purity was not the only inheritance seized from the alternative tradition of the novel. The tradition of surrealism and modern fantasy was strongly alive, and found one important expression in the work of Lawrence Durrell, a writer far quirkier than Beckett, and lacking his philosophical authority, but a fine explorer of the elaborate arts of complex narrative. He too had been a Parisian expatriate in the 1930s, working with Henry Miller, and publishing, in *The Black Book* (1938), a remarkable work of social despair and sexual extremity in the tradition of radical decadence. With *The Alexandria Quartet* (*Justine* (1957), *Balthazar* (1958), *Mountolive* (1958) and *Clea* (1960)) he offered a flamboyant reminder of the erotic, exotic and experimental sources of fiction, in a complex sequence of mirror novels, narrated by multiple voices, reflecting and refracting the Freudian and Einsteinian dimensions of story. No doubt it was the eroticism and exoticism, rather than the hermeticism, of the sequence that made it appeal so strongly to British readers. But his work – like a good deal of new postwar writing – turned fiction back to its alternative roots in the arts of displacement, enigma, narcissism. So, in another way, did William Golding's *Lord of the Flies* (1954), a novel that stepped away from the social convention by placing its action in the boy's book world of the island of shipwreck, allowing Golding to develop a complex metaphysical allegory about human nature and original sin. Like Durrell, Golding belonged in a tradition well outside conventional social realism – the lineage of what Robert Scholes called "fabulation". "Fabulation, then, means a return to a more verbal kind of fiction," Scholes explained in *The Fabulators* (1967). "It also means a return to a more fictional kind. By this I mean a less realistic and more artistic kind of narrative: more shapely, more evocative; more concerned with ideas and ideals, less concerned with things."

The fact was that the return to realism and the tradition that was said to exemplify 1950s British fiction was greatly over-emphasised. Indeed many of the so-called angry young men quickly broke away from the frame in which their first books had been perceived. Angus Wilson, Doris Lessing, Iris Murdoch, Anthony Burgess, Muriel Spark and David Storey were all to prove, as their work developed, very doubtful realists, and in some cases they were from the start. Iris Murdoch's *Under the Net*, read as an "angry" novel because its hero is a detached drifter, was in fact a philosophical surrealist text dedicated to Raymond Queneau, influenced by early Beckett, and alluding in its title to Wittgenstein. It derived in part from her reaction to Sartre's definition of prose, and pursued his failure to see it as "creative of a complete and unclassifiable image". Murdoch called herself a realist, and insisted on the opacity and specificity of the novel, which must be, as she said, "a fit house for free characters to live in". The recovery of a liberal realism was indeed an important feature of British writing in the 1950s, and it indeed paralleled the development of the existentialist-realist novel of Sartre and Camus, or the Jewish moral realism of American writers like Bellow and Malamud. It refocused the debate of British fiction and it has had important implications for a whole generation of novelists whose work was to develop through it but also often away from it. But the recovery of liberal realism was never the only tendency, and many of the best writers, like Murdoch, were to oscillate between it and the claims of a much more reflexive and fantastic view of the novel.

This was apparent in the subsequent careers of the best of these writers. Some of them stayed within the confines of a comic realism or a social naturalism, though often these have proved the least interesting. Far more important for the moving debate of the novel has been those writers whose works moved away from the mood of empiricism and provincialism that flavoured the Fifties. An important example was Angus Wilson, whose earlier novels were praised for their satirical analysis of Anglo-Saxon attitudes, their panoramic range and their moral energy. Wilson's novels of the 1950s were much concerned with these matters, along with a strong sense of chaos and dissolution underlying the social level of life and the liberal view of morals. But the fantastic and grotesque were always part of his writing, and his later work extended this remarkably. *The Old Men at the Zoo* (1961) was a troubling future fantasy, and *No Laughing Matter* (1967) is a radical pastiche of his earlier work, taking the form of the Galsworthyian novel, the panoramic novel of class, history and family, but undercutting its structure through telling the story not from a firm base of realism but through imitating and parodying the discourse of other writers; the book's dominant image is of the distorting system of mirrors in which, in the opening scenes, the members of the central family see themselves distorted, upturned, turned into grotesque identities. *As If By Magic* (1973) parodies the provincialism of 1950s fiction and moves on to become an international, indeed a global novel largely set in the Third World.

Anthony Burgess's novels always had a strong linguistic preoccupation and a Joycean flavour, but he left the relative realism of his earlier works for the complex lexical and musical codes of *MF* (1971) and the ebullient mixture of moral anxiety and literary pastiches in *Earthly Powers* (1980). David Storey's fiction turned from the northern social accuracy of *This Sporting Life* (1960) to works of psychological myth, with strong Lawrentian echoes and a very powerful aesthetic manner. Muriel Spark's work from the start explored the fictional ironies. Her first novel, *The Comforters* (1957), was already a piece of fictionalist self-questioning, a Catholic novel in which the analogy between God and the novelist is explored, and one character persistently objects to her presence within the author's text and plot. The theme becomes sharpest in her work of the late 1960s and early 1970s, notably in *The Public Image* (1968), *The Driver's Seat* (1970) and *Not to Disturb* (1971), works of very precise economy, short, usually present-tense, tightly plotted, end-directed, with a powerful authorial presence but a revolt inside the text from characters who dispute the occupancy of the driver's seat. In much of this writing, the discourse of social and moral realism becomes the material for re-examination, so that we ask again what a book is, what a character, a plot, an order, an ending. That reconsideration of realism was to become part of the rising theme of fictional enquiry that was to run through British fiction in the 1960s.

6 This rising mood of experiment and textual enquiry clearly had analogies with developments in the novel taking place elsewhere. The French *nouveau roman* had developed during the 1950s; a kind of fiction was now emerging, said Roland Barthes, where character retreated into consciousness, and consciousness into fragmentation, and the novel becomes "man's direct experience of what surrounds him without his being able to shield himself with a psychology, a metaphysic". "Nobody knows whether the world is real or fantastic, that is to say, whether the world is a natural process or a kind of dream, a dream we may or may not share with others," wrote Jorge Luis Borges; " 'Reality' is a word that means nothing except in quotes," wrote Vladimir Nabokov; these two great survivors of modernism were between them to have enormous impact on the fictionalist enquiry that developed in American fiction during the 1960s, and extended and intensified in the 1970s. Each of these tendencies emphasised certain features of contemporary fictional possibility over others, and each was deeply shaped by the national fictional tradition in which it arose. The French *nouveau roman* indeed owed much to the impact of existentialism, and the belief that the French novel had changed little since Flaubert; modern American writing owes much to the way earlier American novelists adopted naturalism and then crossed it with modernism.

The English novel was largely stabilised in the nineteenth century through a commitment to liberal realism attentive to the double progressive historiography of individual moral development and social growth, and many elements of it persisted through modernism and into the 1950s. It was this tradition that began to be altered and re-examined by novelists like Wilson, Lessing, Spark, Murdoch, Burgess and others as their work extended. These developments may be logical ones within any fictional career, but it is relevant that they coincided with developments elsewhere. And what they implied was a new attitude toward the constituents of a fiction – a new concern with the status of a text, the nature of a plot, the substance of a character, the sense of an ending – that kept on returning to the 1960s. At the same time what they alter and affect is the social and moral consensus about fiction that had grown up among many in Britain in the 1950s – though they retain the gravitational tug of realism, the concern to maintain the novel as a moral and humanistic form, that has always had great meaning in the British tradition of writing.

During the 1960s many of these preoccupations and emphases were to be extended. There were novels that pointed toward the direction of the French *nouveau roman*, like Ann Quin's *Berg* (1964), Christine Brooke-Rose's *Out* (1964) and *Between* (1968), and Gabriel Josipovici's *The Inventory* (1968). There were others which seemed to show a strong imprint from American experimentalism, like Alan Burns's *Babel* (1969), with its "cut-up" method. But a good deal of this fiction retained a strong sense of realism, like the work of David Lodge, which moved between fictions of a strongly realist kind and the marvellously parodic *The British Museum Is Falling Down* (1965). B.S. Johnson, whose tragically early death cut off a striking career, beginning with *Travelling People* (1963), with its explicit debt to Laurence Sterne, went on in later books to use elaborate techniques exploiting the book-as-object (novels as loose sheets in boxes, holes in the page), but with a very strong autobiographical preoccupation and the aim not of reflecting fiction's inherent falsehood, but of getting rid of "all this lying". For, he said, the nineteenth-century concept of the real was "clapped out": "Today what characterizes our reality is that chaos is the most likely explanation." In many of these fictions the laws of realism are challenged but not overthrown, and they are not quite the "metatexts" of some French and American writing. Rather they are experimental mediations between the liberal realist novel and new forms, works in which fictional invention and fantasy are released on new levels.

Perhaps the spirit of this change in fiction is best exemplified by two novels from the 1960s, two of the best works to come from the decade. In 1961 Doris Lessing interrupted her sequence of powerful socially and politically realist novels, *Children of Violence* (1952–69), to publish *The Golden Notebook*, a work of considerable literary self-examination, an attempt at a book that "would talk through the way it is shaped". Its central figure is a writer, Anna Wulf, who acknowledges but also questions the fact that "Most novels, if they are successful at all, are original in the sense that they report the existence of an area of society, a type of person, not yet admitted to general literate consciousness." What Anna seeks is a new kind of book, "powered with an intellectual or moral passion strong enough to create order, to create a new way of looking at life". But first the task is dissolution, and she turns to a "formless account" that will capture life before it is falsified by fictional activities: "Why not, simply, the truth?" But truth is chaotic and its elements – the social, the historical, the sexual, the psychological, the autobiographical – do not cohere as a whole, especially in an era of fragmentary female personality. Lessing's own book remains in the fragments of four notebooks, reflecting on each other and on the processes of fictional distortion. But she retains the hope of a coherent "golden notebook", a fiction that can attain to the status of an overarching truth. Her aim remains to recover for the novel a humanist authenticity, a capacity for knowledge of life and society which allows an element of realism to remain. Lessing's is an ambiguous text, suspended between possibilities, as too is the work of John Fowles, probably the most interesting novelist to emerge in Britain during the 1960s.

Fowles's first book about the power of books, *The Collector*, appeared in 1963, and his second, *The Magus*, about the forgery and power of art, in 1965, with a revised edition in 1977. They display a fascination with the pursuit of the enigmatic symbol and the problem of the relation between the historical and the formal world. These themes were to be concentrated in *The French Lieutenant's Woman* (1969), a novel which takes the spirit of realistic and omniscient Victorian fiction as a prototype, but teases it with the narrative doubts of an author who locates himself as a contemporary of Robbe-Grillet and Roland Barthes. The result is a superb pastiche of Victorian fiction, telling one of the age's archetypal fables and using the manners and types of Victorian narrative, while at the same time imposing on this the modern author not as omniscient God but as modern forger and impresario. The plot itself deals with historical evolution, and part of the evolution it describes suggests the forces of secularisation and transformation which generate fictional change and the modern novel. There is a liberal realist ending, in the middle, which is retracted, so that an existentialist world-view arises from the independence of the central female character. This opens up two more endings, set in the decadent spaces of a Pre-Raphaelite artist's studio, where the characters have the opportunity to emerge as modern figures, free of the narrative authority of the author. The final endings, left open to the choice of the reader, in fact are intended not so much to emphasise the fictionality of the text but the self-realisation of the characters, making this an existential rather than a meta-textual conclusion. Like many British writers, Fowles is concerned to protect the concept of character, and therefore a kind of realism. His novel, poised between realism and anti-realism, a strong sense of narrative authority and a sense of its counterfeit nature, is an ending from the middle ground. And this perhaps is appropriate, for it is much the point that the debate within the British novel reached at the time – leaving the way open for the much freer sense of form and possibility that marked the spirit of the British novel in the 1970s, when another generation, far less oriented to realism, far more internationalist in perspective, began to find itself.

PART THREE

Contemporary Writers

UNHAPPY FAMILIES ARE ALL ALIKE
Ivy Compton-Burnett and the modern novel

" 'All happy families are more or less dissimilar; all unhappy ones
are more or less alike,' says a great Russian writer in the beginning
of a famous novel (*Anna Arkadievitch Karenina*, transfigured into
English by R.G. Stonelower, Mount Tabor Ltd., 1880). That
pronouncement has little if any relation to the story to be unfolded
now, a family chronicle, the first part of which is, perhaps, closer to
another Tolstoy work, *Detstvo i Otrochestvo* (*Childhood and Father-
land*, Pontius Press, 1858)."

Vladimir Nabokov, Ada (1969)

1 The R.G. Stonelower translation of *Anna Karenina* that is
referred to at the opening of Vladimir Nabokov's novel *Ada* has
proved, for this reader at least, mysteriously unobtainable; and
perhaps this is as well, since its first line appears to reverse the
conventional view of what Tolstoy wrote, and it therefore seems to
want merit. Nonetheless it serves as a sound introduction to Nabokov's own tale of dynasties and descendents, decadences and incests,
a tale occurring in an America which, mysteriously, has many of the
same attributes of Russia, or rather a nineteenth-century Russian
fiction, itself. It is also a salutary reminder of the fact that one stable
ingredient of the novel, especially the old novel, is the family, and
especially the unhappy family. The best crimes are often the most
domestic, and incest, patricide, matricide, filicide, adultery and
malfeasance form, like families themselves, a narrow but potent circle
of life. As the church tells us, the family that plays together stays
together, often to the very end, preferring homogamy to exogamy; and
from Greek tragedy to nineteenth-century fiction it has kept writers
in vital material. All this, manifest through the techniques and
divergences of parody, is very much the stuff of *Ada*, but it is equally
the stuff of one of our finest modern novelists, Ivy Compton-Burnett.

To call her novels parodies may be a misnomer, but in their ritual
and stylisation, their exploitation of the predictable variables of the
genre, they form an art so classically precise that her books, domestic

without ever being domesticated, function like a fine literary allusion.
The laws of tragedy and classical epic – the laws that make dynasty a
potent mythical matter, and turn family duty and dominance into the
stuff of history – somehow obtain here, despite the history of the
novel, where greater naturalism usually occurs, and the issues are
made homely. But not, somehow, in the work of Compton-Burnett.
Her novels draw the laws of living from the domestic space, a.
domestic space that once might have been perfectly real but is
rendered for us as the basis of a dramatic ritual. Here ego can abrade
ego, power and patriarchy struggle with filial freedom and erotic
need, sex struggle with sex and tribe with tribe. History and society
may have something to do with these large battles, but they are kept
marginal, for history itself is a kind of stasis allowing the battles to
acquire their full ritual significance. Like Nabokov's America, which
will do as nineteenth-century Russia, what seems to lie behind Ivy
Compton-Burnett's fiction is not contemporary life but some prior
nineteenth-century novel.

The books of Ivy Compton-Burnett in fact came from life, as
Hilary Spurling makes very clear in her brilliant biography. But, like
one of her own characters in *The Last and the First* (1971), who has
seen some life, "a thing I have always wanted to see", but wants to see
no more as long as she lives, she was remarkably able to ritualise her
powerful early experiences into the basis of a lifetime's art. She was
not only one of the best but one of the most long-lived novelists of her
generation, and indeed her writing life is so marvellously extended
that it is quite hard to say artistically what her generation actually was.
She died after a spell of bronchitis on 29 August 1969, at the age of
eighty-five, writing up to the very last. It could be said that by the
familiar standards by which we test artistic lives hers had been a
notably quiet one; as Elizabeth Sprigge notes in her biography – it is
somehow appropriate that Compton-Burnett should end up with two
biographers working at the same time unbeknown to each other – she
described herself as someone who hadn't been at all "deedy".

This is true, but the life of the family, and then the escape from it,
was to prove largely enough. Her father was a well-known
homeopathic doctor who married twice and produced two families,
having six children by his first wife and seven by his second. Ivy, the
first of the seven, inherited parental responsibilities after the parents
were gone, and never married. But she had much experience of
family power: "From now on," Spurling comments about her
decision to become a writer, "she looked clearly at things obscurely
sensed in the past, chief among them that love of power which
[Samuel] Butler had taught her to recognize in a domestic setting and
which [Goldsworthy] Lowes Dickinson called 'the most disastrous, if

not the most evil, of the human passions'." And in due course a certain timelessness surrounded her. She lived largely in the flat in London she shared with Margaret Jourdain up to Miss Jourdain's death in 1951. There was little travel, and she was not much engaged in historical affairs or politics; like Evelyn Waugh, whose collapsing minor gentry compare interestingly with her own socially similar but far more enduring brand, she was good at making masks to keep out intruders and history. She wore her hair low on her forehead in the classical style retained from her youth, habitually voted Conservative, and maintained and expected polite manners. Her life was local yet touched with sharp tragedies, the worst of them the death of a brother on the Somme and then the loss of two younger sisters, who during the First World War were found dead in bed from overdoses of veronal in strange circumstances. And the hideous impact of this, the war itself and a consequential depressive illness helped generate what Spurling identifies as her essential literary quality, a casual acceptance of harsh facts.

It was out of such a life that her writing was generated, and the lessons of it were the guiding lessons of her books. Her first novel *Dolores* appeared in 1911 and she came to disown it; the last was pieced together and published posthumously, being written in her last days. This made an oeuvre of twenty novels, though the real achievement is usually properly dated from the publication of *Pastors and Masters* in 1925. Here it is worth noting that 1925 was a year of publication of many of the major modern novels – Fitzgerald's *The Great Gatsby*, Dreiser's *An American Tragedy*, Stein's *The Making of Americans*, Woolf's *Mrs Dalloway*, Kafka's *The Trial*. It is in short one of the peak years of modernism, and Compton-Burnett's work fits oddly and interestingly into the spirit of modern fiction. You might say that like William Faulkner with *Sartoris*, published a few years later, she had discovered a universe of her own that she was to continue populating – though where Faulkner covered a whole region and a large lump of American history, she held to a much tighter space, and therefore was able to define a firmer stylistic convention.

The curious splendour is that her novels began to look more modern the further away from the time of their setting she grew. For forty more years, then, years of fundamental change in modern fiction, she sustained a manner which she had now begun, across the period of modernism, across its decline, and into the postwar world, when somehow her work actually seemed to reach its peak. Yet this does not mean her novels played no part in the modern movement. Indeed she had a complex relation to it, and was to be seen by writers like Nathalie Sarraute as a major precursor. The fact was that although she seemed to have fixed her world and held it in the past, her tone functioned differently. Savagely aphoristic and ironic, clear in its definitions and firm in its economy, it came to seem an embodiment of modern irony.

2 Ivy Compton-Burnett's novels have clearly been read very differently by the many readers who bought them, in their shy yellow Gollancz bindings, and with the sexual ambiguity of her chosen signature, "I. Compton-Burnett". "Ivy Compton-Burnett embodied in herself a quite unmodified pre-1914 personality," said Anthony Powell of her, but Hilary Spurling offers a view of the way that, by dividing her life at the First World War, she made of the experiences of the first thirty-five years of her life the stuff of the novels of the next fifty. Her books could thus serve her readers with a double function; for all their unreassuring tone, they could afford a kind of ritual assurance, as nostalgic works marked by wit and malice yet offering in continuous pastiche the spirit of the novels of the nineteenth century; or, for all their reassuring tone, they could be read as works of high moral savagery, and works of high artistic precision, reticent and sensational, compact and morally devastating at once. The ambiguity is interesting in part because it bears on our view of the development of British twentieth-century fiction. Compton-Burnett's thinking and writing were not deeply affected by the spirit of the modern movement that surrounded and coincided with her early years; Samuel Butler, indeed, was a far stronger intellectual influence than Henry James or James Joyce. But the novel of English evocation was itself to have a strong and strange history in modern writing: in the work of Waugh, of Anthony Powell, or Henry Green, all of whom bear the heavy trace of the nineteenth-century heritage in a fiction that has a peculiarly and powerfully modern feel. By stylising the novel of the past they were able to write the novel of the present, and the crucial significance of this tradition has been apparent to a good many writers who have been their inheritors. Antecedence and inheritance are, of course, one of the essential areas of exploration in her novels, and one of their main sources of anxiety. Her own place in the family of English fiction seems to follow the same track of general acquiescence and cunning refusal that is often the mark of her characters' behaviour.

In a curious way, as Nathalie Sarraute pointed out, Compton-Burnett therefore seemed to minimalise fiction, so releasing its underlying tropes and structures. Another excellent modern critic, Wolfgang Iser, has reflected on this, saying that "By refusing to select particular aspects of a particular world and pass them off as a truth complete in itself, she has laid bare an inexhaustible fund of new possibilities, and the more artificial her technique of presentation, the more possibilities she unfolds." She does not, that is, select in order to produce realistic recognitions, familiarities; her families are unfamiliar in many senses. This recognition of her artifice and stylisation has been strong in much modern criticism, and some commentators would say it was exaggerated. Yet the secret ceremonial of surprise in her novels is generally recognised as remarkable, as if in her hands the novel is quietly being changed from one kind of thing into something else. Her novels have all the apparent properties of social fiction, and all the air of management that belongs with moral fiction. But this is not precisely their impact. Rather it seems as if an archetypal world or fiction that began in the nineteenth century as a basis for social observation and moral comedy, as in the work of Samuel Butler, translates itself into something else which possesses the more enduring properties of a fiction.

These were not necessarily characteristics she was herself prepared to acknowledge: "My writing does not seem to me 'stylized'," she once said. In part the stylisation came from her capacity to retain the images of a world that had gone so long that they became a world of abstract form. As any devoted reader will say, each novel is different, and that is part of the pleasure. Yet collectively the novels have the force of a continuing fiction, and one in which the pleasure lies not in the representation but in the presentation. In the spirit of the famous exchange in *Pastors and Masters*:

> "We may as well imagine the scene."
> "No, my mind baulks at it."
> "Mine does worse. It constructs it."

3 A useful book by Violet Powell, *A Compton-Burnett Compendium* (1973), helps us think about some of these questions. Amongst other things, it recounts the plots of her novels and identifies her characters, in one way a futile exercise, because, as Wolfgang Iser says, "If Ivy Compton-Burnett's characters tend to lose their identity in the reader's memory, this is because the centre of attention is not themselves, but their unpredictability." Certainly there is to be reckoned with the famous underplaying of the normal methods of fictional characterisation, and the method of presenting largely through dialogue, so that clear personal characteristics are often subordinate to the total intercourse of the particular scene in which the speakers play their part. The essential dramatic formulae of the novels from *Pastors and Masters* on are often set out in the titles – *Brothers and Sisters* (1929), *Men and Wives* (1931), *A House and Its Head* (1935), *A Family and a Fortune* (1939), *A Father and His Fate* (1957), *A Heritage and Its History* (1959), and so on. In these spaces come the familiar struggles for power, precedence and required affection, as well as the problems of the disposal of fortunes and inheritances; and this suggests a limited range of variation on potential themes, always presented on the carefully articulated understanding that human nature will utter itself fully and frankly in these understated rooms and under-described houses by the all-too-articulate dramatic performers.

This is one reason why her novels read like ur-novels, in which the families become all families, and open up unending yet familiar vistas of that struggle for power, money and love which we pleasantly call family life. The types of the stories refer to earlier types, including those of the Greek drama Ivy Compton-Burnett studied while at Royal Holloway College. Moreover, it is a drama whose nature is totally known to the participants, who share the rules and assumptions of the dramatic process, and, while capable of any violation, including incest (*Brothers and Sisters*) or patricide (*Manservant and Maidservant*), still maintain the laws of the dialogic game.

One of the means by which we know these rules and practices is that they are manifested in every novel as part of a fixed and ritualised social world. Historically we can roughly date and place it. This is England, its landed gentry, in the period around 1880–1900, a period belonging to the time of the author's birth and early maturity. This world, historically arrested, is kept very pure by the author, like some Amish community resisting modernisation from the improvements that came subsequent to its foundation. Its citizens usually employ horsedrawn carriages, maintain landed estates in adverse circumstances, produce large families, frequently sired on two or more wives, have many unmarried dependents, and, despite the struggle for money, maintain a servant corps and probably a governess. As Violet Powell says in her book, quite as interesting as the professions and social habits that are followed are those professions that are not followed, and those habits that do not prevail:

> No one is, or has ever been, in the service of the Crown. Country gentlemen never join the yeomanry . . . . No faint note of a bugle, no rumbling of a distant gun-carriage, disturbs the landscape in which purely domestic campaigns are conducted . . . . Organized games are not permitted to any grown-up or child . . . . The county assemblies and hunt balls, which might be expected to play their

part in settling young ladies in life with suitable husbands, are not frequented, or even mentioned. Consequently the marriages among first cousins (sometimes double) are hardly surprising, though after *Brothers and Sisters* no incestuous marriage occurs.

All fictional societies are, of course, fictional, but this is notably so. Moreover the fictionality clearly owes something to previous novels. "It doesn't seem to matter everything's being in books already; I don't mind at all," says Charity Marcon, the writer in *Daughters and Sons* (1937) who gets the books she is writing out of the British Museum. And clear parts of Compton-Burnett's books also start in the British Museum, in Jane Austen, the Victorian governess novels, Edmund Gosse, and above all Samuel Butler, who has to do not just with her social world but, as Hilary Spurling makes abundantly clear, her angle of moral attack on it. So her novels do not so much belong to a period as conventionalise an historical phase that suits her own history, her temper and her sense of human nature. And they are not so much historical novels in any conventional sense as conventional novels in an historical sense; that is, history disappears as a force to be replaced by history as a stylisation.

For of course the great advantage of the historical setting is that it takes as a case of society a time when the family was at its apogee, reinforced not simply by an apparatus of servants, governesses, family solicitors and inheritance laws which give her not only her casts but her plots, but also by concepts of power and patriarchy which are also interwoven with religious beliefs. Her books also are set on the edge of this phase of things, for the attack on the family was already being conducted at the time of which she writes, and books like Butler's *The Way of All Flesh* and Gosse's *Father and Son* show how a potent dissenting irony can be constructed, and how patriarchal duty can be revealed as egotism or Christian faith as plain hypocrisy. So in many respects Compton-Burnett's novels do offer themselves up as if they were contemporary with such works, works of a time when realism was turning toward naturalism and moral fiction toward harsh irony. Yet Compton-Burnett fully exploits her temporal distance from the period, to make it vastly more artficial, far less relevant to immediate social and historical knowledge, and therefore much more indurant in its forms of behaviour, much more open to her commanding irony. And this gives what she is doing the hard manner of much more modern novels, where detachment from characters and suspicion of the stuff of conventional story are part of the story. Her characters and subjects themselves know their own condition of historical stylisation, and display it in the fiction. As one critic puts it, "Her conversational method creates, as it were, an external stream of

consciousness, in which the characters overtly voice what the traditional novelist usually explains about them."

Indeed the self-awareness of the characters is a crucial method of
creating the peculiar assurance of her form. So in her world even
children know and utter the conditions of their own household tenure
(" 'Will she be over Grandma, or will Grandma be over her?' said
Hengist"). Cunning reticences are practised by the characters in
collusion with the author, reticence being both a way of accepting the
social laws and a device for testing them. The kind of action being
performed is extremely well-known to all its performers (" 'What a
day it has been!' " declared Hugh in *The Mighty and Their Fall* (1961),
" 'There is material for an epic. The fall of Lavinia; the return of
Ransom; the uplift of Ninian . . . ' "). The characters then engage in
the active explication of fictions, and carry fundamental roles of
literary expression; and we can surely see the trace of this in many of
our more self-aware literary contemporaries, like Muriel Spark and
Iris Murdoch.

The comparison with classical drama that is so often made
therefore reveals much, but not everything. For the complicity with
convention is a curious and special tone, and of course a comic one –
generating a prototypical form of fiction which links dramatic types
and practices with those of the more ambiguous world of fiction. Ivy
Compton-Burnett is surely a very modern writer, though it is a
curious form of modernity. Her novels seem to hunger for an absent
morality. Her methods pare down toward rapid plot-motion, simple
character presentation and a telling held close to the mechanics of
dialogue, but they deal with large experiences. Meanwhile behind the
talk there is a pervasive and rigorous level of anguish:

> "We have not settled the best thing in life," said Lavinia.
> "Human friendship?" said Egbert.
> "But it is sometimes shared," said Hugo
> "And it is uncertain," said Teresa. "We want something we
> cannot lose . . . ."
> "What should we really choose?" said Ninian. "We have not
> said."
> "An affection that would last," said Teresa; "in ourselves as well
> as in someone else; that would be a basis for our lives."
>
> (*The Mighty and Their Fall*)

The myth, then, has in it the basis of serious thought and
humanity. And if it sometimes seems that Compton-Burnett ignores
the possible emotional gains of her stories in the satisfaction of
exposing, like some Marxist of the family, the substructures of
interest by which it is constructed and through which it functions, we

must also acknowledge that her irony has a serious moral passion to it. At times it has something carping, bitter and very modern to it, a large distance that turns the book into a sharp text. But something more than the currents of the linguistic surface begins to tell with us; there is a sense of philosophical and moral depth that makes comparisons with a writer like Jane Austen not absurd. If sometimes her surfaces seem to mock and undercut the kind of English novel that went before her, at other times she seems to make some of its most rooted and analytical methods usable again. But her truth functions like a modern paradox:

> "She goes to church," said Muriel. "And she does not have to go, does she?"
> "If she were religious, she would not go," said Frances. "She would have thought about her religion and lost it."
>
> *(Daughters and Sons)*

EVELYN GOES TO HOLLYWOOD
Waugh and the postwar world

"Presently he heard footsteps approach and, without moving, could
see they were a woman's. Feet, ankles, calves came progressively
into view. Like every pair in the country they were slim and neatly
covered. Which came first in this strange civilization, he wondered,
the foot or the shoe, the leg or the nylon stocking? Or were these
uniform elegant limbs, from the stocking-top down, marketed in
one cellophane envelope at the neighbourhood store? Did they clip
by some labour-saving device to the sterilized rubber privacies
above?"

Evelyn Waugh, The Loved One (1948)

INTERVIEWER: Have you found any professional criticism of your
work illuminating or helpful? Edmund Wilson, for example?
WAUGH: Is he an American?
INTERVIEWER: Yes.
WAUGH: I don't think what they have to say is of much interest, do
you?

Kay Dick (ed.), Writers at Work (1972)

1 The years right after the Second World War saw an enormous
increase in Anglo-American literary and intellectual contacts, following on from the changed balance of power. For very obvious reasons
the image of the United States acquired an obsessive and anxious
significance in Britain and throughout Europe, and everywhere there
was a preoccupation with the forthcoming process of Americanisation, and the merits and harms of American civilisation and the global
distribution of its commerce, its culture and its version of the modern
way of life. The newspapers and the magazines analysed the change,
and many British writers – drawn by a variety of different attractions,
from the lure of life in a non-austerity economy to the novel
gratifications of becoming the writer on campus – began to take the
new westward Grand Tour, and write about the experience. Sometimes, as in the case of Dylan Thomas, their entire reputation
changed as a result, as American readers, critics and indeed faculty

wives responded to these interesting and often flamboyant transatlantic presences. These tours were not, as such, new. Throughout the nineteenth-century British writers had stepped westward, producing their reports and commentaries on their American experience, often from the standpoint of a certain condescension. In fact ever since the first discoveries of the West, the American motif haunted the European and the British imagination, becoming the "brave new world" of Shakespeare's *The Tempest* or John Donne's eroticised "Newfoundeland". The story of voyage to the New Eden began to complicate in the nineteenth century, and Charles Dickens's *Martin Chuzzlewit* became the great counter-myth. Here the new historic journey to the New Eden becomes a journey to a pestilential swamp; human selfishness replaces romantic opportunity and the new start. Dickens questioned Eden, challenged Paradise, and discovered America to be the dominion of the Mighty Machine and the even more Almighty Dollar. He thus offered the disappointed British realist's response to one of the most rooted of Renaissance and eighteenth-century Enlightenment myths.

The sceptical tale of American travel was in fact to be a familiar expression of Anglo-American relations in the nineteenth century, through from Mrs Frances Trollope in the 1830s to her son Anthony who, forty years later, tried to amend the impact of his mother's scornful book, but still, on his tour, found the American cities without depth, history transposed out of its proper place in the past and into the future. The French might mythicise America, and frequently did; and among the libertarians of Europe as well as the migrant masses the United States was the beacon of freedom and the promise of the world. But the British, along with a number of European wines, did not travel the Atlantic quite so well, had a more paternal view, and presented a more critical portrait of the American dream and myth.

Indeed, up to the end of the nineteenth century, the United States, in British fictions, was usually treated in the manner caught by that master of comic condescension, Oscar Wilde, in *The Portrait of Dorian Gray* (1890), where it is observed that America had never been discovered but merely detected (" 'Oh! but I have seen specimens of the inhabitants,' answered the Duchess, vaguely"). However, as Peter Conrad shows in his useful study of this imperfect transatlantic intercourse, *Imagining America* (1980), as the century turned, so the image did. Wilde himself saw America as an innocent space open to his aesthetic despoliation. Rudyard Kipling celebrated its epical Anglo-Saxondom, and Rupert Brooke its futuristic and mechanical eroticism. For H.G. Wells it was a place of Things to Come, a perfect figure for the technological future we all faced but America faced and exulted in especially. To D.H. Lawrence the American Indian inheritance led the way back through white deathliness to primitivism; for Aldous Huxley cultish California was generating its own psychic remedies for the modern mechanical world. When Auden and Isherwood moved or fled to the United States at the outbreak of World War Two, their paths, earlier close, divided. Auden stayed in New York and began, as Conrad says, to scourge himself theologically, for his own self-mortification. Isherwood chose California and developed "a uniquely self-detached narcissism", a curious and energetic agelessness stimulated by the permissive world under bright blue skies. Even the ambiguities of film-work for Hollywood came to satisfy, transience in artistic endeavour fitting the transience of the landscape and the bodily and erotic celebration it seemed to offer as reward. For the postwar generation of British writers who went to the United States, the path was already contradictory and complex, a challenge to their reaction to modernity and the modern ego itself.

As for the American reaction to British paternal condescension in literature, it has sometimes been ambiguous but quite frequently and not surprisingly unfavourable. The great Dickens was never forgiven, the Trollopes and Marryats thought unkind, Wilde regarded with suspicion. In the twentieth century, as American cultural confidence and political power increased, less than noble motives were attributed to British fictional treatments of America and Americans. When Graham Greene published his quite notable and politically shrewd novel *The Quiet American* in 1955, the critic A.J. Liebling, reviewing it for the *New Yorker*, saw it as a book of old resentments revived in a state of political fear. The novel was, he said, an exercise in national projections which

> made me realize that Mr Greene ... trapped on the moving staircase of history, was registering a classical reaction to a situation familiar to me and Spengler. When England, a French cultural colony, outstripped the homeland after Waterloo and the Industrial Revolution, all that remained for the French to say was, "Nevertheless, you remain nasty, overgrown children." The Italians of the Renaissance said it to the French, and I suppose the Greeks said it to the Romans. It is part of the ritual of handing over.

This touchiness was understandable, even though American readers might now be readier than this to admit that Greene's portrait of the interventionist sensibility of a new generation of Americans active in the processes of world power-politics has had its moments of disaster, especially in South East Asia where Greene sets the book.

The dialogue of transatlantic refraction has been fundamental to the development of the Western novel, and in the images of comparison and otherness that have crossed and recrossed the

Atlantic, filling European fiction with images of America, American fiction with images of Europe, there has been a powerful and formative Atlantic trade which has shaped the direction of Western arts and writing, encouraging expatriations and emigrations, international movements and mutual relations. But that dialogue has never been easy, especially between Britain and an America struggling to define itself both in relation and in reaction to Europe. The images have always been political as well as aesthetic, Oedipal as well as literary. And in the twentieth century, when the roles changed, and, said Scott Fitzgerald, something subtle passed to America, the style of man, they have been even more complicated still. For Europe was no longer experience and American innocence, London capital and New York or San Francisco province. The European chaos and the two world wars it bred seem to confirm Spenglerian convictions, and the notion that Europe was the waste land and the United States decidedly not.

When American money, assistance and intellectual realliance flowed into Western Europe after the Second World War, a new generation of American literary travellers visited Europe to discover its disorder and dependence. Edmund Wilson, the American critic, travelling in the Mediterranean and Britain, found a cultureless waste kept going by American assistance, and in his *Europe Without Baedeker: Sketches in the Ruins of Italy, Greece and England* (1947), reflected on "how much better we were at home". Leslie Fiedler, in his *An End to Innocence* (1955), found a new collusion, between the now quite uninnocent travelling American and the European air of decay and corruption. Indeed as American popular culture and mythology now began to dominate Europe he saw there only a mirror, a world of "mechanical lust and meaningless violence", that was modernising itself into Americanness: "The new American abroad," he said, "finds a Europe racked with self-pity and nostalgia (except where sustained by the manufactured enthusiasms of Stalinism) and as alienated from its old traditions as Sauk City; he finds a Europe reading in its own ruins *Moby Dick*, a Europe haunted by the idea of America." The old myth of American cultural deference toward Europe was now more or less faded, and the likely future for Europe was reconstruction *à l'américaine*. Many British intellectuals agreed with this broad diagnosis, and its cultural and political consequences have been considerable. It has played its part in literary change and development, and some would say that what we have seen since the war is the final shifting of literary originality in the English-language line across the Atlantic, from Britain to the United States, a shift that from Melville and Whitman on has been much anticipated but exceedingly hard to date. But the story has its complicated elements, and it is useful to look at one of them: the moment of somewhat improbable transatlantic intercourse that, just after the war's end, took place between the United States and Mr Evelyn Waugh.

2 Waugh is to my mind one of the great modern British writers, but he belonged to a generation of novelists whose work has never quite had the attention that was due. It was the generation that came into place in the 1920s and 1930s, roughly matching the achievement in America of Fitzgerald, Hemingway, and Faulkner, and writing about many of the same things. One of these was the impact of the First World War on the relationship between the generations, and the dark discovery of generational isolation. Fitzgerald's "the beautiful and damned", Hemingway's "lost generation", and Waugh's "bright young things" always had a good deal in common, and part of this was an intense imaginative engagement with the life of what all three of them called "the younger generation" ("the topic of the Younger Generation" spreads "like a yawn" through the party at Anchorage House in *Vile Bodies*) coupled with an intense criticism of the modern sterility that guided and emptied their lives. This required an intense, hard modern style, and all three writers became perfectionists in this particular art; Waugh indeed seems to me a writer of intense stylistic originality. But, as David Lodge has pointed out, writers like Waugh, Compton-Burnett and Henry Green, who have much in common, have never quite been granted their innovations and originalities in the way that happened with their American contemporaries, in part because they were overshadowed by the strong modernist generation that in Britain preceded them to a far greater extent than happened in the United States. Up to the outbreak of World War Two Waugh's work manifests the double force of intense engagement with the modern, the contemporary and the chaotic, with the futile wars and the dark places of distant travel, and a strong satirical displacement of these same materials, so that they acquire the force of an image. But Waugh – he tells us the story very thoroughly in the *Men at Arms* trilogy – was affected by the Second World War, a war to which he gave strong allegiance and then came to interpret as a betrayal of civilisation, as the forces of Russia and the West conspired together to produce the Age of the Common Man. With the change of feeling went a great change of style. The changes wrought by war were the theme of a book written on a troopship, *Put Out More Flags* (1942), while the sense of a world lost and finished was expressed in the delightful, promising and unfinished *Work Suspended* (also 1942). By the end of hostilities, Waugh was ready to declare himself as a

new kind of writer, and this he did with *Brideshead Revisited* (1945).

Brideshead Revisited, he explained on the dustjacket, was not meant to be funny: "There are passages of buffoonery, but the general theme is at once romantic and eschatological." The book was an ambitious, "perhaps intolerably presumptuous", attempt to trace "the workings of the divine purpose in a pagan world . . . . The story will be uncongenial alike to those who look back on that pagan world with unalloyed affection, and to those who see it as transitory, insignificant, and hopefully past." Thus the book could only please those who share his hope "not . . . that anything but disaster lies ahead, but that the human spirit, redeemed, can survive all disasters." The novel indeed rigorously explored the social experience of the interwar decades, and is fascinating on that score. But it did so in a manner far more romantic, snobbish, religious and explicitly Catholic than any before it, expressing its dismay meanwhile about the age of the common man.

When Waugh reissued the book with changes in 1959, he noted that it had been written "in a bleak period of present privation and threatening disaster – the period of soya beans and Basic English – and in consequence the book is infused with a kind of gluttony, for food and wine, for the splendours of the recent past, and for rhetorical and ornamental language, which now with a full stomach I find distasteful". Waugh also noted that the book "lost me such esteem as I once enjoyed among my contemporaries and led me into an unfamiliar world of fan-mail and press photographers". The loss of esteem and the sense of isolation he felt in the egalitarianising and blunt-intellectual mood of the postwar years hurt Waugh greatly, and the book was not in general kindly treated by the critics. In particular Waugh was hurt by a review of the novel by Edmund Wilson, with whom he had had an uneasy meeting during Wilson's postwar visit to London, and who, having admired Waugh's early work, now declared himself disappointed by the exoticism and Catholicism of *Brideshead*. He also remarked on the novel's sentimental bestseller characteristics, quite unlike those of the great social satirist of the 1930s. And indeed the irony was that Waugh's "unpopular" book was to be an enormous bestseller, quite transforming Waugh's financial fortunes as well as his image of himself and his readers' image of him.

In all this were the seeds of a new and complicated relationship between Waugh and America, the power that seemed to be transforming the postwar world and even taking command of its religious direction and future. Wilson's own essay appeared to share Liebling's view that the British were failing to acknowledge their own cultural defeat and taking refuge in snobbery to deny the emergence of new American cultural power. Yet this situation precisely allowed Waugh to forge a new and unusual contract with American readers, who enjoyed the snobbery and style Waugh assumed as his postwar persona. *Brideshead* clearly satisfied the needs of a British age of austerity with its images of glut and its social nostalgia, but it also delighted Americans with its richness and its evocation of the British aristocracy in its state of splendid decadence.

So the book became a Book-of-the-Month Club selection, and sold three-quarters of a million copies, earning Waugh a good deal of money which, as he frankly explained to American readers, was promptly removed from him by the British taxman. It also aroused an enormous correspondence, from American readers who wanted to know all about British society and about the author himself. Explaining that he did not believe in leaving letters unanswered, Waugh responded in an article in *Life* magazine. As he put it, "I have momentarily become an object of curiosity to Americans and I find that they believe that my friendship and confidence are included in the price of the book." He went on to display himself as an old-fashioned British figure, living in a well-established and secluded social world. In his youth he had gadded, "among savages and people of fashion and politicians and crazy generals", but he had now ceased to enjoy this and given himself over to his abiding interest, the English language. And, he promised, his future books would have two things to make them unpopular: "a preoccupation with style and the attempt to represent man more fully, which, to me, means only one thing, man in his relation to God".

Waugh was thus already constructing the conservative, irascible, and historically alienated mask of his later life, and doing it in some degree in collusion with his American readers. And this Anglo-American aspect of Waugh's life was soon to develop very dramatically. For, in 1947, he was asked to go to Hollywood to discuss a film version of *Brideshead*, upon which Metro Goldwyn Mayer had taken out an option. He travelled to New York and Hollywood in February-March of that year, and was received well. But after seven weeks of discussion, in which it became clear that the studio saw the novel as essentially a love-story with some religious top-dressing, and that in any case the sexual aspects of the tale took it into problems with the film censors, the arrangement finally collapsed. Waugh was to comment on all this in an essay on "Why Hollywood Is a Term of Disparagement", which explained the film as an art of the common man, and observed that each book that is taken for adaptation probably has something remarkable about it: "It is the work of a staff of 'writers' to distinguish this quality, separate it and obliterate it."

The visit was thus far from being a success, which might have been predicted, as it might have been predicted that, though Waugh's outrageously mannered and dandyish style would have some appeal for Americans, they would have somewhat less for him. Yet in such suspicion Waugh always found promise. Hollywood and California, the most aberrant and extreme yet in some ways the most typical part of America, the place where the American Dream turned into pure fantasy, where the frivolous and strange was not only to be found on the film lot but outside in the streets, in the new religions and strange utopian desire that covered the landscape of bulldozed hills and slipping canyons built over earthquake faults, stirred up a sense of extravagance that was not to be gained from austerity Britain. Here was a milieu of comic extravagances and outrages, and Waugh's hunter instincts were raised to the highest pitch.

For one thing, in its dealings with Waugh Hollywood had evidently lived up to type. Waugh had long been fascinated by film, and technically influenced by it, and the wiles and absurdities of the film world had already been treated in previous Waugh books. *Vile Bodies* contains the Wonderfilm Company of Great Britain, always hampered by lack of capital and the failure of the cameraman to put in a new roll of film. A delightful short story, *Excursion in Reality*, tells of a young novelist, Simon Lack, known, like Waugh, for his dialogue, who is asked to write a film scenario of Hamlet, constantly summoned from meal or bed to conferences that rarely take place and, if they do, involve the dismemberment of the play, granted an emotionless affair with fellow writer Miss Grits, and finally ejected back into a so-called real world which now is unreal, for, notes Lack, "for the first time in my life I have come [in the film-world] into contact with real life".

Now the same surreal real life was on offer in California. Moreover, Waugh had also presented glimpses of Americans and American life before: there is Mrs Melrose Ape and Judge Skimp (". . . that's an American . . . ") in *Vile Bodies*, the American "Loot" in *Men at Arms*, and in *Brideshead* the brief American interlude where Charles Ryder, returning from his withdrawal to the Central American jungle, meets again his wife *and* the "civilization" of New York City ("in that city there is neurosis in the air which the inhabitants mistake for energy"). The glimpses might be thought glimpses of a larger fictional possibility for the writer who had claimed, in his travel-book *Ninety-Two Days*, to be interested in "distant and barbarous places, and particularly in the borderlands of conflicting cultures and states of development, where ideas, uprooted from their traditions, become oddly changed in transplantation". In particular Waugh had always been fascinated by those special cultural crossover points where barbarism interacts with absolute modernity. Now he had found another.

There was also the matter of religion. The popular forms of

American salvation evidently came to fascinate the ever more re-
ligiously occupied Waugh very greatly. "You're angels, not a panto,
see?" the salvationist Mrs Ape – clearly derived from the vaudevillian
gospelist Aimée Semple McPherson, who made a million dollars with
her message until, after a supposed kidnapping, she was found in a
love-nest with one of her co-workers – had declared to her little
troupe of revivalists in *Vile Bodies*. God seemed to do a different sort
of work in the United States, and Waugh pursued the matter.

Like most visitors to Los Angeles, he was during his visit taken, by
Lady Millbanke, to see Forest Lawn Memorial Park, the creation of
another charismatic Californian salvationist, Dr Easton. The well-
advertised cemetery, art centre and tourist attraction cannibalised and
parodied Europe for its decor (Michelangelo's David, the Wee Kirk
o' the Heather, and Leonardo's *Last Supper*, vibrantly imitated and
modernised, improved in size or materials, are among its treasures
and trophies), just as its multidenominational eclecticism seemed to
parody the world's faiths. For a writer like Waugh, obsessed with the
grim comedy of memento mori, and fascinated by finding the relics of
European civilisation stranded away from their cultural source, the
insight into Californian death-practices proved the culmination of his
American visit.

What followed was another article for *Life* magazine, a savage and
well-illustrated piece called "Half In Love With Easeful Death" that
examined Californian burial customs from the standpoint of the
future archaeologist after the destruction of Los Angeles by drought.
As he said, "Without the testimony of tombs the science of archaeol-
ogy could barely exist, and it will be a commonplace among the
scholars of 2947 that the great cultural decline of the twentieth
century was first evident in the graveyard." Waugh quotes a guide to
Forest Lawn by Bruce Barton, presumably the same Bruce Barton
who in the 1920s brought Christianity and American commercialism
into perfect consonance by describing Jesus as the first great
businessman, which points out that the cemetery contains no ghastly
monuments suggesting a pessimistic view of death, but only images of
immortality; he also reflects on Dr Eaton's credo at the entrance: "I
believe in a happy Eternal Life." As he notes, the traditional warnings
of mortality associated with burial are all therefore reversed: the body
is prevented from decaying, the cemetery itself is earthquake-
proofed, and images of eternal childhood abound. The park –
segregated not by denomination but by price and race – eliminates all
the theological meanings associated with the last things, rendering
them absurd, and the soul goes straight from Slumber Room to
Paradise. Indeed Dr Easton is, says Waugh, "the first man to offer
eternal salvation at an inclusive charge as part of his undertaking

service". Waugh, claiming civilisation and a sense of human mortality and mutability, had found perfect vulgarity, and he knew it. Cemeteries, he announced, were "the only real thing in Hollywood – a deep mine of literary gold".

This was the gold that Waugh went on to mine in *The Loved One: An Anglo-American Tragedy* (1948), Waugh's one novel with an American setting, and to my mind his greatest postwar novel, and a quite remarkable work. This was not to be the view of Edmund Wilson, who reviewed this novel too. The book won considerable esteem among the American public, and gave Waugh another enormous success. However to Wilson it was vitiated by its Catholic standpoint: "To the non-religious reader . . . the patrons and proprietors of Whispering Glades [the cemetery in the novel] seem more sensible than the priest-guided Evelyn Waugh," he said. "What the former are trying to do is, after all, to gloss over physical death with smooth lawns and soothing rites; but, for the Catholic, the fact of death is not to be feared at all; he is solaced with the fantasy of another world in which everyone who has died in the flesh is somehow supposed to be still alive and in which it is supposed to be possible to help souls advance themselves by buying candles to burn in churches."

Wilson seemed most dismayed by the fact that the qualities that in earlier novels had expressed themselves as powerful satirical outrage now were put to the service of traditional, conservative and quaintly British religious and social attitudes. It is very certain that Waugh's was not a liberal-hearted novel, but I think Wilson's postwar distrusts led him to misread the book. He did, though, point to one very fruitful comparison, between Waugh's novel and the pre-war American surrealist and black humorist Nathanael West. At his best, Waugh too is one of the great twentieth-century black humorists, and his social and theological distrust of the modern world may have dismayed his liberal-minded contemporaries, but they fed his bleak and surreal vision. He saw a world around him where, as Philip Roth once put it, "The actuality is continually outdoing our talents, and the culture tosses up figures almost daily that are the envy of any novelist." Waugh was always stirred by such a challenge, and never in a simple way or from a simple standpoint. Hollywood was indeed a deep mine of literary gold, and *The Loved One* was to show it had an enormous yield. Like many an American novelist, Waugh wrote his decadent western, in which, like West, he explored one decadence from the standpoint of another.

3 "What a damned impudent woman," cries Lady Circumference, in *Vile Bodies*, on the occasion of Mrs Melrose Ape's performance at Margot Metroland's party, when she asks the company to search their souls; her response is "the organ voice of England, the hunting cry of the *ancien regime*". There were many after the war who – knowing Waugh's view that the world was passing from civilisation to barbarism, rather than progressing to egalitarian enlightenment – believed that Waugh's fiction was a cry of much the same kind. In the book he published just before *The Loved One, Scott-King's Modern Europe* (1947), Waugh had submitted his hero, a simple classics master, to the world of state socialism and European cold war politics. When on his return his headmaster asks him to teach not classics but modern economic history, Scott-King has a ready reply: "I think it would be very wicked indeed to do anything to fit a boy for the modern world . . . . I think it is the most long-sighted view it is possible to take." It was in fact not a new theme with him: Waugh's novels depend on a persistent comparison between the safe city of order and the barbarian wilderness, ever-encroaching, and therefore rendering all serious human action absurd. Yet it is precisely that anarchic absurdity, the ever-present barbarian challenge to humanism, that makes his comedy. *The Loved One*, too, is indeed a satire on or an anarchic comic exploration of the modern world in its most modern place, the United States and Hollywood. And indeed at first the joke seems to be done from the standpoint of traditional, arrogant, aristocratic British culture. "I never was much good at anything new," says Sir Francis Hinsley, one of the "English titles that abounded now in Hollywood, several of them authentic". And evidently Waugh too is not much taken with the stuff of modernity: plastics, uniformity, homogeneity, and Kaiser's Stoneless Peaches, which taste "like balls of damp, sweet, cotton-wool". And he portrays (as many writers have) an America where everything seems sterilised, even sexual relations, so that the women are Bergsonian mechanical objects, their "uniform elegant limbs" apparently "marked in one cellophane envelope at the neighbourhood store", and above their nylon stockings there is little of human interest.

No-one can miss Waugh's bitter distrust of a liberal and secular age where a hopeful historicism seemed to replace a classical sense of transcendence. In *The Ordeal of Gilbert Pinfold* (1957) he invented a central character who clearly is a version of himself – an irascible Tory, all tastes negative, bored with the world, living among the first and the last things. "The tiny kindling of charity which came to him through religion sufficed only to temper his disgust and change it to boredom. There was a phrase in the Thirties: 'It is later than you think,' which was designed to cause uneasiness. It was never later than Mr Pinfold thought." Pinfold is outrageous; this in turn is a protection of his modesty. But it is just that modesty which is assaulted and exposed as paranoia internalises all the forces he most fears, and the wilderness beyond invades the body itself. Pinfold wishes to live in a classical wholeness, his very writing a well-made object not personal to himself. But the story of Mr Pinfold is exactly the opposite, a confession, an agony, a product of the wilderness inside the self. What is excluded is also incorporated; the process of incorporation becomes the work of art.

And this is very largely how Waugh's comic vision had, and was to continue, to work. Civilisation and sanity stand in place, comic anarchy enters; the force of disorder is also the force of comedy, which is not a stay against misfortune, a mode of preservation of the eternal things, but an amoral and destructive vitalism. Always a novelist of the Twenties, Waugh was preoccupied with barbaric vitalism as were so many of his generation. It gave an art of assault, an art of moral dismay, and it depended on an imaginative collusion with the barbarities which in classical seriousness one would distrust or consider a basis for tragedy. The result was a decadent art, an art of amoralism, mannered, aestheticised, indifferent, and very funny. Humour masked the inroads seriousness was making by building its own conspiracy; and the form that emerged was a humour of mortal resignation, a black humour, a laughter in the ruins.

In February 1948, the readers of *Horizon* – a magazine teasingly referred to in the novel's opening dialogue – were in fact treated to a sneak preview of *The Loved One*, which occupied the space of an entire issue. The editor Cyril Connolly introduced it by observing that "In its attitude toward death, and death's stand-in, failure, Mr Waugh exposes a materialist society at its weakest spot, as would Swift and Donne if they were alive today." Waugh himself also provided a note, predicting that because the book dealt with two serious subjects, death and America, it would cause "ructions". He also explained its stimuli. "The ideas I had in mind," he said,

> were: 1. Quite predominantly, over-excitement with the scene. 2. The Anglo-American impasse – 'never the twain shall meet.' 3. There is no such thing as an 'American'. They are all exiles uprooted, transplanted and doomed to sterility. The ancestral gods they have abjured get them in the end. 4. The European raiders who come for the spoils and if they are lucky make for home with them. 5. *Memento mori*.

It is an economical and useful account, and as it seems to suggest it draws on a memory-bank of European-American contacts and myths. "Through no wish of my own I have become the protagonist of a Jamesian problem," reflects Dennis Barlow, the book's central figure, an English rogue-poet down on his luck, and he also recalls that most such relationships end in tragedy. Waugh indeed subtitled the book "An Anglo-American Tragedy", and there are many overtones from classical tragedy built into it. But if it is a tragedy it is a very cool one, with an absurd death and even more absurd burial from the tragic heroine, producing from dark events a comic result. The ancestral gods do indeed get Aimée in the end; the European raider does go home with the spoils; and his role in the book is that of one who has been in Arcadia, or in other words *memento mori*. Some of these motifs remind us of *Brideshead Revisited*, but done in Waugh's coolest and most indifferent manner. And the result is surely no tragedy but a very black comedy.

But was it a comedy of English condescension, in, say, the same spirit as *Martin Chuzzlewit*, a novel that was long to rankle with Americans even though its vision bore a marked resemblance to that of many American writers, and particularly to Melville? James Russell Lowell once complained that "for some reason or other, the European has rarely been able to see America except in caricature", and in Waugh's books there is by definition no shortage of that. In fact Waugh's book seems quite learned about the "Jamesian problem", and the tradition of international fiction, in which of course it is an entrant. The American myth, and the depiction of America in literature, European and American, was forged in the space between the two continents. And in particular it has always depended upon the Edenic or Arcadian motif, fundamental to the entire process of American discoveries and settlement; Columbus, discovering his New World, believed he had lit upon the terrestrial paradise of which, from Classical times on, the European imagination had long dreamed. It was the New World in every sense, spared the fallen nature of the old, offering history a new start and restoring mankind to the primal garden of Edenic innocence, the green world prior to sin. In Shakespeare and Donne we can find the famous motifs; they are there in Michael Drayton's poem "To the Virginian Voyage", which sees paradise ahead for the westward traveller, and a world governed by the natural laws of the Golden Age.

This has been crucial to American sensibility, and American writing, ever since, from William Bradford's journey of arrival in the New World to Fitzgerald's Gatsby, that twentieth-century Columbus staring at the green light on Daisy Buchanan's dock. It was also the theme that Dickens explores to structure *Martin Chuzzlewit*, that

journey to a depraved Eden that claims paradisal innocence but which
is marked by materialism, the Almighty Dollar, and the crime of
slavery. Dickens, who of course is as bitter about Victorian Britain as
he is about America, simply suggests that the United States is part of
the world, and spared neither history nor sin. In this it was a fable of
European experience looking sceptically at the American claim of
innocence, and this theme was to find its powerful reverse expression
in a good many American novels of the reverse voyage, from
Hawthorne's *The Marble Faun* to the complex mythological transac-
tions of Henry James's novels of innocence and experience.

It is thus highly appropriate to the tradition that Dennis Barlow,
caught through no wish of his own in a Jamesian problem, should
journey to a terminal Arcadia, death's Utopia, Whispering Glades.
"Behold, I dreamed a dream and I saw a New Earth sacred to
HAPPINESS . . .," declares the marble plaque at the entrance to the
cemetery, which contains a list of pastoral and Arcadian desires for
this green and innocent place, signed "Wilbur Kenworthy, Dream-
er". And Whispering Glades indeed belongs with all the other places
of innocent pastoral in American fiction, from Cooper's wilderness to
Hawthorne's Blithedale, or for that matter Dickens's New Eden.
Dennis Barlow, the postlapsarian, European decadent, knows it for
what it is, and also knows its opposite, the world of gothic and dark
romanticism that has always functioned in American as well as
European writing both to explore and challenge the dream. His
natural home is in a parodic version of the myth, and he finds his due
place in the nearby animal cemetery, for animals, we are told, are "a
headache in cemeteries", and their soulless fate is indeed a grim form
of memento mori. For him, Arcadia is too bland, a denial of the
tragedy of experience; but far from provoking him into detachment it
demands his engaged delight, his dark romantic investment in all that
is on offer. A true romantic poet, he is half in love with easeful death,
the very thing that Dr Kenworthy and his acolyte Mr Joyboy, that
cosmetician of mortality, put on offer. And Barlow in fact finds
himself in a place of inescapable excitements and, like his creator,
"over-excited by the scene", quickly "goes native" under the pressure of his decadent Muse.

So *The Loved One*, like all of Waugh's best novels, becomes a work
of comic delight in which the famous conservative distrust and the
late indifferent classicism is drawn over into an endless and deep
fascination with its opposite. Waugh's best heroes, from Margot
Metroland to Basil Seal and now Dennis Barlow, are delighted comic
users of the world in which they find themselves, becoming effective
survivors in the modern world of social decline, irrevocable modernity, fleeting relationships, new manners and life-styles. Like Waugh,

they enter with anarchic delight into the most barbaric and surreal of modern milieux, and in its mixture of innocent Arcadianism and absolute modernity Waugh could have found no better field for his talents, Dennis Barlow no better sphere for his fate, than here on the American West Coast and amid its funerary practices.

Waugh's American Arcadia is certainly a place of barbarism; the book begins on the edge of a desert, where three English voyagers, "the counterparts of numberless fellow-countrymen exiled in the barbarous regions of the world", converse. An evening breeze shakes the palm-leaves and swells "the dry sounds of summer, the frog-voices, the grating cicadas, and the ever present pulse of music from the neighbouring native huts". We must turn three pages before we discover that this desert watering hole is Los Angeles, and that we are among the British film colony, the actors and socialites who have been imported to Hollywood for their mannered Britishness and must now preserve it.

Here, as usual in such imperial communities, the danger is of going native, but the satirical note is turned as much against them as their world, and it is just their stance that Dennis Barlow refuses, as he does indeed "go native" in a spirit of delighted immersion. He is a European raider, and out for his own survival; but he is also a writer, and out not so much for innocence as, in both an emotional and a literary sense, experience. He retains his detachment, which allows Waugh a very classical note of satire with all the privileges of European wisdom: "American mothers, Dennis reflected, presumably knew their daughters apart, as the Chinese were said subtly to distinguish one from another of their seemingly uniform race, but to the European eye the Mortuary Hostess was one with all her sisters on the air-liners and the reception-desks. She was the standardized product . . . but Dennis came of an earlier civilisation with sharper needs." From the standpoint of a more rooted culture he is able to see American culture as essentially parodic, rendered empty by transplant. So he listens to the tape in the University Church at Whispering Glades (a good deal of the parodic sense here is gained by simply copying the truth):

> In 1935 [it says] Dr Kenworthy was in Europe seeking in that treasure house of Art something worthy of Whispering Glades. His tour led him to Oxford and the famous Norman church of St Peter. He found it dark. He found it full of conventional and depressing memorials. "Why," asked Dr Kenworthy, "do you call it St Peter-without-the-walls?" and they told him it was because in the old days the city wall had stood between it and the business centre. "*My* church," said Dr Kenworthy, "shall have no walls."

This is staple Anglo-American comedy, but Waugh takes it further. Dennis listens to the tape, its tones "so often parodied yet never rendered more absurd or more hypnotic than the original", and finds that "His interest was no longer purely satiric." "In that zone of insecurity in the mind where none but the artist dare trespass, the tribes were mustering. Dennis, the frontiersman, could read the signs."

Waugh's novel, I am suggesting, comes, like all his best comedy, from that "zone of insecurity in the mind where none but the artist dare trespass", and it becomes a gothic novel, the novel that was always invested with the paradoxes and the labyrinths that lie behind the faces of innocence. As Leslie Fiedler points out in *Love and Death in the American Novel*, its themes of Eros and Thanatos have obsessed the American creative imagination; they obsess Waugh's. Dennis, led onward past his sense of standardisation and plasticity, is brought to Aimée Thanatogenos, whose name is virtually a translation of the title of Fiedler's book, which of course Waugh could not have read, since it appeared later. Aimée is one of Waugh's most brilliant creations, a figure of standardised American surfaces beneath which Dennis glimpses more, an immigrant atavism, indeed a rich glint of lunacy. She is "unique. Not indefinably; the appropriate distinguishing epithet leapt into Dennis's mind the moment he saw her: sole Eve in a bustling hygenic Eden, this girl was a decadent" – like Dennis himself. She displays the experience within the innocence, the tragic base within the parodic culture:

> brain and body were scarcely distinguishable from the standard product, but the spirit – ah, the spirit was something apart; it had to be sought afar; not here in the musky orchards of the Hesperides, but in the mountain air of dawn, in the eagle-haunted passes of Hellas. An umbilical cord of cafes and fruit shops, of ancestral shady business (fencing and pimping) united Aimée, all unconscious, to the higher places of her race.

She is divided between her heart, "a small inexpensive organ of local manufacture", and her ancestral instincts, the Attic voices that speak of "Alcestis and proud Antigone". And she is likewise divided between the claims of Mr Joyboy, the "ethical," Mom-obsessed embalmer of Whispering Glades, and Dennis, the gross intruder, the decadent European poet and employee of the cemetery's four-legged rival, the Happy Hunting Ground pet cemetery. They speak in quite different voices to the serious objects of her contemplation, which are Art, Love and Death; while Joyboy woos her with his artefacts, the beautifully embalmed and smiling corpses he supplies for her attentions, Dennis does so with his plagiarised poems which plunder

European and American romanticism for images of love and death
("in the world I come from," he explains when caught out, "quotation
is a national vice"). Joyboy is "ethical" and Dennis is sometimes very
sweet and loving but, as she tells her newspaper adviser the Guru
Brahmin, "sometimes he becomes unethical and makes me feel
unethical too."

It is all a tragedy, for Aimée, thus split betwen present and past,
modernity and atavism, ethics and passion, America and Un-
Americanism, commits suicide in Mr Joyboy's laboratory. But with
appropriate decadent indifference, Aimée's death becomes a triumph
for the comic spirit. Now Dennis can both assist his embarrassed rival
and suitably celebrate the ancient spirit of his loved one by having her
cremated at the pet cemetery. And, as the fire burns in the oven, and
Dennis arranges for a greeting card to go annually to Mr Joyboy
saying "Your little Aimée is wagging her tail in heaven tonight,
thinking of you," Dennis, his return passage home securely contrived,
sees the meaning and end of his quest:

> On the last evening in Los Angeles Dennis knew he was a favourite
> of Fortune. Others, better men than he, had foundered here and
> perished. The strand was littered with their bones. He was leaving it
> not only unravished but enriched. He was adding his bit to the
> wreckage; something that had long irked him, his young heart, and
> was carrying back instead the artist's load, a great, shapeless chunk
> of experience; bearing it home to his ancient and comfortless shore;
> to work on it hard and long, for God knew how long. For that
> moment of vision a lifetime is often too short.
>   He picked up the novel which Miss Poski had left on his desk and
> settled down to await his loved one's final combustion.

Like the true decadent artist, Dennis has all the time been following
his Muse. Her message, like the message of most rigorous art, was
never finally one about the power of sentimental love, as he had
divined: "It was about Whispering Glades, but it was not, except
indirectly, about Aimée. Sooner or later the Muse would have to be
placated. She came first." Evidently she is a muse of hard experience,
which in two senses is what Dennis reaches. There is experience as
antithesis to innocence, which Waugh's America appears to lack
except as an atavistic instinct; there is the "experience" which forges
the stuff of art, the stimulants and sufferings that, passing through the
"zone of insecurity in the mind where none but the artist dare
trespass", transmute into literary wholeness. America offers, in its
barbaric modernism, and its sterilised blandness set over the pain of
life, one kind of decadence; Europe, anarchic and "unethical", its
classical and tragic forms corrupted to comic roguery, is another.

Like Vladimir Nabokov in his brilliant transatlantic novel *Lolita*, that story of European corruption seeking the timeless arrest of innocence-not-quite-become-experience in his American nymphet, only to find that time works in America too, Waugh takes a spirit of decadence forged in Europe and allows it to explore, with a sense of infinite delight and pleasure, another. Yet the theme was not new. Indeed, we can find it throughout the history of American writing. Waugh's gift was to invest it with his gift for macabre comedy.

4 "You don't have to read much of him," Dennis tells Mr Schultz at the Pet Cemetery, who does not know Henry James. "All his stories are about the same thing – American innocence and European experience." "Thinks he can outsmart us, does he?" asks Mr Schultz. "James was the innocent American," explains Dennis. Waugh, evidently enough, is not the innocent American, and he could be accused of outsmarting his subject; I have tried to suggest that the balance of relations is far more complex. *The Loved One* seems to me, like *Lolita*, a major late novel in the tale of transatlantic relations, and filled with its complicated contradictions and motifs. And precisely because it was so, it seems to me essential to read it in the context of the history of complex refractions that have constructed a whole transatlantic genre of fiction, one in which the artistic engagement of European writers with America, and American writers with Europe, has constructed a distinctive art of mutual investment. The trade has not simply been one in literary images but in literary forms, creating not an aggressive hostility between American and European writing, but a formal intimacy. This, said Henry James, was the "complex fate" of the American writer; it has become part of the modern fate of the European. American modernity has become a classic test for the makers of modern forms; similarly the modern forms of European art have been constantly assimilated into the artistic apprehension of American life by American writers. Waugh, I have suggested elsewhere, is one of the great inventors of modern comedy, the comedy of modernity; and his styles have to my mind some relationship with the styles of much modern American fiction, especially the fiction that has attempted to encompass American life through the comic vision.

Waugh was by no means the first writer to think of the world of Hollywood and southern California as the appropriate subject for the surreal comic western, or see its practices of fantasy, love and death as essential material for modern art. In the late 1930s two major American writers turned their attention to precisely this subject. Both were working as screenwriters in Hollywood, and captured its surreal world in their two last novels. Both, like Waugh, were writers whose style had been founded in the 1920s, and who had presented us with some of our most powerful modern images of both the lure and the corruption of the great American dream.

One of these was F. Scott Fitzgerald, the novelist who had seemed to celebrate the essential spirit of the American 1920s, but who by the end of the 1930s was working out his last disappointed days as a Hollywood scriptwriter, capturing that experience lightly in his Pat Hobby stories, but transfiguring it into profound material in *The Last Tycoon* – the book he left unfinished when he died of a heart-attack in 1940, so that it was published incomplete in 1941, in a text edited by Edmund Wilson. The other was his friend Nathanael West, also working as a screenwriter when he wrote his novel of Hollywood, *The Day of the Locust*, also a final book, for West was to die in a car accident within days of the death of his friend. There had been Hollywood fiction, California fiction, before, but in their work we can see a sequence that would persist. They located an essential American fantasy-land which was filled with the myths and distortions of the American dream, a westward drift of the haunted imagination drawn into facile images of life and then into revolt against them. Their theme was not simply the surreal vision of life that comes from screen-images, but the surreal nature of the world and the community that itself creates them. And from the artist drawn into such a world, as many modern writers have been, it in turn requires a new surrealism of method, as in turn Waugh had seen and suggested in his earlier novels. All this, it seems to me, might suggest why Waugh might seem to us not a writer remote from the American literary interpretation of contemporary American experience, but one who seems to contribute very directly to it.

As Edmund Wilson said, there is a comparison of profit to be made between Waugh and Nathanael West. West had begun to write in the late 1920s and early 1930s in expatriate Paris, an episode which confirmed an already held interest in surrealism. He was also essentially a comic writer, an author of the modern grotesque whose characters habitually live in a state of semi-crazed desire which is the mask for an inward suffering, as he showed in *Miss Lonelyhearts* (1933), a black farce about a newspaperman who actually tries to respond to the sufferings revealed in the letters sent to his agony column. The problem is the artist's, incapable of providing an adequate form of response to the kind of world he sees about him; and West continued to be a novelist who dealt in a world of suffering, unmitigated by the traditional religious deliverances, a world of festering non-redemption. In *The Day of the Locust* there is, as there is in Waugh's book, a scene in a Californian funeral chapel; a recording of Bach's "Come Redeemer, Our Saviour" is played on the electric organ and to it the mourners, "hoping for a dramatic incident of some sort", and drawn to the funeral entirely for that reason, respond only when, for a moment, the music hints at impatience with the Saviour's absence. There is also at the centre of the book, as in Waugh's, a central character who is an artist searching for a story in Hollywood, an artist who is thrust toward stoical indifference and an art of modern grotesquerie. Tod Hackett is a painter, and his name suggests his associations with death and cruelty, the subjects that are summoned into his art by his experience. He has come into the studios as an illustrator, but his own world is a revolt against the glossy realism he is asked to produce. His own style is driven by experience toward the extreme, towards a *Guernica*-like modernism. And he achieves it by emotional withdrawal from others and by his prediction of and then participation in an apocalyptic disaster: the book ends in a great urban riot of the disappointed crowds unable to match dreams to realities, and there Tod finds the subject and method of his painting. Tod's uncomfortable response to the suffering of the lost dreamers who surround him is plainly shared by West, who also artistically uses the literary equivalent of Tod's grotesque art of "Mystery and Decay".

West's novel is therefore set on the fringes of the Hollywood studios, where the dream tarnishes and grows ambiguous: around its backlots and dream-dumps, among its extras and its castoffs, and the surrounding tribes of the rejected and discontented who have been lured to Hollywood by its power as national dream. Here everyone would like to be an actor, exposing identities both falsified and underneath pathetically real, and in the seething crowd of those who have come to California for leisure, sunshine and oranges the "terrible boredom" of mob bitterness is everywhere: "Every day of their lives they read the newspapers and went to the movies. Both fed them on lynchings, murder, sex crimes, explosions, wrecks, love nests, fires, miracles, revolutions, war. This diet made sophisticates of them. The sun is a joke. Oranges can't titillate their jaded palates. Nothing can ever be violent enough to make taut their slack minds and bodies." All this is West's California, which he presents very coolly, going for a comedy of almost parodied agony, of distortion, perversion and misdirected desire. The ambiguity of the film studio turns into the ambiguity of reality itself: acted battles suddenly become real, the faked scenery of the backlot matches the architecture of Los Angeles itself, and the relationship between the stars and the boiling and discontented crowd is both one of extraordinary yearning and violent hostility. In the home of grotesquerie, the grotesque becomes truth. "It is hard," the book notes, "to laugh at the need for beauty and romance, no matter how tasteless, even horrible, the results of that need are. But it is easy to sigh. Few things are sadder than the truly monstrous." West is an expert in the truly monstrous, and he sighs while at the same time maintaining the rapid, elliptical and coolly detached means of his comedy, which is an art of agonised laughter at the grotesque world.

West's book is itself clearly an early work of modern "black humour", a novel where pain, suffering and tragedy are transmuted into the comic mode and human figures lose their conventional humanity and become, themselves, grotesque victims of a grotesque and cruel universe. His characters are object-like, and are made so not just by their own inner distortions and perversions, but the conditions of an American dream itself turned into surreal nightmare. They are also, of course, the product of the techniques of fictional dehumanisation characteristic of West's surrealism. Each of them – the dwarf Abe Kusich; Homer Simpson, who is described as being like a poorly-made automaton; Faye Greener, the novel's sexual centre, whose invitation "wasn't to pleasure, but to struggle, hard and sharp, closer to murder than to love" – is the invention of a sensibility given to seeing the human in a dehumanised and mechanical, or a Bergsonian and comic, light. Like Tod Hackett, whose greatest painting is the apocalyptic "The Burning of Los Angeles", caused by the final riot in which Homer Simpson is lynched for "perversion", and in which depravity runs wild, West *needs* a sense of disaster to yield him form and art. The matter and the manner thus come together in images of physical distortion and emotional extremity in a world drained of solid significances, and the result is the tone of what Jonathan Raban once called "aesthetic sadism", the dark comic surface over the persisting but irremediable sense of pain.

Fitzgerald's *The Last Tycoon* was, of course, not a comic novel, and its treatment of the Hollywood subject was a good deal more realistic, its manner more humane, and it is a tale of the movie business from the inside. But it is constructed from the haunting sense of decadence that marks all of Fitzgerald's work, and intensified in his novels of the Thirties, as the world to which he has attached himself burns out in self-destruction and corruption. His "last tycoon", the movie producer Monroe Stahr, possesses many of the characteristics of Fitzgerald's classic heroes, a powerful and transcendent inner dream of his own which drives him and compels the world around him, but he is a man at the end of his possible existence, a failing hero: "There was no world but had its heroes, and Stahr was the hero . . . . The old loyalties were trembling anew, and there were clay feet everywhere; but still he was their man, the last of the princes." But he is surrounded by an absurd, half-finished landscape of plasticated dreams and desires, and they also exist within him, half surreal and half ridiculous. History itself is distorted: Stahr is compared with the great Presidents, but Andrew Jackson's home is closed, and "Abraham Lincoln" appears in the commissary, "his kindly face fixed on a forty-cent dinner, including dessert", an actor in the fantasy. And the fantasy he has created begins to destroy him, as his world moves toward extremity and collapse, grows apocalyptic. Fitzgerald surrounds him with surreal images – of the two girls floating down through the flood on the head of the property Goddess Siva during the ominous opening earthquake; of the phone-call from the President of the United States, who turns out to be a talking orang-utang; of figures like the negro on the beach who hint at the end of the power of Stahr's old stories, and those like Minna who indicate his own search for death and extinction. Like *The Great Gatsby* it is a novel about the ambiguity and potential corruption of those who seek to interpret and present the American dream, an image of the empty nightmares that lie beneath it, a work of anxious decadence that sees at once both magic and tawdriness.

And this apocalyptic and anxious theme has gone on in a good deal of the fiction of southern California and Hollywood ever since; so has the surrealism and extremity of presentation of a world which has already constructed its own images in the forms of the fantastic and the grotesque. The apocalyptic note passes on into Norman Mailer's still powerful *The Deer Park*, where he presents a culture utterly dead and then, through a new politics of sexuality, attempts to reconnect the circuits, through to the grotesque abstraction of Thomas Pynchon's remarkable novel of southern California, *The Crying of Lot 49* (1966), which presents in the mode of tragic farce a universe utterly technologised and system-linked, where images of self and story become narcissistic and driven towards their possibly empty centre. It is again a world hungry for revelation but caught in meaninglessness, where most signals are empty or at the least enigmatic, and the Word itself has been lost. We can read our way through from these novels into the works of black humour that were to become so crucial to the American novel in the late 1950s and 1960s, when the nihilist-absurdist mode acquired a new power in the face of modern horrors and the sense of human irrelevance.

Waugh's books are, perhaps, black humour of a distinctively British kind, forged out of a conservative distrust of change coupled with an endless delight in the outrageousness of its absurd opposite. But in the dark tradition of modern comedy Waugh was surely one of the great modern exponents, and his achievement is consonant with the contemporary mode of macabre and apocalyptic writing which has indeed become one of the pre-eminent forms for dealing with the

dehumanisations of a disintegrating world. The critics who condemned Waugh for his anti-humanism have often not seen how close he
has been to the fundamental modern artistic developments; indeed,
when we survey the writers of the last thirty years or so in both the
United States and Britain we can sense a continuity on from Waugh,
if not a direct influence – on the brilliant, sharply intellectual and
profoundly macabre performances of Muriel Spark, his co-
religionist, and on other successors, including Angus Wilson and
Anthony Burgess, but also on the outrageous comedy of physical and
metaphysical violation practised in America by writers like John
Barth, Joseph Heller, Kurt Vonnegut, Terry Southern, James Purdy
and Donald Barthelme. Waugh, I have said, is one of the great
modern writers; but at his best – and *The Loved One* is Waugh at his
best – he is also amongst the most relevant and contemporary,
creating a complex collusion between detachment and investment in
modern anarchy which has made him a power in a world where the
older humane comedy has grown harder and harder to write.

5 *The Loved One* did not conclude Waugh's involvement with the
United States. In 1948 he returned to America with a more sober
purpose, to lecture in Catholic universities on converted British
writers like himself. Thereafter he was to retain a persistent interest
in Catholic America, and the hopes and disappointments of the
evolution of faith there. In particular he took pleasure in the signs of
monastic revival he for a time detected in American Catholic life. As
he said in his foreword to *Elected Silence*, the title of the English
edition of Thomas Merton's *The Seven-Storey Mountain*, a powerful
and very popular devotional work written "in fresh, simple, colloquial
American" by a Trappist monk: "There is an ascetic tradition deep in
the American heart which has sometimes taken odd and unlovable
forms. Here in the historic Rules of the Church lies its proper
fulfilment. In the natural order the modern world is rapidly being
made uninhabitable by scientists and politicians . . . . As in the Dark
Ages, the cloister offers the sanest and most civilized form of life."
And he told Randolph Churchill in a letter that "the best hope of the
world is in the remarkable increase of Cistercian vocations among the
yanks". But the part played by American Catholics in the modernisation of the faith dismayed him, and there were other annoyances. His
celebration of Trappist life in America caused him to suggest it was
an escape from other vexations, like overheated rooms, American
radio, and bubble-gum; and he came in for considerable criticism in
the American press. "It so happens that I like visiting America, love

and respect countless Americans, and, knowing their peculiar sensitiveness, take pains not to make the kinds of criticisms of them that I should freely make of any other nation, most of all my own," he said by way of explanation. For the remainder of his days, the United States seems to have been largely conceived by him as a contrast between the embalming room of Whispering Glades and the Trappist cell.

But the story does not quite end there. Metro-Goldwyn-Mayer, in 1965, did make a film of one of Waugh's novels: *The Loved One*. The script was by Christopher Isherwood and the black humorist and *Dr Strangelove* writer Terry Southern. But Isherwood resented Waugh's novel and its criticism of the religious spirit of California, with which, like Aldous Huxley, he considerably sympathised; there was another tradition of British treatments of this volatile subject. Whispering Glades therefore becomes a space pad for firing bodies out into the stratosphere (as usual, life follows art; this commercial proposal has newly come onto the American market, and had many takers) and Aimée is the first to be disposed of, along with the entire content and significance of Waugh's novel. *Brideshead Revisited*, in its turn, was to become an upmarket Granada television serial, beautifully made, sexually frank, concerned with the religious as well as the sentimental story, and inexhaustibly nostalgic about aristocratic Britain and the great British country house (Castle Howard was substituted for Madresfield); it won world-wide audiences. As for Waugh, he died himself in 1966, and his memorial service followed the Latin rite. There then arose the question of how to inter his papers. They passed, in fact, to the store of the University of Texas, where many of us consult them, travelling to the United States to do so, and staying in overheated rooms. We do not have Waugh's view of this, but we might recall what he wrote about the message of Forest Lawn:

> To those of us too old-fashioned to listen respectfully, there is the hope that we may find ourselves, one day beyond time, standing at the balustrade of Heaven among the unrecognizably grown-up denizens of Forest Lawn, and, leaning there beside them, amicably gaze down on Southern California, and share with them the huge joke of what the Professors of Anthropology make of it all.

It is not hard to imagine that gaze then shifting across to the Professors of Literature at Austin, Texas, not so many hundred miles away.

As for the plot of Anglo-American literary intercourse, that changed too, as is the way with things in a mutable world. No doubt partly in response to the changing balance of power, the reaction against the sense of European decline and the temptations of American openness, the fictional image of America became decidedly more exhilarated, and the traditional plot frequently reversed. Cultural contacts with America increased, and with Europe diminished; the era of the Fulbright travel grant and the charter flight drew many British writers across the water, following a new myth of voyage. A new America-centric generation took its place in British fiction, one for whom Europe was more likely to be innocent and America the place of contemporary experience. Kingsley Amis's *One Fat Englishman* (1963) is somewhat close to the Waugh model, in that the rogue-hero goes to the States in a mood both of curiosity and English superiority, but the superiority itself is undermined, and he suffers one of fiction's sharper defeats: "I sometimes get the impression that you think some of the people in this country don't like you because you're British," he is told. "That isn't so . . . . It isn't your nationality we don't like, it's you." During the 1960s a new species seemed to emerge, in books like Wilfred Sheed's *A Middle Class Education* (1961), Anthony Bailey's *The Mother Tongue* (1963), Andrew Sinclair's *The Hallelujah Bum* (1963), my own *Stepping Westward* (1965), Thomas Hinde's *High* (1968) and David Lodge's *Changing Places* (1975), where the Englishman is frequently an innocent, the voyage is toward a liberation beyond shame or guilt, and the myth itself is consciously rewritten again, much as Waugh had himself rewritten it, but in a new balance. And with the change has gone on a change of literary forms, a vigorous creative intercourse between American and British ways of writing. Waugh himself would probably have had little regard for these writers; he found the Butler Education Act an arrangement for "the free distribution of university degrees to the deserving poor", and the generation of writers it appeared to have produced as "sour young people coming off the assembly lines in their hundreds". Yet there are few of them on whom he did not leave a trace; and it is hard not to see his own Anglo-American tragedy as, not late in an old line, but forceful and central in a new one.

"DESIGN-GOVERNING POSTURES"
Malcolm Lowry and modern fiction

" . . . he had suddenly a glimpse of a flowing like an eternal river; he seemed to see how life flowed into art; how art gives life a form and meaning and flows on into life, yet life has not stood still; that was what was always forgotten: how life transformed by art sought further meaning through art transformed by life; and now it was as if this flowing, this river, changed, without appearing to change, became a flowing of consciousness, of mind, so that it seemed that for them too, Primrose and he, just beyond the barrier, lay some meaning, or the key to a mystery that would give some meaning to their ways on earth: it was as if he stood on the brink of an illumination, on the near side of something tremendous, which was to be explained beyond . . . . "

Malcolm Lowry, Dark As the Grave Wherein My Friend Is Laid (1968)

" . . . if it is true, and man is a sort of novelist of himself, I can see something philosophically valuable in attempting to set down what actually happens in a novelist's mind when he conceives what he conceives to be the fanciful figure of a personage, etc., for this, the part that never gets written – with which is included the true impulses that made him a novelist or dramatist in the first place, and the modification of life around him through his own eyes as those impulses were realized – would be the true drama . . . . "

Malcolm Lowry, letter of 1950

1 Malcolm Lowry is today one of our best-known neglected novelists. When he died in 1957, under saddening circumstances, after taking a semi-suicidal combination of drink and drugs, he was a maverick figure in modern fiction. He was the notable author of *Under the Volcano* (1947), a novel that even at that time of revolt against modernism one or two prescient critics thought one of the great works of the age. But such success as the book received, and the high regard it brought him from many, was soured for Lowry by a general lack of recognition in his native Britain, a few bad reviews, and the belief that somehow another novel – Charles Jackson's *The*

Lost Weekend – had pre-empted the attention due to him. Even the signals that success gave seemed negative, and in the event that was the last real moment of lifetime glory.

For ten more years he wrote on and on, but the vast body of material he produced never found a proper home. The publishers seemed no longer to take him seriously, and he became in his later years a massive creator of manuscript, of texts which turned into other texts and never seemed to reach completion, as he chased through paper the mystery and tragedy of his own artistic necessity – a necessity always touched by his considerable capacity for self-destructiveness. Misfortune and misadventure struck him repeatedly: the unhappy pattern of his first marriage, his persecution and jailing by the Mexican authorities, the loss of manuscripts, the burning of his house, the breaking of limbs, the general refusal to understand. If there was a destructive streak in Lowry himself, fate seemed to collude and conspire with it, ironising his talent, turning his destiny toward obscurity and defeat. As with other *poètes maudits*, the driving energy of creation was also an energy of destruction. He suspected himself that there was some deep failing or weakness that declared itself in the words of his text and their effect on others; the stories he told were frequently stories of self-destruction, neglect and decline. Writing indeed was a quest through the destructive principle, though he always hoped or believed that it would have a redemptive outcome, and that the inferno was on the path to paradise.

Three things conspired, in dangerous equation: the plot of his life, the plot of his art, the plot of his age. In all of them there was something infernal, but perhaps a code, a clue, a pastoral promise of restoration to the primal garden. In the last letter he wrote to be printed in *The Selected Letters of Malcolm Lowry* (1967), which comes from a return voyage to Britain, he records a journey to the garden of the Lake District and a visit to Wordsworth's house, where he finds on the desk a passage the poet had written about the writer's two conflicting selves. Shortly after he was dead in Sussex: the coroner's verdict was "Death by misadventure".

There is no doubt that Lowry was sadly neglected as a writer over his lifetime: he never made things easy for himself, and he wrote against the prevailing mood. There can equally be no doubt of the recognition that has properly come to him since. *Under the Volcano* is a Penguin Modern Classic and is seen as one of the major modern novels; and Lowry has been claimed as a major monument of contemporary Canadian, British and indeed American fiction, the obscurity of nationality and relationship to tradition being a key part of his story. He is a writer of the greatest importance, whom we can now see much better than before: because of the gradual release of his manuscripts, because the cult of realism that dominated the latter part of his writing lifetime has now lifted, and because we can sense behind us a postwar tradition of British fiction – if we can claim him for that – which was a good deal more experimental and complex than was thought in the decade of his death.

At the same time the aroma of neglect persists, coming off the pages of his books themselves, especially the late tales of powers wasted and talents unrecognised. These are stories of inordinate ambitions and incomplete results, of great writers who cannot declare themselves and are uncertain whether they possess vision or talent at all. Lowry believed that we are the novelists of ourselves, but the novel he lived was one that always moved near tragedy or defeat. This is understandable; few recent writers have indeed suffered creative misfortune on Lowry's scale. Writers often lose manuscripts by fire, theft or carelessness, but he did so with extraordinary frequency; the pattern indeed shifted to his wife, Margerie Bonner, one of whose detective stories appeared lacking its last chapter, a postmodern episode that was not however meant, and destroyed the book. Writers also over-produce, but Lowry's production of text was inordinate, as he tried to attach meaning to all available experience, generating a seamless narrative in which each new version attempted to express what was being written now but also everything that had been already written and published. He hungered for form but also for formlessness, driven by a sense of significance always threatening to overwhelm him. As his biographer and editor Douglas Day has put it: "Lowry was nothing if not a symbolizer: whatever happened, whatever he heard or saw, had to *mean* something, however obliquely." Yet at the same time in most of what he did there is a sense of creative direction never quite fully achieved, of signification not properly elaborated, of bewilderment about the potential public meanings of his kind of creativity.

And yet one of the reasons why Lowry compels us is precisely that among modern writers he is rare in the degree to which he experienced that creativity; it was the guide of his life, and he was indeed particularly taken by the notion, which he derived from Ortega y Gasset, that we are the novelists of ourselves, creating our fates and setting in process the machine of our own reality. We develop what he called "design-governing postures", a sense of significance that gives to the random the weight of artistic meaning. The story of the artist, even the imperfect artist, is the story of the construction of life. Lowry's accumulated work is the story of the endless predicaments and collapses of composition, the hunger for expression and the unease with it. The process is cumulative, involving the writer in the fictions, so that Lowry's late writings persistently allude to and parody the work already written, which is still conceived as being within the process of composition. New writers encase the written, and they become self-surrogates of various kinds, competing with each other for the mastery of the fiction, the position outside the narrative which will let them be the author of it all. Yet it was as if Lowry was determined that there could be no outer writer, that one never evaded the state of the written, that cosmic Laws of Series never freed the text for the author of it. The world itself was a novel, very modern, and also rejected. "Indeed it was the first thing you learned:" reflects his author-surrogate Sigbjorn Wilderness in *Dark As the Grave Wherein My Friend Is Laid* (1968), "the reader does not want to hear about your rejected play. That was true: still, why not? Half the world was like a writer who has had his play rejected. Indeed the world at times seemed very like a rejected play itself. Or a rejected novel, like, for instance, *The Valley of the Shadow of Death*, by Sigbjorn Wilderness. A world in suspense, a world in delirium, a drunken world in fear." Neglected fiction goes with a neglected world; all the metaphors collude, and so one functions as a writer.

2 When postwar British fiction comes under assault for its failure to develop the artistic directions and intentions of the modernist movement, then Malcolm Lowry – along perhaps with Samuel Beckett and Lawrence Durrell – is one of the names we can produce to refute the charge. *Under the Volcano* has fairly been called by Walter Allen the finest book by an Englishman in the 1940s, and there is now a substantial body of other work to inspect. There is the early novel *Ultramarine* (1933), which is also in its way a late book, since he revised it in a form that was posthumously published in 1962. There is the slim and posthumously reconstructed *Lunar Caustic* (1968), written over the period 1935–41, in several versions, a work that reveals his expressionist devotions as well as his fascination with the infernal modern nightmare city; there is *Under the Volcano* itself, the one clear and solid monument; there are the interlinked and box-in-box stories of *Hear Us O Lord From Heaven Thy Dwelling Place* (1961), and, related to them, the two big attempts at post-*Under the Volcano* fiction, *Dark As the Grave Wherein My Friend Is Laid*, written three times and then abandoned, and *October Ferry to Gabriola* (1970), mostly written between 1952–54 and still under way on Lowry's death, both of these intended to moderate the great book and incorporate its meanings into a larger sequence.

There are other items available, and probably more to come; there are the famous lacunae, like the novel *In Ballast to the White Sea*, lost when Lowry's shack in Canada burned down. We have *The Selected Letters*, fascinating amongst other things for the glosses and reinterpretations, the proposals and counterproposals, attached to the fiction, a remarkable, anguished and often buoyant compilation interesting to anyone at all concerned about the emotions, crises and indeed self-deceptions of creativity. It all now amounts to a substantial and significant if confusing creative enterprise, one that makes clear that Lowry indeed conceived his work as an absolute life-dedication, the dedication of a man of great intelligence, considerable critical sense, and wide if chaotic reading, attempting a full and responsible achievement. For Lowry it was all part of a continuous enterprise, what he called "The Voyage That Never Ends", the title he wished to give to the sum of his writings and, presumably, to his own life.

The large scale of the enterprise and the kind of self-investment that went into it is unusual in contemporary writing. George Steiner has noted the importance in our modern arts of the literature of the unfamiliar and the artist of "extraterritoriality", and remarked that much of our best modern writing has come from writers "unhoused". In a literal sense this was true of Lowry, and he was always fascinated by multiple territoriality; in "Through the Panama" (in *Hear Us O Lord* ...) he reflects on the plight of "an Englishman who is a Scotchman who is a Norwegian who is a Canadian who is a Negro at heart from Dahomey who is married to an American who is on a French ship in distress which has been built by Americans and who finds at last that he is a Mexican dreaming of the White Cliffs of Dover". What he shares both with Beckett and Durrell is a very angular relation to the British literary tradition and British culture, and an essentially expatriate commitment to a cosmopolitan and internationalist view of art. Like them he travelled extensively in the 1930s, assimilated many of its avant garde attitudes, and carried forward and transformed some of the essential preoccupations of modernism, so that his work, like theirs, has a vital continuity with the radical experiment of fiction that, up to 1930, seemed to be shaping the best art of the century.

But where their expatriation was based on well-forged cosmopolitan links – Beckett went to Joyce's Paris, a basic modernist centre, and Durrell first to Paris, though his was the Paris of Henry Miller, and then to the Mediterranean – Lowry was inclined to expatriate himself *away* from the places of art. He went to Bonn, and Scandinavia, and assimilated some of the lore of expressionism. He went to Spain and then Paris for a spell, and married there, unhappily. But he soon moved to the United States, following the path of voyage, jazz and Melville, and then went on to Mexico. And when he did settle for fourteen years, it was typically in a cabin with almost no facilities, built, under pioneer's rights, on the foreshore at Dollarton, British Columbia, inconveniently over the US-Canadian border and virtually inaccessible at times through the mails – something that added to the persistent confusions with which his literary life was bedevilled. When Jacques Barzun unfavourably reviewed *Under the Volcano*, with its massive intertextual allusions, as "an anthology held together by earnestness", he protested in a letter: "Having lived in the wilderness for nearly a decade, unable to buy even any intelligent American magazines (they were nearly all banned here [Canada], in case you didn't know, until quite recently) and completely out of touch, I have no way of knowing what styles were in fashion and what out, and didn't much care."

This letter deliberately conceals a good deal; Lowry was indeed a very literary writer, was widely read in a fund of mixed sources, including Kierkegaard, Kafka and Hesse as well as Dante and Melville, and he had taken in a very great deal from the twentieth-century moderns – after a Joycean punning bout he speaks in a story of being "Joyced with his own petard". Powerful literary influences are impressed all over his work, and the basic conception of his fiction is derived from a speculative modernist spirit. Nonetheless he differs strongly from a writer like Beckett, that unmistakeably major figure, a writer of the most exacting literary economy whose work is coherent with our own sense of modern absurdity, of fiction pressed toward silence, of existential exposure, of the recessive motion of text and writer. Durrell's writing, like Lowry's, moved increasingly from a predominantly political vision of despair toward hermetic complexities and cabbalistic themes; his most substantial achievements, above all the four books of *The Alexandrian Quartet* (1957–60), that remarkably composed sequence of psychological fictions in which the characters represent less discrete personalities than interlocking facets of love and desire, have a formal splendour but also a certain cultic privacy. Lowry, though, is a writer whose clear modernist dimensions, his narcissistic and speculative forms and his dominant awareness of the claims of the universe of fiction-making, contained an essential inheritance from romanticism. His two greatest modern literary heroes were characteristically oblique ones – Conrad Aiken and the Norwegian writer Nordahl Grieg, both novelists of voyage to whom *he* voyaged in youth, shipping on freighters to the United States and Norway in order to meet them. The signals of modernist influence are clear enough in his work: the deep literary allusiveness, the quality of strain and anguish that (as Stephen Spender said in a useful introduction to the 1965 reprint of *Under the Volcano*) links Lowry with other modernists in his concern with "the modern breakdown of values", the interlocking structures of his fictions. But, as Spender also says, Lowry's view of life is individualistic in a way that that of most of our modernist writers is not, for through them a consciousness both historical and collective speaks. And his work is primarily based on *self*-projection, so that the surrounding world tends to be solipsistically merged with that of his hero, who is in almost every case a clear surrogate for the author himself.

Modernism is an art filled with portraits of the artist, but, as with the most famous of all of them, Joyce's, the drive is toward the mode of impersonality, moving away from the lyric to the dramatic. Indeed in much contemporary thinking, the very presence of the author in our thoughts about text is an anxiety; as Michel Foucault puts it, we like our discourse to develop "in the anonymity of a murmur". Lowry saw a world constructed as fiction, but in it his presence as the author as well as the authored was a central fact. His essential assumptions about art were thus romantic ones: art was seen as imaginative voyage and representative suffering, all this in the cause of a final transcend-ence, the fulfilment of an oceanic, a paradisal opportunity. It is against this that he associates, modernly, a sense of tragedy; his primary themes are the despoliation of the garden of the world by man, and the tragic state of the serious spirit in the modern world. His heroes move through landscapes of destruction and waste, hellish scenes in which symbolic ruination abounds, seeking the restitution of the paradisal garden.

The tragic sense derives from a feeling of inevitable identification with this world, and in some of his work this is supported by an intense historical awareness. But the tendency toward self-destruction seems, in his work, to exceed the exterior conditions of it, and the work itself celebrates a degree of nobility in the destruction. Crea-tivity is based on a scaled-up dream of the self, the principle by which we compose our lives. This, though, is often violated by reality, and in many of the stories of *Hear Us O Lord* . . . we see a growing power of self-criticism, a hunger for equilibrium, as in "Through the Panama" ("And yet there has never been a time in history when there was a greater necessity for the preservation of that seemingly most cold-blooded of all states, equilibrium, a greater necessity for sobriety (how I hate it!)." Lowry's compulsive rewriting was largely to do with this, a diminution of what he called "character", which largely meant portraits of the author, in favour of writing as such, which led in turn to rewriting, an endless speculative reinterpretation of autobiographi-cally generated material.

And this in turn led to the delays on the late books. Over the final years his editor Albert Erskine, probably with the experience of Thomas Wolfe, that great author of egotism, in mind, was pressing

the delaying, defaulting and ever-cunning Lowry to complete his
work, while at the same time warning him of the dangers of
autobiographical over-investment. Lowry responded by both acknowledging and subverting the criticism, admitting that an interfering
creative daemon was driving his books onward into complication and
altering them. It was a daemon that insisted on making a fiction from
the author's own sense of neglect and suffering, a romantic self-
justification: "*Gabriola*," he wrote, "may not be the artistic triumph I
sometimes think it is, but if I have any knowledge of the human
psyche at all it is . . . a psychological triumph of the first order . . . the
bloody agony of the writer writing it is so patently extreme that it
creates a kind of power in itself that, together with the humour and
what lyricism it may possess, takes your mind off the faults of the story
itself, which, incidentally, are of every kind . . .".

On the other hand, the gratification of the author's own ego was
not the intention of his writing: "The real protagonist of the *Voyage*
[the novels past and present all seen as an entire sequence] is not so
much a man or a writer as the consciousness – or man's unconscious." Like many of his immediate friends and contemporaries,
including poets like Dylan Thomas, Theodore Roethke and Delmore
Schwartz, Lowry was fed by a double principle. There was the spirit
of the romantic to placate, a spirit subjective, self-justifying, oceanic,
mythical, concerned with the great themes of artistic damnation and
redemption; and there was the spirit of the modern, ironic, self-
doubting, text-centred and formalistic. Between the two there was
tension and conflict, generating deep artistic contradiction, one that
led for Lowry not toward silence but toward a troubled articulation
that was never quite to satisfy either him or the publishers whom he
so persistently managed to disappoint. Yet it is for just this reason that
the growing availability of his creative enterprise matters so much,
because it is the testing place of a major intelligence attempting to
resolve the most fundamental contemporary artistic issues.

3 It is partly because of the dependence of Lowry's writing on his
own life and experience, as well as because of the dramatic content of
his personal story, that he has become an obvious subject for artistic
biography. Douglas Day has given us a valuable Freudianised
account, which has in turn been valuably amended by Professor
Muriel Bradbrook, who adjusts some key mistakes about Lowry's life
in England, many of them deriving from Lowry's own inclination to
make his personal story one of dramas and cruelties, and Tony
Kilgallin, who adjusts some of the Canadian part of the story. Lowry

liked to emphasise strange and polyglot origins: a Manx background, a Norwegian one. In fact he was born in 1909 in a conventional and reasonably religious upper-middle class British commercial background; his father was a Liverpool cotton-broker, and there was indeed a maternal grandfather who had been a Norwegian sea-captain. Lowry was even able to give dramatic value to a very conventional minor public school education, recalling extreme social and sexual miseries. Certainly he felt himself at odds with his family background, and in 1927, after leaving the Leys School in Cambridge, he shipped as a deckhand on the *SS Pyrrhus*, out of Liverpool, bound for the Far East, the experience that provides the material of his first novel *Ultramarine*.

If this was partly an act of revolt, it was also a very literary voyage, fed by some of the authors he most admired, who included Herman Melville, Nordahl Grieg and Conrad Aiken. Subsequently he liked to paraphrase Melville's claim and say that a cargo ship was his real Yale and Harvard. But in fact his formal education continued and he attended Cambridge in the early 1930s, taking the English tripos at a time when many notable figures, including William Empson and I.A. Richards, were about; Muriel Bradbrook's brief book gives a very sound account of this, showing that despite all protestations otherwise Lowry *was* an educated writer, and "without doubt the greatest novelist (except possibly E.M. Forster) whom Cambridge has produced". The break with the family worsened, partly because of Lowry's drinking, and Lowry went on to Spain, Paris, and then, extending the necessary voyage, to New York City, where he was hospitalised for drunkenness, the experience behind *Lunar Caustic*. It was now that the major phase of his expatriation began, making his experiences on the American continent the material of a fabulous plot which was to structure much of the rest of his writing.

The nightmare experience of New York was therefore only the start of a journey toward a greater primitivism. Lowry continued his "tooloose Lowrytrek", going to California in the hope of becoming a screenwriter, but sailing onward in 1936 to Mexico, where he arrived on the Day of the Dead, the kind of symbol he did not forget. His experiences there turned infernal; he was briefly imprisoned and his marriage broke up finally. *Under the Volcano* was begun in Cuernevaca that year, and continued until 1938, when he moved to Los Angeles; here he started a second version. In 1939, as war broke out in Europe, he moved to Vancouver, was joined by Margerie Bonner, and after a gloomy start found an end to many of his miseries. Dollarton, where they settled, was to become "an undiscovered, perhaps undiscoverable, Paradise", a geographical myth to set against infernal Mexico.

He was now in effect a literary solitary, a wilderness writer; he took the word to name a central alter ego in his fiction. The break with his family was now severe, and when *Under the Volcano*, revised yet again, was accepted for publication in 1946 in both Britain and America, the poor British reviews did not encourage him to return home. He was happy, if wished, to acknowledge himself a Canadian or an American writer, very much in the mood of the hero of "Elephant and Colosseum" (*Hear Us O Lord* . . .), a Manx author living in America because "the people who believed in him were all Americans, and even here in Europe – once more came that inexplicable childish pang, yet so deeply he couldn't believe its cause was mean and unworthy – he'd received no word from the heart." Yet the hope for a word from the heart was clear; the Dollarton paradise, Eridanus, was by no means secure, and at times he raged against his Canadian exile. Now it became especially appropriate to emphasise the lonely nature of his genius, his separation from literary influence, even his ignorance. "I am capable of conceiving a writer today, even intrinsically a first-rate writer, who *simply cannot understand*, and never has been able to understand, what his fellow writers are driving at, and have been driving at, and who has been too shy to ask," he has Sigbjorn Wilderness write in his journal in "Through the Panama" (*Hear Us O Lord* . . .). And Wilderness, he explained in a letter to Erskine, who had evidently questioned the autobiographical nature of the fictions he now wrote,

> is not, in the ordinary sense in which one encounters novelists or the author in novels, a novelist. He simply doesn't know what he is. He is a sort of underground man. Also he is Ortega's fellow, making up his life as he goes along, and trying to find his vocation . . . . According to Ortega, the best image for man himself *is* a novelist, and it is in this way that I'd like you to look at him . . . . Moreover he is disinterested in literature, uncultured, incredibly unobservant, in many respects ignorant, without faith in himself, and lacking nearly all the qualities you normally associate with a novelist or a writer.

Wilderness is the writer as innocent, but the innocence is perpetually exposed to forces outside and beyond him, the powers that signal to him and to some degree construct him. The fictionality of exterior mechanisms now seemed increasingly important, threatening the timeless paradisal innocence that was one part of writing with the demonic and infernal processes that for Lowry had always interwoven with it. The plot of life, moreover, increasingly troubled the plot of art. And by 1954, the theme about which he had always written, eviction from the paradisal garden by the powers that governed modern mechanism and chaos, became real again; the Dollarton foreshore was being developed and the Lowrys had to leave the shack for New York, Italy and then Britain. Lowry entered on the new voyage with a certain troubled gaiety, but it was already filled with dark premonitions. Lowry himself was in a state of growing depression and alcoholic debilitation, and along with the physical wasting the literary confidence was dying fast. He worked on the late Canadian stories with their repeated theme of expulsion and potential damnation, of fear of silence and fear of destruction, but also of possible renewal.

But the voyage that never ends was indeed ending, and in 1957 he died in a Britain that had still not really given him any word from the heart, in every sense an author of his own misfortunes who had always had a sense that he had never quite learned who the true author really was. He had come to see the imperfections of his own work as severe, his fiction of self a fiction that could not complete itself. Yet the aim had always been more than confessional: as he told Erskine, " . . . what if one should give a real turn of the screw to a subject that is so often treated half-heartedly? I think unquestionably what one is after is a new form, a new approach to reality itself." Lowry's new form was obviously more lyric than dramatic, but it was fed by a sense of laws governing the quest for significance. Yet it was a process of literary as well as personal discovery, concerned with the hidden plots of meaning and significance that illuminated contingency and gave art. Even as he sought to make the sum of his work into one whole, he discovered the labyrinths of division and deviation that fragmented it again. This was not a natural plot of the 1950s, but a good many writers since have found it consonant with our most contemporary literary difficulties, and recognised not just in Lowry's successes but his confusions an artistic experience central to our time.

4 Lowry's literary quest covered three and a half decades and a number of radically different forms of writing. His first book, *Ultramarine*, was begun on the turn into the 1930s and published after one lost manuscript and much revision in 1933. It is in many respects a very Thirties novel, about the young middle-class boy who finds himself put in contact with life by work and comradeship with workers. The nineteen-year-old hero, Dana Hilliot, of British-Norwegian parentage, follows Lowry's own experience by signing as a deckhand for an Asian voyage on a ship called the *SS Nawab* (in the late-life revised version, this was changed to the *Oedipus Tyrannus*, this being the name of the ship that Hugh signs on to run arms in *Under the Volcano*; so all the stories were to interlink). Hilliot is in revolt against the family but cut off from the crew both by his

background and his sexual prudishness and inexperience. But he wins their respect when he stands up to and reaches community with the man who taunts him most. Here the period message is very clear: the romantic search that the sea so powerfully invites can best be fulfilled by fraternal acceptance of one's fellow men in the forecastle. But Hilliot's wandering, harbourless, dispossessed and essentially lonely characteristics are crucial, and his "wild self-dedication" is metaphysical, for he desires not only to prove himself to others but achieve a delight beyond despair. He is obsessed by his "incapacity to position things and see them in their places", and his desire for order is both a personal and a symbolist's literary need. It also has a strong psychological, an Oedipal, dimension; Hilliot is also driven by his break with his father and the need for his substitute. As he says in a grandiloquent drunken speech, "I assume the guilt of a mother, or of a father, or of a heredity, imagine it completely, to be able on the one hand to give an adequate explanation of my more inexplicable actions, and on the other in order to be clothed in a dark, blood-stained dignity. Some of these points are raised, and you may have read for yourself, in my much maligned and certainly dangerous and misleading work, *Hamlet* . . . ".

It is after he has been accepted by Andy, in a fatherly role, that the chaos and disunion of the ship's machinery, which he has seen as a mechanical inferno, now falls expressionistically into place: it is all pitiless regularity, interdependence. Now sexual love and desire can become a romanticised "sublimated all-embracing love for mankind", and a romantic oneness with the universe achieved: "Then at last again to be outward bound, always outward, to be fighting always for the dreamt-of harbour, when the sea thunders on board in a cataract . . . ".

Ultramarine has an ostensibly social theme, but it is a story of ironised self-discovery, and its prose is appropriately mannered and modernist, especially indebted to Aiken, to whom it is dedicated, and Grieg. But Lowry's book of the later Thirties, about his New York experiences, was to take on a quite different form. The published version, *Lunar Caustic*, in fact conflates three versions or related endeavours, variously called *The Last Address*, *Swinging the Maelstrom* and *Lunar Caustic*, which seem, from the various notes in his papers, to have been guided by a reaction to a letter of Chekhov's about a story of victimisation where a man attempts to squeeze the slave out of himself. The central character was variously a political Left-winger, a reforming journalist, and a musician; he is sometimes called Sigbjorn Lawhill, taking his name from a ship, the *SS Lawhill*, and indeed he thinks he is one. But in the published version he is Bill Plantagenet, an Englishman travelling the Atlantic for two reasons: to find his missing American wife and to bring his jazz band to its spiritual home. In each version the theme is the same, of the hero moving through a city of terrifying modern signs and signals which have chaotic but potent meanings for him to the door of Bellevue Hospital, there to receive mental treatment for an alcoholic breakdown; but the modern pain remains. The New York of the book embodies "all the horrors of war"; it is the "last frontier", but in the form of a city of wild images and ciphers, a Dante-esque inferno. The controlling style is expressionistic: images of dereliction and imprisonment, of the machine-like rhythms of work routine, of "mechanic calamity", dominate the tale. And the overall vision is apocalyptic, of the great city of misery and destruction, its terror captured in the final thunderstorm:

> An iceberg hurled northward through the clouds and as it poised in its onrush, tilted, he saw his dream of New York crystallized there for an instant, glittering, illuminated by a celestial brilliance, only to be reclaimed by the dark, by the pandemonium of an avalanche of falling coal which, mingled with the cries of the insane speeding the *Providence* on her way, coalesced in his brain with what it conjured of the whole mechanic calamity of the rocking city, with the screaming of suicides, of girls tortured in hotels for transients, of people burning to death in vice dens, through all of which a thousand ambulances were screaming like trumpets.

Lunar Caustic is a novel of the modern waste land, of breakdown and psychic extremity, a visionary work. But it is also a work with deep literary traces. Lowry describes the story as "about a man's hysterical identification with Melville". And Lowry's New York recalls the city of *Redburn*, while Plantagenet, the innocent, is treated by a Dr Claggart, and in one version it is important that he be told his name comes from *Billy Budd*. These allusions are not slight; Lowry sought to mirror in modern form the spirit of the great writer not just of seafaring but of incipherability, the novelist who knew obscurity in every sense and had written of the demonic in art and vision.

But *Lunar Caustic* was also conceived as part of a larger enterprise. As Douglas Day explains it:

> Apparently, if Lowry had lived long enough to give *Lunar Caustic* the full symbolic treatment, a journey from Europe to New York, and then to the rest of America – with Mexico and Canada – would have been something like a voyage from Inferno to Purgatory to Paradise. But Lowry, one is sure, would never have made it that simple: journeys for him are never only geographical, and hell never in one place.

Lowry's scheme as he put it in a 1946 letter was somewhat different:

Lunar Caustic was to be the purgatorio, *Under the Volcano* the inferno, and the lost *In Ballast to the White Sea* the paradiso in a Dante-esque trilogy. But whatever the order it is clear that the long period of composition allowed Lowry to conceive of a sequence both psychic and mythological, and to some degree historical too. For Lowry's theme in *Lunar Caustic* is also a world of mad contemporaneity rushing toward disaster and war, and this sense of universal historical extremity was to carry over into the writing and rewriting of the book that has always mattered most to us, *Under the Volcano*, started in Cuernevaca in 1936, but, through the complex process of composition characteristic of Lowry, dealing with the events of the Day of the Dead 1938, seen from the standpoint of Laruelle as he looks back from one year later, from a world now already entered upon a World War. Indeed the book we have is in effect Lowry's fourth version, and it is constructed on an extraordinary process of incrementation. Thus many of the autobiographical events included involved experiences subsequent to the moment of first composition: the breakdown of the marriage to Jan Gabrial in late 1937, the subsequent drunks, Lowry's arrest by the Mexican police under suspicion of spying, and yet later happenings – the imaginary future the Consul projects for himself in his letter is clearly that Lowry led with Margerie Bonner at Dollarton. In fact the book derives as we have it from two essential versions: the version of 1941 submitted to publishers but widely rejected, and the rewritten version accepted in America and Britain in 1946. The final version added a new double perspective to the book: Geoffrey Firmin, the Consul, ceases to be closely identified with Lowry's own experience and vision, and his paranoia, once Lowry's own, about pursuit and spying becomes dramatically separate; and, spaced by the war, the novel becomes a work of historical retrospect on the Thirties, a vision of an age building itself to war, rather than a book *in medias res*.

    Under the Volcano thus grew into what it is – amongst other things, an eminently postwar novel – through an extraordinary process of incrementation. Lowry describes these in the famous letter he wrote to the British publishers, Jonathan Cape, when their reader complained of the book's lack of structure and excess of local colour. This letter (written on the 1946 return to Cuernevaca) – and another to Derek Pethick, who gave a radio talk on the novel – is "the brilliant defence", and perhaps the best piece of critical writing, or rewriting, the novel has ever had. Lowry's glosses are not entirely reliable, and they have sometimes led critics down strange paths, but they are a remarkable work of self-interpretation, presenting the novel as a symphony, an opera, a horse-opera, a "sort of machine", certainly a book of multiple codes and systems. They also reveal the book's construction as a work of *bricolage*, its chapters coded to the number of twelve but written at different dates and in different ways. They also show how far it moved from being an autobiographical tale with which Lowry characteristically began, turning over time into a fable of a period of suspicion and treachery, of European processes set on top of Mexican events, of events casting their shadows forward through time even as they circle within the mythological space of the narrative. For Laruelle in the first chapter, the individual fates that come to crisis one year are set in a time that "seemed already to belong in a different age. One would have thought the horrors of the present would have swallowed it up like a drop of water. It was not so." Justifying the book's shape in the letter to Cape, Lowry explained that its time structure was crucial: the book was "a wheel with twelve spokes, the motion of which was something like that . . . of time itself". Thus the story is set amid major historical processes, in the world of contemporary Mexican politics and the struggles of world powers that are building to war between the liberal democracies and the totalitarian states, already prefigured in the war in Spain; but it is structured, in modernist fashion, against historical time, to give the mythological and the metaphorical matter space in the novel, and the tragic curve of Firmin's fate the place of dominance.

Lowry's letter makes it clear that the myth of the novel is indeed infernal, a tale of expulsion from the paradisal garden into a damnation with which, nonetheless, Firmin himself temperamentally conspires. He has no real alternative to damnation in this sense, since the universe to which he is bound on a wheel of fire is an infernal machine, a destructive principle itself. He is caught in the Day of the Dead, itself, as a form of stasis in history, potentially more threatening than is Bloomsday. But the destructive cycle is an ultimate human state as well as an historical condition, and Lowry explains that the novel is about those forces in man – guilt, remorse and doom – which cause him to be terrified of himself. The novel's underlying mythography therefore appears to allow the Consul little freedom of choice, little chance to define his acts for himself; his quest can only lead to ruination and damnation, and his doom begins from the start. Having thrown up his post, broken with his wife, and acquired advanced dipsomania – his "abuse of magical powers" – he can only seek destruction heroically. When the redemption he desires becomes possible with his wife's return, he can only reject it, and it is by encouraging the suspicions of the vigilantes and accepting their provocations he brings about his own death in the *barranca*.

In this sense the book seems to be a fable of romantic damnation, the tale of a "Faustian gent", a shattered prince who becomes an aristocrat of suffering before he becomes a random victim and a discarded corpse. The gnomic signs of the universe through which he moves confirm this, forming a Law of Series that takes his path downward through external confirmation. Yet the counter-movement is offered too; towards the end of the novel Firmin becomes aware of love as a transcendent principle and an upward movement, through which things have greater distinctivness and separateness – so "had he desired it, or willed it, the very material world, illusory though that was, might have been a confederate, pointing the wise way". Nonetheless Lowry was to suggest that the Consul's abuse of magical powers and his consequential damnation was a general condition of consciousness, the process that led the world toward war and indeed to the discovery of the atomic bomb.

Under the Volcano is clearly meant as a mid-century tragedy and as a symbolist and multi-significant text, one reason for the extraordinary variety of readings that can now be found of it. It is also a text of massive allusion, filled with the "borrowings, echoes, design-governing postures" that Lowry worried about inordinately, afraid in those days before we had the word "intertextuality" that he would be accused of plagiarism. He considered providing a system of footnotes rather like those to *The Waste Land*, to explain the many guiding codes and systems, taken from astronomy, cabbalistic theory, and a vast number of other writers, including not simply obvious sources like Dante, Marlowe, Goethe, Melville and Joyce, but other writers of Mexico like D.H. Lawrence and B. Traven. But the design-governing postures are present directly within the text as well as forming a code of hidden allusions that need to be sought for; like Bill Plantagenet, Geoffrey Firmin is a man following signs, the seemingly contingent notices – street signs, advertisements for films, the random Spanish phrases, which in their very ambiguity or false translatability become coded messages pointing the pathway to damnation. The very composition of the book was based on the collation of seemingly random data which was then capable of being constructed – or rather, constructed itself – into significance, for to Lowry coincidence was rarely accidental. The plot that the artist constructs is in some sense being constructed externally, by life itself; and if Lowry found an infernal system within it he read it not simply as an aesthetic choice (as when a writer simply decides that what he will write next is a tragedy) but as a structure the world had signalled to him. *Under the Volcano* is most autobiographical in this particular respect: to Lowry in his time there, Mexico had signalled itself in the form of tragedy. Firmin, Lowry liked to say, is not so much a character as a consciousness; indeed the four central characters of the book – Firmin and Yvonne, Hugh and Laruelle – are a common consciousness. But if they, and especially Firmin, have some magical control over their own inter-related fate, they are under the rules of a larger process. And it is in part because the book is constructed in this way that Lowry never could conceive of it being totally completed.

Under the Volcano is certainly at base an autobiographical novel, started from the writing down of daily life in the way Lowry always wrote it down, but following its own signs to the point where it becomes monumental – a great work where romantic sensibility transforms into expressionist modernism, becomes a totally con-structed artefact, a coherent if at times obscure unity, an *agon* of whose excellence there can be no doubt. Yet, having constructed his monument, Lowry felt some evident need to challenge or deface it, as if it obstructed him as a writer. It was centred on a highly romantic form of self-dramatisation, and it expressed not only a tragic but, in Melville's way, a diabolic view of the world. We can see why Lowry might feel the theme of auto-damnation oppressive and artistically over-coherent, and why, having by now settled down in his Dollarton "paradise", he would come to believe that it should be amended by a *paradiso* which affirmed, as Lowry thought a writer should affirm, the goodness and the immanent meaning of life. But even this idea of a tripartite work on the Dante-esque model did not suffice him. With the war and *Under the Volcano* behind him, he began to recast his writing plan. He came to conceive of a sequence of six or seven books to be called *The Voyage That Never Ends*. The books already written and published – *Ultramarine* and *Under the Volcano* – would be in the sequence; so would the books written and not yet published, like *Lunar Caustic*; so, indeed, would the book written and lost, *In Ballast to the White Sea*. This idea was radically different from the earlier structure he had devised, being essentially open-ended. Like the famous letter to Cape, each writing would be a commentary on writing already done, each book a gloss on other books, in an ever-proliferating system. The books already in the canon would become hostage to books yet to be written.

Lowry was now deliberating an idea of continuous creation, not in the conventional form of the *roman fleuve*, but in that of a structure of interlocking connections, where every work is perceived as a fictional refraction of an ever-more elaborate set of author-surrogates. *Under the Volcano*, refracted by restoring to it its working title of *Through the Valley of the Shadow of Death*, would stand in the middle, but be written by Sigbjorn Wilderness, the central but not the only literary alter ego Lowry provided for himself. The plan was daring and radical; we have had other versions of such a conception, before or since (in the late work of John Barth, for instance), but rarely on this sort of scale. It was also overwhelming, and in the event became a process of endless deferral, as the commentaries never completed themselves and the confessional or autobiographical material veered away from drama and toward pure contingency.

One thing that determined the plan was the return visit to Mexico in 1946, a visit filled with disappointments and ironies. It contained many troubling events: the arrival of the reply to the letter from Cape, which appeared to dismiss the book, Lowry's growing self-doubt and his feelings of passive victimisation, a suicide attempt, and, yet again, an expulsion from the country. Lowry's journals of that trip were to make the basis of his next book, *Dark As the Grave Wherein My Friend Is Laid*, which we now have in a version retrieved from over seven hundred pages of manuscript, and which is among other things a systematic qualification and questioning of *Under the Volcano*, an undercutting of the romantic Mexico of the earlier book, and an undermining of its elaborate tragic codes with the materials of contingent reportage. The great volcanoes that dominated the earlier novel are now extinct and dull, no longer legendary; and dull fact is substituted for high fictionality, a vague sense of hope for the sense of tragedy, a redemptive marriage for a disastrous one, and, as Ronald Binns has pointed out, the book is a kind of parody of its predecessor, a partial dismantling. The mode is confessional, and the central character is now obsessively a writer, overwhelmed with his devotion but doubtful about and critical of his own talents: and negative confession is important, in the manner of a dark journal. So Sigbjorn Wilderness reflects, in a way typical of the general self-challenge in the book: "Descriptions were his weak point and probably he should not be a writer at all. He was fooling himself."

The book refuses any form of dramatisation other than the despairing self-dramatisation indulged in by its hero, preferring to lay itself open to its own and life's contingency. The conception of an art of pure open-endedness arises, an art that distrusts formal completions. Sigbjorn imagines himself reading a book that "had not yet been wholly written, and probably never would be, but that was, in some transcendental manner, *being* written as they went along". Daily life itself writes fiction, flows into art as art flows into life, in a great flowing of consciousness with an immanent meaning at the end of it. It is a writer's book, a cry of literary despair based on aesthetic disappointments and a justified sense of personal neglect which is then redeemed by extra-literary hope, an exploration of the intricate voids and blanknesses of the writing process, a theory of deferred creation. Lowry's own notes for the book make it clear that he conceived it as one where significance is not encoded but endlessly postponed, making it a writer's quest not for meaning but for "sufficient greatness of soul to accept unflinchingly the existence of a meaning and the knowledge that he will never know precisely what it is".

Another part of the Mexican experience was to go into *La Mordida*, which nowhere near reached completion, but the late major project was *October Ferry to Gabriola*, where Lowry reconceived matters again. The book again arose from incidents in his own life, above all his sense that the Dollarton paradise was endlessly and necessarily threatened. The book, he explained, deals "with the theme of eviction, which is related to man's dispossession", and initially it was conceived as a joint work with his wife, a solution to literary passivity he had explored in *Dark As the Grave* . . . . Its central character Ethan Llewelyn is a Canadian-born lawyer, bearing a guilty burden but living in Lowry's British Columbian paradise of Eridanus. As Lowry told Erskine, the whole plot is really "the difficulty of the future taking any shape at all", the implicit anxiety of *Dark As the Grave* . . . . And it shares with that book an iconography, a landscape, a psychic set where loss of the paradisal garden, the burning of the domestic house, the incomplete benison of a good marriage, the wandering through a seemingly random yet finally very managed landscape which promises both damnation and potential redemption. But in the end it differs, for despite a devotion to expressionist montage it does seek dramatisation and objectivity, a firm form. It bears, as Lowry said, the signs of "the bloody agony of the writer writing" which would, he hoped, justify its imperfections, and like all Lowry's late work it seeks the path back to Eden that would constitute the affirmation *Under the Volcano* lacked.

October Ferry . . . attempts to give coherence to open form; it is essentially and by choice an undramatic work, and by conventional standards it disappoints. By less than conventional ones, too, it seems not fully to enter its own difficulties, emphasising the feeling of suffering rather than finding it as a condition of the text. Thus the place where we can best find Lowry's later resolutions is in the later short stories, most of them collected in *Hear Us O Lord From Heaven Thy Dwelling Place*, where the refractive processes of his postwar and post-*Under the Volcano* writing are most on display. In one story, "Ghostkeeper", omitted from that collection, the writer hero, Tom Goodheart, becomes intensely conscious of the endless potential multiplicity of narrative: "no sooner did poor Goodheart come to some sort of decision as to what line his story should take than it was as if a voice said to him: 'But you see, you can't do it like that, that's not the meaning at all or rather it's only one meaning – if you're going to get anywhere near the truth you'll have twenty different plots and a story no one will take.'" *Hear Us O Lord* . . . is an elaborate system of multiplying narrators and multiplying codes, of ever increasing author-surrogates, both bringing closer and further distancing Lowry's versions of himself.

   These writer-characters have distinctively similar histories, British, Manx or Scandinavian. They live in a world where fictions multiply but are persistently violated by reality; so, in the excellent "Elephant and Colosseum", fictional codes – taken from prime romantic sources, including Keats and Scott Fitzgerald, whose *Tender Is the Night* Lowry had adapted as a brilliant and unfilmable screenplay, called a "masterpiece" by Christopher Isherwood, and with whose Dick Diver Lowry had a natural identification – are seen as temptations of false feeling and false rendering. The multiplication of literary surrogates becomes a way not only of multiplying the experience of life and its unstructured plurality of stories, but shows the variety of interpretations the author is capable of seeing, softening the romantic core. And in "Through the Panama", subtitled "From the Journal of Sigbjorn Wilderness", Lowry offers us his best late work, a tale that fractures, splits into discrete signs, a collage, a doubled text we may fairly call postmodern in the spirit of many of our best contemporaries. The split is the splitting of Lowry's own conception of art, which both asserts life and divides from it, romantically experiences it and modernistically textualises it. In its divergence lies a crucial dilemma, one that he could not resolve and which left the whole open-ended, self-questioning construct in the incomplete state in which we now have it. It has its large monument, and its self-critical commentaries; it has its own inbuilt destruction, and its compelling seriousness of attention. A writer of subjective confession, he became in the end an explorer of the insufficiencies of literary form; a writer hungering for permanence who was also his own destroyer, a writer who sought assertion but left us with plurality and ambiguity.

5 Lowry was very much a writer's writer, and part of his fascination lies in his semi-mystical notion of creativity, forged out of his own experience and also from a number of philosophical and literary sources from Ortega y Gasset to Melville. To read it crudely, it suggests that creativity is an instinct for ordering natural to us all, manifesting itself as an evolutionary force transcending the nature of reality and giving meaning and mythology to existence. Life is constructed as a fiction, and the most revealing aspects of art are therefore those which make explicit those laws and machineries which make a writer a writer, causing him to modify life and create its simulacrum. Yet Lowry was never sure of the right and final order,

and this forged a complex relation between his writing and his life-story, in which one of the essential facts was exactly that he was a writer. But his heroes would be figures not only for himself but men of consciousness and conscience, a body of multiplying and changing personae whose own previous works are necessary historical facts, forms of past consciousness that must retreat in order to give way to present ones. The complex interweaving, the incremental process of creation, is therefore associated with the idea of the writer as an agent of unconscious powers – like Sigbjorn Wilderness, the writer must know himself not only as author but as the authored, not only as the writer but the written. Thus he must put himself in accordance with some mystical Law of Series, some pattern of creative coincidence that will lead to redemption. If Geoffrey Firmin has aligned himself with Laws of Series that point to damnation, then the reverse too is possible. As Lowry said of the hero of *In Ballast to the White Sea*, "in effect both the life of the imagination and life itself has been saved by A's having listened finally to the promptings of his own spirit, and acted upon those promptings . . . ". The creative operation of the soul hungers for the transcendental; Dana Hilliot finds this through fraternity and voyage; Bill Plantagenet finds the negative collusion, the dark law of series; the Consul discovers the sequence of damnation; the late heroes attempt the path of restoration and follow Lowry's desire to see creative coincidence as a moral force. But Lowry's problem lay finally in granting to the creative power, which ought to be moral power, a complete and genuine coherence; the divergence between transcendental possibility divided him, as a man and a writer. The romantic dream remained a dream, and creativity meant endless obstructions, fractures, lost directions, new starts. Yet here in fact are many of the difficulties that most interest us, as they drive him deeper and deeper into the meaning of writing itself.

Over time, Lowry has come to seem more and more consonant with our modern understanding of writing, and, even in his crises and imperfections, seemed a major explorer of creativity. There remains, perhaps, the question of his relation to contemporary British writing, and reading. It was a matter on which, in *Dark As the Grave . . .*, Lowry, after receiving the Cape letter, expressed himself bitterly. Sigbjorn's wife Primrose says:

> "You said yourself that English talent has all run to literary criticism. And that they're jealous of anything really good that comes out. And you said something about the national ethos just at present, that while it's always deploring the fact that your national literature has become so feeble when anything threatens that seems to be just the answer to their prayers, they'll do their damnest to kill it."

In 1946 the scale and preoccupation of Lowry's creative enquiry was not fashionable, and Lowry's suspicion of the critical direction was understandable. So perhaps is the neglect. There was something about the essential mythology and preoccupation of Lowry's fiction which made him seem more an American than a British writer. Indeed we can read him as firmly in the line of American romance. The Melvillean trace is everywhere, and even the Volcano was, he said, a White Whale. The Dollarton paradise was Thoreauvian, and Lowry's search for a transcendental pastoralism Emersonian. The romantic agony and the crisis of signification are in the spirit of Poe; the eruption of the machine in the garden recalls to us Hawthorne. Confessional writing is a commonplace structure in American literature, much of which has been a Song of Myself; the modernist tragic epic has been much practised by American writers, along with its antithesis in poems like Hart Crane's *The Bridge*, a writer on whom Lowry reflected a number of times.

American fiction has been greatly about the wilderness, and that surely has to do with the name Lowry chose for his own fictional self-presentation; it has been persistently concerned with the formative myth of the unsullied and prelapsarian garden and the dark mythology of the Fall. Indeed it has been a fiction mythologised rather than historicised, a fiction of solitude rather than society, and this is true of Lowry's work too, which was always concerned with the transcendental and the immanent, the paradisal and the cursed, in ways that have entered the mythology of American fiction and been scarce in our own. Yet there is a scepticism, a testing of the limits of creative powers, an anxiety about the dangerous dominance of the mythic impulse, which we can recognise in relation to the British fictional tradition. In one sense his work asks whether any large truths can be won by art. The fiction of the universe has its significant powers, but it is in the end largely our own fiction, and the word is obscure and rarely pentecostal. Lowry, as expatriate writers do, touches a place where traditions meet, as, in the postwar world, they must; happily a good many British writers have affirmed the importance of his radical inventiveness. His fiction remains an unstable entity; he conceived it himself as a voyage that never ends, that continually rewrites itself, but this is a view now more familiar in writing in an age of diminished certainties, an era of suspicion. And if, in the course of the hazardous enterprise, he left us one complete and coherent book which, despite all the retextualisation and redefinition he essayed, we can claim as a contemporary classic, that is fortunate too.

NEW MEN
Snow, Cooper and the novel of the fifties

"During the last years of the war a literary comrade-in-arms [C.P. Snow] and I, not prepared to wait for Time's ever-rolling stream to bear Experimental Writing away, made our own private plans to run it out of town as soon as we picked up our pens again – if you look at the work of the next generation of English novelists to come up after us, you'll observe we didn't entirely lack success for our efforts. We had our reasons for being impatient. We meant to write a different kind of novel from that of the Thirties and we saw the Thirties Novel, the Experimental Novel, had got to be brushed out of the way before we could get a proper hearing. Putting it simply, to start with: the Experimental Novel was about Man-Alone; we meant to write novels about Man-in-Society as well. (Please note the 'as well'; it's important. We have no qualms about incorporating any useful discoveries that had been made in the course of Experimental Writing; we simply refused to restrict ourselves to them.)"

William Cooper,
"Reflections on Some Aspects of the Experimental Novel",
International Literary Annual, *2 (1959)*

1 When the war was over and a new literary atmosphere began slowly to emerge in Britain, a group of writers which included C.P. Snow, William Cooper and Pamela Hansford Johnson set out, fairly systematically and in the end very influentially, to establish a tone for the postwar novel to come. As with most movements, the tone was experimental – except the experiment was a revolt against an experimentalism, that of what was sometimes called "Thirties Fiction", though its real roots lay in the Twenties and before. Thirties Fiction in practice meant the novels of James Joyce, Virginia Woolf, and some of their successors and inheritors; a kind of fiction which had made notable discoveries but, according to C.P. Snow, had stultified, leaving a cult of experimental imitation in which "Reflec-

tion had to be sacrificed; so did moral awareness; so did the investigatory intelligence." The revolt went wider, and also contained a deep suspicion of the revived Romanticism that had shaped an important strand of writing during the 1940s, evident in the poetry of Dylan Thomas, or the fiction of Malcolm Lowry. So a curious reversal now occurred; it seemed that it was a more social, more realistic and above all a more traditional kind of novel that was less conventionalised, less limited, and more experimental than experiment itself. The times were serious and austere; it was an age of progressivism and reform that had come in the wake of war. The argument greatly suited the mood of a period that indeed expected a moral and historical attention from its writers, a time when George Orwell and E.M. Forster were again becoming dominant literary influences, and the author was being urged toward a public and political role. A good number of writers now began to emerge, some writing on from the Thirties, some new, who emphasised not their bohemian and avant garde novelty, or the prophetic and visionary wisdom of their writing, but their ordinariness and the accessibility of their materials, the social, public nature of their language, and their writerly commonsense. In poetry there grew up a strong quarrel, fed by critical theories that emphasised text over poet, and irony and impersonality over subjective flamboyance, with Thirties politics and Forties romanticism. As Donald Davie put it, ironically, in a poem about the new irony called "Remembering the Thirties": "A neutral tone is nowadays preferred," and so it was. That tone became more or less the spirit of what came to be called "The New Movement", a poetry of sense and detachment that emphasised purity of diction, clarity of subject, and an unromantic irony of approach.

And in the novel . . . well, in the novel a similar and purposeful intention was indeed growing up toward the end of the 1940s, so that it very strongly flavoured the Fifties. It was the mood of what Rubin Rabinowitz has called "the reaction against experiment", which in many ways was not so much a disagreement about literary forms as about the class origins of writing in Britain. For the experimental and the avant garde had been largely identified in Britain with "Bloomsbury", and the new writers sought to assert different social and cultural origins for their work; the new fiction was as much class revolt as formal revolution. It changed the tone of international experimentalism that had been so powerful in the arts since the 1890s, and it signalled a retreat from a good many well-established literary assumptions and allegiances. It found a usable past in the main line of English writing that had proceeded apparently undisturbed by the revolution of modernism, looking back to poets like Hardy and novelists like George Eliot and Dickens. It reactivated the spirit of social attention, and it spoke the language of consensus. Its impact was massive and it still has a strong power in the pattern of British writing, giving it many of its contemporary strengths and many of its contemporary weaknesses. If there remains, in Britain, something like a recognisable and socially available literary language, an art that is familiar rather than estranging, an art of the commonplace and the commonsensical, concerned with humanist values and moral responsibilities, then this quiet literary revolution has had much to do with it. And if British fiction has appeared to outsiders regularly inbred, socially and philosophically narrow, lacking what Paul West once called "the transcendental stare", offering repetitious generic satisfactions and well-made middlebrow objects, and having too little to do with the function of the novel as a form of epistemological enquiry, then it has a good deal to do with that too. The spirit of this modest revolt thus produced some of our best writers and some of our worst instincts, the strengths and the weaknesses of literary provincialism; and indeed the provincial theme, the construction of art from regional sources, was an essential part of the enterprise.

The new spirit in fiction that started after the war was not then particularly new, but it had the novelty and challenge of a social revolt. We can find all this very explicitly in one of its more influential books, Kingsley Amis's *Lucky Jim* (1954), which firmly sets upper-middle-class aestheticism and experimental posturing against the world of common, plainspeaking, comic ordinariness, and cosmopolitan cultural attitudes against local and provincial ones; the argument was one that Amis carried over into poetry too. But the mood for all this had been set up over the years before Amis was writing, both in the newly urgent literary criticism of figures like F.R. Leavis and Raymond Williams and the arguments of writers like Cooper and Snow – who, ironically enough, was to become Leavis's adversary in the battle over the Two Cultures, and be identified by Leavis as a writer whose failure even to comprehend the function of the literary imagination left his work flat and dully mimetic. Yet both shared some degree of belief in the moral power and the mimetic function of literature, and its relation to general cultural expression. Art's version of reality had its roots in the familiar social realities – and increasingly, it seemed, in that middle-ground of existence, that median vision, that came from what William Cooper, in the timely title of one of his novels, called "scenes from provincial life". Neither Snow nor Cooper were new writers, and indeed they had both written Thirties novels – though not "Thirties Novels" – themselves. Snow's first novel *The Search* appeared in 1934, the story of a young lower-middle-class provincial boy who enters the larger world of science and London and becomes both a social and a scientific explorer in

pursuit of modern hope; its structure was to provide the basis for the
much vaster *roman fleuve* that from 1940 onward Snow undertook in
Strangers and Brothers. Cooper's *Scenes from Provincial Life* (1950)
appeared at the time to be his first novel, though he then proved to
have published fiction before under his real name of H.S. Hoff. Snow
and Cooper had the appearance of being fictional twins, both having
come from similar provincial and scientific backgrounds and having
worked together in the scientific civil service. Indeed Snow is an
important character in the sequence of novels that Cooper started
with *Scenes from Provincial Life* and developed into a four-book *roman
fleuve* of its own. The two writers seemed to set a new direction for
fiction, and, as Cooper has said, they did not lack success for their
missionary efforts. The common ground between them is obvious
enough (though one of the main themes of Cooper's Joe Lunn novels
is Snow's apparent doctrinalism and the literary rivalry between the
two) but of equal importance is the difference between them, a
difference that has some implications for the multiple directions of
realism which writers rather younger, who seized on the dominant
mood, actually came to pursue.

2   It is worth thinking why the *roman fleuve* became so popular a form
in the years around and after the war. For there were, indeed, a good
many of them: Evelyn Waugh's notable *Sword of Honour* trilogy
(1952–61), Olivia Manning's excellent *Balkan Trilogy* (1960–65), later
followed by the *Levant Trilogy* (1977–80), Paul Scott's *Raj Quartet*
(1966–75), and, the sturdiest and longest lasting of them all, Anthony
Powell's twelve-volume *A Dance to the Music of Time* (1951–75). It is
surely significant that all these narratives ran across the war, and so
suggested some fundamental continuity running through English life
and culture, though they also gain their power from displaying the
fundamental discontinuities as well. Nonetheless they are generally
versions of the family saga, and indeed suggest the power of survival
of the tribal families and friendships that appear to guide so much of
English life, which may change, age, pass from generation to
generation, yet retain some interlocking power. They are stories that
thread processes of connection between the past and the future, and
in them not only family, generation and recurrence of experience but
time and memory are likely to play a crucial part, not simply
constructing the architecture and the edifice, but becoming matters of
speculation, as indeed they have done in a good deal of the major
fiction of our temporally disoriented century.

But in all this there can be no doubt that Snow's *Strangers and*

Brothers sequence is central and significant, and it has made its bid to be regarded as one of the great documentary and recapitulative works of a century not easily susceptible to documentation, a chaotic century of multiple forms of self-expression, where realism itself has seemed hardly possible. Snow's edifice represents one of the more ambitious ventures of contemporary British fiction, and it was to run to eleven volumes, cover thirty years of publication, from the initial *Strangers and Brothers* (later retitled *George Passant*) in 1940 through to *Last Things* in 1970, and tell a tale that reached across some sixty years of British social, domestic, public, political, intellectual, scientific, strategic and emotional history. Since the story began long before its first volume was written but was then designed to continue long beyond it, it was inevitably an open-ended construct, hostage to fortune. It is also a story of time and memory; Snow may have quarrelled with modernism, but he greatly admired Proust, and less the Proust of formal and aesthetic sensitivity than the Proust who could construct, through the operations of memory, the great social edifice of French life and pursue and develop it through a lifetime. But where Proust's is a fiction of consciousness, Snow's is a fiction of history, personal and public, the history of one man constituting the history of a culture. And memory is a mode of retrospect, linking origins and background to future events and possibilities and the great changes and crises of the contemporary world.

So born, fictionally, just before the age of nine, in an English provincial town left deliberately unnamed but created with enough specificity to be recognisable as Leicester, Lewis Eliot (later Sir Lewis), initially a solicitor's clerk, then barrister, committee man, scientific administrator, higher civil servant, fellow of a Cambridge college, and universal mediator, husband first to Sheila and then to Margaret, father to David, becomes witness and agent in an essential lineage of contemporary British social history. The sequence of the books is dominated by his narrative privilege; he has told us these novels in his proper person, entered each room, collogued on each staircase, taken each taxi, caught each train on the way to history.

Much of the time he is centre stage in a meritocratic fable, the story of the ascent of the "new men" of society and their rise to access, affluence, and social and scientific responsibility. On occasion he has been the wise ghost on the edge of other tales and other lives, ever ready with a sagacious thought, a solution, or, usually, a compromise. He begins the sequence in the mean streets, looking in on the lighted windows of real life; he ends it, fictionally, with the dying fall of *Last Things*, only just surviving the novel and telling his tale with the raging impotence of old age. But in between he has been one of our most ubiquitous and prolific narrators, tracking his way through twentieth-century British history and society, sustaining his intimacy with many of the larger events and choices of modern times: in *The New Men* (1954) he is in at the birth of the British atomic bomb; in *The Corridors of Power* (1964) he is sorting out the aftermath of the Suez Crisis; in *The Sleep of Reason* (1968) he is involved in a court case closely resembling the Moors Murder trial. Each of the eleven volumes has its own distinct subject of concern, but the sequence is linked not simply by a common narrator but a belief that this narrator is intimate with the very nature of history, a history which has constructed not just his ascent through the social order but also the movement of a certain kind of decent, optimistic and rationalist mind toward pre-eminence in the affairs of men.

Strangers and Brothers is told like a Victorian novel and written in much the spirit of a Wellsian one. Snow conducts the sequence in an efficient, semi-timeless prose, highly discursive; and the entire narrative clearly depends on a strong autobiographical content and a reportorial social and historical attentiveness, which is an appeal to recognition and resemblance, an invitation to look to the record. Eliot is his own first-person narrator, but he functions very like a diarist for Snow himself, while engaging in the fictional function of effective dramatic presence at the appropriate barricades of modern history; indeed in some sense history must be that which is near to him, as he must arrange to be near to history. In this way he is one of our larger history men, and the curve of modern events is very much the curve of his life; we feel that the world is young when he is, ages as he ages, that it feels much what he feels, and does not feel what he does not. Each volume is civilly constructed as an independent tale, told in good chronological order and made dense with the local stuff of the time in which it is set; every volume also participates, until the end, in the larger open-ended structure of a permissive and historically alert whole.

Lewis Eliot is an observant narrator, though famously unimaginative, and his world is not a place of imagination; his manner is emotionally flat, often indifferent, increasingly pompous, and finally irascible. He is a public man, and what we know of public men is that they are not quite like private ones. He has some sense of his own weaknesses, and the tale teaches him some insights into himself and his limitations, but he is seen largely without irony. He has a critical and moral intelligence and a sense of decency in human affairs, though this is somewhat ambiguous, for it is not simply an angle of vision but a social commodity enabling his success and his access. His famous gift for compromise may make him dull, but it also opens all doors to him, which is both socially and narratively convenient. He is in every sense a realist who has found his way to the places where reality does its daily public work, in that realm which he calls "the world", meaning the world of social life, power, political influence, public responsibilities. As his critics have pointed out, there is an awful lot of the world that is not his world, but from time to time he sees this, renouncing his attachment on occasion, though once back to private life he is in general both short-sighted (the metaphor is used) and emotionally tedious. But his world is close to the social reality we think we know as the form of our general life, and he presents it to us so familiarly and so flatly that we think we know it already, indeed that we can scant it. It is presented to us with a low-key discursiveness which may leave much unsaid and a lot more unfelt; but how well we know it. This gives the impression, as much realism does, that it is all virtually unconstructed, partakes of the pure contingency of life. In fact the truth is that it is highly constructed, according to a clear historiography, or perhaps rather two historiographies that come frequently into conflict.

For Snow is a fairly exact heir of Wells and other early twentieth-century evolutionist writers who made their plots out of the belief that the emergence of a new class was a manifestation both of the life-force and the growth of scientific wisdom. Like them, he tells a story of the "new men", with new ways of thinking, bearing the radical wisdom and ethical anxieties of science, the liberal programme whose task is not simply research and discovery but also reform and social amelioration. It is on just this basis that Snow can consider the classic story of the successful scholarship boy, the tale of one young man's emergence from the obscurity and the new forms of social thinking of a British provincial city through to the corridors of power, as a progressive plot of history and a principle of general hope. It is a peculiarly British plot of meritocratic advancement, a story that has always had considerable national appeal, and counted for a good deal in the 1940s and 1950s.

But it is also a story of rational social development, the kind of development that a lot of scientific thinkers in the early part of the century saw as a possibility; man would make a decent and humane society out of the capacity to mediate his own survival, and Snow in fact becomes the chronicler of the testing time, the period of social experiment and scientific explosion in the years of wartime and after. History would grow and times change, generation give way to generation; but the important thing to realise is that this was a Whiggish evolution, and find the right ways of decently administering it to create a society of human promise. Hope is freedom from limitation and possessiveness: "I should like to add that people get on best when they're given freedom – particularly freedom from their damned homes, and their damned parents, and their damned lives," cries George Passant in the opening volume. So one essential story is the story of an agnostic liberal optimism, one essential plot that of the Time of Hope, where the decencies of the good family rise to the top and allow reason to triumph. Snow's model of life came to seem that of the great committee of mankind where the business of the agenda is the decent survival of the species. But beyond that man was prey to his Tolstoyan fears about his own place and function in evolutionary history, and this led to another plot, darker, bleaker, and one no longer open to the pervasive spirit of reasoned liberal optimism.

This tale is Wellsian too, but in it life is a biological struggle, reason does not always prevail, and instinct and aggression frequently overwhelm virtue and decency. Its implications are tragic, and its threats great; the individual is left, in a rational and agnostic universe, to seek personal validity and human assuagement alone, in a mortal solitude and amid private pain, neurosis, and consciousness of final extinction: "We die alone." Snow's self-seeking and intransigent men, his arrogant, powerful and neurotic women, are embodiments of a life-force that is both intemperate and curiously fragile. They are the possessors of a lonely *angst*, a stoic or angry awareness of tragic isolation. In the New Men, then, there has always been the Old Adam; and beyond the firelit rooms of reason where Lewis Eliot likes to sit there is a darkness of strange desires and disorders, opening out into a different history where liberal decency does not serve, the good committee of life frequently fails to agree, lives go wrong, conflict grows, suffering cannot be alleviated. Snow once said that Lewis Eliot begins by observing the human emotions in others, and finally finds them in himself. And the depredations on reason and the tragedies of solitude he has recognised in others do have a way of coming home to roost. The plot of Time of Hope gives way to the plot of the Sleep of Reason, which has always been there, constructing many of the dramas and conflicts, but which by the end of the sequence seems to be dominant, giving the entire venture a bleak tragic fall.

Snow is not a novelist usually associated with tragic powers, and he was frequently accused of blandness. But *Strangers and Brothers* was finally to work, in its contingent way, toward a darkness of vision. On the face of it it is a tale of great meritocratic success, and the achievement of liberal intentions. By the end Sir Lewis Eliot has his world; he has come a long way since he was the young stranger, peering in from the dark into the bright, lighted windows of other people's exciting lives, and now it is his hand that is on the switch. His gifts long ago brought him to power and success, his capacity for compromise to a guiding role in postwar culture. Intelligence and reason are doing the best they can; and yet, it seems, liberalism is only liberalism, reason is only reason, and the world goes its own way. In the early volumes, which densely evoke the period prior to the time of writing, an evocative realism serves very well, and the books have an appropriate sense of confidence and completeness. But, as the sequence extends and comes closer to the present and the ominous intimations of the future, the sense of despair clearly increases.

For this is also a story of ageing, and there grows a proper terror about mortality, and a history that indifferently outruns the life of the creator. Fictional realism is a kind of mastery over society and time; the very mastery that the power to narrate gives is itself now at risk. The world that Eliot has known and guided into good sense begins in one way to shrink, in another to grow vaster and more uncontrollable. Consciousness of a history where liberal reason may have gone astray grows, especially in the penultimate volume, *The Sleep of Reason*, where a none too exciting tale about a Vice-Chancellorial appointment in a new university gives ground to a story about a murder trial in the same town, closely resembling the Moors Murders trial. A lesbian couple have tortured and killed a small boy, and it is apt that one of the couple is related to George Passant, and gives a kind of comeuppance to his search for freedom. But here the rational enterprise of the century reaches its point of danger, as it comes to seem that the move toward human liberation was not a move toward more and better selfhood, but a release into expression of the obscene and brutal face of human nature. Against George Passant's cry for freedom in the first volume comes Martin Eliot's despairing judgement here: "I have seen freedom," he says, "and it rots."

This late dismay passes on into *Last Things*, a book that declares itself as the end of the story and the end of the life of the storyteller. Snow once suggested that his aim was to bring the tale to the edge of death, and this is indeed what happens; in the course of the volume Eliot suffers a three-and-a-half minute cardiac arrest during an eye operation, as severe a threat to the future of narration that fiction can offer. He comes through to the end of the novel, but this is a story of closure. The novel ends on an obituary roll-call; death has undone many of the main participants of the story: George Passant, Francis Getliffe, Austin Davidson and a few more. The big world that was "the world" seems powerless now, and, as he has before, Eliot comes close to renouncing it. Power is in the hands of others whose values are not invested by the same sense of moral urgency and virtue; the sense of things snuffed out dominates the tale. The world's processes continue, but it is a world now not of strangers and brothers but of enemies and sons. An old story continues, but in new circumstances; at the end of the tale Eliot's son David steps loose and out into the world, much as the young Lewis had done at the end of *Time of Hope*.

But it is a world vastly altered and seemingly more depraved, and the promise must be that much more ambiguous. And while the healthy young drift with new forms of radical feeling into the new history, in the old world hospitals and sickbeds dominate. Yet in the end his is a story of survival, and not an elegant one: Eliot achieves his place at the end of the book with all the bitter irascibility against the human condition, as well as against those who tend him, that old age can bring to bear. But, in the rational, agnostic world he has inhabited, where of the four last things (death, judgement, heaven and hell) he can logically comprehend only one, death itself, biological non-existence, survival is everything. However muted it may be, his survival to the last page is a sort of triumph, one that means that there is a tomorrow not only for the race, the society, the family, but for him as well. He has lasted: "That night would be a happy one. This wasn't an end." And the book does finally confirm the human cycle, its final sequence being a roll-call in significant order, a list not of births, marriages and deaths, but of deaths, marriages and births.

The critics have not always been kind to Snow, and this was perhaps understandable. He had made his kind of novel into a test case for the novel of liberal realism, an opposite to the fiction of literary experiment and literary despair, and his own weaknesses came to seem emblematic. Leavis found his work banal; Lionel Trilling, similarly sympathetic to realism, found in him "No strange or violent or beautifully intense vision of life," and a body of modestly simple notions: "It is not much to make novels with," he imagines Snow thinking. Eliot's limitations have been obvious, and he has none of the powers of a legendary hero, being the voice of a conventional vision that has lived by watching a world of more powerful figures whose existences and conflicts form the main substance of his story. His inadequacies are in many respects self-confessed, but they have muted the world he writes for us, avoiding the full depths of psychological suffering, the deeper notes of fictional exploration. Eliot's irascibility with the human condition in *Last Things* is in part an irascibility with himself. He has not been much of a man, and his loving and his giving have been muted and wanting. He has made a decent, but not a very vivid and living, self. He is not entirely likeable, and certainly not entirely complete. Yet the end of his story becomes a kind of ultimate evocation of Snowland, that bleak landscape of tragic isolation beyond and outside the power game where the self passes from today to tomorrow in the inadequate and unsatisfied solitude that is all, as biological individuals, we have. Snow's work had always seemed to point the opposite way, making the stay against this circumstance the solid, substantial world of family and regional locality, the club, the committee, the college. Now it is a more brutal reality that diminishes the power of culture, the claim of the socially real. And this, from a writer who, it is often said, has lacked the power to move us, is indeed a terrible story.

3 Snow's achievement was in the end an influential one, and both in its way of drawing on the practices of the fictional tradition without a sense of greater disturbance, and in its troubled and often tragic spirit of progressive goodwill, it helped encourage younger writers toward a fiction of contemporary society. Yet in the end it was perhaps less Snow than a writer who stood in somewhat impish relation to him, William Cooper, who was to have the stronger influence on the generation of writers who came next. Appearing at a timely date, in 1950, when new fictional directions were still uncertain, and no clear postwar trend or movement had really declared itself, the book that appeared to be his first (though it wasn't), *Scenes from Provincial Life*, became a fairly obvious forerunner of a whole sequence of novels which were to treat local British life and the familiar and ordinary experience of recognisable people with a fresh, youthful, critical curiosity. "Seminal is not a word I am fond of," wrote one young writer, John Braine, about it. "Nevertheless I am forced to use it. This book was for me – and I suspect many others – a seminal influence." And there can be little doubt that not only Braine but a number of other writers, including David Storey, Stanley Middleton, Stan Barstow, and indeed myself, were encouraged by it to find a sense of direction in the period after the decline both of modernism and the political fiction of the 1930s.

Cooper's novel bore many of the same marks as Snow's sequence, but expressed itself in a rather different spirit, lyrical, comic, and challenging, and if there was a modest literary revolution which guided the spirit of the 1950s, a decade when all revolutions were modest, then it seemed to voice it. Like the first part of Snow's sequence, it was set in a midlands city left deliberately unnamed ("I will not describe our clock-tower in detail, because I feel that if you were able to identify our town my novel would lose something of its universal air"), though again it is identifiable as Leicester. It dealt again with the ordinariness of familiar life, though it did so with a bright comic delight. It was set, like a good many novels of the time, not in the contemporary scene but in the formative ground of it, right at the end of the 1930s, among young provincial intellectuals over the crucial months of change and crisis leading up to the outbreak of the Second World War. It dealt with large international troubles, and the consciousness of a group of young and nonconformist provincial radicals who know they are somewhat distant but troubled witnesses of the world's great events, but whose life finally becomes engrossed in their own complex sexual relationships, so that conflict arises between the force of history and the force of the familiar and everyday. Fearful of a German occupation of Britain, they plan their exiles; but the day-to-day world of provincial life is in the end all that matters, and with a familiar devotion they finally opt for it. The characters, like Snow's, are the "new men" (Cooper, indeed, was later to write a novel about scientific and technological life called *Memoirs of a New Man*) and were to be associated with the fable of meritocratic ascent as the sequence continued over three more volumes. So, like Snow, Cooper's fiction began to relate the world of ordinary origins to the required decencies of public life, and, like Snow, his realistic pleasure in the world was associated with the sense that the world is actually open to talent and mobility. But Cooper's was also a comic story, as Snow's was not, and it had a tonal excitement that made his work seem immediately accessible and usable.

Scenes from Provincial Life certainly does not have the obvious qualities one would expect in a "radical" book. It is a simple (but artfully simple) lyrical novel set in the English provinces, self-conscious about the ordinariness of the life it deals with and the particular limitations and innocence of the youthful central characters, the town's intelligent but not quite intellectual young people. They do not quite belong, their roles do not quite fit ("What *can* I behave like?" wonders the narrator, Joe Lunn, science master at the local grammar school, when he is told he does not behave like a schoolmaster), but this is part of provincial life too. They are schoolmasters, accountants and commercial artists who are also writers and poets and painters, with yearnings for a life beyond the provinces which nonetheless do not separate them from their world. Joe is cautious about the proprieties; the bohemianism of the group is modest; even the record-playing sessions of Joe's mistress, Myrtle, and her late nights are thought to be going a bit too far. The point is that they all of them feel their place, as well as their independence from their place, and this is as true of Joe Lunn, the detached and retrospective narrator, as it is of the characters of his story.

Throughout the book they talk of leaving, going to America in the fashion of Auden and Isherwood under the fear that Britain will soon be occupied and become a totalitarian state ("Though we were three very different men, we had in common a strong element of the rootless and the unconforming, especially the unconforming. We had not the slightest doubt that were some form of authoritarian regime to come to our country we should sooner or later end up in a concentration camp"). But the impending disaster is only half real, and the novel refuses to be a political tale ("For some reason or other political sentiment does not seem to be a suitable subject for literary art," Joe slyly comments), for there is daily life to be lived out too. It is all a story of innocence, told from the standpoint of a later time and a bigger world; "We were completely serious about [the state of the world], and we became even more serious even as our actions became more absurd." They do not leave, and choose the familiar; in retrospect the choice becomes historically right, and their stories can continue, for the familiar wins the war after all.

The contrast between the power of history and the power of the diurnal is indeed the book's main concern, and the heart of its strength. The characters regard themselves as free, but they are drawn, like Joe himself, "by something like instinct", back into their culture, the people, the time, the place. They are intelligent and bright-minded people struggling to make sense of artistic desires and their historical situation, but also their environment and their immediate passions. They share together a comic edge that undercuts pretentiousness and, to some degree, history itself. They are governed by a certain kind of decency and a sense of moral duty; as Joe Lunn says, this becomes all the more important if one believes one *isn't* a good man.

The book is indeed a lyrical comedy, warm with its own note of nostalgia, something of a report but more the evocation of a feeling, an attitude to life which is both loving and ironic, intensely aware of the quirky and the absurd. The story is scenes indeed: illuminated glimpses, moments of meeting and parting, episodes of friendly conversations, of love-talk and love-making, all presented in the spirit of the culture in which it occurs, and all coming together as an emotional whole. The tale is slight, an inset into history: the action simply covers a series of small episodes in the lives of the four central characters over the ominous spring and summer of 1939. The two essential relationships – that between Joe and his mistress, Myrtle, the commercial artist, and between Joe's accountant friend Tom and his homosexual protégé Steve – have started well before the tale does, so what we catch is their elusive ebb and flow. Over Joe hang two threats, both equally serious, Hitler and marriage, as the relationship with Myrtle finally comes to contain "too much ebb and not enough flow". With the war coming, the culture threatened, it is necessarily a story of ending, half unwanted:

> The end. And I knew with certainty [Myrtle] was there at last. I did
> not know the reason. I supposed that something I had said or done
> during the last few days must have been the last straw. I do not even

know what it was, and if I did I should not believe in it as she did.
To most of us the movements of the soul are so mysterious that we
seize upon events to make them explicable.

Myrtle ends the story in a state of tragically betrayed hope; the novel
ends, like Snow's sequence, on a roll-call, of subsequent marriages
and subsequent war-service. But the comic tone survives all, Joe's
tone, with its air of rare authenticity; his late comment on Myrtle –
" . . . I can only say that to the very depths of my soul I was fed up
with her" – has a comic truth quite rare in fiction.

Scenes from Provincial Life is in fact a comedy of a bad time, its
loving familiarity powerful but turned into both nostalgia and irony by
the events to follow. And indeed they follow in ways that favour the
characters, most of whom will become the new men and women of
the postwar world, leaving behind their provincial life to enter the
London scene, the offices and clubs of Whitehall or the familiar
routines of middle-class marriage and adultery. Joe Lunn's story
would thus go on for three more volumes, plotting the development of
his life as scientific adviser to government, as married man, as writer.
Scenes from Metropolitan Life, written in the 1950s, but delayed in
publication because of a threatened lawsuit until 1982, takes the tale
into the corridors of power, and renews Joe's relationship with the
now-married Myrtle. *Scenes from Married Life* (1961) turns the
celebration of bachelorhood into the celebration of marital existence,
a theme not common in the testing emotional world of fiction. *Scenes
from Later Life* (1983) brings the tale into the late 1970s and the
experiences of retirement and parental death, but despite a rising
quota of pain the characteristic Cooper good humour and the sense of
celebration of the familiar prevails; over the lifetime of a generation,
the sequence retains the same buoyant spirit with which it started.
The dark solemnities of Snow's novel are not here; Joe Lunn may
indeed be a new man, and he may have followed the course of
meritocratic advance to status and influence, allowing the stories he
tells to deal with the public and political world. But he has not
acquired sobriety; the comic principle, touched, as it always was, with
a sense of lyrical pathos, survives continuously through the four
volumes. Cooper has remained a novelist of life about its usual and
even banal business, detailing with affection, understanding and a
deep sense of the quirks of human nature what happens to intelligent
and sceptical people as they marry, breed families, have affairs, work
at routine jobs, and worry about their mortality, their sexual lives and
their salaries in a very knowable world.

But Cooper's novels are also portraits of an artist, an artist of a
certain kind. We meet Joe Lunn as a book of his has been persistently

refused (he is given to literary misfortune and misadventure) but he remains determinedly a writer. But it is out of familiarity – the strains of daily life – and his feelings about it that he makes his art, an act of recollection, turning "authentic" experience into "material", "delightful and disastrous, warm, painful and farcical. I reach for a clean new notebook. I pick up my pen." Life is a sequence of felt moments which, if viewed, as Joe views them, with some detachment will become the stuff of writing ("I think of all the novels I can make out of them – ah, novels, novels, Art, Art, pounds sterling!"). Here are no modernist ironies of artistic difference, however, simply those of a writer who is determined to live and then transmute the life into art. The assumptions and technique are ostensibly simple, but at best it is extremely self-conscious and adept, though "Joe" subjects his writing to much the same ironies as he does his life. He can be compared with H.G. Wells, whom he admires ("I loved it, enshrining Wells's message of optimism," Joe writes of *The History of Mr Polly* in *Scenes from Later Life*), and he has a similar gift for capturing youthful, buoyant pleasure in existence. But there is a powerful balance of reminiscence, sentiment and irony so carefully composed as to recall major works of "artistic" realism, like Turgenev's. His novels, like much good realism, take their place as an important social record of particular cultures, phases of social history, felt private emotions and historical reactions; but they are also morally and aesthetically illuminated, shot through with literary perspectives, in a way that Snow's are not. This evidently had a good deal to do with the way a good many writers in the 1950s found a way of balancing a sense of cultural observation and moral analysis of their society and an idiosyncratic comic viewpoint which became a way of living in the present. If, over that period, the judgements of what the reviewers liked to call an "irreverent" fictional attitude became commonplace in British fiction, Cooper seemed to have a good deal to do with it.

4 The impact of Snow's and Cooper's views of the possibilities of fiction on the writers of the 1950s was considerable. "We meant to write novels about Man-in-Society as well," said Cooper, explaining his belief that Joyce had brought the modern novel into a cul-de-sac, and that the form needed an invigorating renewal by being brought back toward an art of recognisable and lived-out values. The progress of the novel has always depended on an oscillation between two parts of its nature, its referential and discursive and its aesthetic function. According to the famous distinction of Iris Murdoch, novels divide between the "journalistic" or the "crystalline", or, in another way of

putting it, between the metonymic and the metaphoric. The modernist revolution – which, said Virginia Woolf, set the writer free, led him from the kingdom of necessity to the kingdom of light, allowing him to dispense with the traditional obligation to plot and character, with Victorian materialism and Victorian "reality", in the interests of an art of expressive form – was an art of the crystalline, the metaphoric, the symbolist. By the 1950s the distinction between its achievements and those of other writers was being noted; the contrast was between "experiment" and "realism", the "moderns" and the "contemporaries". And in the regular oscillation of fiction it seemed to be that the novel of realism was in favour, that of experiment in decline. The need was to point the way to an art of familiarity, of lived-out and recognisable values, and of the contours and shapes of ordinariness, visibly seen in the places of ordinariness – provincial life, lower-middle-class experience, the world of domestic life and the world of work, of shops and Kardomahs and market places and getting on and growing up. The novel, Snow, Cooper and others suggested, should not be an aesthetic distillation of experience, but of experience as it was known and felt, experience as a given. It arose not from the intense speculation of an artist working solely in fiction's special universe, but the sharing of the extant world with others through the medium of fiction's local powers of attention. Art has humanist powers, and we need no formal abstraction to understand our experience and interpret or relish it. Life is dense, substantial and complex enough, taken on ordinary terms; and the power of the novel was its ability to take it on such terms.

In a time when, in the literary traditions of other countries, the break with the past was severe, the case was attractive and strong. In due course it was to reveal its limits; as Angus Wilson once observed, the 1950s saw in Britain a revival of the traditional novel "for reasons which are really extraneous to the novel but which are something to do with the social battle inside England, and which should never have played a part in deciding the form". The cult of provincialism indeed had something to do with a social reappropriation of fiction, and it was for a time to narrow literary horizons significantly. Yet it also provoked into existence a good many excellent writers, and it did restore to the novel some of its humanist powers. Snow's and Cooper's novels are a fiction of our offered and given culture, an art of its habitual intonations and its agreed forms of commonsense; they reassert the power of the grativational tug of realism which has always played a very large part in the history of British fiction.

Yet in the event their fiction worked in quite different ways, though it shared common ground, just as in Cooper's tales Joe Lunn and Robert share an office and a club together. Snow's was a fiction of public history, a writing of social record as this can be measured against the fragility and finitude of individual human lives, and it endeavoured to give weight and meaning to the novel of public affairs to an extent that had been largely missing from fiction for a generation. Cooper's was an ostensibly more modest and playful venture, in the end at odds with large historical solemnities, a fiction of personal feeling guided by an intense comic vision and a sharp artistic control. The vision was ironic and set within chosen limits; it had a deep sense of the absurd that regularly played over the habits and hopes of human life; what it wrote of it lit with a sense of human oddity and surprise. Their novels tell us, like George Eliot's, that one thing that can make an artist is the power to have intelligently seen, known, and then shaped and illuminated the processes of the ordinary world. It is certainly not all there is to art, and it is indeed a view from provincial life. But it is enough to give us an art of power and force, as Snow and Cooper, in their different ways, were able to show us.

A MATTER FOR SERIOUS SCRUTINY
F.R. Leavis in the 1950s

1 F.R. Leavis, who died in 1978, is one of the very tiny handful of critics in our time who will take a central and significant place in a critical tradition he did so much to make explicit, and then urgently and actively to extend into the kind of literary and cultural world in which we live. Ours is a time abundant with criticism and alert with literary theory, but we attach no great meaning to the activity, separating it off into academic institutions and allowing it little play in the general functions of culture. Leavis was an academic, urgent in enlarging English studies into something much more than historical scholarship or abstract theory, or a release of subjective emotions; he saw the task ·of valuation and judgement as an essential task of culture. It was work that he began in the late 1920s but which perhaps attained its greatest power in the 1950s, when I was an undergraduate. Indeed of all the intellectual influences on my early life F.R. Leavis's was unquestionably the strongest. My convictions about the fundamental importance of the literary imagination, my sense of the artist as the essential critic of public life and personal experience, come very much from him; and that has had a good deal to do with my attitudes as a writer, my critical interests, and my long-term preoccupations as a reader. In more recent years the sense of influence has shown up more as a quarrel than an agreement, and my consciousness of the limits as well as the strengths of the positions he took up, though not of the critical commitment he urged, has also intensified greatly. These words could probably be repeated by many who came as new students to literary study in the 1950s and took their sense of literature's value from the claims he made for it. For this was the time when the impact of *Scrutiny* and Leavis himself moved magically through the English departments of most schools and universities; to a subject which was largely a form of literary history leavened by nineteenth-century nationalist philology, Leavis gave a rigour, a sense of purpose, and a moral meaning deeply needed.

I was never one of the inner circle; I never contributed to *Scrutiny*, and did not study at Cambridge (indeed I scarcely knew where to find it) but at a small redbrick. But I was one of many who plunged his head deep into the blue-covered journal whenever a new issue appeared. I met Leavis only once, on a characteristic occasion, when he came to my redbrick to lecture on "The Principles of Literary Criticism". In such universities someone is always lecturing on the topic, but the name of Frank Raymond Leavis caused enormous flurry; Leavis, in any English department at the time, was contentious, and people hurried back to the bound files of *Scrutiny* in the library and worried about how much they dared to support him. In due time, he appeared, wearing a shirt open at the neck and carrying a knapsack clearly purchased at the army surplus store; it was rumoured that he had hitch-hiked. There was a dinner given by the college principal, which as an officer of the student literary society I attended. Leavis talked throughout the meal, as he was free to do; while we carved the roast beef, he consumed little save a number of healthy and life-enhancing pills. And so, at the lecture afterwards, did we. Leavis, as he would have said himself, was nothing if not polemical, assaulting the teaching of English, the domination of the socio-literary metropolitan clique who made the possibility of writing serious literature impossible, and the broad failure of the culture to display a critical attitude. It was an occasion doubtless repeated in most universities and colleges during the very early 1950s, and in each it was probably memorable. For Leavis was, as everyone records, a compelling and compulsive lecturer in a manner of stinging yet uplifting severity, and everyone felt both better and worse for his coming.

At the time (it was 1952), as he pointed out himself in his lecture, Leavis's qualities as a major literary critic, one of the few we can claim in the modern British as opposed to the broad international tradition, had attained surprisingly little recognition, either in the academic world or in the broader literary circles to which his magazine *Scrutiny* persistently addressed itself. *Scrutiny* was not simply a review of academic literary criticism, and it had a determinedly public role, engaging in contention with all the other magazines and with the general flavour of literary activity. Unlike most critical journals, it studied the past and attended to the major canon, but it also firmly reviewed the present. *Scrutiny* had started in May 1932, and it expired in October 1953; but over those years, as Laurence Lerner once said, it built up "a body of practical criticisms, of substantiated literary judgements, that has surely no equal in extent and quality". Behind its founding by a group of research students were two strong influences; one was the excellent earlier review *The Calendar of Modern Letters* and the other *Fiction and the Reading Public* (1932), a

study of decline in popular taste in fiction by Leavis's wife, Q.D.
Leavis. Her book examined the workings of "a number of tendencies
which, having assumed the form of commercial and economic
machinery, are now so firmly established that they have run on their
own and whenever they choose", and concluded that if this were to be
reversed, it must be done by conscious effort, taking the form of
"resistance by an armed and conscious minority". "If this way offers
no hope," she concluded, "then there is none."

   Scrutiny thus started with apocalyptic concerns and missionary
passions: "The general dissolution of standards is a commonplace
. . .," said the opening editorial. "A review is necessary that combines
criticism of literature with criticism of extra-literary standards."
Leavis himself announced in the first number that "the arts are
something more than a luxury product . . . they are 'a storehouse of
recorded values' and, in consequence . . . there is a necessary
relationship between an individual's response to art and his general
fitness for humane existence." Art was concerned with sustaining the
clarity and vigour of thought and opinion in society, and "with
maintaining the very cleanliness of the tools, the health of the very
matter of thought itself". The paper struggled through the political
conflicts and dissensions of the 1930s, the publishing difficulties of
wartime, the austerities of the later 1940s, and its demise in 1953
came sadly just at the moment when its influence was beginning to
become very extensive indeed. This, in a sense, confirmed the
prevailing conviction, which was that the struggling minority could
and should struggle, but in the context of an ever-declining and
militantly middlebrow culture. Yet, though its death intensified the
gloom of what seemed a gloomy and culturally depressed time, it
came around a moment of change and development, for good or bad,
and in that change the impact of Leavis and the magazine with which
his name was so much associated was very considerable indeed.

   Leavis's aim was the intervention of serious criticism into culture,
and he had little regard for what passed for criticism in the rival
magazines, the Sunday newspapers, and the general debate surrounding the arts in Britain. His complaints sounded right, for the
situation was notably disappointing; it is still not greatly better. As for
the serious intonation of criticism, that meant for Leavis something
very different from what the term might mean today. In Leavis's eyes
literature itself was both the subject and the essence of criticism, and
he granted to literature a moral and human weight far remote from
the hermetic and phenomenological modes of interpretation now so
widely practised in literary study. The critic was a purposeful and a
moral agent in culture, engaged – he took the phrasing from Eliot,
who was both mentor and adversary – in the common pursuit of true

judgement. Critical judgement involved, he said, particular immediate acts of choice, which cannot advance literary thinking in any good way unless there has been a real and appropriate responsiveness to the literary work. Yet it was not enough to read as if nothing had gone before; in writing and in living there are guiding traditions. When pressed (by René Wellek) for some general account of his principles, he offered this: "Traditions, or prevailing conventions or habits, that tend to cut poetry off from direct vulgar living and the actual, or that make it difficult for the poet to bring into poetry his most serious interests, as an adult living in his own time, have a devitalising effect" (*Scrutiny*, March, 1935), and terms like "vitality", "maturity", "responsibility", and "morality" were the measures of the standards that could set Milton below Donne, or Dickens below George Eliot.

This sense of living, if threatened, tradition gave the direction and vitality to Leavis's work, which was itself a version of, an informed, studied and felt hypothesis for, a contemporary literature; this was why, though he liked few contemporary writers, potential writers like myself were often deeply stimulated by him. Like a good many at the time, he looked to the novel as a primary form of great critical literature, and if his book *New Bearings in English Poetry*, first published in 1932 and reissued in 1950, offered some significant guidance to the new poets of the time, his study of the English novel *The Great Tradition* (1948) probably had even more compelling influence on the shape of postwar British fiction. Leavis's account of the central tradition of the English novel is famously selective, but the principle of selection was utterly clear: literature enhanced awareness of life, and the primary lineage that concerned him was of those "major novelists who count in the same way as the major poets, in the sense that they not only change the possibilities of art for practitioners and readers, but that they are significant in terms of the human awareness they promote, awareness of the possibilities of life". Leavis's ur-English and very canonical account of the past of the English novel was to familiarise a view of it that still survives. The line is essentially that of the novel of social and moral realism, its history passing from Fielding and Richardson, through Jane Austen, Dickens, George Eliot, Hardy and Henry James, to the great early twentieth-century figures of Conrad and Lawrence. If Sterne was dismissed, the gothic novel seen as a distortion, the Brontë sisters as "sports" (in the biological sense), and much modern fiction as primarily trivialising, this was because they were all marginal to the evolution of the progressive, critical tradition of the novel as an essential and primary form of moral and social judgement.

A small quarrel in the book suggests exactly where Leavis's feeling for tradition came from, and it is the tradition of British nonconformity at, you might say, its firmest and best. He quotes Lord David Cecil, in *Early Victorian Novelists*, on George Eliot:

> But the moral code founded on that Puritan theology had soaked itself too deeply into the fibre of her thought and feeling for her to give it up ... her standards of right and wrong were the Puritan standards. She admired truthfulness and chastity and industry and self-restraint, she disapproved of loose living and recklessness and deceit and self-indulgence.

Leavis responds with characteristic sarcasm in saying that he differs from Cecil in *sharing* those standards and beliefs, and they seem to him productive of serious literature; and, he goes on, "I will add (exposing myself completely) that the enlightenment of aestheticism or sophistication that feels an amused superiority to them leads, in my view, to triviality and boredom, and that out of triviality comes evil." It was not surprising that Oxford did not always favour Leavis (he considered that Cambridge did not either). The fact is, of course, that Leavis's great tradition is a Puritan one, and it omits much that the contemporary reader might find in it, and much that a modern writer might want to use: the experimental and the self-begetting, the fantastic, the gothic and the grotesque. Leavis's modernists seem to lack many aspects of their modernity, his expatriates many aspects of their internationalism, his aestheticians their aesthetic devotions; and Leavis's tradition can be said to have foreshortened our understanding of the way in which the path of realism has not been the only path for British fiction.

Leavis was later to write on American fiction, inclining to agree with the then familiar view that it was an alternative tradition, given over not to the novel but to romance, though he found in it a critical force that many commentators had overlooked. But it was all a potent reading of the relevance of the novel to life and society, and to its imaginative dispute with the instrumentalisms and the aesthetic trivialities that vitiate literary and human culture. And though he saw contemporary culture as itself so deeply vitiated in this way as to be incapable of generating a fiction with a full "awareness of the possibilities of life", he was and remains perhaps the only modern British critic to exert great influence over contemporary writers, offering them not only a usable fictional past but a kind of orthodoxy that has laid a powerful trace over the postwar British novel, redirecting it toward the tradition of social and moral realism he spoke for.

2 Leavis, in fact, spoke with the voice of a cultural revolt that became very relevant to the 1950s, a revolt that summoned back into creative play the kind of provincial and nonconformist strenuousness he took as a human essence. No doubt his appeal was in part to the lower-middle-class meritocratic mood of the times, and to those for whom new doors had opened to university education and expression in the world of letters and the groves of academe. To them, as to Leavis, dilletantism and the "amused superiority" of the mannered and the sophisticated were not a sufficient account of culture, and it was very appropriate that Leavis should have had a special appeal to those like myself who had been not to Oxbridge but to one of the "redbrick" provincial universities founded as a result of the broad spreading of nineteenth-century education, and touched with the values of hard work, getting on and keeping decent. Such institutions had a rigour of tone and an aversion to the manners of upper class and metropolitan life, and made no claim to urbanity, wit and taste in the politer senses of these terms. In offering in *Scrutiny* a rigorous conception of "taste" very different, far less elite, Leavis touched on a social and moral quarrel that ran deep in his own contemporary culture. The quarrel took on life in the cultural press. "The school of Leavis and Richards was severe, sometimes sour, sometimes absurd . . .," Philip Toynbee observed generously, in *The Observer*. "But high prejudice is needed somewhere. We cannot do without the defiant setting of a standard which the Cambridge critics achieved for so long." "*Scrutiny* today represents an influential but isolated point of view . . .," G.S. Fraser said in *The Modern Writer and His World* (1964). "Crudely generalising from him, a reader might say that, in spite of the rather grim severity of tone, what he is always looking for is the embodiment of positive life-enhancing values . . . . But . . . may it not be a good thing for young readers to have passionate and immature admirations?" The "grim severity" became famous, and Leavis's judgements, especially on his contemporaries, were famously considered "grudging".

But more bitter accusations were levelled. John Hayward saw Leavis as "a cold intellectual", his enterprise a "methodical and uncompromising destruction of reputations". Stephen Spender wrote of "Dr F.R. Leavis's anti-university Cambridge where the Leavisites devote some of their critical faculties to being embarrassed much as the Quakers did to quaking," and he saw the whole enterprise as "the rebellion of the lower middle brows", a spirit of "provincial puritanism" that sought to regard creation as an offshoot of critical analysis.

Leavis took his revenge by asking in *Scrutiny*'s last number: "How, there is still (it seems) some point in asking, was it possible to get Mr Stephen Spender established as a distinguished writer? There is no mystery about the processes by which it was done; the portentous fact is that they met no resistance (except in *Scrutiny*) . . .". John Lehmann entered the fray by attacking "Provincialism, one of the blights that is always in danger of settling on our literature". Leavis belonged in the mood of assault on Bloomsbury, of the large-scale condemnation of what he called "the Auden ethos", where promising writers were arrested at the stage of undergraduate brilliance, and the domination of the literary magazines by a metropolitan elite of trivial and mannered tastes. And, though he did not like the work of Kingsley Amis, and despised that of C.P. Snow, he was very much linked with that cultural reversal that passed through the 1950s as the old cultural standard-bearers – those who, said John Wain, indulged in "the bland assumption that Culture is Culture No Matter What" – found themselves confronted by a new generation of different social and cultural values, values that, very often, had much to do with that provincial and neo-puritan tradition Leavis summoned up. In criticism his logical heirs became cultural critics like Richard Hoggart and Raymond Williams, and the much more socially and then theoretically oriented criticism of the 1960s. In due course the heirs became apostates, as the cultural and critical climate again changed significantly in the 1960s. But in the bitter cultural quarrels and reconstructions of the 1950s Leavis and *Scrutiny* were central, and they gave a vitality to a very vitiated and critically uncertain literary scene which remains part of our contemporary imagination.

3 *Scrutiny*, then, marked a very remarkable moment, the moment when somehow the activities of literary criticism and the broader literary debate came for a moment together in a vital and interesting meeting of critical activity and general culture of a kind we now entirely lack. The moment came when the Modern movement had collapsed and so had the schools of the 1930s, and when, in the postwar climate, many were turning to literature to find a moral and social vision that was better than politics and more complex than an abstract philosophy. But Leavis's, and *Scrutiny*'s, origins also went back to the 1930s, and it is interesting to see how they found their place there, and how this particular spirit, liberal and critical, but also puritan and provincial, forged itself. As I have said, *Scrutiny* was founded in 1932 by a group of collaborators, mostly young research students, at Cambridge, and Leavis himself did not appear as the editor until the fourth number. They were part of a new academicisation of English as a serious university subject, in which Cambridge led the way. Their intellectual credentials were serious and interesting, owing a very great deal to the critical activity which had surrounded the emergence of the modern movement over, during and just after the wartime years, and where the two most notable voices were T.S. Eliot and Ezra Pound, both Americans expatriate in Britain but very closely in touch with continental influences. Their attempt to teach people How To Read, as Pound put it, had much to do with the transformation of verse they were undertaking, an attempt to begin art anew which could, they both acknowledged, be done by elaborating a new attitude toward the tradition; the task of "constructing the past" has to be begun again, for every significant new work of art, every change of form, changed the past order.

This meant breaking with the Victorian and Georgian modes of poetry, identifying an alternative tradition, distinguishing the "dissociation of sensibility" which had weakened poetry from Milton onward, and discovering the new "objective correlative." Leavis announced his indebtedness to Eliot's *The Sacred Wood* (1920) in particular, and read in its critical reappraisal a significance for all modern judgement of literature. But a good many of Eliot's influential principles had complex international sources, and today it is not hard to see the alliance between Eliot's "modernist" criticism and the work of the Russian formalists and others – work that by the 1950s had become distilled, condensed, Americanised and turned into something called "the New Criticism", a tendency of which Leavis is usually seen as a member. Other figures of great importance in the map of Leavis's critical view were I.A. Richards and William Empson, Cambridge critics who appeared in the early issues of *Scrutiny*. Richards in particular was associated with the "practical criticism" which was also part of the *Scrutiny* spirit, but again his work was close to many continental sources and theories, in particular the linguistic revolution following on from Saussure, the language-theorist who was in due course to be massively revised as a support for structuralism. Another strong influence was Edgell Rickword, editor of the 1920s critical-and-creative magazine *The Calendar of Modern Letters*, who subsequently became a Marxist and edited *The Left Review* in the 1930s. Leavis also famously talked with Wittgenstein, and owed some small indebtedness to his language theories.

So, when *Scrutiny* started as a critical review, it was part of a web of international aesthetic, critical, linguistic and cultural theories which had a great deal to do with the Modern movement. But the magazine had some firm resistances: to Eliot's move toward "classicism", and to the developing arguments of Marxism ("we intended

Scrutiny to stand for the human tradition as something to be fostered apart from any religious [or political] creed; and the fostering of a free play of critical intelligence we thought of as essential to the tradition. In this sense *Scrutiny* invites the description 'liberal' "). Nor did it acknowledge the international spirit of modernism, or the broad movements of internationalist aesthetic theories. It was part of *Scrutiny*'s power as a cultural force that it Anglicised all these things. Thus Leavis's book *New Bearings in English Poetry* helped construct Eliot as a poet in the same British tradition as Hopkins and Yeats, and in much the same way the modern movement in fiction came to appear either as a tendency of trivialising aestheticism or, as in the case of Conrad and Lawrence, as a form of culturally rooted social and moral criticism. By the 1950s many of the ideas that did relate to the broader map of Western thought had been given a new acquaintance with the British way, the spirited critical tradition which had moral and social roots in commonsensical and morally exacting English life, and this humanisation and familiarisation, reinforced by basic ideas of human soundness and moral maturity, made the tradition that Leavis was describing seem essential standards of culture. Leavis was finally to acknowledge this power himself, saying that *Scrutiny*'s judgement, so strongly disputed at first, "invariably turned out to be right", and that "after what was often the most indignant resistance in the world of literary fashions, they have been accepted, and now pass current as what was always known".

In the "Valedictory" to the last number of *Scrutiny*, Leavis permitted himself a sad joke to the effect that "a rich subject awaits some (probably American) researcher: the discrepancy between the official or conventional agreed valuation of *Scrutiny* and the evidence of a decisive influence exerted". By 1953 that evidence was unmistakable, and it remains a potent part of our cultural and intellectual history. Leavis represents, I suppose, an essentially British view of literary criticism, one marked by its strongly personal tone, and yet its sense of association with the communal debate, a view of "things that have found their bearings with regard to one another, and not a theoretical system determined by abstract considerations". Leavis's criticism seemed more like a form of humanism than a theory, and in that he indeed summoned up something crucial in the British empirical tradition. In terms of his academic place, we might suggest that he belonged to a moment before a crucial change already in train had fully developed, of which in a way he was a part, and criticism became massively institutionalised and professionalised, constantly refining its theory. In terms of his place in the culture, he not only captured but helped distil a moment, one in which that feeling for criticism as a form of literary urgency, focused around "values essential for profound and intelligent living", came increasingly to matter. It cast its implications into the spirit of writing, gave us the sense that the artistic imagination could intervene in society's central places, and helped, I believe, summon up a sense of creative possibility in a discouraging moment. Few recent critics have achieved as much, and our cultural life feels, I think, the less for it.

4 Towards the end of his life, Leavis was honoured by a Professorship at the University of York, and lectured yet more widely; a book by Leavis and his wife and long-term collaborator Q.D. Leavis, *Lectures in America* (1969), declared the later opinions of them both. It is short and in some ways surprisingly disengaged, three of the four essays – Leavis's on Eliot and Yeats, and Q.D.'s on *Wuthering Heights* – concerning themselves less with culture than with a precise effort to see in the long view the creative endeavour of the writers discussed. In the essay on Eliot Leavis remarks that matters of fashion and immediate cultural direction are "not my business now", and, whether because the audiences were American or the preoccupations had changed, the emphasis is different. The essay on Eliot is a classic (perhaps *the* classic) justification for the work of a poet whose influence was now waning, finding in that work a centre of "pure, significant, achieved creation, qualified . . . to exercise the profoundest kind of influence". The centre lies, Leavis now argues, in the *personal* quality of the poetry, that side of his work concerned not with the famous "impersonality" nor with the social affairs of a public world which Leavis had emphasised earlier, the side less to do with *The Waste Land* than with other poems – "La figlia che piange", "Marina", and *Ash Wednesday* above all – where poetic technique "is a technique for sincerity". These are the poems where memory and love play most part, functioning as "some vital node of experience" against despair. A related claim is made for Yeats – that his great poems are only a small proportion of the whole, and that it is in those poems where Yeats confronts the complexity of experience faced that he is at greatest force. The force comes, Leavis suggests, from discoveries emerging from the process of composition, rather than from Yeats's famous preoccupation with "artifice'" or the chill cast of the cold eye over culture. In his later judgements, indeed, Leavis was looking away from the poetry of culture to the poetry of feeling, as was his wife in her essay on *Wuthering Heights*, itself a reading of the book's moral and emotional effect.

This leaves the fourth essay, "Luddites?, or There Is Only One Culture", which returns to contention, and to the famous and acrimonious "two cultures" debate Leavis had engaged with C.P. Snow, who had complained of the lack of scientific awareness in British culture, and its over-dependence on the artistic and humanistic imagination. Leavis argues that his assault had been largely misunderstood, and that indeed his was not an attack on material standards of living, or on scientific culture as such. "I was merely insisting," Leavis says "that there *is* an intrinsic human nature, with needs and latent potentialities the most brilliant scientist may very well be blank about, and the technologically directed planner may ignore – with (it doesn't need arguing) disastrous consequences." The tone in some ways sounds resigned, the cultural adversaries – and there are plenty about, as they still are – hardly engaged, and the implication now different. Above all the essay seems there to reinforce the suggestions of the other essays in the book. For Leavis was not now insisting on art's essential criticism of culture, and was arguing that it is the personal density and texture of artistic experience, sufficiently encountered and judged, that makes for the literary and creative intelligence. There *is* one human nature, and art speaks to it when it speaks with the most complex sincerity. It is in a way a stand above the argument, perhaps even a transcending of or a floating away from it. The one culture, the single human nature, has a detached value in an enraging world. Perhaps it was a change of view, or perhaps something Leavis always taught us carefully to notice: a sign of the times.

"NO, NOT BLOOMSBURY"
The comic fiction of Kingsley Amis

"While he explained, he pronounced the names to himself: Bayswater, Knightsbridge, Notting Hill Gate, Pimlico, Belgrave Square, Wapping, Bloomsbury. No, not Bloomsbury."
Kingsley Amis, Lucky Jim (1954)

"I'd rather go to bed,' she said in her habitual monotone.
"If you're tired some food'll perk you up."
"I don't mean that. I don't feel tired. I mean sex."
This was exactly the sort of thing that Ronnie, in his role as a graduate student of Britain's youth, was supposed to know all about. But, for the moment, his reaction was a simple though uncomfortable mixture of lust and alarm, with alarm slightly to the fore. "Fine. Nothing I'd like better, love. We'll grab a taxi and go to my flat."
"I can't wait," the girl droned. "I want it *now*."
"But you can't have it *now*, for Christ's sake."
Kingsley Amis, I Want It Now (1968)

1   The French have always had a fondness for writers who profess themselves intellectuals, whether they are or not. On the other hand, being different, the British prefer their writers not to be, however philosophical or high-minded they may happen to be in private life. This helps explain something of the difference between most British and most continental fiction; the British have rarely produced the philosophical novel, the serious political novel, or the novel of aesthetic exactitude. What they have produced is the writer of many mediations, the writer who is party to the commonplace and ordinary stuff of life, the realist, the observer, the humorist. Political and social attitudes, even strong ideas, may play a part, but it is best if these are presented as prejudices, instincts or eccentricities rather than theories or ideologies. Indeed, one of the things that has mediated social, political and intellectual life in Britain is its capacity for manifest humour. And this may be why one of the triumphs and pleasures of the British fictional tradition is the comic novel. We have a strong comic line in the novel, and it still goes on. But even in this

matter the British taste has been generally for the untheoretical. Two lineages started in the early days of fiction, one with Henry Fielding, the voice of good-humoured benevolence, the maker of one of our great comic heroes, Tom Jones; the other with Laurence Sterne, who invented and abstracted the anti-novel almost before the novel form had begun, and so became one of the great heroes of experimental modernism, as well as the discoverer of comedy as a form of response to pain and mortality.

In general it has been the lineage of Fielding that has prevailed. Jane Austen, commonsensical as well as sharply ironic, familiarises us to the difficult world of social manners. Dickens was a man of exacting social ideas, but a great writer of the familiar and the popular. Joyce is, in *Ulysses*, a most remarkable comic novelist, the supreme parodist of text; but Evelyn Waugh, fiercely and splendidly prejudiced, his social attitudes often dismaying, his compassion nil, is surely the best twentieth-century British comic novelist to date. His fiction is darker and sharper than it often seems, but like much modern comic writing it refuses many of our most serious notions of literature, and is more *against* ideas than for them. Indeed, the ideologically or philosophically obsessed have usually seemed, in British comic fiction, the enemies of reality and the true comic instinct – Thackum and Square in *Tom Jones*, the dreaming transcendentalists in *Martin Chuzzlewit*, and so on to Professor Welch and his Bloomsbury artistic coterie in Kingsley Amis's *Lucky Jim*, a novel that undoubtedly owed as much of its success to maintaining the eighteenth-century fictional tradition as it did to providing a radical view of its own time, the 1950s. This is not the only place where Amis does homage to Fielding, and in British fiction he has been far from alone. *Tom Jones*, said Gibbon, "may be considered the history of human nature", and the comic novel of human nature has long been found the true British way of doing fictional things.

This in turn may explain how we treat our writers, which is not quite as intellectuals but as outrageous observers of our institutions, mores and political practices. Comedy becomes a way of pursuing offence without offence, and to this day we are capable of producing, and thinking very British, authors whose manner is both spikey and clubbable, aggressive and affable, writers who both outrage and delight us while generally refusing to be our leaders of thought, our makers of political judgement, our constructors of philosophy, our severe critics, our metaphysical explorers. Waugh himself is one of the chief modern examples – a writer of distinction and originality, whose irascible disguises served to hide him from readers, strangers and much of the argument of the world, who was able to sustain at the highest level of arrogance a virtually unattainable intellectual and social position, and in general to claim as the very centre of writing the proprietorial, seigneurial rights of the English eccentric, whom it would be quite inappropriate to gainsay or interrupt. As it happens, and as it does often happen, Waugh possessed powerful intellectual qualities – a strong sense of history, which he had manoeuvred into a theory of a decline and fall that had started with the end of Catholic dominance in Britain and was now quite irredeemable; an unusual aesthetic taste, which could be presented as very proper in a gentleman; a great studiousness which he chose to call "a little learning", and presumably hence a dangerous thing, though less dangerous than a lot of it; and above all a compelling sense of style which could appear at once an art form and a normal possession of a man of rank, but never as a modernist novelty.

Thus *A Little Learning* was the appropriate title for his recessive fragment of autobiography: no tale of an intellectual or an artistic upbringing but an account of personal and social relations invested with an apocalyptic sense of faith, a certain sense of acquired position, and a general instinct that the world is a place of follies. We can understand it, therefore, when Sean O'Faolain, in his book *The Vanishing Hero* (1956), chooses to characterise Waugh's work in much the same way, describing Waugh as "a writer of purely brainless genius, which he had amplified by the possession or development of enormous technical skill". This probably pleased Waugh perfectly well, though it happens to be enormously unfair; Waugh at best is a novelist of very considered powers and devastating human judgement. But we can see how it feels true; Edmund Wilson, who had a good deal of Waugh's temper, and admired him greatly until he met him and found himself treated, as an American, with contempt, aptly identified his fictional and social manner with that of Jowett's advice to the gentleman: "Never apologize; never explain." Waugh did not explain, or not in public; the diaries explain, and explain him, a good deal. He invented remarkable new techniques for fiction, but professed dislike for the modernist avant garde – indeed, as time went on, for everything that had happened in his own lifetime, a fact which made him one of the comic historians *of* modernity. His mannered conservatism hid a pessimist's dismay; his late florid face was a facade over pain. He unlocked all this once, in *The Ordeal of Gilbert Pinfold*, hinting at the general human treachery which drove him to take up his mask – a hard facade that in fact had made him one of the greatest stylistic and comic interpreters of his age in the form of the novel.

2 When World War Two ended, Waugh's style, shaken by the experiences of wartime and the coming of the welfare-state world that followed, seemed half-spent. His later fiction reflects a good deal on this break, and the problem of writing the tale of the new age of dishonour. The new generation of the 1950s gradually emerged, their air apparently puritanical and socially of the lower middle class, their tweedy sports jackets hanging badly off their shoulders, their mildly Left-of-centre social principles everywhere being asserted. It was not, it seemed to Waugh, a climate for his kind of writing, and he raged against it. As for the most comically assured of the new writers, Kingsley Amis, whose impact on the 1950s came to rival that of Waugh on the 1920s, he seemed in almost every respect Waugh's antithesis. Waugh had portrayed British society in a state of irremediable historical decadence, a world of social, political and sexual treachery in which a few inheritors from the past hinted at the better, more stable and fixed world that was falling in, like the roofs of some of our best country houses, on top of us; Amis mocked the past and its styles and manners, and spoke straight from the plain and ordinary present. Waugh had found in the Catholic English past an older history to which he could convert and from which he could gain some sustenance; Amis attacked all that was nostalgic and medievalising in the British character, every notion of a Merrie England, and found his sustenance in the commonplace, the provincial, the bottle of beer and the blonde. Waugh had a religious and metaphysical rage with the contemporary world; Amis seemed full of secular delight in its stuff and its ways. Waugh's first hero was the weedy Oxford student Paul Pennyfeather who falls foul of rogues and rascals far more interesting than he; Amis's hero is the anti-scholar who wins out against the flamboyant adversaries and pretenders in the interest of simple honesty.

Waugh and Amis therefore looked like literary opposites, and the distinction applied equally in political matters. Waugh was not simply a writer of conservative instincts; he offered himself as the one true conservative. Amis, on the other hand, appeared part of the New Left that was emerging in postwar Britain, in an era when there was a new appeal for literary commitment. At St John's College, Oxford, in 1941, he had been an undergraduate communist ("the only party I have ever joined"), of course at a time when Britain and Soviet Russia were allies. During the 1950s he was announcing himself a probable lifetime Labour voter, and explored his Fabian allegiances in a pamphlet called *Socialism and the Intellectuals* (1957), a title that was hardly likely to go down well at Combe Florey. Amis was also not just a striking novelist and a fine young poet writing in the way of the "Movement", but also an academic, teaching English at a British "redbrick", Swansea, and writing fine and rather severe critical essays on which the impact of Leavis and the spirit of new critical intensity was apparent. Thereafter, forsaking the "redbrick" world about which he had written, he went to a fellowship at Peterhouse, Cambridge, with every prospect of a career that united the academic and the literary, the critical and the creative functions. None of this was in the Waugh spirit, except as stuff for the making of satirical fiction. But in the event a sharp break came. Cambridge did not suit, whether because of its often backbiting attitude toward those with literary ambitions, or because criticism itself was in any case being pushed heavily toward more theoretical preoccupations, is not quite clear. It is now that Amis entered on the life of the full-time writer, with great success, and indeed he was to pass the gene on to his son Martin, who has done the same.

Even so matters were changing. *Lucky Jim* and the books that immediately followed were enormously successful, and caught the temper of the times, coupling brilliant comic effects with a sharp sense of social process and even social protest. The poetry was admirable in the new, rational-critical, anti-modernist movement way, and displayed comic vision, good feeling, and commonsense, a much needed voice in the era of purity of diction and a strong sense of anti-romanticism. Amis's essays were forceful and accessible pieces of literary criticism, and he was clearly a central figure of the new "Movement" mood. But the manner was shifting, along with the political sympathies and the mode of social exploration in his work. Amis might well protest that it was the world that was changing, he remaining much the same; but the fiction seems to record a different story. At any rate Amis's politics moved toward the Right, and today he defines himself as a non-wet and so presumably Thatcherite Tory "with a few liberal bits", on hanging, homosexuality, abortion. But the "liberal bits" are only occasionally noticeable, and in the history of post-Orwellian liberalism, which has a lot to do with modern fiction, Amis did not continue as a striking example of the cause. The writer who began to write in the spirit of a humanist commonsense in a postwar time (you might say commonsense was to his world view what post-Heideggerian existentialism was to Jean-Paul Sartre's) took on rage and spleen, sometimes invested against morality and the human condition itself, as in *Ending Up* (1974), one of his deepest novels, and sometimes in a latter-day social ire arrayed against the modernity of the modern world. The writer who wrote compassionately in *Take a Girl Like You* (1960) of the change in sexual and emotional manners became in late books like *Jake's Thing* (1978) a notable misogynist in the age of feminism; the critic who had admired the radical impact of American fiction in the 1950s began to rage against the worthlessness of American writing.

In many ways Amis seemed slowly to have inherited the role of the Comic Bad Man of English Letters which Waugh had so powerfully sustained a generation earlier. Now the similarities began to look very evident. Both of them had begun as spectacular Young Turks, writing the novels of their new age in which, as at Waugh's Anchorage House, the topic of the Younger Generation is much discussed, and had turned into Angry Old Men. Both had captured, in subject and style, the manners, moral upsets, cultural dislocations and social instabilities generated by a recent war. Both of them were strictly anti-romantic writers who carried somewhere in their work a secret but gradually more explicit nostalgia. Both revolted against the extremities of experimentalism and the impact and significance of the modern movement. Both darkened deeply with the years, taking on a pervasive awareness both of the absurdity of the social world and the hideous weight of mortality into which human life is born, so that their comedy is touched with pain. Both turned youthful attitudes that seemed fresh and exciting into something crusted with an air of powerful prejudice, and protected those prejudices with an engaging but troubling comic conviction. Both, as they grew into public figures, turned their comic masks into public faces, into a manner that was both clubbable and crusty, amusing and bitter, rotund and misanthropic, a disguise that did not quite seem to disguise everything. Both started with a complex social awareness and an extraordinary cunning of observation, and nurtured it in the direction of an enraged dissent from most of what was observed. And both – this can certainly be said of Waugh, and I think we will say it of Amis – turned, with their virtues and their faults, into major writers whose mixture of basic craft, remarkable social perception, comic vision and gift for rage and outrage managed to construct a lifetime of writing of extraordinary dimensions and decided influence. It has been said that few contemporary comic writers can get free of the intonations of Amis, and the tradition of modern comic fiction in Britain has an inescapable source in Waugh, who will, I think, be seen as one of the great black humorists of the century. Both suggest that the comic is both a stylistic capacity and a form of human pain, and both indicate what I think is a very British way of dealing with it which may have striking limitations and peculiar strengths. And, as a result, both are difficult to write about, provoking both annoyance and respect, a sense of a talent often imperfect yet of an extraordinary force.

3 Literary dates have a calendar of their own, referring not just to the clock but to styles, moods and visions in writing which have their own momentum. Today the literary Fifties seems a distinct period in fiction, drama and poetry, an artistic, intellectual and critical community which still half guides us but also seems remote. Its sensibility, in which Amis himself was central, is marked by a burst of new writing in which a serious progressive severity, a new critical instinct, took hold, and much of that critical instinct was turned to the immediate past. The new tone seems determined to dispense with the experimentalism of the 1920s and 1930s, with the romanticism and apocalypticism of the 1940s (the exemplary figure was Dylan Thomas, still a target in Amis's most recent novel to date, *The Old Devils* (1986)), the Beckettian despairs emanating from Paris, though there is an underlying existentialist influence. Amis's Oxford friend Philip Larkin came in poetry to exemplify the new voice, plain-speaking, exact, observant, pessimistic, anti-romantic; he also helped prepare the way in fiction by publishing his early novel about Oxford life, *Jill* (1946). The connection reaches further, for Larkin is the dedicatee of Amis's first novel *Lucky Jim*, which became a summative work of the new spirit in fiction much as John Osborne's *Look Back In Anger* did in drama. There were other books to reinforce it – from John Wain's earlier *Hurry On Down* to Iris Murdoch's slightly later *Under the Net* – and so to suggest that a meritocratic, critical, comic and youthful voice was sounding across the entire literary scene.

One thing that seemed to feed the new tone was the social background and the education of these newer writers, speaking from a lower-middle-class, and just occasionally a working-class, orientation, though usually with a college education. They looked across a landscape that was deeply changed by the world of the welfare state, was divided by war from the past generation, and was probably more comfortable than the depression age of the 1930s, even though it was pressed by nuclear anxiety. Mores, manners and social accents were changing, in life and fiction, and the writing was amenable, open, speaking plainly, from recognised social positions, in clear rhetorical tones; it had few oblique angles, few signs of avant-garde displacement, and it offered to return the literary arts to the accessible ways that prevailed before the coming of modernism; an artistic spirit, Philip Larkin suggested, that could only interest Americans and had as its two main concerns mystification and outrage. It thus seemed painstakingly British, and it painted British culture in a time of relative liberal recovery, touched by social hope even if at times with a stoical despair. All these elements seemed present in Amis's work, and had much to do with the cultural success of the early novels, in which liking it here and wanting it now were very much the theme and the basis of the amenable vernacular tone. In an age which lacked strongly ideological feelings but had a powerful sense of generational transition, Amis's fiction had a generous comic rapport with the times, an appropriate social feeling, and a distinct moral vitality.

No doubt the success of *Lucky Jim* came largely from these elements, though we should also add that it was and remains one of the funniest modern comic novels. But the success was not entirely simple. The book had been round several publishers before it came out in January 1954, and it took something like another year before it acquired its popular if not mythical status. Nor was it quite what it seemed at the time. When it appeared, in a climate hungry for a postwar fiction, it was largely acknowledged as a work of the New Anger, and read for its social rage and protest. To reread it now does not confirm this, for like many books in the 1950s it seems to have been a reassessment of the 1930s and the shadows left over a world that suddenly seemed very different. Jim Dixon's seemingly dangerous adversaries are largely variants on what Angus Wilson had already named the "darling dodos', those of waning social power who still hung on to the mannerisms of the past. Jim is the traditional innocent comic hero, as well as the man who is pleasantly attuned to the present in its plainest forms. According to a traditional comic plot (the plot, we might say, of *Tom Jones*), he is rewarded by comic good fortune, becomes "lucky" Jim, winning a job in commerce and the prettiest girl in the story, freeing himself of the disguises and moral pressures that have kept him restrained. The plain form of the novel is justified by artistic presumptions developed in the book, as in several more of Amis's novels. For the danger of art is Bertram's danger, mannerist pretension, and that above all is represented by Bloomsbury. The way Jim is pointing is quite clear. "No, not Bloomsbury", he thinks to himself, when the lure of modern London beckons at the end and he searches for his right address.

Lucky Jim declared itself and a mood surrounding itself in a great many ways that took their place in postwar literary style. It had little to do with the aesthetic mannerisms, or indeed the ideological allegiances, of the generation gone just before. It turned from political matters to commonsense moral vision, throwing off not just Bloomsbury but provincial sexual repression, conventional intellectual behaviour, academic respectability and social snobbery. To express all this, it captured (much as in the United States J.D. Salinger captured in *The Catcher in the Rye*) a workable vernacular voice, comic and loosely argued, a voice that did sound like a voice and spoke out against unnecessary complexity, instituted social deceit, disguises and hypocrisies, and detected false intonations. It set the unfaked against the faked, the unphoney against the phoney, the unpretentious against the pretentious, the near-at-hand against the far-away, the allusion to close domestic gods against mystificatory and distant deities. A redbrick university was an ideal location for Jim Dixon's story, since here the manners of other places – the traditions and snobberies of privileged Oxbridge colleges, the mannered eccentricities of upper-middle-class donnish style, the constant appeal beyond the here-and-now to an imaginary Merrie England – prevailed in a world which gave them no support.

The story, however, could easily be shifted elsewhere, to many another department of British social life, and it touched on the nature and spirit of literary life itself, one reason for the unease of many of the critics of the previous generation who attacked the new phenomenon. The vernacular voice of Jim, which is so clearly the deployed voice of the author, speaking the author's own mind, constructing his distinctive world, coercing by a teasing sentence-structure the true way of saying things out of the false way in which they are usually said in writing, can thus become, in Orwellian fashion, the voice of commonsense itself. It is a knowing voice, tugging at sense in order to gain the commonsense, showing itself not so much angered, rather as fundamentally appreciative – of the good simple things that speech and life give us, like girls, money, drink, and a sturdy language that is not laid upon us by our social betters.

Here were the dominant virtues of the book, which have not stopped sounding in Amis's later works, though they sometimes take strange turns. For its language was able to construct a sceptical social and moral realism which found sense, dismissed aesthetic over-formulation, knocked against pretension, and gave to the stuff of ordinary life a comic enjoyment, a reinvigoration of the banal. Amis, indeed, was a moralist inside the moral tradition of the novel, just as the shape of its fiction was the shape of romantic comedy, surrounding the hero – anti-hero, said the reviewers – with the stuff of good fortune won by moral and linguistic persistence and generating an alliance between his simple commonsense and the comic muse. Jim has to live in social disguise for much of the novel, to hold down his intellectual job. When drink releases him from the intellectual convention he is forced to practise, we see this as a satisfying comic explosion of truth, though it could just as well be a naive reaction to ideas or a form of prejudice of its own. As David Lodge once observed, the triumphant moment in the book comes when Jim no longer has to hide his vernacular vision in his thoughts but comes right out and speaks: "The bloody old towser-faced boot-faced totem pole on a crap reservation, Dixon thought. 'You bloody old towser-faced boot-faced totem pole on a crap reservation', he said." This is classic comic gratification, the victory of the small over the not so very big, the silent over the expressive. But the freedom it expresses is the freedom of the comic spirit itself, at least accounting for its own feelings. In the tradition of the social and moral novel, as in Jane Austen for example, *Lucky Jim* takes the bearers of false and hypocritical sentiment to task and replaces their world with one of true feeling. But it was the old novel in a new form, sounding a fresh, impertinent, culturally active voice and giving it fictional energy.

For several novels thereafter Amis wrote in much the same spirit, good-hearted and morally critical of the pretentious social world. *That Uncertain Feeling* (1955) took on a long-lasting adversary, contemporary Wales, the home of a spirit of bardic pretentiousness epitomised in the work of Dylan Thomas and those who have used it to justify a sentimental and nostalgic Welshness of a kind that still haunts his most recent fiction. Other novels and some short stories caught aspects of a related theme: the shabby gentility and banality of much of wartime and postwar British life, and the way it was lit and excused by false justifications. Certain distinctive gifts became not-able, and Amis grew expert in presenting the social character who is just off-key, voicing loud claims and understandings that do not quite sound right, and then playing in the sound that does. The comedy stayed intimate with realism and common life, and grew more observant about manners and mores. Not all previous writers admired the tone, and Somerset Maugham condemned the new writers like Amis as "scum".

It was ironic that Amis should now win the Somerset Maugham Prize for Fiction, even more ironic that the consequence of this travelling prize was travel, and to Abroad, which Amis famously did not like. He chose to spend the booty in Portugal, perhaps because their pillar boxes are like ours; the fruit of the voyage was *I Like It Here* (1958), the story of a writer called Garnett Bowen who suffers the selfsame fate. Another plain-speaking hero constantly caught in what he calls "bum" – bureaucracy, restriction, pretension and formality – Bowen goes off to Portugal to find there an expatriate writer who is the absolute antithesis of himself. This is John Wulfstan Strether, a parodistic figure who clearly owes much to Henry James and something to Bloomsbury, and who suffers from severe logorrhea and high-flown artistic pretensions. Bowen longs for home, the "here" of the title, but finds his reward in discovering in Lisbon the grave of Henry Fielding, the eighteenth-century British novelist who showed us, as the novel puts it, that fiction could express "a moral seriousness that could be made apparent without evangelical puffing and blowing". The homage is clearly that of Amis himself, and is the most interesting thing in a rather loosely constructed book. Like many another postwar British novelist Amis was writing into his contract with the novel a sense of its tradition, and its continuing power. The novel of comic morality, of benevolence, good feeling and good judgement was capable of revival in postwar British circumstances, and Amis's fiction for a time seemed set to confirm this.

Certainly this was appropriate to Amis's next novel, *Take A Girl Like You*, which is one of his best, and seems to mark a decided change in his work. The farcical tone and the comic male hero here give ground, as larger issues, broader social observations and greater moral complications enter the novel. Interestingly the underlying eighteenth-century reference point here is Fielding's adversary and object of parody, Samuel Richardson, and the novels alluded to are *Pamela* and *Clarissa*, while the central theme of the novel is the Richardsonian principle of procrastinated rape. Amis here sees the story largely through the eyes of his heroine, Jenny Bunn, though he complicates matters by acknowledging the need for a stronger male character, Patrick Standish, and hence plays against Richardsonian themes the kind of criticism Fielding made of them. In any case, where Richardson's standpoint is that of a rising merchant class elaborating a controlled economic and sexual morality, a growing Puritanism and Victorianism, Amis is writing of a time when the inherited lower-middle-class standards largely derived from this were giving way to postwar notions of sexual liberation and permissiveness. Amis's aim here is clearly to write a capacious and compassionate novel of contemporary morality and changing sexual roles, about morality as inherited standard and the making of morality for oneself.

Jenny is a contemporary girl who is granted a strong moral sense, and is caught in a familiar crisis about right and wrong, focused on the price, value and meaning of her virginity. The high value she sets on it is contested by her lover-adversary Patrick Standish as the product of a "bloody little small-town conscience". Her friends cannot help her define the prize she seeks to retain: "I thought it was all to do with arranged marriages and betrothals and all that." Amis's writing takes much of its force from his sense of contemporary mores and social detail, and the theme of changing sexual moralities has been crucial to his work since. He creates Jenny's values and ways as a vital and comprehensible compound of juvenile innocence, traditionalism, and a desire not to be exploited or discarded, in a world that, for a girl like you, the girl of the advertisements of the time, is a series of sexual confusions and traps. In this world the men in turn look for immediate sexual pleasure and gratification, and the story of the rape is told as a kind of enforcement of historical necessity. Jenny is left with appropriately ambiguous feelings: "she could hardly pretend that what she had got was not worth having after all", what she gains by her loss of virginity being access to contemporary experience. Patrick, with his own shivers of mortality, becomes an interesting hero, a rake with a strong sense of modernity – and also a precursor of the shit-hero who would figure in several books to come.

Take a Girl Like You is Amis's most balanced book morally, and shows his debt to the literary tradition. But it also opened the way for Amis to take on a new kind of writing, in which the 1960s mood of sexual liberation and then of growing male-female conflict were to be dominant themes. The Amis shit-hero, a kind of echo of Evelyn Waugh's Charles Ryder, becomes a common character in these books. Waugh also seems echoed in the subject of *One Fat Englishman* (1963), in which, like Waugh in *The Loved One*, Amis responds to the image of booming, materialist, liberation-hungry, opportunistic America with a good deal of suspicion. Like Waugh he presents this by having his hero out-exploit the exploiters, and the book, like several of Waugh's later novels, is a conflict of unattractive opposites. The book came from a teaching visit Amis made to Princeton, and this apparently confirmed him in his sense of "Britishness" as a writer. (Some of his work had, strangely, been compared with that of the American "Beat Generation".) Amis evidently did have his roots in the tradition of moral fiction that flourished in the British 1950s. But during the 1960s the liberative mood that had showed in Amis's earlier work was changing, growing more dangerous, and the task of the critical observer and analyst, the interpreter of manners, becoming harder. This showed in part in the change away from moral fiction and towards more open, random and spontaneous forms of writing, what Philip Roth called a "letting go". Amis's writing had depended on a degree of social certainty as well as a gift for capturing the generational mood, and as the new manners seemed to break away from the old morals Amis's 1960s fiction began to show the strain.

4 Liking it here and wanting it now had been very much Amis's theme; but as the moral intonations of the 1950s gave way to the freer, franker, and often more frantic liberationist attitudes of the 1960s (we can see their price paid in the world of punk, money, success and disgust explored by Martin Amis later), his subject seems to have grown more difficult and elusive. The issue is one he confronts directly in *I Want It Now*, the novel he published in the key year of 1968. Here the hero, Ronnie Appleyard, is a television interviewer, a specialist in contemporary mores, and a self-described

shit who meets an androgynous boy-girl, Simon Quick, at a party. It is the Sixties, she wants it now, and all that seems needed is to gratify the sensual satisfactions indicated by the title. For this the novel shows much sympathy but also much anxiety; this is Amis, and some moral explorations have to be conducted before gratification comes. So, just as *Take a Girl Like You* depends on the principle of procrastinated rape, *I Want It Now* depends on the notion of deferred orgasm. Simon is frigid, and Ronnie seeks a semi-psychological account of the cause. This, in the end, proves to be an overwhelming mother, a female ogre-figure from the familiar Amis stable. This permits Amis to shift the novel into more usual Amis territory, into the world of the darling dodos, in which Ronnie can administer the usual putdowns and commuppances. Moral examination can be conducted before we reach a final mood of reform and renewal, which even affects Ronnie himself. "I was a shit when I met you," Appleyard declares at the close. "I still am in lots of ways. But because of you I've had to give up trying to be a dedicated, full-time shit. I couldn't make it, I hadn't the character. Which is a pity in a way, because when you fall back into the ranks of the failed shits or amateur shits or incidental shits you start taking on responsibility for other people."

In short, Amis ends the book the contemporary moralist, as he always was, trying to capture the temper of the times but also trying to relate it to a conception of decency, responsibility and virtue. So, if his heroes were now becoming less bastard-detectors than bastards themselves, they retained a capacity for self-improvement and permitted the story to provide a moral gratifiction. Amis's heroes from the start had been heroes of prejudice, excused because they are attractive, have history and the spirit of change, as well as the muse of comedy, on their side, and possess the gift for exposing bastards far greater than themselves. Thus it was always possible to embody their preferences, instincts and prejudices in the basic linguistic tone of the book, and make them sound like the voice of a truth. But it seems just to suggest that by the later 1960s Amis was finding it harder to construct convincing contemporary heroes, delineate them with cultural precision, and still give them some moral authority. Ronnie is an apt example. It is the shit in him that makes him continue to pursue Simon after their first hopeless lovemaking, because she is an heiress. This brings him into contact with her family, and lets him shine as a bastard-detector among various tattered lords and neo-fascistic American southerners. The trouble was that, in a tale for the times, the boorish rich no longer appeared particularly potent material for satire, and when Ronnie finally lures Simon's mother onto a television programme and gives her her comeuppance in public the result seems slight and trite, a routine and contingent victory, part of Amis's taste for setting up characters in order to knock them down. What is important in the book is that Amis clearly is seeking, generally, to widen the confines of the social and moral novel, and attempt a new range, one that will capture the flavour of contemporary culture in its fashionable, frantic, elusive turnover. The change in sexual mores is an essential concern, as is the new androgyny represented by Simon Quick, and the use of sex as therapy. But the novel ends not on some strong emotional discovery but in accordance with the familiar habits of comedy, as Ronnie defeats the wicked mother, releases the sleeping beauty, loses the base inheritance but acquires a happy romantic relationship in a conclusion of classic comic and moral shape.

5 In the late 1960s and early 1970s it was hard to see what direction Amis's work was taking, some of his novels, like *I Want It Now* and the later *Girl, 20* (1971) being telling reports on contemporary mores, pointing toward a new kind of book about an age of moral nullity and opportunism, and others testing out a playful variety of modes. Amis now tried detective fiction, briefly assumed the mantle of Ian Fleming to write a James Bond adventure (*Colonel Sun*, 1968), and explored another genre that interested him, science fiction, or what he called "future fiction". But there were books of stronger personal feeling and more powerful vision, the most notable of which is *Ending Up*, a work that brought to the centre of his writing a theme that had long belonged to it, that of the pains of ageing and mortality. The sense of mortal sadness in that novel deepened his work, but the pattern of his early success, where the vernacular of the age yields up values sufficient to construct a vision of it, seemed to elude him more and more. This is one part of the disturbance that seems to afflict *Jake's Thing*, the book in which the sexual moral comedy of his earlier work suddenly goes sour on us. An angry mortality had become part of Amis's central theme, and with it goes a deep sense of the failure of the body to provide its appropriate satisfactions, a vision of lost joy that is answered by rage. If the ageing and fading powers of the hero provide part of the story, so does the revolution in sexual relations which has led less to a general emotional liberation than to the rise of feminism and aggressive and hostile male-female relations. After the mechanical libidinousness and polymorphous perversity of the 1960s comes the feminist revolution of the 1970s, abrogating the effective sexual contract, the love-relation, on which so many of his own earlier novels, like so many of the novels of the past, had been based.

Jake's Thing, a painfully miserable book, is a tale of fundamental sexual manipulations and exploitations, written in what seems a masochistic rage. It is a story of an age of fashionable therapies and chic models of interpersonal relations and group dynamics, of sex-therapies, of Masters and Johnson, of women who can do everything without men, and the shit-hero has turned into the shit-heroine. Jake Richardson, sixty years of age, an Oxford don who also happens to live in London, has had a healthy sexual past, of "more than a hundred women". But now he is suffering from a loss of libido, a word he is not even sure how to pronounce (libeedo? libighdo?), and requires treatment. This leads him through the world of the new behaviourism and the fashionable spirit of sexual engineering – the late 1970s waste land. And Jake is notably *not* in tune with his times. "I don't particularly object to oral sex or anal sex or the rest of the boiling, I just don't enjoy that kind of thing as much as the . . . straightforward stuff," he says. His problem comically causes him to stand trouserless in lecture theatres, study pornography, and have measuring devices attached to the once private parts he loves so well. He is the male chauvinist who has turned from hero into victim, and who sees his world in collapse, as his Oxford college starts to admit women, female roles everywhere change round him, and gentrification hideously transforms the surrounding landscape, while even the buses are driven by Asians. The tone of the book, like that of several of Amis's novels, works two ways: it can be seen as a punishment vested on a presumptuous male chauvinist and a hero of prejudice, but also as a reverse satire, assaulting the modernisation of the world all the way from the social landscape to the bedroom, and to this extent a vindication of Jake and his irritation. Jake is an uncomfortable figure, the shit-hero caught in the bitterness of late life, a bundle of savage prejudices and decencies which are virtually impossible to disentangle tonally, for even the decencies are prejudices, as they always have been. But the lesson of the book is clear: Jakes's lost potency comes not simply from his physical ageing but from the intrusive claims and the modern attitudes of the women themselves; and in this novel Amis turns into a striking, disturbing, splenetic novelist of contemporary male sexual pain and persecution.

There is, of course, no reason why he should not. In an age of female and feminist fictions the raging, pained, felt voice of the male should have its place in return. But the form sounds uncomfortable in the work of the writer who had once celebrated women as nicer than men and who had made the commonplace world of sexual relations the basis of a moral feeling. These difficulties return in *Stanley and the Women* (1984), a novel which deals with a sequence of darkly troubling events which suddenly overtake the life of the central character, the obscure Stanley Duke, an advertising manager for a tabloid newspaper, who is confronted with the madness of a teenage son who thinks he is being watched and programmed by strange cosmic powers. Stanley, twice married, but living now in Amis's late-life world where males drink themselves stupefied in order *not* to be sexually possessed by their women, finds himself an accused victim. His son's schizophrenia is first treated by chemo-therapy, but then it passes into the hands of a woman psychologist who treats the family as the cause, and Stanley is placed in the role of the guilty father. The women in Stanley's life all seem to betray him, and appear not as comically incomprehensible figures but an actively malign force. In one passage Stanley turns to a male psychologist for help, asking if all women are mad? No, the psychologist tells him, they are terrifying and logically sane in their use, and misuse, of the male. It is clear from the tone that this is no simple moral comeuppance vested on an old lothario overproud of past sexual victories. Both these books, in their way disturbing in their open truth, are explorations of the dark punishments women eventually impose on male sexuality, as well as on the loss of joy and the emptying of meaning that has come when behaviourism and commercial modernity have come along to displace, and replace, a more deeply felt human culture. Both seem to expose rather than interpret the pain they display, as the moral world seems to dissolve before unreason.

These are powerful books, striking because of their edge of pain and their sense of cultural disorder. Their theme is strong in modern fiction, for instance in Ford Madox Ford's Tietjens tetralogy, where the man of honour from the old world, the man who would not, finds that world corrupted by sexual treachery and brought to collapse. A similar fate befalls Waugh's hero of prejudice and hopeful virtue, Guy Crouchback, who in the *Sword of Honour* trilogy goes off to fight for the chivalric virtues he hopes quixotically to maintain, only to find that the war's purposes are corrupt and women themselves help corrupt it. The image of perverted sexual relations has been a powerful one in modern fiction, a key figure for the way in the modern world the attempt to sustain history as innocence and virtue collapse, virtue grows stained, and moral purpose is defeated. Amis's later fiction thus seems to have taken a familiar if terrible shape, toward a late-life vision of cultural emptiness, sexual corruption, and mortal exposure; the world promised by Jim Dixon, the world of commonsense taking its victory over pretension and hypocrisy, and social clarity over social falsehood, has not done well, and moral competence can no longer be sustained. Yet the naked frankness and force remain, to remind us that Amis is one of our most disturbing contemporary novelists, an explorer of historical pain. In these two novels the pain does not acquire the largeness of a vision, but in *The Old Devils* (1986) the theme is extended, and indeed this novel is surely the best of his late books.

The story of a group of retired middle-class couples living a notably drink-soaked existence amid the pleasant landscapes and modernised miseries of contemporary Wales, *The Old Devils* returns to the more complex feeling of *Ending Up*, and even carries something of the joy of the earlier books, for these are ageing versions of Amis's young characters of the 1950s, a time to which they look back. It is not entirely an easy read, the boredoms of ageing and Wales being heavy, sometimes banal material, which even the famous Amis vernacular cannot always stir into joy. But the writing is spirited, the language attentive, and the subject considerably felt; while the now very familiar Amis tricks – the elaborate putdowns and comeuppances, the large bursts of rhetorical complaint, about the modernness of the modern world and the awful youth of the young – take their place in an inclusive vision. Amis chooses to tell his story not from the standpoint of one single male hero but from several angles, and *The Old Devils* is, perhaps as befits its Welsh setting, unusually choric. This is a tired and contingent world; for the couples, sex has virtually died, marriages are hostile, egotism prevails, the body is a trouble. Drinking starts early, if it ever really ceases; few novels are as washed in wine and spirits. The men gather daily for their "Bible" session at the Bible and Crown, the local pub; the women gather in each other's homes to pull the cork on the first bottle of Soave and begin the day. Drink opens up the voices, which grouse, complain, hold the floor, or otherwise upstage. Their speeches deal with Welsh pretentiousness, the vulgar tastelessness of modern improvement, the ruination of town and landscape, the misbehaviour of the young. Behind all this sounds the chatty Amis vernacular, making the characters sound a communality of voices speaking against the banality of the world, which lies over most things.

The banal, troubled couples are stirred to life by the return of two of their former number – Alun Weaver, a successful media Welshman and a local lothario, and his wife Rhiannon, with whom two of the men have been in love. Between them they stir up the old emotions, past glimpses of joy and error, the remnants of past feeling. All this Amis recreates with loving care and a strong map of emotion, the woman characters as strongly felt as the men. The mannered rage against the modern world is mediated and made part of the sadness of what has been lost, and the present even summons up some striking notes of moral maturity in several of the characters. Wales itself becomes less a comic issue than a state of mind that has to be accepted, and the story comes to a compacted, symbolically appropriate, even hopeful end. This troubling but strong book contains the most painful kind of anger, against the mortal human condition itself, for which none of us has the cure. The Angry Young Man may feel like a Bitter Old One, the moral seriousness of the early novels open to defeat; but his writing can still contain a moral desire, a sharp, self-challenging honesty. Amis remains one of our most troubling comic novelists, still directing his assault on the way we live now, and on the pain, the self-enclosure, but also sometimes the secret joy, of ageing life itself.

THE NOVEL AS PASTICHE
Angus Wilson and modern fiction

"There was nothing for it, Gladys thought, but to make them laugh. After all, she'd suggested the mirrors, so she couldn't let them spoil the afternoon. But when she saw herself she was too disconcerted to speak. 'Look,' Sukey cried, 'Gladys is upside down.' And so it proved – at the top of the glass, white boots in reverse; at the base, a plump face grown red with surprise. They all at last could laugh. To keep the fun going Gladys stood on her head on the shiny, linoleum floor . . . ."

Angus Wilson, No Laughing Matter (1967)

"How can we combine caring with shaping?"

Angus Wilson, in an interview (1977)

1 In 1983, when Sir Angus Wilson celebrated his seventieth birthday, a very large party was held – most suitably, for he is a novelist of large parties – in the unusual but appropriate setting of the London Zoo. Wilson's novels frequently begin with large lists of dramatis personae, the repertory of a very social novelist with surreal inclinations. So *No Laughing Matter* announces as its additional cast "Husbands, wives, lovers of various kinds, university teachers, and undergraduates, Russians, members of Society, politicians, journalists, members of Lloyds' and the Bloomsbury Group, Cockneys, German refugees, staffs of preparatory schools, English residents abroad, Egyptians, actors and actresses, Moroccans, financiers, Scandinavians, and representatives of the Younger Generation". The guest-list of the zoo party seemed calculated to prove that such exotic communities really do exist, not only in fiction but in real life. And to them were added the friends and acquaintances of a central literary lifetime – famous writers and famous critics, fellow-novelists and fellow-knights, fellow-Dickensians and fellow-Powysians, fellow-biographers accompanied by autobiographers, fellow reviewers and fellow literary journalists, fellow men-of-letters and literary hostesses, publishers and poets, gay couples of both sexes, radio reporters and

television directors and a camera crew or two. They were making a television film that summer of *The Old Men at the Zoo*, Wilson's most apocalyptic novel, about Britain in a time of nuclear holocaust, and about the strange parallelism between human and animal nature, set in this very same zoo. Everything colluded with Wilson's troubled story, including the weather that evening. As the party started thunder cracked and torrential rain fell, the animals and birds in their cages began to chatter and scream; and the guests fled indoors, adding to the screams from the animal enclosures the party screams of human social life.

Parties in Wilson's books are usually troublesome. In *Hemlock and After* (1952), Wilson's brilliant first novel, there is the opening party at Vardon Hall, where an eminent Man of Letters who also remains an Enfant Terrible, Bernard Sands, watches a "general crumbling of good manners and a lifting of emotional lids", and finally sees the event, the culmination of several troubling weeks, turn into "a tapestry of obscene horror". Thirty years on, Wilson himself was now both Enfant Terrible and eminent Man of Letters; happily his party was not a Wilsonian rout but a social success, a mark of the high recognition that belonged to one of the great figures of our age. For, when we consider the tiny handful of recent British writers who can be claimed as major, as of long-term importance and lasting representativeness, then Angus Wilson is clearly one. To many of us he stands as the most developed and impressive novel-writer of his generation, the generation that follows on after James Joyce, Virginia Woolf, Evelyn Waugh, Graham Greene, Anthony Powell and Ivy Compton-Burnett, and made its mark after World War Two – a writer who carries an enormous substance in his work, has produced some of our bulkiest and socially most solid fictions, who has expanded extraordinarily from the witty, economical brilliance of his sharp and often malicious early stories to become, in books like *Anglo-Saxon Attitudes* (1965), *The Middle Age of Mrs Eliot* (1958) and *No Laughing Matter* (1967), a novelist of extended historical and human scope. He has brought alive the possibility of a substantial, a compassionate modern fiction of moral urgency and historical power; he has humanistically re-activated the tradition of the past, so that to read him is to feel the force of what great past novelists from Jane Austen to Dostoevsky might pass on to a true contemporary. He has also lived a central cultural life as a social observer and a critic, worked indefatigably in the interests of writing generally, and been in the broadest sense a modern Man of Letters, his vision and his interventions in literary life having central importance for his fellow-writers and of course his readers.

Wilson is unmistakably a key figure for us. But that said, it must also be observed that his high reputation is very mixed in its basis, and founded on a wide variety of different judgements, different *kinds* of judgement. And nearly every critic who has written on him has felt an ambiguity of perspective and emphasis in his writings, seeing this either as part of his creative power or part of the confusion his books can sow in their readers. Wilson has encouraged this sense of ambiguity, pointing for example to that "fierce sadism and a compen- sating gentleness" which leads to a very mixed view of his characters, to his sense of the dual nature of all action, which may be both morally competent but also self-gratifying, and to his awareness of the strange personal obsessions that drive and compel any writer. The ambiguity of *all* writing is something he has reflected on, both in his powerful biographies of writers, Zola, Dickens, Kipling, and his comments on his own work in the splendid self-analysis of *The Wild Garden, Or Speaking of Writing* (1963), one of the frankest books about creativity and composition we have by a modern British writer. Knowledge of writing as both self-justifying and counterfeit is quite common in modern literature, but it is clear that Wilson possesses it. This leads toward the strange positional insecurities that many readers have found in his work, especially perhaps in more recent novels like the highly pastiched *No Laughing Matter*. Those who see his work as predominantly a realistic fiction of social range and moral maturity have this aspect of his writing to come to terms with; those who think of him as a textual experimentalist have to acknowledge that he is a writer of moral power, that his work possesses a striking and singular moral maturity. Yet to overlook the self-doubt and self-mockery would be to overlook something essential, something that helps us understand him as modern.

One way to consider this is in the light of comedy; Wilson is a great comic writer, but a writer of a very protean kind. For his American namesake Edmund Wilson it was evident where Wilson stood – as the natural successor to Evelyn Waugh, the devastating satirist of his time and his class, the malicious and sharp-edged analyst of postwar Britain. *Hemlock and After*, his first novel, is a brilliant work of liberal moral analysis. Bernard Sands has progressed from *enfant terrible* to moral scourge: "If he had forced from the public and the critics respect and hearing for his eternal questioning of their best-loved 'truths', he must never allow them to feel they were indulging the court jester. They should continue to take from him exactly the pill they did not like, and take it without any danger of whimsy." We can feel the author behind this, but Wilson is also the moral scourge of a moral scourge, going on to observe: "If on occasion he mistrusted his own powers, it was not a mistrust he intended others to share." Wilson has a gift for multiplying ironies, and is capable of establishing that morality and humanism can arise from impure motives and psychological inconsistencies. This he does by establishing a narrative tone that contains equal parts of moral wisdom and toughness – the kind of thing that Jane Austen and George Eliot give to the British novel – and something quite close to malice. The moral toughness brings out responsibility and self-knowledge; the malice suggests something puppet-like, theatrical and absurd in all our actions. And this is one reason why Wilson's apparently very realistic and substantial novels, moral comedies of contemporary life, often dissolve somewhat as we read them into a distinctive kind of modern grotesque, one that suggests an unusual set of perceptions about our social and human nature. It points in its way toward humanism, moral duty, the need to follow the path to clarity of vision and truth; it points also toward an emptiness at the centre of all human action, manifested in the persisting theatricality which informs it. Life is a role or a performance, society a theatre, the masks and disguises are always there and irrevocable. The selves we try to live truthfully with are counterfeit, and this situation touches the novelist too, who is at once both a moralist and a comic mimic, apeing the persistent grotesqueries of life.

Wilson is often seen as the prototypical postwar British novelist, and in many ways his career serves as a central example of many of the preoccupations and directions of the contemporary British novel. There is the sense of tradition, which is in some ways that famous great tradition, the tradition of the social and moral novel. The comparisons here lay somewhere between George Eliot and Dickens, and his comedy has qualities that refer back to both. Yet there is also throughout his work, and intensifying in the later books, a decided questioning, both moral and technical, of just that sort of novel. Wilson has remarked himself that the social novel has often gained its solidity at the expense of psychological depth, and that a modern novelist cannot ignore those psychological depths: "We are on the threshold of a psychology for which the older novel forms do not provide," he once said. Any account of Wilson's importance and influence, any description of the way he seems to shape a significant postwar direction in British writing, has to come to terms with this consciousness, his clear awareness of the moral uncertainty of the novelist in an age when the power of unconscious motive is accepted, and when neurotic, disordered and perverse experience has to take its place near the centre of fiction. Wilson's own changes of direction as a novelist, his shifting of allegiances, has had to do with this; if he possesses a good deal of the repertory of the traditional novelist, he has also persistently engaged himself against those forces in modern British writing that make traditionalism into the safe haven for literary and moral nostalgia. From the start there was a tonal revolt in his writing; over time it has intensified. His later books, like those of many of our best writers who began to write in the 1950s, have been a kind of quarrel with their own condition, an exploration of the troubled spirit of the serious novel in contemporary Britain.

2 British fiction since the war has had a strange relationship with the novel of the past, acknowledging it, using it, parodying it, and, from deeply changed historical circumstances, quarrelling with it. In the case of Angus Wilson, the troubling and apparently intensely mischievous writer of the early stories was soon to become intensely reassuring. The large and panoramic novels he wrote during the 1950s and early 1960s seemed clear in their allusion to the nineteenth-century heritage, calling up again for modern use the powers of fiction variously practised by Jane Austen and George Eliot, Charles Dickens and Fyodor Dostoevsky. In particular Wilson seemed to acknowledge the force of the socio-moral tradition of fiction, the line concerned with the moral life in society, and to bring that critical and humanistic lineage that came through Jane Austen and into E.M. Forster to the condition of postwar uncertainty. Like other writers at the time, he declared his dispute with modernism, and its use of interior monologue and aestheticised form, and asked for a fiction of "external observation, social setting, character set firmly in narrative and scene". He wrote appreciatively of many writers in this tradition; he praised, in a 1958 article, "Diversity and Depth", the attempt of a number of postwar writers to restore "that social framework in which human hopes and despairs must be viewed if duty and responsibility or defiance of duty and responsibility are to have full meaning". He has always created his characters as members of society, and society as a dense and historically specific web in which we are all involved. His may seem a selective society, typically upper or upper middle class, vaguely intellectual, decidedly stylish; but he has constantly sought to expand it, socially and geographically, and his later *As If By Magic* (1973) is a profoundly ambitious attempt at a global novel.

He also powerfully displays a key feature of this tradition, its controlling moral concern. He is unmistakable in his tough-minded attention to moral awareness and responsibility, and at times unsparing in his satirical power of moral exposure. Even as he relishes his world for its stylishness and flamboyance, he measures and judges it according to an ironic comic rule. And, as in Forster, the irony is specifically directed to what can be called a humanist centre, showing up self-deceit and hypocrisy in the realm of personal relations, moral and emotional atrophy. If, as Ian Scott-Kilvert tells us, his prime aims are satiric and his targets "the facade of middle-class values and manners, the hollowness of the respectability, the decorum and the apparently 'progressive' virtues which can mask hypocrisy, meanness, immaturity exhibited to a pathological degree, and above all cruelty", then that indicates a central concern we can all recognise, a liberal-radical spirit we cannot miss, speaking for tolerance, sanity and individual decency against the powers of deception.

This appeared to place him as part of the revolt against modernism that belonged to the 1950s, and in his essay "Diversity and Depth" he seemed to put this allegiance very clearly: "No sharpening of visual image, no increased sensibility, no deeper penetration of the individual consciousness, whether by verbal experiment or Freudian analysis, could fully atone for the frivolity of ignoring man as a social being, for treating personal relationships and subjective sensations in a social void," he said of his modernist and Bloomsbury predecessors. But Wilson was to repudiate some of this later, and the view never did quite encompass his full quality, as he said himself. "That I have . . . been interested in writing novels about man in society in a decade when some other English novelists have been laying stress on the social novel, has perhaps associated my novels with theirs, but the connection seems to me very flimsy," he wrote in *The Wild Garden*, where he also acknowledged the role played by the unbidden, the unresolved, and the pressure of unspoken psychological needs, in the process of fiction-making. In 1951 he challenged the attempt to return to "the great tradition", complaining of the over-tempting role the conventional middlebrow novel, about "the same world, the comical, jogtrot, not too bad, awfully plucky old world that novelists have been portraying for the last hundred years", was playing in current fiction. When he wrote on Dickens, he portrayed a radically different, vastly more troubled Dickens than the figure who had taken his place with *Hard Times* in Leavis's Great Tradition. An article on John Cowper Powys, whom he greatly admires (I do not entirely share the admiration), complained of the "deplorable tendency to identify the novel's purpose with some kind of 'felt' sociology", and in writing to Rubin Rabinowitz, who was compiling his book *The Reaction Against Experiment in the English Novel, 1950–1960* (1967), and was to identify Wilson as "one of the most devoted exponents of traditionalism in fiction on the contemporary English scene", he remarked: "I think my position has been greatly modified, even strongly changed by my own development as a novelist – my feeling that the traditional form was inhibiting me from saying all I wanted to say."

As he said himself, then, there was indeed a struggle in his writing between "diversity" and "depth" – "diversity" having to do with traditional narrative skills and the powers of storytelling, "depth" to do with the realisation of psychological intensity, a power required of great modern writing. This pressure became ever clearer in his fiction, some of it directly dealing with the relationship between traditional literary meanings and understandings and modern life-crises. In *The Middle Age of Mrs Eliot* (1958), Meg Eliot is a devoted serious reader who finds herself cast into a world where the great expectations afforded by literature no longer function. In *Late Call* (1964), Sylvia Calvert, a former servant girl living in a blank modern New Town, finds the anodyne fictions she reads no longer serve her: "the great comforting engulfing whale of fiction seemed now to have died on her, so that she looked through its ribs into nothingness; and even that skeleton was decaying into dust from which nothing more came to her than the sweet sickly smell of romantic fantasy." Wilson seems to suggest that old fictions cannot tell the truth about our changed and more grotesque world; this seems to have had to do with the surreal, grotesque mode he took for *The Old Men at the Zoo* (1961) and the pastiche techniques of *No Laughing Matter* (1967), a form of the modern self-examining novel.

There were other reasons why the authority of fiction was ambiguous. In *The Wild Garden* he reflects interestingly on storytelling as deception, remarking on his early discovery that one advantage of telling tales was to exert charm, and win attention and success. "All fiction for me is a kind of magic and trickery – a confidence trick, trying to make people believe something is true that isn't," he told his interviewer in the *Writers At Work* interview (1957). This view of fiction as trick and counterfeit is, of course, ancient; but it has had major claims in modern and modernist thought. What Wilson chose to emphasise was the relation of storytelling to mimicry and clowning, and also to the unbidden and the unconscious. "The general relation of my life to the themes of my work is perhaps more apparent than in many authors," he tells any potential biographer helpfully in *The Wild Garden*, "for I started to write at the age of thirty-six and in unconscious response, I believe, to a definite crisis to which my earlier years had steadily moved." The obscure powers of fiction have long concerned Wilson. His fictional characters often possess awareness of them, depending upon, and telling, stories, and sustaining an often mannered, self-mimicking tone which suggests a mixture of intense self-knowledge and camp self-deceit.

So do the books in which they appear, books which offer themselves as at once realism and magical invention, mimesis and trickery. The result is a texture famously hard to read, a texture mixed from traditional and modern elements, from realism's objectivity and fantasy's subjectivity, from moral exactitude and playful mimicry. If Wilson is pre-eminently a "social" novelist, he is harder to accept entirely on that plane than many of his contemporaries, and there is always something intensely self-critical in his manner. Criticism has shown the contradiction, sometimes seeing him as the exemplary modern liberal humanist writer, creator of what Anthony Burgess calls "the contemporary novel of the middle way", sometimes as a writer of very high extravagance. As Wilson himself has emphasised, the social novelist can have another side. Thus he told Frank Kermode: " . . . there is a great deal of what you call the George Eliot approach. But above all that, and mixed with it, and perhaps swirling it around and distorting it . . ., is a great lump of a kind of Dickensianism . . . . I have got this – how can I say it? – this grand guignol side. I am sure that I have in my character strong sadistic impulses which do come out in my books . . . ".

About this "grand guignol" side Wilson has been very explicit, especially in his remarkable study of Dickens, *The World of Charles Dickens* (1970), and various essays about him. "The intense haunting of my imagination by scenes and characters from Dickens's novels has continued and developed into my middle age," he wrote in "Charles Dickens: A Haunting", adding that he is aware not so much of the wholeness of Dickens's novels as parts of them, of "an atmosphere and scene which are always determinedly fragmentary". Dickens's social vision was, of course, notably different from that of most of his contemporaries; society does different things to his characters and gives them different natures. Raymond Williams has helped explain this; Dickens's characters, he said, "speak at or past each other, each intent above all on defining through his words his own identity and reality; in fixed self-descriptions, in voices raised emphatically to be heard through and past other similar voices". Character is presented through a kind of flattening, a self-dramatisation which is also a powerful simplification; the characters by strange interaction construct a striking and extreme society in which the social and the psychological are locked together. The comic method composes a world both familiar and alien, lifelike and distorted, containing evil and nightmare as well as benevolence and community. Wilson notes how Dickens's "unspoken atmosphere" is made up of wanderings, imprisonments and flights, of disguises, theatrical deceptions and false-seeming. Society is vividly here, but not in George Eliot's way: the world is a strange and unreal city, creating distortion and stress, atomisation and social fragility, miming and exaggeration. The point of the method is to release energy and invention, generate fable, and explore the texture of cultural feeling. Dickens is less a novelist of sure moral poise than an extraordinary inventor, and a good deal of Wilson's work falls in with this tradition – where judgement functions not as a classical irony but as a sense of generalised human feeling, and flamboyance and theatricality are fundamental features of the writing.

What is striking about Wilson's work is that both of these two traditions are there, and co-exist. The analytic and ironic moralist is evident, but so is the writer of running inventiveness, the mimer and player. In places the ironic mode of Jane Austen seems dominant, as in *Hemlock and After* and *The Middle Age of Mrs Eliot*, though even here we are sometimes asked to apply the test of moral realism to characters whose reality is in doubt. We seem to observe a telling flaw of character, a quality of cruelty or snobbery, which is there for excoriation; we then find it the material of delighted invention. We see the bondage of the family, the endless wars of parents and children, husbands and wives, and they seem to be charged with the sins of selfishness and lovelessness; but then they also appear as the actual stuff of all existence, which is universal exploitation. In political judgements, Wilson seems persistently progressive, condemning snobbery and class values against the standard of tolerance and egalitarianism. But here again the attitude is elusive. The world of equality and welfare statism, the New Town world of *Late Call* for example, may be historically realised but it has little flavour of regeneration about it, and if Wilson at times writes like a radical humanist he also is one of our sharpest observers of the dulled communitarianism and the bureaucratic managerialism of the welfare state world.

Much the same uncertainty attaches to Wilson's fictional technique. In keeping with this method as a social novelist, he has normally used the method of traditional omniscience to present his fiction as a realistic narrative. "In *Hemlock and After* and *Anglo-Saxon Attitudes* I chose quite naturally the 'God's eye view' in frequent use among the nineteenth-century novelists I admire. I was surprised to find how unfamiliar this had now become; indeed, in the United States it had to be explained as a revival (I am glad to say successful) of an archaic form," he observed in "The Novelist and the Narrator" (1961). It has of course been the most commonplace form of contemporary British fiction, especially for comedy and satire, but Wilson generally uses it very openly and freely, moving from character to character, seeing through many eyes, presenting extended sections of exposition, and allowing himself acerbic moral points and judgements; more precise technicians might find this random. This allows Wilson a characteristic place within his mock-theatre of fiction, acting, presenting, lighting, directing.

Yet this secure God-like manager is granted many insecurities of his own, and these have increased considerably in later novels. Similarly that note of verisimilitude so essential to realism has been opened to question, allowing a large intrusion of fictional self-consciousness. Perhaps we need two (at least) Angus Wilsons for our critical reaction to him. One is the writer of liberal realism and great moral power and seriousness, exposing the pain and muddle of our class history and our present progressive illusions; the other is the writer of a more extravagant and freely inventive disposition, often distinctively experimental, and growing more so as his career has developed. Realistic and estranged, mixing mimesis and comic pastiche, his fiction seems to carry the tensions of much postwar British writing as it sought to relate the half-broken tradition of the past to the needs and pressures of a difficult present.

3 Wilson's writing is very much that of our time. He began his work as the war ended – he dates the start in November 1946 – and it grew in part from emotional and psychological upsets, as well as the changing social flavours, that belonged to the period itself. The stories he published over the next years in various magazines made him into the new era's sharpest and most satirical chronicler, and publication of these stories in the two collections nicely titled *The Wrong Set* (1949) and *Such Darling Dodos* (1950) (there was a later story collection, *A Bit Off the Map*, 1957) settled his reputation as the voice of the new generation. It was a powerful debut, all the more unusual for being made in short fiction, a form with which British writers rarely make their reputations. But his stood out for several reasons. One was that he seemed to speak both for the virtues and the contradictions of an era of revived liberalism, drawing somewhat on Forster and Orwell for his spirit, but expressing it with a modern sharpness a good deal closer to Evelyn Waugh. They were mood stories, splendid period vignettes, a wonderfully cunning portfolio of a declining upper middle class caught just as their time was running out but their vitality was far from spent. To Edmund Wilson the inheritance from Waugh had clearly passed on to a writer of unusual sharpness who had caught the spirit of a rare social struggle: "In this struggle, though they keep up certain forms, [the characters] are always jeering and jabbing: they do not flinch from frank hatchet work. They all dislike one another, and the author dislikes the lot." Even if this was not quite true (there are odd glimpses of characters who are morally favoured), it catches the spirit in which his early work was received. For these were indeed stories where social dislocation and dispossession is a haunting theme, change is everywhere in the

air; and nowhere in modern British letters has the cry of social impoverishment been quite so shrilly sounded.

At the same time Wilson was also a devastating explorer of the postwar world itself, with its uncertainties of intellectual direction, its mood of cultural confusion and historical disorientation. Thus the stories in the two volumes collectively captured a good deal of the history of the period through from the 1930s and across wartime, their social satire infused with a strong historical and cultural awareness; it was appropriate that one of them was titled "A Story of Historical Interest". It was, like many Wilson titles, very ironic indeed – a tiny moment that can seemingly be dismissed into the past acquires an intense historical approriateness. The sharp personal bite of the tales somehow gave the flavour of a central social process, a change of feeling and life-manners that went from the bourgeois *rentier* anxieties to the pre-war period into wartime's enforced democracy and then on into the austere and bureaucratic spirit of postwar life, when the bourgeoisie found themselves displaced persons and sounded their rage ("It was of course true that this sort of thing [lesbianism] was on the increase and Trevor said it was the ruin of England, but then he said that about so many things – Jews and foreigners, the Labour government and the ballet" ("The Wrong Set")). They drew clearly enough on the milieux of their author's own life – the a-little-bit-down-at-the-heel-but-still-trying-to-keep-up-appearances hotel world of his childhood, the professional and governmental institutions in which he had worked (the story "Real-politik", for example), the tweedy progressive intelligentsia who had left their Thirties causes but felt they had a new part to play in the socialist welfare state world.

Wilson eyed them all with a mocking sympathy, a half-involved satirical delight; the very title stories of the two volumes spoke directly to the new social and moral confusion. In "The Wrong Set" a young man goes to London and finds himself caught between two environments, one the seedy nightclub scene where the raffish, enraged petty bourgeoisie, like Trevor, gather, the other a Fabian pacifist household: which is the right set? Wilson's sympathies here are clearly on the "progressive" side, but in "Such Darling Dodos" matters are more ambiguous, with both the old Toryism and the spirit of Thirties progressivism set into ironic juxtaposition. Wilson has a liberal sympathy with change, but his taste is not exactly for the heroes of the flattened postwar world. Indeed his stories raise moral issues without creating predictable moral solutions, and this has a great deal to do with their devastating tone. We catch occasional glimpses of virtue, a feeling for a world that might be moved away from hypocrisy and illusion toward truth and decency – as in the possibility of homosexual friendship displayed in "Et Dona Ferentes", the hopeful release from the entrapping mother in "Mother's Sense of Fun", or error corrected in "A Flat Country Christmas". Wilson said himself that most of the stories are about "cherished illusion" that might be overcome by frankness, decency and unselfishness. Yet the moral note is a little bit sharper, and the "cherished illusions" have a more unusual role.

This is apparent in Wilson's very first story, "Raspberry Jam", where the two eccentric elderly sisters, who appear so "odd, fantastic, and highly coloured" to the young boy's eyes, are in one sense unmasked, but in another colluded with; illusions may be necessary. In "Fresh Air Fiend", Miss Eccles, the fiend of the title, determines to assist Professor Searle, whose wife has turned into a neurotic grotesque, by devoting herself to unmasking the truth, and so letting "a breath of fresh air into a very foetid atmosphere". The truth produces not release but breakdown; the irony turns against the truthteller herself. Wilson is very capable, in fact, of delighting in his moral grotesques, and reacting against those who oppose them. He gives us both the malicious power and the curious camp charm of his old illusionists – the sponging fathers, the ageing and raddled hostesses, the plucky widows and raffish old sports, the smooth bureaucrats and the liberal progressives – who may outrage us, but take on a strange obsessive splendour, enriched by Wilson's gifts of mimicry. They are well-trained survivors of old struggles, and though they look back in nostalgia they have never been secure. "Frightful" they may be, but Wilson animates frightfulness with a histrionic delight, until what we feel is not the need for their reform but the skilful complexity of their grotesque manners and gifts for distortion and exploitation. In fact, in these hard, cunning and clever stories, usually turned on some sharp social contrast, we can find a very protean spirit of comedy, made partly from the energies of moral satire and partly from an engaged fascination with oddity and psychic distortion.

This hard, analytic and observant tone, alert with a sense of the social flavours of the time, Wilson carried over into his first novel, *Hemlock and After*, written in a four-week leave from the British Museum, and still one of his most rigorous and economical books. It is a classic novel about the fate of liberalism; again, though, the bite is a mixture of sharp moral assessment and delight in the grotesque, as if the spirit of Jane Austen had met the world of Ronald Firbank. The book is set in the summer of 1951, in a cold-war mood, and against an atmosphere of mounting world crisis which is steadily cracking "the uneasy paste of hope and optimism of which so much confidence is compounded". This corresponds to and colludes with the moral crisis and the rising awareness of evil, both outer and inner, which begins to erode the life and beliefs of the eminent liberal humanist at the centre of the book, the writer Bernard Sands, fifty-seven and at the peak of his success. He has just won a liberal victory against "authority" by acquiring unconditional government sponsorship to start a colony of young writers at Vardon Hall, only to find that this requires that he take on the mantle of authority himself. Gradually he is forced to recognise "the dual nature of all human action", as his own sense of moral virtue is challenged. A "growing apprehension of evil" begins to disrupt his portrait of the world, and when he sees a young homosexual arrested for importuning in Leicester Square he finds he shares the "hunter's thrill": "A humanist, it would seem, was more at home with the wielders of the knout and the rubber truncheon." Having judged the Tory complacency, moral neutralism, and psycho-pathological decadence of others, he finds their equivalents in himself. But if the book is an ironic moral comedy about the dangers of leading the moral life, it is also about the dangers of *not* leading it – of living, as Hubert Rose does, only by "despairs and desires", or by adopting Celia Craddock's "life-loving" view ("If life, in fact, had proved too big for her moral values, she had at least proved as big as life itself by setting them aside"). In this hard, exacting moral comedy there can be no victories, and Bernard fails, but at a high testing point. The object of irony, he is also treated with compassion, and that cunning balance was to become the mark of Wilson's writing in the much more socially ambitious novels that were to follow.

Wilson's next book, *Anglo-Saxon Attitudes*, was to take on the large characteristics of much of his following work: a big cast of characters, an extended historical action, and a sense of dealing with the primary moral contradictions of British behaviour: "He's an Anglo-Saxon Messenger – and those are Anglo-Saxon attitudes. He only does them when he's happy," runs the splendid epigraph from *Through the Looking Glass* that Wilson seizes on for his title. Evidently the moral instincts of Anglo-Saxondom will be a potent theme, and Wilson has much to say here about the relationship between public and private morality, and about the ambiguity of the puritanical sense of British virtue. The moral theme that so much concerned the 1950s is itself heavily tested: "You take up something where somebody's in the wrong and make an arbitary decision about the goats and the sheep and then start making moral noises," says Elvira Portway. "It's just an English parlour game . . . and what's so *ghastly* is that it's got into our literature." "Moral noises" sound throughout the novel, generating a crisis of moral ambiguity that engages not just with the life-crisis of the central character, Gerald Middleton, a retired professor of history who is forced to re-examine his own sense of truth and decency, but the British sense of tradition itself.

In the fable of the novel, built around various historical and emotional falsifications, a crucial one is an archaeological fraud which suggests a rather more priapic past for the founding fathers of the church than is generally allowed. Middleton himself we meet as a man killed by compromise, "a failure with a conscience", who has "no right to judge", but is now forced to face his own inertia, and acknowledge that both as a family man and a historian he has given way to easy self-deceit. One notable feature of the book is that Gerald is a hero who grows in the course of the narrative, acquiring moral insight and a position beyond illusion from the testing experiences he suffers. Wilson's next novels were increasingly to be focused around heroes – and yet more strikingly round heroines – who have the potential for self-discovery and the insight to grasp the difference between the false and the true paths of life. Wilson, who observed that he "still feels that there is a sense of something real under the social surface", is thus able to grant Gerald a place modestly beyond illusion at the end of the book.

As some critics noted, this increased moral seriousness required some muting of Wilson's harsher satirical powers, if in the interests of a deeper sense of life. This was to grow clearer in Wilson's next novel, *The Middle Age of Mrs Eliot*, a novel of severe feeling which nonetheless must hold a place among Wilson's very best books. The story of Meg Eliot, who has to rebuild the entire social and moral basis of her life when her husband is accidently killed in a terrorist incident at a foreign airport, is a tale both unsparing and notably compassionate, perhaps Wilson's most thoughtful mediation of the mode of moral realism which has always drawn him but does not clearly characterise all his work. If this is the book where Wilson's satire and sense of free and flamboyant invention are kept most in check, this allows him to express a sense of measured and mature affirmation. At the same time it is a comment on the kind of literature it is, and above all on the "great tradition" of moral literature. The heroine's name, Meg Eliot, seems laden with literary overtones, and her nature as a character owes much to those heroines from Anne Elliot to Dorothea Brooke or Isabel Archer whose task it is to confront life's variousness and complexity and come to terms with it. Meg is an avid reader who makes such comparisons, with Maggie Tulliver and Emma Wood-house, and her author clearly calls up such literary comparisons to set both a standard and a contrast for her judgement of life. "I wouldn't be interested in novels if I wasn't interested in real people," Meg declares, defending the novel's *vraisemblance* – to be answered by her brother with another, academically familiar view: "A narrow conception of the art of the novel . . . that would receive short shrift from any literary critic." Wilson's sympathies lie evidently enough with Meg, but the point of the book is that the conceptions of life and moral maturity Meg takes from her novels hardly meet the pressures of contemporary life, anarchic history, current evil. As with *Don Quixote*, the old books cannot quite be true to life, and Wilson draws on their imprint not to reconstruct them as they were but as a new book of life now must be, which is essentially something different, made of modern truth.

The Middle Age of Mrs Eliot may properly be called a work of contemporary moral realism, a kind of skilled rewriting within the tradition Wilson at this time was affirming. This makes it all the more interesting that he followed it with *The Old Men at the Zoo*, which mixes the dystopian futurism of Orwell with an extraordinary capacity for surreal fantasy. Set in the future at a time when the sense of European conflict present in most of Wilson's fiction boils up into nuclear war, the book – which seemed eccentric to Wilson' work at the time, but does not since – concerns itself with the need for the contemporary imagination to face violence, evil and terror, as an aspect not simply of exterior political events but of inward animal nature. In the face of such a vision the liberal competence to maintain judgement and decency is brought to an extreme edge. Though quite consistent with the running themes of Wilson's work, and above all with his concern with the evil in the world to which humanistic values offer us thin guidance, the book also made it clear that Wilson did not feel at all bound by the limits of the social and moral realistic novel, even though its imprint is still visible in the way the story is told, and was seeking to widen its boundaries and escape its familiarising and conventionalising habits (and his literary criticism at this time confirms as much). It is relevant too that the book was published at the beginning of the 1960s, when there was a considerable change occurring in the texture of fiction; the same year, for example, saw the publication of Doris Lessing's *The Golden Notebook*, a novel that remarkably breaks open the frame and assumptions of the serious romantic novel its author so evidently admires.

When Wilson came back, then, to a more familiar kind of fiction with *Late Call* he was ready to bring to the task a kind of bravura that would give to his second novel about a heroine forced to encounter the troubled realities of the world a flavour rather different from that of *The Middle Age of Mrs Eliot*. Partly it is that this is a novel seen from the level of commonplace life, its central character a servant girl who becomes a hotel-keeper and then a resident in a modern New Town. The book starts by undercutting the safe sentimental world of the everlasting Edwardian summer which has so often served as base-camp for modern British fiction, and which is in several of Wilson's novels the starting point for his version of twentieth-century English social and moral history. Sylvia Calvert, the heroine, has grown up in a world where the dominant images all conflict with the actualities of her existence. She too has been given fictions, and depended on stories that, unlike Meg Eliot's, are not tales of moral maturity but sentimental romances, though for Sylvia they constitute an essential level of reality. She has part of her mind and her life constructed for her by the romance novels, the Thirties films and the television series which, with parodistic delight, Wilson constructs for us repeatedly in the book. For Sylvia they represent a perfected reality – she reflects that they have spent "time and money enough on the films to make things real" – which overlies the actualities of her commonplace and dull existence. But by recognising them as incomplete, and facing resiliently up to that existence, and using it, Sylvia does become a contemporary heroine. Yet for Angus Wilson the controlling images of commonplace reality are a central form of consciousness in history, and, by parodying and pastiching them, he is able to use them as a language in the novel. He was to do the same again, in a far more ambitious way, in *No Laughing Matter*, to me his most experimental novel, and a book that belonged to the changed fictional equation of the 1960s as much as Meg Eliot's story did to the 1950s.

4 "But then the English novel is not an aesthetic novel, it is a social novel. *The Forsyte Saga* has great importance as the mirror of the British high bourgeoisie" – so says Herr Birnbaum, the German-Jewish children's novelist and refugee who plays a minor part but makes a major point in *No Laughing Matter*. The observation has, of course, much to say about Wilson's own *oeuvre* to this point, and especially to some parts of it. Wilson's work had itself largely been a mirror of the British high bourgeoisie, and it had tended to favour the social novel over the aesthetic novel, if with many complications. But where Galsworthy's novel is essentially a monument to society's realism, Wilson's work has been otherwise. From the start the mimicry, the sense of social absurdity and the satirical drive had been strong, and Wilson's work had moved in several different directions, in a pattern less like a direct growth than a process of disintegration and reintegration, taking up familiar energies in fiction and shaping them into new forms. As for *No Laughing Matter* itself, it was indeed a social novel, and as ambitious a mirror of the British bourgeoisie as Wilson had tried. Indeed we can see it as Wilson's closest approxima-

tion to the "Condition of England" novel, an extended social and historical tale based in the history of a family which was to reflect upon and explore the history of British culture from the last days of Edwardian and Galsworthyian security through to the period of new economic miracle materialism in which the novel was being written. *No Laughing Matter* is the bourgeois novel in the form Wilson had made of it, the story of a social history growing ever stranger and more insecure over a lifetime, roughly the lifetime of the novelist himself, a story, too, of life stunted and perverted and then released into strange paths in the modern world.

No Laughing Matter uses many of the methods of the modern historical novel. There are five books and nine different time-sections, chosen to illuminate both the development of the family and the key historical moments of modern times. The World Wars enter, but perhaps more importantly the apolitical age of amusement in the 1920s, the darkening economic and the sharpeningly more ideologic spirit of the 1930s, the collapsing of the British Empire and the conflicts of Suez in the 1950s, and the bleak emptiness of the modern economic miracle in the 1960s. There is a great deal about class relationships and changing social structure; much concern with money, and its general and specific functions; and a good deal of attention to sexuality and particularly its exploitations. On all this the book is knowledgeable, detailed and eclectic, the work of a trained modern historian with a vision of the gains and losses involved in the making of modern life. But it is also a book filled with styles: styles of life, styles of self-expression, styles of art, both in popular and serious culture, styles in which we see the changing clock of history and feeling. There is a broad geography centred in Britain but covering Europe and North Africa, a geography which is also a politics. And politics, and history, administer, as usually in Wilson's books, some salutary shocks and anguishes. Variously the characters encounter the outrages of Hitler's fascism, the spirit of pre-war anti-Semitism, the bombings of war and the new conflicts of peace. In all this the centre is the Matthews family, six children of awesomely feckless parents who move (with some typological neatness) into various areas and fields of modern work and experience, and whose lives, multiply-narrated, separately followed but brought back into conjunction at various key points, are given over a long span and over many fundamental changes. Through their different lives, we see different ways of seeing the world's crisis, and follow its peaks and troughs, from for example the post-World War One hopes of a new world through to the Depression, and from the new expectations of the 1950s through to the post-Suez world of "hire-purchased Hoovers and sleeping-pill salvation".

Family world and historical world are held in interesting balance, being seen essentially through the eyes of the different Matthews children. In the making of the match some major historical events, especially the wars, are represented only obliquely; the main time-slices are 1912, 1919, 1925, 1935, 1937, (briefly) 1942, 1946, 1956, 1967. Some key event-years (like 1926, the year of the General Strike) do not feature, so that the emphasis falls on compelling public events mainly in the 1930s and in 1956. Wilson, then, is not precisely concerned with bringing his characters into direct confrontation with the conventional landmarks of modern history; this has something to do with a key theme, which is that of evasion. So Sukey's gentility, Marcus's narcissism, Rupert's and Margaret's artistry, Gladys's evasion of full financial responsibility, and even Quentin's politics, flavoured with a strange sexuality, become largely forms of escape from major history, and this in turn makes a significant history. Not only does the novel become a saga of the British high bourgeoisie; it also seems a compelling condemnation of it. If the dynastic bourgeois novel as we have it in forms from *Buddenbrooks* to *The Forsyte Saga* is a very material and substantial species of fiction, able to give us a great sense of social substance as well as of familial rise and fall, the telling point about *No Laughing Matter* is that it is not like that – the family is not a coherent communion, there is little substantive relation between the individual and the culture, and from the start the family is in dissolution, on from the one happy moment at the beginning when we see them in a "union of happy carefree intimacy which it has securely known before and was never to know again".

For a moment there is a communal daydream, as the family walk out with all the confidence of their class, until the scene collapses in squabbles, the financial dependence of their parents on *their* parents (and later on their own children) is made apparent, and the images of domesticity are turned into grotesquerie. What is lost at the start is desperately sought again by the next generation, first by forming a substitute, game-like family of their own, then by seeking to begin again. All, in effect, fail, and nearly all of them end exiled out of Britain, in the Algarve or the Moroccan desert of dryness and exile: "There [Marcus] lay on his stomach in the hot sand among the broom bushes and pressed himself deeper and deeper into the dryness . . . . Didn't she . . . know anything of how he had let himself be measured and dried by life until he was at peace with the hot sand?" The other characters seem dried too, as history moves beyond them, leaving the book dominated by the sense of the failure of a generation. "As we get older," says Rupert, "we don't distinguish greatly between what might have been and what is." But we feel the novelist doing that, portraying a world that has failed to connect with reality, and a mask of illusion hiding the relationship between the characters' situations and the world of modern politics. When Quentin indicates his Marxism as the Matthews children play their famous Game, the point seems clear:

> I thought when I retired I should have to condemn you [their parents] as a generation, or rather as two generations, indeed as all the older generations, perhaps as the embodiment of accumulated history. You are, after all, all we know of the past. It's you who have put us in the soup and you don't seem prepared to help us out of it for fear of scalding your fingers. Not to put any pretence on it, you are a guilty lot. But as in my moment of retirement I reflected, I soon saw that this business of generations would not do. Here we have a system and a class in decay . . . .

This suggests that *No Laughing Matter* is Wilson's most political novel, his most explicit condemnation of the British bourgeoisie. Yet that is not quite true; for all its accusing sharpness, the book depends on the endeavour of the characters, who are granted great invention and intelligence, to create a response to history, a sufficient contemporary image of existence.

5 This depends in part on the book's extraordinary styles and mannerisms (to which I will return) and partly on the key role of the Matthews family, whose lives make the central story of the book – one of the strangest families in Wilson's fiction (which has offered us many strange families), all of them self-aware, camp, high-style histrionic performers, specialists in self-caricature and the caricature of others, and variously appalling and charismatic. On their various forms of virtuosity, which includes capacious invention in fiction, theatre and social activity, the book acquires its tone and construction. From the start, when they appear before the distorting mirrors at the Kensington Wild West exhibition, they take on the role of social and emotional comedians, to be caricatured in turn by a novelist who will use here some of his most flamboyant, protean and creatively energetic devices. They are chameleon figures who use false-seeming for a variety of purposes; in this respect *No Laughing Matter* is very much a laughing matter, or history read as a kind of strange farce. The farce is itself conditioned, for one feels that the absurdity and extremity derive from a society which is itself a strange theatre, and the image of theatricality dominates the book. Theatre has meant much to Wilson in earlier books, there in the *grand guignol*, in the list of dramatis personae, the text that functions like a kind of play in

which the author himself participates, as actor and mimic, as well as director and dramatist. Here that metaphor becomes exact and extensive, a figure for illusion, the social illusion that allows the bourgeois family to believe that, whatever is happening in history, they stand centre-stage. To do this they cast off character and take on roles, becoming artificial players who take on other identities. From the start the Matthews children are self-knowing actors, mocking others, mocking themselves, speaking in an elaborate, self-parodying discourse, drawn from stage, music-hall, popular culture, general cliché ("His Nibs"), playing a part in life that is filled with role and society and empty of selfhood, staged against the parts played by others and depending on lines already pre-written by the conventions of theatrical interaction.

This has a good deal to do with the fundamental insecurity and unreality of the family structure, based as it is on sentimental illusions without real underpinnings, and on the disjunctive images of a declining class. But it also appears in the novel as a decisive image of life. Not only is society based on a theatre of illusion, but so, it seems, is all human identity, the product of many images and perspectives. This virtuoso theatre transforms somewhat as the novel progresses, and a more realistic register from time to time emerges. But in the early part the emphasis is on self-caricature and self-display, and it takes up the main world of the fiction, indeed takes over the novelist himself. For Wilson seems very conscious of the way theatricality has become a central image in modern life, one of disturbing and multiple significance. In sociology the "dramaturgical analogy" (to take Erving Goffman's phrase from *The Presentation of Self in Everyday Life*) became a commonplace; *homo sociologicus* is a role-player, his performance already ascribed by the total social theatre in which he takes part, his nature made up of interaction with others, his individual contribution small. In psychology the theatre is pre-eminently mental, arising from the play of early relations, constantly remanifest in later ones. The analogy arises in a good deal of modern fiction (John Fowles's *The Magus*, Muriel Spark's *The Public Image*), frequently considering the role and nature of the impresario. And the impresario's is an histrionic art, an art of game-playing and counterfeiting, one that makes him *pasticheur*, puppet-master, miming and playing his characters, appearing and dissolving.

In *No Laughing Matter* a good deal of attention is given to all this, so realising in several forms the problems of appearance and reality which are the inherent problems of art. The central Game which runs through the novel has much about this. The Matthews children begin it by attempting to mime their parents, in order to try them before Quentin, as Mr Justice Scales. But can the roles be played?

"Was the man or the woman able to be another also the most suited to defend that other's interest? Yes, for simulation, whatever its motive, demands identification. But was he or she sufficiently detached to be able to offer a defence intelligible to others as defending counsel should, without the confusion and blurs of subjective statement? Yes, for simulation and mimicry also demand observation: in them compassion is tinged with mockery or mockery by compassion, and identification is distanced by the demands of technique. But could this simple mixture of opposites which mimicry requires, of affection with distaste, of respect with contempt, of love with hatred – be justly defined as a sort of reasoned apology? Yes, if it passed through the tempering fire of the scrutiny of Mr Justice Scales. The rules established, the Game could now proceed."

The novel itself proceeds according to this answer, and is very game-like, especially in the earlier part, where the virtuoso temperament of the novelist is engaged in just the same activity. Later a stronger sense of history as real and onerous enters, but by then the novelist has other games to play, using the methods of pastiche and parody to produce simulation and mimicry based on observation and identification. The book is built as a wonderfully rococo world of images and perspectives, narrative and theatrical registers and collocations of motifs from various levels of culture; there is much comedy, much parody, much camp, much allusion. The theatre is very variously conceived, and levels of "reality" multiply; the devices are used for many ends, for establishing an histrionic manner common to all the characters, presenting social styles and manners, displaying the personal relations of one character to another, representing unconscious psychic and social fantasies, and allowing the author a large freedom of texture and tone.

This sense of multiple perspective, of endlessly angled mirrors, is created at the start, with its extraordinary plethora of images – the new screened images from Gaumont Graphic and Pathé Pictorial of the Kensington Wild West Exhibition, itself an absurd confusion of motifs, which lead us to the actual Exhibition and the Matthews family visit. They, "as they came that hot July afternoon through the crowds . . . might so easily have been frozen and stored away in the files of the National Film Institute", to catch the eye of "the costume designer, the lover of moments of good cinema, or the searcher for social types", are offered to the multiplicity of image-collectors, and the author is evidently all of these things. Yet the camera will not do, for "no recording machine yet invented" could preserve their happy carefree intimacy – an intimacy made of yet more images, passing from consciousness to consciousness and structured in turn around the motifs provoked by the Exhibition. They are presented as "free" or "unconscious" mental monologues; but Wilson complicates the device by interfusing them, making his own point-of-view position obscure. We then pass from what the book identifies as the "para-psychological" stage to the social one; the shared communion also links the family's social being, their *public* image: "Many in the large crowd turned with amusement or surprise to see these posh youngsters singing so loudly in public. Mr Matthews, by now conscious of the public gaze, smiled and swung his walking stick a little at the attentions of the passers-by; his wife smiled too, to see him smiling. 'Billy loves public notice, don't you, darling?' " In this he does not differ from any in the family, each of whom seeks a stage to perform from. Acting "themselves" and their desires, acting what others expect them to be, performing to please and to be liked, staging themselves in solo and group turns, dissolving into fragments like Aunt Alice ("she [Margaret] had to hurry home to let Aunt Alice fall apart into all the various unrelated persons that she now knew bobbed up and sank down like corks in the ocean inside the old raddled body as inside all our bodies").

Flamboyant multiple images, interlocked registers, multiplied points-of-view – these had all been used in Wilson's work before, but here they are displayed with a distinctive and abundant virtuosity. The changing angles, the long shots and the close-ups, the stored actuality, the accumulated surrealism of the unconscious, are the materials being given play. Inside the frames are the performances, each character casting roles for the others or inventing one to play to the world, as in the complex case of the comic cockney servant Stoker, with her Wild West fantasy:

> Needed indeed now and again by Miss Stoker who, a good-natured, true serving cockney, will do anything, does anything, for her charges. Yet in Miss Stoker's mind is the clear realization that faced by buffalo, grizzly or Indians it is she, the "down at the Old Bull and Bush I shall shortly own 'er, walks among the cabbages and leaks" Hetty Stoker who (in her masters' version), for all her gallery roaring, heart-as-big-as-the-Elephant-and-Castle loyalty, will panic, take fright, pee her knickers or otherwise betray her lowly origins instead, as the legend should be, of dying by sucking the poisoned wound of her youngest charge (Master Marcus) when the Indian arrows are flying and furious . . . so fortified, her version takes in theirs and, Comic Western to the life, she falls over the prickly pear, mistakes the porcupine for a camp stool . . . .

And so on. If we find the language difficult, the flowline hard to find here, that is because the language arises from everywhere: cultural clichés, social attitudes, popular songs and children's dirty jokes,

cockney and mock-cockney, story and crude stereotype. The multiplying images are multiplying languages, generated from what people
say about each other and the not entirely separate things they might
say about themselves; the narrative angle weaves freely between
Stoker's own inner consciousness, the consciousness of those who
see her as clown, servant, protector, and from the novelist's own
obvious delight in mimicry. A large social consciousness exists,
opening out into a different kind of oddity and unreality for each
character, but holding each of them to their types and the typings that
others impose on them. Endless mummers and muggers, the characters guy their own parts, as Gladys does, elaborate them into stylistic
excess, as Marcus does, to turn them toward art, as Rupert and
Margaret do. The Matthews can do all society in different voices:
"Giggling and imitating, it was some time before they went to sleep."
But their theatricality, used for self-mockery and farce, is also used
for moral judgement and recovery. This is the function of "The
Game", "born of their need to relieve their pent-up shame, distress and
anger in histrionics, to heal their hurts with mimicry's homeopathic
sting, and no doubt as well to indulge some sexual urges".

6 If the world of mimicry and pastiche, reflection and refraction that
is focused in the Matthews family is a form of cultural interpretation
and large-scale social satire, it is also something more – a writer's
commitment to a virtuoso technique. The technique itself has been
one close throughout to Wilson's writing, but with *No Laughing Matter*
it seems to become a commentary on what has gone before. Wilson
had seemed the novelist of a contemporary realism, yet the cunning
contents of realism – apparent social mimesis, along with mimicry and
sound artifice – now are dissolved into their constituents and made
part of the story, subjected themselves to history and analysis. The
famous omniscience thus dissolves into an enormous divergence of
points of view. The apparently continuous realistic base divides into a
variety of narrative types: direct narration, sketches and playlets.
Culture is a palimpsest and a pastiche; palimpsest and pastiche
become dominant methods. And above all there is parody, where the
borrowed stylistic modes and the rhetorical mimicry become identifi-
ably focused – in an Ibsen parody, a Shaw parody, a Chekhov parody,
a Beckett parody. If throughout Wilson's fiction the registers are
unstable and less than definitive, here the process reaches its most
overt. Wilson had always been a novelist of quotation, of stylistic
citation (as at the opening of *Anglo-Saxon Attitudes*). His characters

write and perform; Margaret's Carmichael stories are quoted here. They are readers too, their minds shaped by discourse and structure, as Meg Eliot was, and Sylvia Calvert; the structures of past writing and image-making shape present lives. One reason for realism's apparent stability is that it is able to allude to previous writing as if it had made language universally safe; we can see past the words, the types and the characters to an accurate representation of life. The problem of realism and its inheritance becomes specific in *No Laughing Matter*, and this is why it is Wilson's most testing book.

So we can feel Wilson's novel, in perhaps a very British way, using all the modes of ambiguity, distortion, multiplication and refraction, of pastiche and parody, while hungering, like his own characters, for some authentic register, a stable language, a stable text, a coherent vision. Within this novel, Margaret the writer bears this burden. Her writing is a fearful activity, constantly at risk – "these imposed patterns falsify" – but also a psychic necessity. Through it she quells anxiety, avoids relationships, relaxes through "the familiar stringing together of words". This advances her far into irony and form; she becomes something of a writer's writer. Yet the dangers are there, of escaping life, of her characters turning into "figures and lettered proportions". She is an ironic anti-Dickensian; in this she is detached from her author, who offers in turn a sense of thriving life. Yet he too seems implicated, his own methods of caricature posing a related problem. "Never," says one critic, Herman Servotte, "except perhaps in James Joyce's work, has the pull between the two opposing tendencies in the novel, between its desire for an accurate 'realistic' rendering of life and its desire for an autonomous creation, been so clearly demonstrated as in this novel." This is exactly its interest, and also its problem, one that belongs to a good deal of contemporary writing. For Wilson would like to have the ebullient energies of literariness that make for mimicry and parody and those that create mimetic truth and life's true feel on the same side. Since they cannot quite be there, this produces an equivocal form. The novel raises its large questions, about life, moral and historical authenticity, human wholeness as well as emptiness, seeking to reconcile his ebullient first pages and the sense of emotional desert that haunts the last ones into a single vision.

My own sense is that this brilliant novel does not find its balance, and can hardly do so; art is indeed built from contradictory impulses and it frequently displays them. Indeed the point seems made in the book, as Quentin, in the role of Mr Justice Scales, attempts to reach a verdict. The family protests: "Billy," Marcus calls, "Billy, is that God prosing away there, impertinently forgiving us all? Turn Him out of the house at once. Just because He's always been out of all the fun and games is no reason why he should bring his great self-pitying feet in here, ruining my carpet . . . ". In the end Quentin's judging world and Marcus's camp one angrily co-exist. And so do the two main elements of this realistic *and* game-like novel. It is a book which seeks rigour of judgement, but that can exist only if we take the characters as more than image-constructs or creatures of language, human representatives who have led a "real" life; it has great freedom of fictional invention, but it is precisely that which takes its characters out of any stable base in reality. The imbalance was there locally in many of Wilson's earlier novels, but here it becomes the stuff of high literary risk, a risk that in his later books Wilson has gone on taking. In *As If By Magic* the flamboyance and fictional extravagance is played over a world map and focused on a serious moral issue, that of world hunger itself; in the more muted *Setting the World on Fire* the scene returns to a tempestuous English world.

Wilson has stepped a long way away from the world of British 1950s fiction, and I believe his later achievement has not had the recognition due to it. We may explain it partly as a freeing of an enormous creative ebullience and versatility that was always there, a writer's imaginative battle to break away from some of the realistic confinements that surrounded his earlier books into that grandeur of radical invention that must be a prime task for any writer; we may see it as part of a larger process of the return to fiction's powers of versatile allusion which has allowed the postwar novel to pass beyond traditionalism and into a recognisably modern form. Whatever the reason, *As If By Magic* is a novel by a major contemporary writer, a novel that rightly takes extravagant chances, a great release of creativity, a remarkable, buoyant comic creation, loose, rich and playful, and as humanely and intelligently done as it can be.

"A HOUSE FIT FOR FREE CHARACTERS"
The novels of Iris Murdoch

"We are not isolated free choosers, monarchs of all we survey, but benighted creatures sunk in a reality whose nature we are constantly and overwhelmingly tempted to deform by fantasy. Our current picture of freedom encourages a dream-like facility; whereas what we requiᴤe is a renewed sense of the difficulty and complexity of the moral life and the opacity of persons . . . . Literature must always represent a battle between real people and images; and what it requires now is a much stronger and more complex conception of the former."

Iris Murdoch, "Against Dryness" (1961)

"Love has a thousand shapes. There might be lovers whose gift it was to choose out the elements of things and place them together and so give them a wholeness not theirs in life, make of some scene, or meeting of people (all now gone and separate) one of those globed compacted things over which thought lingers, and love plays."

Virginia Woolf, To the Lighthouse (1927)

"[Sartre's] inability to write a great novel is a tragic symptom of a situation which afflicts us all. We know the great lesson to be taught is that the human person is precious and unique; but we seem unable to set it forth except in terms of ideology and abstraction."

Iris Murdoch, Sartre: Romantic Rationalist (1953)

1 Iris Murdoch is unmistakably one of our great contemporary novelists. Yet, like a good many of her own literary characters, she exists in a curious, half-magical state of elusiveness. Those who have written about her work – a greatly increasing number – find her strangely hard to define or interpret. She began writing in the climate of realism that surrounded British fiction during the 1950s, and is perhaps the one recent British novelist who has written persuasively and fully thoughtfully about the enduring value of realism in the novel, that kind of realism she celebrates in the great nineteenth-century novelists George Eliot and Tolstoy: "The social scene is a

life-giving framework and not a set of dead conventions or stereotyped settings inhabited by stock characters." Yet her own realism is not of that kind, and some of her best critics – like Robert Scholes, who calls her a "fabulator" attempting to find "more subtle correspondences between the reality which is fiction and the fiction which is reality" – have understandably read her writing in almost the opposite spirit. She is a philosopher, and her works possess a clear philosophical power; yet they are not philosophical novels in any usual sense, and she has conducted a particular quarrel with the abstract inclinations of that genre (criticising, for example, Sartre's fiction, "stripped and made anonymous by extremity"). She has an *oeuvre*, a body of work that evolves, changes, and aspires toward a wholeness; yet it is a prolix and in some ways meandering sequence, seeking not the hard clarity of a small number of books but the elaborateness of a vast and sometimes apparently repetitious production. "If one has a thing at all one must do it and keep on and on trying to do it better," she has her character Arnold Baffin say in *The Black Prince* (1973). "And one aspect of this is that any artist has to *decide* how fast to work. I do not believe I would improve if I wrote less. The only result of that would be that there would be less of whatever there is." On the other hand Bradley Pearson, in the same book, has a different view; most artists, he says, drift too readily from the stage where the work is unformed to that where it is ready, and "This is of course a moral problem, since all art is the struggle to be, in a particular sort of way, virtuous" – a fully natural state of creative power is rarely attained. She is most certainly a serious novelist, yet her books can be and have been read at many levels, from the most metaphysical to the most romantic and sentimental; her various readers can thus construct her in very different ways, and she seems constantly and teasingly to reconstruct them, giving them a good deal of the probable and an element of the unexpected. Her own speculations about the novel form suggests that she regards it as very plural and heterogeneous, and her books and her many useful essays give us not so much an aesthetic of contemporary form as a theory of human nature and then a broad philosophy of art. It is this that leads her back to the lasting need for realism in art, and points her own fiction back toward the great social and moral issues of the nineteenth century. Yet she is much taken with the magic of art as artifice, produces work of high stylisation and often complex literary and mythological allusion, and has generated a sequence of very distinct conventions, to the point where the landscape of Murdochland is today considered unmistakable.

Murdoch is both a very modern and a very British novelist (like many British novelists she also has an Irish flavour); and there are many who would say that the two elements are irreconcilable. That brings us to her notion of the novel's innate liberalism, a liberalism that in her later work has passed through a transcendental stage toward a kind of religiosity. For Murdoch the novel is the natural repository of character, the complex human figure, "a fit house for free characters to live in". At the same time she has thoughtfully observed that we do not live any longer in the world of nineteenth-century liberalism in which the concept of the free individual flourished, and in philosophy and in art alike we need to derive a new concept of the person, a concept that presumably implies a changed manner of mimesis of the figure in art. Yet at the same time she clearly reads in great and serious art something transcendent. No philosopher and hardly any novelist, reflects Bradley Pearson in *The Black Prince*, "has ever managed to explain what that weird stuff, human consciousness, is really made of . . . . How can such a thing be tinkered with and improved, how can one change the quality of consciousness?" She has been very taken by the Platonic paradoxes surrounding the nature of art and the role of the artist, and her own commentary seeks from the artist "a sober truthful mind" and the power to reject consolatory fantasies. Her own novels show this trouble, frequently seeming to quarrel with the established conventions of art and their habitual resolutions, and hungering for a form of expression and human action which transcends art's limitations.

This is powerful and right, an essential aspect of her fiction as a mode of thought and knowledge; but there is a way of reading her own books, especially some of the earlier ones, as consolatory romantic fantasies, and certainly as very formal and mannered works. She has quarrelled with a good deal of the argument in behalf of an "experimental" modern fiction, but some of her books – *The Black Prince* is an example – move quite closely in tune with many of its speculations. Her books secrete large metaphysical and mythological structures, and they depend on an essential notion of art as discovery, especially in the realm of the good and the true; yet they have a taste for a contingent social realism, for local detail or commonplace narrative satisfactions, which seems to struggle with their larger intentions. Unlike another kind of philosophical novelist, Iris Murdoch is to me a writer who has always struggled in the midst of things. And that very fact seems to sustain the prodigious production, the continuing enquiry, and make her less an artist of clear resolutions than a busy and active agent of the imagination.

By now we have many books – twenty-two at the present count – to guide us to a view of her. Yet to some degree the centre of her talent as a novelist seems more elusive than ever; no single book concentrates it, and no book seems completely to close a phase or constitute a complete affirmation. Her very productivity indeed has sometimes seemed to challenge her obvious brilliance, and certainly has turned it into a kind of continuous practice. However, any serious reader is bound to note the substantial differences that exist among her novels, and the sharp changes of direction that have brought her along a path that puts a large separation between her first published novel *Under the Net* (1954) and, say, the recent *The Philosopher's Pupil* (1983) – even though there is, as it happens, a marked similarity of preoccupation between the two books. If *Under the Net* appeared an angry novel, her second book *The Flight From the Enchanter* (1955) appeared a fabulous one; by her sixth, *An Unofficial Rose* (1962), her work seemed to become a form of bourgeois romance, a novel of sentiments, with a strong erotic charge and a structure of sexual permutation. Then there was *The Unicorn* (1963), drawing strongly on the stuff of Gothic fiction and the spirit of romance, to be followed not long after by a social and political novel set amid the Irish troubles, *The Red and the Green* (1965), the most specific of her books. *Bruno's Dream* (1969) seemed a complex meditation on the relations of memory and love and death; *The Black Prince*, with its framing devices and its challenge to the authority of the narrator, came close to the spirit of much recent fictional experimentalism. In later work the strength of her preoccupation with the conditions of death and power that surround the act of love becomes very dominant, but so does a new religiosity and a concern with sainthood and relevation. Theatre and opera seem heavily to have guided both the staging and the ceremonial of her latest books; there is also a clear new texture of Shakespearean allusion and a sense of an art shaped by the laws of his later comedies. Indeed her own late comedies are marked by a much more profound contemplation of art, a new complexity of form, and a texture of moral maturity, while yet remaining part of the insistent quest for an honest and serious art that has marked even the more bizarre moments of her entire endeavour.

Thus, if her variety is striking, so is her persistence. There was and there still is a familiar Murdochian world, with certain ummistak-able kinds of character – the Love-Prisoner, the Near-Saint, the Deathbed Contemplative, the Spoiled Priest, the Failed Artist, the Plotter and the Enchanter – and a certain kind of social landscape, centred around the British bourgeoisie, the civilised upper-middle-class educated who are either leisured or in professional life, and extended into a half-stylised fringe world of aesthetes, bohemians, raffish young people who usually trouble the interwined and often ancient emotional web of relationships that the novel proposes to examine and challenge. The Murdochian landscape and cityscape is also familiar; sometimes it is intensely social, like the busy London of some of her novels, and sometimes it is notably a-social, gothic and mythical, a landscape of sea and caves and natural features which form a map in which places of wonder and power open her characters to often testing and terrible challenges by water or entombment. All this makes it a society and a landscape strangely angled toward familiar life, this of course being part of its power and compulsion – a world in which sexual and emotional expectation itself is often unusual, fornication has a distinctive elegance, strange sympathies and mysterious contracts unite or divide the human figures.

Then, too, there are the presiding themes: the concern with love, the committing centre of human action, and with its surrounding web of magic and fantasy, power, possession and imprisonment; the concern with death, and its challenge to memory and desire, and the question of mortal centrality; the concern with art as power, so that her novels, with their extraordinary psychopomps (Mischa Fox, Honor Klein, Hannah Crean-Smith, the dying Bruno, and so on), contain figures who stand close to the artist in possessing the gift of plotting and transformation, and help turn the books they are in toward mystery. There are, as in the novels of Vladimir Nabokov or John Fowles, the narcissistic anxieties of creation itself, often concerned with the question of whether art is accidental and factitious, or integral and morally and formally whole, a theme itself intimate with the question of love, which is both a transcendent dream and a given case of personal relationship. Miss Murdoch reflects much on the practical anxieties of life, especially in its form as love or acknowledgement of connection and otherness; but she also, and with increasing flamboyance, does indeed practice fiction. Old Murdoch hands grow expert at guessing which cards are being stacked to be dealt out later; Miss Murdoch, knowing we know, plays the game with cunning. Her own powers of magicality are now quite openly on offer, and if this depends on surprise, then one surprise is indeed in the way she steps beyond the previous case, in each new novel doing something new, as in the marked change of landscape she achieves in *The Philosopher's Pupil*.

2 All this has greatly altered the way in which her work has been discussed. The 1950s novelist of anger, the conflict of art and commitment, and Sartrean shadings, has largely gone from sight. Antonia Byatt, in her brilliant 1960s book, *Degrees of Freedom* (1965), on her first seven novels, changed the picture by presenting her as a novelist of strong social and moral inclination who was much concerned to depict the opacity of the world as the field for the testing of human freedom. To Robert Scholes she was a "fabulator", her work in tune with the experimental break away from the limitations of realism that marked so much contemporary fiction in the United States as well as in Britain; more recently, in a rather severe study by Elizabeth Dipple, *Iris Murdoch: Work for the Spirit* (1983), she has been displayed as a novelist of broadly religious character whose aesthetic and moral attitudes are ways of fighting "our modern dis-ease", defending the spirit of true – as against false or indulgent – art. The view of Frank Baldanza that she is "a traditional realist" seems in many ways peculiarly inappropriate, though it survives as an issue because she appears to insist on it. "I've always wanted to be a realistic writer in the tradition of the English novel and to portray real people and real problems . . .," she once said in an interview. "But, of course, any kind of theoretical interest one has as a novelist has to fight, often rather destructively, against one's desire to be realistic and portray real character." Her own great interest in the process and force of the imagination, uttered in the early disputes with Sartre, developed in her later commentaries on Plato, discourage any simple and empirical view of the fictionalising process; her speculative intent, always clear, has grown clearer, leading even within her novels to curious interweavings of formality and contingent empiricism, of large myth and local narrative. Such matters of necessity and contingency grow from time to time very explicit, as in *An Accidental Man* (1971), and they retain the trace of the arguments of and with existentialism. But the commitment to the realistic and the liberal tradition is real, especially when it means that capacious humane realism found in British Victorian novelists or in Tolstoy, or more recent Russian writers whose achievements have been explored by her husband John Bayley in criticism. Murdoch is a writer of our time, and a post-existentialist novelist; but like many British novelists she has held firm to some decisive idea of realism and its power as an explanation for our need for imaginary friends and fictions.

A powerful early essay called "Against Dryness" (1961) went into much of this; it is one of a number of substantial pieces in which she has explored her view of the imagination and given theoretical support to her work in a way fairly uncommon in Britain. Here she notes that the liberal view of man has not entirely sustained us speculatively, and led to an inadequate relation between our view of the person and the background of transcendent values and realities: "We no longer use a spread-out substantial picture of the manifold virtues of man and society. We no longer see man against a background of values, of realities, which transcend him. We picture man as a brave naked will surrounded by an easily comprehended empirical world." We have appropriately ended up with two kinds of novel – the "crystalline" novel, "a small quasi-allegorical object portraying the human condition and not containing 'characters' in the nineteenth-century sense", and the "journalistic" novel, "a large shapeless quasi-documentary object, the degenerate descendant of the nineteenth-century novel, telling, with pale conventional characters, some straightforward story enlivened with empirical facts". The distinction seems a familiar one now, between, as it were, the novel as reportage and discursive prosework, and the novel as self-begetting art, though the phrasing suggests a contrast closer to that Virginia Woolf made between her work and Arnold Bennett's. Murdoch's analogue for the crystalline novel, the novel of dry symbol, seems to be the lonely self-contained individual; that of the journalistic novel is that of naively free selves moving liberally against a commonplace reality.

These quarrels and contrasts were, as I have suggested elsewhere, powerful in the postwar debate that led toward the making of contemporary fiction. And to a degree Murdoch's strongest declaration appears to be against "crystalline" fiction, the fiction of serious modern experiment, the fiction that disputes metonymy and lies in the tradition of symbolism. Yet the discursive novel clearly does not suit her either, as the quarrel with Sartre shows. She is an aesthetic novelist, but aestheticism is an essential object of anxiety, for what it points to is the containments and consolations of form. One way to quarrel with this is through an argument for realism, one which asserts the destructive but necessary power of the "now so unfashionable idea of character". The "Against Dryness" essay is early and perhaps depends too much on the term "realism", now notoriously volatile, and sometimes seeming to mean a sense of density and social texture, sometimes a more mysterious apprehension of exterior potencies. But another way is to argue, as she does in *The Fire and the Sun* (1977), from a Platonic position, claiming the need for recognition of the ethical responsibilities of the imagination, and the necessity of an art that provides "work for the spirit". In one sense this argument, refusing the standpoint of Modernist symbolism, of existentialism, and evidently of Marxism, is making an aesthetic utterance in behalf of liberalism – or to be more precise a post-Kantian unromantic liberalism that still recognises the density and complexity of the moral life and the opacity of persons; and we might think it very English. But it is a liberalism presented with a high imaginative flourish, and it is not hard to sense that in recent fiction it is acquiring a distinct new religiosity.

Perhaps one way of saying this is that Iris Murdoch would appear to be a theoretical empiricist, an odd thing to be. Her novels are in flight from concepts; they conceptualise the flight. They resist the dominant acquisition of the world by language; and use language to say so. Their drift is toward the grasping of the contingent, but this is done by way of a theory of flexible necessity, or growth into the coherence of form. Her critical argument disputes the fiction of symbol and myth, at least of the "dry" modernist symbol, which, she says in "The Sublime and the Beautiful Revisited" (1959), "has the uniqueness and separateness of the individual, but . . . is a making sensible of the idea of individuality under the form of necessity, its contingency purged away", but this would not be an unsufficient description of her own novels. She has refused a broad theory of experiment, but spoken of a method of composition whereby "each novel will suggest its own technical innovation". The object of her anti-symbolist, or realist, theory seems predominantly to protect, both philosophically, in terms of a definition, and imaginately, in terms of a method of writing, the substance of unique human personality or character. As she tells us in the same essay: "Contingency must be defended for it is the essence of personality. And here is where it becomes important to remember that a novel is written in words, to remember that 'eloquence of suggestion and rhythm' of which James spoke. A novel must be a fit house for free characters to live in; and to combine form with respect for reality with all its contingent ways is the highest art of prose."

The "fit house" sounds rather Jamesian too, like his loose baggy monsters in which human figures move freely. Yet this theory, which has a profound moral attractiveness, seems to pose problems in practice. Not only is liberalism itself qualified and questioned in her work; there is also a dominating preoccupation with pattern and form. In fact Murdoch's notion of "unutterable peculiarity" is not so much a literary instinct as a moral and aesthetic theory captured by a writer of enormously fertile literary talents. And what it has encouraged her to construct with those talents is certainly not some modern version of the nineteenth-century novel, but a distinctive form of the contemporary novel with a strong philosophical perspective on human relations and art, and a firm moral urgency.

3 Thinking about all this, it is useful to go back to the beginning, to the middle of the 1950s, when the postwar novel in Britain was being established and Iris Murdoch was seen as an important and central figure in the activity. *Under the Net* was not her first novel; five earlier works had been written but not published. But in 1953 came her fine brief book on Sartre, and the following year *Under the Net* came out, to great praise, but in a distinctive climate. Other novels – John

Wain's *Hurry On Down* of a year before, Amis's *Lucky Jim* of the same year – surrounded it, and in that year *The Spectator* announced a "New Movement" and found Murdoch firmly within it. *Under the Net* was itself brought in under the net of anger, social and moral realism, and a new fictional spirit much concerned with territorialising, in a commonsense way, the world of welfare-state Britain and its rewards and alienations. Thus some of the book's dominant features – its direct philosophical preoccupations, its strong figurative qualities, its strange ornateness – did not receive much recognition, though they are some of the strongest Murdochian marks upon it. And though some of the existential implications were noted, it was not much seen that the book related to the challenge to Sartre Murdoch had expressed in her book on him, where she held him "blind to the function of prose" insofar as it was "creative of a complete and unclassifiable image", and questioned the concept of the abstractified philosophical novel.

There were other issues to do with language and silence close to the centre of the book; if Murdoch had been in existentialism's orbit, she had also been in that of British and Viennese linguistic philosophy, and her novel's title comes out of Wittgenstein. Beckett too was in the background (Murdoch had responded warmly to *Murphy*), and so was the dedicatee, Raymond Queneau, who has surely something to do with the strong surrealist flavour unmistakable in the novel. Art as sound and art as silence, theatre and theatricality, the relationship between the discursive and the symbolic, are all there: the role of non-discursive art – mime theatre, the image narrative of film, even the mute animal film-star – come to the centre of the story. But (as would prove usual in Murdoch) these playfully presented aesthetic and linguistic issues were related to a concern with the proper conduct of human relationships, and the acknowledgement of the otherness of others. Though shaded with absurdist and existential concerns, the gesture was notably romantic; what was pursued was the wonder of the world, the vivid existential otherness of things and persons, the discovery of opaque significance.

Certainly, then, Murdoch was not an Angry Young Man: not angry, not quite young, being an established philosopher of thirty-five, and not a man – though one distinctive feature of *Under the Net* was its remarkable act of male impersonation, the story being told in the confessional first person by a young male narrator who indeed had some of the qualities of the "outsider" anti-hero of the period. Jake Donaghue, like Colin Wilson's famous alien, bore a consciousness of alienation, an existential burden, an awareness of a world that was contingent but not yet necessary. He is a comic *picaro* with a number of Beckettian qualities: Irish origins, Parisian connections, the job of a translator between French and English. He is without "commitment", an intellectual and social free-floater in an alien bourgeois society, with traditional bohemian failings ("There's nothing that irritates me so much as paying rent") and a policy of appearing penniless even when he is not. He observes: "It is not my nature to make myself responsible for other people. I find it hard enough to pick my own way along." He has "shattered nerves", and cannot bear to be alone for long ("I am therefore a parasite, and live usually in my friends' houses"). An intelligent rebel and sleeper on other people's couches, he is also in a philosophical impasse which is the book's main theme. He is conscious of the competing claims of the aesthetic and the social, the literary and the political; he seeks detachment without isolation, and creativity without fixed definition. He disputes with his culture and his age: "Nothing is more paralysing than a sense of historical perspective, especially in literary matters," he says, and the perspective teaches the lesson so strong in the 1950s season, for Jake shares the prevailing conviction that he lives in an age when novels simply cannot be written. In a sense, the lesson of the book is that they can be, by Jake, which means, in turn, by Iris Murdoch too.

Other things strongly associated the book with its season. There was the knowing and impressive account of the artistic-bohemian landscape that underlay the literary life of the time: a well-understood and explored London, both necessary and contingent, with its pubs, river, people and street geography; a Paris flavoured with the bittersweet mood of postwar anxiety; a world of film studios and national health hospitals where the prevailing austerity and the welfare state feel are firmly present; a political atmosphere in which strong Left-wing arguments were requiring writers to define their direction and their commitment. All this indeed gives the novel period qualities and a peculiar kind of radical appeal that her work did not subsequently repeat. Murdoch herself has confessed that she sees the novel as a very "young" book – of course it was also a very distinguished one, and distinguished in a way that finally separated it from the work of her contemporaries. The social accuracy was not the essential concern: "That was just self-indulgence. It hadn't any particular significance," she told Frank Kermode when he asked about the high level of actuality in the book in his "House of Fiction" interview with her in 1963. And certainly the novel is dominated by an imagination of a different and decidedly more mythical and fanciful sort, while Jake's sense of separateness and disaffiliation derives less from his social quest than a linguistic and metaphysical need. Thus, as Murdoch explained to Kermode: "[The book] plays with a philosophical idea. The problem which is mentioned in the title is the problem of how far conceptualising and theorising, which from one point of view are absolutely essential, in fact divide you from the thing that is the object of the theoretical attention." With many more novels to guide us, we can see how central this is as a preoccupation in Murdoch's novels, returning to clear attention, for example, in her recent *The Philosopher's Pupil*.

Under the Net is, then, a good novel about contemporary life, but it is also a good novel about virtue. Nonetheless it possesses a form rather different from anything later, the form of comic picaresque. The basic structure comes from a series of events over a brief phase in Jake's life, leading to a change in his emotions and interpretation of events. His story starts with him homeless, jobless, with only an accommodation-shop address; it ends with many of these things not greatly altered – after much talk of love he remains alone, and after much exchange of money his bank balance remains low – but with his vision of the world changed and renewed. Above all, he has ceased to be a translator and become a writer, following a similar change in the theories of the French writer whose work he translates; and he has lost his original state of "shattered nerves" and his paranoiac awareness of contingency ("I hate contingency. I want everything in my life to have a sufficient reason") and come to a sense of the world's wonder. He has a new apprehension of solitude, a new apprehension of others. Much of this has come from his recovery of a sense of the nature of literary art, and its instrument, language: this is the philosophical idea. But to some degree it is a comic enlighten-ment, and the philosophical idea is treated with much play; one of the striking features of the novel is indeed its distinctive Murdochian baroque, the ornateness of mind, the fondness for objects rich and strange, the elaborate figurative invention (Jake in his bearskin, Anna fleeing without her shoes), and, of course, the strong characteristic sense of mystery associated with the essential feelings and affections of the characters, and their distinctive "otherness".

Jake's story is indeed a quest through language, and its relation to silence. Appropriately his acquaintance includes three people who offer him versions of this. One, Dave Gellman, a linguistic philo-sopher committed to the spoken word only, and to an open and very spartan philosophy of life, lives in "contingent" London; his flat is next to, and dominated by, the cold walls of a modern hospital; and he expresses a spare and utilitarian view of the world. He sees Jake as the "incorrigible artist" and wants him to take a useful job as a hospital orderly. By contrast there is Anna Quentin, who offers a more aesthetic world, of silks, toys, and romantic passion. But she too is preoccupied by silence; a former singer, she is now devoted to mime, "very simple", "very pure". Murdoch's way of conveying what are clearly very speculative notions through characters, objects, places and lines of action is nowhere more evident than in the chapter – dreamlike and surrealistic, dominated by ideas of and images of silence – where Jake searches out Anna in the miming theatre at Hammersmith. Appropriately in a book where the male mind and male characters are so sharply rendered, the female ones are rich romantic objects; and Anna is an ornate person done in an ornate style. She is first shown in a vast toyshop of rich objects – "amid the enchanting chaos of silks and animals and improbable objects that seemed to arise almost to her waist she looked like a very wise mermaid rising out of a motley coloured sea" – and she is "like a great doll". Her silence is artistic purification; where the singer exploits charm to seduce, the mimer is more aesthetic and more "honest". And likewise in love: Anna tells Jake that love is not a feeling or an emotional straining for possession, but action and silence. Jake resists his temptation to shake the thundersheet, left over from the old theatre Anna is about to sell, accepts the new silence of the place, and spends the night there sleeping in a bear's skin.

But the character who dominates the first part of this novel, and the direction of Jake's philosophy, is Hugo Belfounder, whom Jake describes as "my destiny". It is really his acquaintance with Hugo that is the book's theme, Jake says, and he explains he has unfinished business with him. Belfounder's history is carefully filled out; of German stock, he has inherited an armaments firm which, because of his ardent pacifism, he has converted into a firework factory. He is dedicated to the impermanent and perishable arts and sees the firework setpieces he makes as an art akin to music, calling for "both manual dexterity and creative ingenuity". If, as seems intended, the mythological story of Vulcan, Mars and Venus is used to provide a loose framework for the novel, Belfounder would seem to stand for Vulcan. (This framework, as I long ago suggested in writing about the book, seems worked out with such surrealist ingenuity – even down to the use of locales like Hammersmith and such arts as fireworks, film and watchmaking – that I remain convinced it is there, even though in talking to A.S. Byatt when she wrote *Degrees of Freedom* Miss Murdoch quite denied the intention.)

However, unfortunately for Hugo's theories about an imperma-nent and momentary art, art is mediated by society. His fireworks are soon being classified into styles by the newspapers, and his next venture, into expressionist film, turns into box office success, if only because he is, accidentally, extremely good at business. Hugo is another of Murdoch's flamboyant early characters, but his primary impact on Jake is a philosophical one. When the two of them are immured together in the typically Murdochian setting of a cold-cure research centre, Hugo expresses in conversation a theoretical attitude which enormously impresses Jake, an attitude which lacks "both the practical interests and the self-conscious moral seriousness of those who are usually dubbed idealists", and manifests an objectivity and detachment which shows "less like a virtue and more like a sheer gift of nature". To Hugo, everything has a theory and yet there is no master theory – "I never met a man more destitute than Hugo of anything which could be called a metaphysic or general *Weltanschauung*. It was rather perhaps that of each thing he met he wanted to know the *nature* ... ". But the conspicuous feature of Hugo's philosophy is that it is opposed to description; he believes we make too many concessions to the need to communicate, that language is a machine for making falsehoods, that only actions speak. The consequence is that Jake, impressed, starts making notes of the conversation, and in a comic paradox which is also a form of bad faith, produces a book called *The Silencer* in which a touched-up version of both their arguments appears. A part of this argument is reproduced, and Hugo's position here emerges as the case that theory obtrudes at the moments when one is most warmly involved in life, and that it is dispensable:

> ... the movement away from theory and generality is the movement towards truth. All theorizing is flight. We must be ruled by the situation itself and this is unutterably particular. Indeed it is something to which we can never get close enough, however hard we may try as it were to crawl under the net.

Even art, he holds, works against theory, and for almost all of us truth can be attained only in silence. This evidently poses the problem of the book, and Jake's problem in particular, which is that of picking one's way between the opposite camps of theory and silence, and between the "unutterable particularity" of individual sensations and their expression in art. But when Jake rereads these words from *The Silencer* he reflects that the opposite view can be strengthened, and the novel provides a dialectical adversary for Hugo in the person of "Lefty" Todd.

Todd, the leader of the New Independent Socialist Party, is the man who represents the case for a practical, political unity between theory and practice, and it is significant that throughout the book Hugo in fact regularly yields to him. Todd represents the very Fifties path of "commitment", and all Hugo's worlds of art and silence are displaced by the insistent weight of the NISP. Lefty defines the role of the intellectual, for Jake, by quoting Marx's view that social being is the foundation of consciousness, and taking this to mean that political parties exist first to think and then to act. Lefty observes that Jake needs to become involved – "As soon as you do something and knock into people you'll begin to hate a few of them. Nothing destroys abstraction so well as hatred" – and advises him to write plays, by analysing current successes and then filling in the political "message". Jake does not accept this crude demand, but it does define his artistic dilemma. It is after the NISP take over the mime theatre that he finds that he can now shake the thundersheet, and afterwards he reflects that "my previous pattern of life was gone forever". Shortly after this he is pushed into the expedient of stealing Mr Mars, the film-star dog, and releasing him from his cage, an image of his own change.

Jake remains imprisoned himself in his intellectual role, by its very nature isolated. Indeed, refusing the offer of a scriptwriting job, he nonetheless elects his own solitude and poverty. In Paris on the 14th July he experiences the sum of his isolation. Like Polyphemus on the fontaine des Medicis, all he can do is overlook the lovers; and when he sees Anna and pursues her, all he is left with are her shoes. When he returns to Dave Gellman and takes a job as a hospital orderly, he does, though, find a way of reconciling the aesthetic and the social. As he later explains:

> It occurred to me that to spend half the day doing manual work might be very calming to the nerves of one who was spending the other half doing intellectual work, and I could not imagine why I had not thought before of this way of living, which would ensure that no day could pass without *something* having been done, and so keep that sense of uselessness, which grows in prolonged periods of sterility, away from me forever.

And this leads to the radical revaluation that changes him at the book's end. Hugo appears in the hospital as a patient, victim of a headwound sustained at an NISP meeting, and reveals certain facts which show Jake that his account of the world and the relationships of people in it have been quite false. Now Jake simply wants to "get the facts: theories could come later". And the conversation with Jake does restructure his universe: "A pattern in my mind was suddenly scattered and the pieces of it went flying about me like birds," he says – a simile later reinforced by the image of the starlings that live in their hundreds outside Hugo's flat, a mass of noise, finally entering through the open window – like much else from the animal kingdom – at the book's end.

What emerges is that Jake has imposed his theories on everyone, acting throughout as if his own hastily-formed deductions were truth. Hugo's revelations force a sexual re-sorting of a kind that would become familiar in Murdoch's novels. Jake has the love-map upside down; Anna has loved Hugo, probably led him to his anti-theoretical theories, and these she got in the first place from Jake. "I knew everything, I got it the wrong way round, that's all!" Jake cries. His approach to life has not, as he thought, been passive, nor his role contingent. This "wrench which had dislocated past, present and future" thus brings him to a classic Murdoch understanding:

> It seemed as if, for the first time, Anna really existed now as a separate being and not as part of myself. To experience this was extremely painful. Yet as I tried to keep my eyes fixed upon where she was I felt towards her a sense of initiative which was perhaps after all one of the guises of love. Anna was something which had to be learnt afresh. When does one ever know a human being? Perhaps only after one has realized the impossibility of knowledge and renounced the desire for it . . . .

It is an ending strong in affirmations, of the opacity of persons, and the moral need to see things as they are and not as one wishes them to be. The moral discovery is couched in a philosophical frame, and leads to a discovery of emotional and creative energy. Jake seems to end the book in solitude, but it is crowded with possibilities. He spends what is left of his money on Mr Mars, the friendly, useless ex-film star dog; Mrs Tinkham's cat has her variegated kittens, "one of the wonders of the world"; Jake feels like "a fish which swims calmly in deep waters, . . . the secure supporting pressures of my own life." Abandoning translation, he resolves to write originally, and "this possibility was present to me as a strength which cast me lower and raised me higher than I had ever been before." Full of this strength which is better than happiness, he finds it is "the morning of the first day".

Under the Net is not a book Miss Murdoch now greatly favours ("a derivative book, it's got all sorts of childish games in it, as it were", she has said), but it was among the very best novels of the 1950s. It belongs to the season of commitment, realism, and existentialist issues, and the novel carries this weight. Thus the ending seems filled with allusion to *La Nausée* – the radio love-song, the parable relations between animal and human life, the discovery of writing – though most of the implications are opposite: Jake is carried past silence and imitation into a sense of original truth. It is a novel of considerable social density, but notable for its baroque and fantastic invention, quite as rich as anything as Murdoch has ever done. It deals very certainly with the problems of constructing a contemporary novel, and is a work of self-begetting in the modern manner, a novel about the becoming of a novel. Like a nineteenth-century novel, that truth is presented not basically in moral but in philosophical terms, and Jake's weakness has not been so much a moral failure as a failure to comprehend the processes, instruments and states of mind through which truth is discovered. If it is a book that in all sorts of flamboyant ways evokes the density of lives, its main task is devising the images and forms that help us to comprehend that density. It lays down many of the prime themes of Murdoch's subsequent work – the search for a form beyond absurdity, an art beyond discursiveness and theory, a language beyond silence, and the direction of enquiry, which is through the apprehension of love and otherness, the one way we might find necessity within the contingent.

But, for all that it implies, it is also a very incomplete guide to what was to follow, a large and extraordinarily productive career that would take Murdoch's writing forward into a wide variety of different forms and places. There were three more novels in the 1950s – *The Flight from the Enchanter*, *The Sandcastle* (1957) and *The Bell* (1958) – already suggesting a prolific and varied talent. Then came a brief break of three years, until *A Severed Head* of 1961, which had the air of being a new step. The prolific production then resumed, and a clearer image of Murdoch's dominant direction, changeable, various, but marked by a sequence of fundamental preoccupations that made her a distinctive author of the time, a time shaped by much larger concerns than those that had seemed local to the 1950s.

4 By the end of the 1960s it was clear that Iris Murdoch had become a very different kind of novelist from the one whose first book had seemed so much to match the mood of the 1950s. The things that apparently had flavoured her initial work – its picaresque note, its relation to French existentialism, its world of flamboyant radical and refugee figures, its urban flavour – had slipped away, and Iris Murdoch was now an author of extraordinary and prodigious production, having produced something very close to a novel a year for over ten years. Her novels were no longer tales of picaresque adventure with clear ethical resolutions; they were usually set in well-defined and ritually contained groups of people, sometimes in a limited or even closed community, increasingly concerned with middle-class rather than bohemian life, and far less to do with the processes of writing. The later novels of the 1950s and then the fiction of the 1960s seemed broadly to become what could be called metaphysical romance, and they were often versions of the novel of sentiments, winning Murdoch a general popular audience which could delight in the love world of the stories without engaging too much with any

broader dimension. Novels of personal relationships and feelings, they also seemed to touch on strange powers and forces, and moved in the direction of surrealism and fantasy. The conventions of the romance and the fabulous novel were drawn on – in *The Unicorn*, for example – and made a part of the repertory. There were a number of critics who thought the case for taking her work seriously was diminishing. But not only was Murdoch's creative variety astonishing; so was the steady underlying purposefulness of theme.

Murdoch's novels, as Antonia Byatt said in her book, persistently pointed toward a serious reading, being much concerned with the way art might represent the good and the true; she remained a novelist insistently concerned with the novel's moral powers, making the task of pursuing a serious moral intent the prime preoccupation of her writing. Great art, she was to say in "The Idea of Perfection" (*The Sovereignty of Good*, 1970), has a "selfless attention to nature" which is of a piece with moral virtue, and "aesthetic situations are not so much analogies of morals as cases of morals". This meant that the novelist should represent characters who possess ethical powers, the competences, freedoms and restraints, known in everyday life. This of course depends on what concepts of the individual we have, what view of the kind of universe in which they live, and what kind of transcendent conditions govern it; in the secular and fictionalist universe in which we live, the problems are notable. Murdoch's novels became speculations on such matters, multiple and various, yet always acknowledging some fundamental relationship between certain kinds of love or attention, and certain kinds of formal making. Love is a moral thrust of feeling that turns toward apprehension of the real and the good, and, she tells us in "The Idea of Perfection", "If apprehension of the good is apprehension of the individual and the real, then good partakes of the infinitely elusive character of reality." The wholeness given by love bears some relation to aesthetic apprehension, or form, but form itself risks becoming consolation, false art, unwilling to seem true, unless it sustains moral pressure as well as aesthetic joy.

Nonetheless the fact remained that Murdoch's theory of "unutterable particularity", which is a moral theory and a theory or justification of the importance of the novel and the novel's way, was indeed strangely transacted into writerly practice. This was partly because her work retained many of the preoccupations of the philosopher while clearly depending on a distinctive and flamboyant delight to be won from the rituals and practices of the novel. Her fiction, working toward the good and the true, also worked toward a greater completeness of form – rather in the spirit of Lily Briscoe as she contemplates Mrs Ramsay in Virginia Woolf's *To the Lighthouse*:

"she brought together this and that and then this, and so made out of that miserable silliness and spirit . . . something – this scene of the beach for example, this moment of friendship and liking . . . stayed on in the mind almost like a work of art." Her books become a fiction of personal relationships and feelings within an instinct for the transcendental, affected more, perhaps, by Simone Weil or even G.E. Moore than Sartre. Like the Bloomsbury novelists, she was evidently drawn toward a fiction where the world of secular relations bore fundamental implications of aesthetic, moral and transcendental possibilities, though here too there seems to be a dispute, one that appears to have preoccupied her at the beginning of the 1960s when she wrote *A Severed Head*; if *Under the Net* appears to represent her interest in, but quarrel with, the Sartrean novel, *A Severed Head* appears to display her interest in and quarrel with the novel of Bloomsbury.

A Severed Head is not a novel all her critics have liked. Elizabeth Dipple firmly speaks of it as "redolent of real evil and . . . uncommonly easy to dislike", for in it satire and pessimism "reduce all the materials of civilization, perceiving them as sheltering devices behind which a primitive ego resides". *A Severed Head* is one of Murdoch's more curious books, a patterned comedy with much rococo detail, a basic cast of six characters, and a series of love-relations which, rather in the manner of farce, offered the reader all the sexual pairings you might imagine, and then one you would probably not. But apart from its strongly ritualised quality what most distinguishes it is the way it appears to comment, half-engagedly and half-satirically, on the fiction of Bloomsbury-like personal relations. The main character has the name Martin Lynch-Gibbon, which appears teasing, and is a wine merchant; the mother of his wife Antonia "came out of the Bloomsbury world, as something of a minor poet and a remote relation of Virginia Woolf"; Antonia herself has "a sharp appetite for personal relations", seeks "a perfect communion of souls", and possesses "a metaphysic of the drawing room". The story is set in and around a wealthy and well-heeled London drawing room world, polite, artistic, elegant, and tolerant (Martin has both a happy marriage and a pleasing mistress, and other relationships are of the same kind). But it is soon dismantled when Martin is drawn toward the anthropologist Honor Klein, and led by her into a world of primitive powers and totemistic forces; and through a sequence of events which involve ritual incest and the dark powers of prophecy he leaves behind his "talent for a gentler world" for a world of force which has "nothing to do with happiness", and experience "remote from love and remote from ordinary life."

Honor Klein is tricked out with the exotica and the erotica of one of those presiding enchanter-and-psychopomp figures who play a considerable part in Murdoch's novels. She has striking characteristics (her hairy lip, which Martin notices as he strikes her violently three times in his cellar), strange skills (with a samurai sword, for example), and she is ceremonially and incestuously paired with her brother Palmer Anderson, a psychologist. These two guardian figures, the anthropologist and the psychologist, preside regally over the book, introducing a world of the primitive and unconscious that leads toward "the dark gods". Honor is not simply the book's disturbing erotic centre, but its emblematic one – an enchanter, "a severed head such as primitive tribes and old alchemists used to use, anointing it with oil and putting a morsel of gold on its tongue to make it utter prophecies". Martin acknowledges that "who knows but that long acquaintance with a severed head might not lead to strange knowledge", and through all this the form of the novel of personal relations falls open, as if D.H. Lawrence had suddenly intruded upon Virginia Woolf. The implications seem clear: the world of personal being and becoming, the conventional novel of liberal character, is not enough, and the real is beyond and outside us, its moral imperative lying however exactly in its irrationality and primitivism, its acquaintance with the mythic and the unconscious. This in its turn has implications for the fictional form; Murdoch's novel may start in the world of conventional sentiments and personal relations, but it must also be open to enchantment, ritual, mannerism, and form, and the social scene as life-giving framework has never quite been the full sum of her reality.

In this light we do well to consider the strange events that occurred on the road to Rathblane, fifteen miles south of Dublin, two nights before the Easter Rising of 1916. Rathblane is the house to which Millie Kinnard has retired on a kind of secular retreat before the great culmination, and Millie is the central female character of *The Red and the Green*, perhaps Murdoch's most conventionally realistic novel. But where *Under the Net* had been clothed in a contemporary social realism, *The Red and the Green* is conditioned by a clear historical specificity, dealing as it does with major public events at a significant time, events of which we have some considerable historical record. Very unlike most of Murdoch's novels of the 1960s, then, where the romance characteristics are strong, this book is not spun primarily from within itself, and is open to the contingency of fact. Yet had you stood on the Rathblane road that night, you would have seen a sight surely strange to the average mind, which respects contingency, though one perfectly acceptable to a regular habitué of Murdochland: four male figures, somewhat heated, passing by separately on their bicycles en route for Rathblane and Millie Kinnard.

The four are in fact the four main personages in the novel. One, Andrew, loses his virginity to Millie; another, Pat Dumay, hard and violent, comes for his own kind of sexual satisfaction; a third, Christopher, to whom she is engaged, feels at the least entitled to see her; a fourth, Barney, a failed priest and elderly withdrawn figure not unfamiliar in Murdoch, comes to spy on her, out of a kind of love. Most of these are related, and in the earlier part of the book Murdoch has given us these characters in great social, moral and psychological detail, separating their lives and exploring them in their distinctive separation, responding without overt literary coercion to their differently defined moral natures and their radically divided political sympathies, and rooting each of them in a dense contingent society and milieu of his own, as well as in the specifics of a Dublin historically recreated with great vigour. The reader may have found in the invention of these four characters a symbolic aptness, finding them micro-cosmically related to the larger struggles of Ireland. Nonetheless, in the tolerant detail through which each one is brought into existence we may find our understanding of what Murdoch means when she says she is "a novelist concerned with the creation of character".

We might then say that something changes as these characters enter Rathblane, commonly impelled on the same night toward the novel's focusing character; and they pass in and out of the bedroom, up and down the stairs, in and out of the front door, hither and thither on their various bicycles. Amid the chaos love is made, to no-one's real satisfaction. It is all very stylish and funny – as Millie says, like a comic opera – the confusion and coincidences taking on more force because of the apparently undirected and unritualised nature of the earlier narrative. It is one of those virtuoso moments that set a Murdochian stamp on things; in it some essential narrative tactic and manner in her work appears to distil.

This is partly because the work contains within itself the idea of distillation (in the Easter Rising itself), and partly because Millie herself is a character made to serve culmination, a human figure with more than human purport, like Honor Klein. She too is tricked out with a special emotional depth and density, and strange associations: her pistol, with which she undertakes target practice in her boudoir, her altar-like dressing table, where she metaphorically celebrates decadent rites. By virtue of being the centre of the sexual interplay of the book, Millie becomes also its emblematic centre – something like a symbol, something more than a character, for through her the narrative firms and distils. If she is partly a surrogate for the emotional powers and violence that will find another expression in the Rising itself, she also serves – like Honor Klein – to urge form or design onto the novel, an urging which is in turn a testament to otherness, to strange powers and mysteries that transcend the individual identities of the other characters. This comes over somewhat unusually in *The Red and the Green* because it is an historical novel, and one where the force of otherness is attached to political dimensions. But if art indeed is "selfless attention to nature", then do such rituals and culminations, which are present in all her books, give us a design beyond contingency, or do they compromise the sense of contingency, the moral substance of relations, the "life-giving framework"?

The questions arise because few novelists today have the capacity or desire to represent a serious moral agent, and few seek to confer through secular narrative a transcendent meaning. Murdoch's characters are granted great competence in moral matters, a separated freedom of being. But she also patterns them, brings them out of accident and into ritual, makes the logic of love into the logic of a formal composition. In short, she gives herself a very dialectical aesthetics, where the writerly task is to pass elegantly between the rocks of realism and symbolism, the slackness but truth of contingency, and the real but potentially dry consolations of fantasy, myth and transcendence. This is the passage made by love, which is hardly love in its liberal and secular sense, but a form of transcendental moral apprehension. Her books unite high aesthetic pleasures with great moral pleasures, which is to say that, in different degrees, they achieve the capacity to construct something elegant while saying something which is humane and true.

As her production has increased her range has in some ways narrowed, in the sense that we feel these issues moving toward higher concentration. Devotees of her work sense, I think, a tightrope walk being undertaken over the dark pit of pure consolation waiting below. But consolation, the loss of the sense of the infinitely elusive character of reality, the failure to be true, is still some way off; for the real strength of her later books, her books from the beginning of the 1970s, which are in many ways her best, is their readiness to consent to the potential of those formalising powers, while sustaining the moral pressure toward truth. As she said in her Gifford Lecture of 1982: "in good art we do not ask for realism; we ask for truth." And, as she said in *The Fire and the Sun*, "Good art, thought of as symbolic force rather than statement, provides a stirring image of a pure transcendent value, a steady visible enduring higher good, and perhaps provides for many people, in an unreligious age without prayer or sacraments, their clearest *experience* of something grasped as separate and precious and beneficial and held quietly and unpossessively in the attention."

5 These concerns have persisted, and today it must seem that the novels where the aim of an art of high moral apprehension has been best served are several of her most recent ones, in which, undoubtedly, these issues have grown more intense. To some degree this has been because Murdoch's later work shows a much stronger acquiescence in the power of form, the form that has always been implicitly asserting itself but which now becomes overt. Indeed the great ritual forms of art, opera, music, and comic and tragic drama, are scarcely hidden allusions behind the fiction that, from about *The Black Prince* onward, have shaped much of her work. In *The Black Prince* the strongest allusion is, of course, to *Hamlet*; and this is one of those novels which, as has happened on occasion within her work, seems to take hold of the formal questions that concern her, and push the matter to the forefront. "I wanted to produce a sort of statement that might be called my philosophy," says Bradley Pearson in that book. He also notes that it is not always possible in art to avoid an elegant complexity: "And then one asks, how can this also be 'true'? Is the real like this, *is* it this?" It is possible that by a kind of "momentary artifice" we can offer a diagnosis; yet the marvels of the instrument frequently interrupt the task to which it is dedicated. *The Black Prince* is a comedy based on these premises, a book of great self-consciousness and wry outcome which will nonetheless compound art's paradoxes. The chaos of life disputes Bradley's grand designs; he falls into comic disaster. His narrative of love is, we are told, "a literary failure". Yet the closing words, by another voice, pose the problem differently: "Art is not cosy and is not mocked. Art tells the only truth that ultimately matters. It is the light by which human things can be mended. And after art there is, let me assure you all, nothing."

Murdoch's serious allusions were to persist. In *The Sea, The Sea* (1978) the underlying text is *The Tempest*, where art is both asserted and abjured. Again love is the central kingdom, a past love re-projected in a very contemplative present. This is one of Murdoch's more magical novels, set in a minimalised landscape and seascape, somewhere in the north, in and around a great Edwardian house, with a view across the sea, that "image of inaccessible freedom", with yellow rocks, a testing watery cauldron, a swimming place, and a nearby small village with a hotel to serve the unexpected visitor. Charles Arrowby, the central character, over sixty, is a retired theatre director much devoted to *The Tempest*, but he has now laid down his staff and drowned his book, hoping to repent in meditation a monstrous egoism. Spareness is all; even his diet comes from a textbook for the new minimalist gourmets, and the very *cuisine* is *nouvelle*. But pasts are not done with, and small intrusive mysteries appear: a sight of a possible sea-monster, poltergeist-like happenings in the house. The isle is full of noises, and, slowly, as if by meditation he has evoked them, those who have populated his memories – old lovers, relatives, friends – fill the economical stage. Above all there is Hartley, his lost first love, whose memory has kept other lovers at a distance and sustained an unmarried state. Beginning in his mind, she appears in his life, in the village, elderly and trapped in a jealous marriage. More attractive mistresses are on offer, but her old face reconstructs young love, and meditation is set aside as he plots to free her, opening the story of those ambiguities of freedom and possession so central in Murdoch. Soon Hartley is his own love-prisoner; violence and death follow; Charles goes through the dark mysteries of desire in conflict with contemplation, and the sea, no longer clean and innocent, engulfs.

Like many of Murdoch's late novels *The Sea, The Sea* concentrates on the dark chill of loving, the conflicts of egotism and sacrifice, desire and death. It is also, like most of them, very elegantly plotted, as the world Murdoch makes on the first page is the one she goes on to spend. That is part of the magic of invention, and that itself is a central object of attention. And, again, though the tale is presented in part for its intricate cunning and flamboyance, it is also offered metaphorically, as an opening beyond conventional reality. Late in the book, Charles thinks, as do many of Murdoch's later characters, of Shakespeare's special powers; in his work, he reflects, "magic does not shrink reality and turn it into tiny things to be the toys of fairies". This in turn has to do with that "secret vital busy inwardness" that drives our lives, but which tends in old age to move toward some final meaning. This becomes a common tone in the later novels, which seek to elicit from life's facts and dreams a meaning, a weight, a sense of the things that matter.

This makes each new book a fresh ritual – in *The Philosopher's Pupil* there is a sudden and unexpected change of landscape, as Murdoch sets her story in a southern spa town which is as populous as the world of *The Sea, The Sea* is spare, and shifts the focus from the artist to the philosopher – and gives each ritual a serious task, a task unusual in modern writing. Rozanov, the philosopher (definitely not of Murdoch's own mould) in *The Philosopher's Pupil*, is markedly uncontemplative, a plotter and planner, who seeks to orchestrate his own love-ritual. Again disorder disposes of grand designs. Rozanov dies by water: accident or murder, contingency or symbol? The questions radiate; Murdoch is still a realist of fantasy, a magician of the contingent. Art's aims are not always fulfilled; and disorder violates shapeliness, but it does not necessarily defeat it. For where is the end of the tale? We determine it arbitrarily, just as we define the limits of a person arbitrarily, says N., the fussy, hyper-specific narrator of *The Philosopher's Pupil*. Persons do not end and stories do not stop, though we close them. "It is my role in life to listen to stories," adds N. "I also had the assistance of a certain lady." So, too, has modern fiction, the certain lady being one of the very best of our novelists – the ambiguity of fictions, and their potency for truth, being one of her fundamental concerns, the command to listen to stories one to which she has made us attend, in the way only a serious artist can.

MURIEL SPARK'S FINGERNAILS

" 'Human nature,' said Sir Quentin, 'is a quite extraordinary thing,
I find it quite extraordinary. You know the old adage, Truth is
stranger than fiction?'
"I said yes."

Muriel Spark, Loitering with Intent (1981)

"The sense of a system saves the painter from the baseness of the
arbitrary stroke, the touch without its reason."

Henry James, "Preface", The Tragic Muse (1890)

1 We should undoubtedly all have noticed it long ago, but the times
were not entirely favourable, and the writer came from mildly unusual
sources; but Muriel Spark is one of our finest and surest modern
novelists, a writer of brilliance and pain who from the start of her
career has been exploring and developing some of the most complex
aspects of the contemporary form of fiction. Her spirit, as many of her
readers would now acknowledge, was at first very hard to catch, and
her seriousness has been masked by such elaborate mannerism that it
has taken time to digest it. She came to fiction out of poetry, and the
poetic part of her career was famously obscure, indeed a kind of
loitering with intent, in a world of vague literary tasks in vague
bohemian locations – the kind of world that Jake Donaghue lives in in
Iris Murdoch's *Under the Net*, and in which many of her own fictional
characters have lived since. That world underlies a lot of her fiction,
but so also do several others – the Presbyterian Edinburgh of her
childhood, the contingent London of the writing years, the Euro-
world of her success in the period since she became a citizen of
Rome. The odd coupling of Rome and Edinburgh to some degree
explains where the fiction starts, for the part-Jewish Presbyterian who
became a Catholic convert (this mixed history finds its fullest
examination in her novel *The Mandelbaum Gate*, 1965) seems to have
converted to fiction at roughly the same time. That dramatic and
intense conversion provided both the impulse and the material, much

of it satirical, for her first novel, *The Comforters*, which appeared in 1957, at a time when British fiction did not seem capaciously open to writers of her temper. As Ruth Whittaker notes in her useful book on Spark, the reviewers did not get her wavelength, and one review entitled "No Angry Young Women?" asked what had happened to the crazy mixed-up girls who should have been brightening the literary scene. To readers who like their fictions to familiarise and domesticate the world, and to present it as a humane place in which to live, Miss Spark did not offer a great deal, and the taste by which she was to be understood was to be slowly acquired.

One thing that helped was the movement away from emphatic social and moral realism that came to the novel after the 1950s, and the more complex view of the nature of fictions that went with it. For *The Comforters* may not have been an angry but it was most certainly a very radical book, and firmly insistent on the difference between fiction and commonplace social realities. As the narrator tells us, "the characters in this book are all fictions", and the firm refusal of all sentimental resemblances is one of the book's most striking features. There are others, from the satirical and grotesque tone to the witty metaphysical enquiry into the nature of fictions, the function of novelists, and the character of their truth, as well as the truth of their characters; one of hers firmly disputes her role in anyone else's fiction. Mrs Spark was writing out of attitudes not very close to the mainstream of the later 1940s and 1950s, though in another way this was exactly her time, or her prime. Her novels and short stories persistently allude to what she calls, in *Loitering With Intent* (1981), "the middle of the twentieth century", when her role as a British writer was forged, a time of poets on the bottle, of hackwork, of girls of slender means, of crises that linked money and art and sex and faith, and God seemed to be behaving, in relation to the visible world, rather like a quirky novelist Himself. Poetry and the novel and literary criticism were very much interlinked then, and Spark was involved with them all, but in rather different ways from, say, Kingsley Amis or John Wain. Her poetry owed something to the bohemian apocalyptic mood, her criticism tended to favour the romantics and the Victorians, and especially those who had some crisis of faith and art, from Wordsworth to Newman to Ruskin. Like other writers of the time, Spark was a comic writer. But where others were writing largely within the tradition of humanistic and social comedy, Spark was not. Indeed it was the 1960s, when humour became more extreme, that offered the right word for her spirit. The phrase "black humour" became popular, and it suited her very exactly. For Spark was essentially a writer of the modern macabre and the *memento mori*, and black humour was just what she was about.

Spark was indeed a Catholic novelist, and even in the Catholic novel she was notably extreme. She wrote of a world so decadent and strange that it could be presented with a hard satirical unconcern. Her tactics of indifference made her aesthetic surface strong, but they were also part of an appalling *moral* manner, a splendid impudence. As with a number of Catholic novelists – and they have contributed a more than proportionate share to the aesthetic speculations as well as the literary achievements of the English novel – her dealings with the form have always been touched with an ingrained casuistry. Her *Memento Mori* (1959), a very black farce about the old, desperately seeking to hold onto the manners of the young and maintain the pathetic significance of their lives, only to be constantly reminded of the facts of mortality, had to come from a novelist with a certain style, a certain and very fascinating version of faith, and a certain kind of detachment from life. Of these powerful qualities, Muriel Spark has made the most ever since. Her formal brilliance and the wit of her plots has always had a great deal to do with the paradoxes of faith and the arbitrariness of human behaviour. Sandy, in *The Prime of Miss Jean Brodie* (1961), freely betrays the teacher she loves; but betrayal is a way of dealing with the call of belief. In the wartime novel *The Girls of Slender Means* (1963) the chances of fatness and thinness have to do with who can squeeze through the window of redemption; randomness, not morality, is the stuff of salvation. This leaves us with little to do in life but be famous for something: 'famous for mathematics' like Monica, 'famous for sex' like Rose in *The Prime of Miss Jean Brodie*, or extremely good at playing oneself, like Annabel Christopher in *The Public Image*, that novel where extraordinary voids and potential significances clash against each other right up to the final image of the book ("Nobody recognized her as she stood, having moved the baby to rest on her hip, conscious also of the baby in a sense weightlessly and perpetually within her, as an empty shell contains, by its very structure, the echo and harking image of former and former seas"). *Not to Disturb*, she called one of her novels; but her novels have managed in general to be morally and metaphysically very disturbing indeed.

Conversion to Catholicism not only started Spark's novels, then, but gave them much of their distinctive flavour. But they also draw on a complex inheritance. She was born of a Jewish father, educated in the spirit of Edinburgh Presbyterianism during the 1930s and its extreme political anxieties (*The Prime of Miss Jean Brodie* tells us much about this), and she married and went to Rhodesia, returning during the war. She experienced the bombing and worked in black propaganda (again there is a book on the matter, *The Hothouse on the East River* (1973)), and it could be said that she has gone on working in it ever since. Her conversion came in 1954, and it somehow encouraged her to write fiction ("I was writing and talking with other people's voices all the time. But not any longer"). *The Comforters* deals with this transition, the step from a raffish literary world to a new world of Catholic companions; the two were to interfuse to extraordinary effect in many of her later books. The tone from the start was satirical, and it was clear that if her works, as they do, depend to a considerable degree on a Catholic aesthetic, it was hardly that of Catholic humanism, of, say, the kind that François Mauriac spoke for in saying that "the heroes of our novels must be free in the sense the theologians say man is free. The novelist must not intervene in their destinies." Spark's characters are indeed free in the sense that some theologians say man is free, which is to say not free at all. And the novelist, like God, does intervene in their destinies, and not always for the best.

Indeed, this paradoxical analogy, between God and the novelist, is the basis of much of her fictional speculation and the stuff of her stories, and, as David Lodge points out in his article "The Uses and Abuses of Omniscience", the results are decidedly unexpected: "The True Church was awful, though unfortunately, one couldn't deny, true," finds Caroline in *The Comforters*. She belongs with the Catholic novelists of detachment, like Joyce, whose God-like writer is indifferent to creation, paring his fingernails; with the Catholic novelists of the unexpected result, like Graham Greene, discovering unexpected redemptions in the corrupt and debased; with Catholic novelists of satirical indifference, like Waugh, who, despairing of God's sensible presence in contemporary history, feels free to present the modern world as chaos.

Spark too presents a universe absurd and macabre, but at the same time offers a sense of what is absent, a knowledge of true things, and last things. Indeed, like Waugh, she is very much a writer of the *memento mori*, and her novel of that title is a central testament – a farce showing the comic unreality of human and historical concerns in the lives of its geriatric cast, while at the same time evoking for the human lot a sense of cool and instructive pathos, and moving toward a solemn underlying seriousness ("Jean Taylor lingered for a time, employing her pain to magnify the Lord, and meditating sometimes confidingly on Death, the first of the four last things to be ever remembered"). But, unlike Waugh, Spark is always and self-consciously the aesthetician, not only because she is a poet as well as one of our most intelligent novelists, but also because she sees the need for wholeness and coherence in her creations. In some of her novels this seems the central preoccupation, and it is the relation between the chaotic and contingent and the possibility of a meaning or a teleology that guides both her artistic and moral interests.

And so, from her first novel on, there has been a preoccupation with the relation of an author to a fiction and its agents; an interest in extravagant, disturbed social milieux, and camp or high-styled figures; an emphasis on the relation between the real and material, and the surreal and supernatural, often introduced by the invention of diabolic or charismatic figures who have some strange intervention to make in human affairs, as does the novelist herself. In the earlier books this frequently went along with the population and elaboration of a large social world and the provision of a large cast of characters, always handled with a quirky moral concern which involved in the novelist a sense of foreknowledge and fate. The future of her stories often guides their present, and this makes plots into destinies.

These themes, as I say, were always there, but they were perhaps not always perceived, for there was much else too – a witty gift for observing contemporary society, manners, and historical changes, and a strong autobiographical charge in a number of the novels. But, as if in revolt against our ignorance, her books during the 1970s began to distil these concerns. Their characteristics grew closer to the manner of the *nouveau roman*, with the text becoming a very hard presence, and the causalities and structure being laid bare. And in a group of short novels in the late 1960s and early 1970s – *The Public Image* (1968), *The Driver's Seat* (1970) and *Not to Disturb* (1971) – she seemed to concentrate all this. Looking back, these books seem to mark a distinct aesthetic phase, not unlike those which occur in the careers of certain modern painters who, by localising certain aspects of a once broader artistic endeavour, have made their forms conspicuous. It may be more simple; Spark clearly found attractive the form of the novella, which publishers very often do not like, but some magazines (like *The New Yorker*, where several of her books appeared in their entirety) do. Whatever the reason, in these books a new authority comes into her work, a form of great tactical precision; in them every compositional decision and every compositional device is traded at the same high level of economy as are Hemingway's best stories. The result is that unusual thing in modern writing, a clear deliverance of style. And though style is not all that Spark is about, it is something that clearly does matter to her, as it should to all of us.

2   What is it that makes these books feel so modern, and very much in tune with the difficulties of the modern writer trying to find the manner in which to present a hard and material world that time and again seems resistant to effective representation? In them and to a

greater degree than elsewhere in her books, certain distinctive things occur, certain sure economies are made. The length is shortened, the expository material diminished, a good part of the substance is conveyed through pointed and ritual dialogue, the narrative is held to one or two days, and the extent of particular scenes – what James calls the "discriminated occasion" of the telling – is increased. The manner grows very exact, the technique abstemious, there is presentation through small and contingent material things, the character's psychologies are not normally entered, metaphor is limited, and the tense is often the present. The present, as it does often in Spark, also points to the future.

For these are all novels of ending, and in a way they all are endings, the earlier part of the possible story being given as prior exposition. The scene begins on the edge of finality, and completes it. Frank Kermode has always been one of Spark's best interpreters, and in his book *The Sense of an Ending* (1967) he seemed to analyse on the general level the elements that matter in these novels. As he pointed out, endings in fiction and apocalyptics in history are analogous, for they turn contingency into design, seamless annal into structure, the simple clock of things into signs, portents and promises. Endings satisfy our desire for structure and our sense of concord, and one of the ways fictions satisfy is precisely because they give to the time of the world a design of significance. Thus endings are a fundamental aspect of narrative desire, but many modern writers, for this very reason, have disputed with them, as does, for example, John Fowles in *The French Lieutenant's Woman*. But, far from disputing, Spark takes them as the essence.

Endings are one of our main means of giving meaning to stories, one of the ways the writer makes the present of the narrative an element of the future. Spark has always had an interesting way with these matters; and, as David Lodge has said, she often appears to sacrifice all narrative surprise in a way that most writers would advise against. What *will* happen is told us in the course of what *is* happening; the outcome often precedes the event. The result is a pressure on the reader to see *how* it is happening, and what the novelist is doing to it. If endings give meaning to stories, the ending of lives gives meaning to those too, and often they are not the meanings we expect; Spark's novellas here are not just end-directed but death-directed, for death is the one indisputable ending we all suffer.

Yet there are, in a sense, ways of disputing it. In *The Public Image* Frederick makes a plot out of his own death, constructing his suicide in order to expose the public wealth and private squalor of his wife, the English tiger-lady actress Annabel Christopher. But the story is really her story, and she is able to reconstruct his plot, developing a profitable alternative. In *The Driver's Seat*, the story moves straight towards its mortal terminus, the newspaper pictures of the corpse of the central character being described to us virtually before we have met her; this very exact story I will return to in a moment. In *Not to Disturb*, a pastiche of an old narrative situation where the events happen to the employers but are told by the servants, those traditional fiction-makers and reporters of crimes of high bourgeois passion, the servants have learned modern manners; they have now acquired press-agents and aspirations to being screenwriters, and they too share with their author a fondness for forward plotting, helping their stories on a little. Since a *crime passionnel* is in the offing, they have no scruple about discouraging callers and encouraging apt developments to ensure that the story indeed accords with their prefigurative fictions; technically innocent and morally implicated, they aid death's business, just as does the *memento mori* novelist who constructs the larger fiction herself.

All these preoccupations are striking because they are the antithesis of that concern for open freedom which has been so much at stake in the modern novel, and is exemplified in Henry James's famous account of the writing of *The Portrait of a Lady*, where, like his own Ralph Touchett, James attempts to construct his plan without over-determination so that Isabel Archer can be truly free. We have learned to value the novel of what has been called, by Alan J. Friedman, "open form": the novel, that is, where tight determinants, inexorable plots and the rules of genre are broken apart in order to catch at contingency, consciousness, the atoms as they fall. James tells us that he determined to make Isabel Archer the "essence", and placed her at the centre of his creative process that she might determine her own "end". In a modern variant, John Fowles in *The French Lieutenant's Woman* describes his permissive relation to his characters, who should, he holds, grow existentially alive, at least to the point where they reach not one ending, but alternative ones.

This is exactly not the way in these novels of Muriel Spark. No author could be surer which way things are going: from these books the beginning, which creates wide expectation and the sense of possibility, and the middle, which both substantiates and qualifies it, appear absent. Her people and their destinies arise from the last, cutting away much of our sense of option and motive, purpose and aspiration. There is no great taking in of impressions, no learning from experience, and in that sense her work conveys significant absences, a feeling of omission. This is why it carries some parallel with a good deal of modern experimental writing and the achievement of the *nouveau roman*, for which Spark has expressed a regard. "The crime consists of stating that there is in existence in the world something that is not man, that takes no notice of him, and has nothing in common with him," says Robbe-Grillet, "The supreme crime . . . is to record this separation, this distance, without trying to sublimate it."

That said, what is not man in Spark is not randomness but a system. In Spark's fictions there is a material world, contingent, solid and in recent novels often expensively decorated by the new materialism: there is an intensive and almost *chosiste* description, in *The Driver's Seat*, of the decor of Lise's apartment, the stuff of the plastic airplane meal. There are characters, often flamboyant, but they have no strongly established psychology, no necessary motives. No pathetic fallacy links the two: things are inert in their quiddity, people move among objects as if they were object-like. The hard world is part of the aesthetic clarity, but it also has a strong contemporary reference. In their want of psychology her people populate an instantaneous and random world, very film-like. In earlier books this is often bohemian or suburban London, but in later ones it grows opulent and internationalist, reflecting her move to Rome. The Rome film-world of *The Public Image*, the northern and southern cities (Rome again?) of *The Driver's Seat*, and the *dolce vita* society of *Not to Disturb* are all part of a modern scenario (to use an analogy that clearly interests her), part of a world of fashion, role and publicity. It would be hard to say Spark loves any world, but she certainly does not love this one; the images of decadence are many, though to her cool eye presumably no more than may be expected. But it is exactly this world of moral contingency that makes her endings so compelling. They unsettle contingency, introduce into randomness those plots, grids and fictions which do move truth, and so they bring into the *chosiste* world the eschatological questions which are so much a mark of Spark's distinctive and troubling manner as a modern writer.

3 All this is very clear in *The Driver's Seat*, perhaps her most precise book, the narrative of a few brief continuous hours in the life of Lise, a middle-aged inelegant shrill woman with a "final and judging mouth". Lise is on holiday from her normal life, leaving her job in an accountant's office in an unnamed northern city. She buys new clothes, insisting strangely on a dress that will stain, makes arrangements for leaving her flat-key, and takes a plane flight to a southern city, also unnamed, where she expects some kind of encounter to occur. Indeed throughout the journey she is ready to meet someone, behaving flamboyantly, drawing attention to herself; various people are encountered and seem to be implicated in her plot. The text meanwhile tells us what will happen, promising significance and publicity in all the newspapers. Arriving, Lise shops in a modern department store, encounters a student demonstration, acquires a car, and in the last lines of the novella meets her death by murder, crying "Kill me" in four languages. Of this ending there is authorial foreknowledge, shared with the reader, but also – and more extraordinarily – with Lise too. Once we have read the book, and read it back, we see that Lise's dress which stains, her deliberate flamboyance, and her selectivity about which acquaintances to develop, are all shaped by her sense of an ending. She is an active murderee, complicit with her killer, and of course with her author. This raises an issue about ultimate morality, and another about form. For Lise, as it were, commits suicide without offence. She takes the driver's seat over from her killer, but also from the novelist, becoming an alternative plot-maker, a giver of form to contingent events. And just like Annabel in the earlier book, she knows she has her public image to consider: she is ripe for a newspaper story, ripe for a fiction.

All this is done with a characteristic brilliance, in a form of hard anxiety. Muriel Spark plants, and plays with, the plot, and displays and preens its elegant shapes and details. Lise, with more to lay down on the line than her author, namely her own, albeit fictional, mortality, seems to play with the author's powers, indeed defeats her originator, not, like Caroline in *The Comforters*, by trying to stand aside ("I intend to stand aside and see if the novel has any real form apart from this artificial plot. I happen to be a Christian"), but by assuming total mastery of it, the driver's seat. She outwits contingency, and this is her victory. For on first reading *The Driver's Seat* reads like a totally contingent book, hard and random in the overt manner of the *nouveau roman*. Places are unnamed, and the central event is a journey from one placeless place to another: impressions, random, sudden, unorganised, given in all their perceptual properties, dominate. The material things of the world appear not to reinforce their human associates: Lise's flat is totally impersonal, and impersonality is the motif of the world. The tight time-span suggests that the book is simply moving through the clock of hours, and the present-tense increases instantaneousness and reduces causality and connectedness. And Lise's motives and sensations are never given, only her perceptions and her actions, keeping the relation between character and author a hard and ironic one. The end-directed telling has the effect of giving a detective-story-like construction, mildly implying outcomes, resolutions, motives we might come to comprehend, coherences we could grasp if we just wait. But what most makes for suspense is Miss Spark's gift for being appalling, and the realisation that in the Sparkian world any surprise is possible. And, as with a detective story, once the ending has been given, the structure unfolds backwards, giving everything not so much here a narrative as an aesthetic coherence.

It is, in a sense, a plot of two victories, both to do with the value placed *on* plot, and its nature not simply as story but as destiny. Lise's victory is that in the chaotic run of the present she has always known a future, and the relationships with strangers, the hints at sexual complication, the passing claims of politics, and the substantial department-store world of material temptations become diverse and multiplying alternatives, put in their place by her own emphasis on her mortality and its moral, philosophical and theological implications. Lise has a soul to consider, and she makes the subtlest use of it she can. With all the casuistry of the higher Spark heroine, and many of them are outstanding casuists, not least the nuns of *The Abbess of Crew* (1974), she partakes of her narrator and makes the most dangerous and extreme flirtation with mortal sin she might; her death is a triumph of confused mortal responsibilities.

Miss Spark's victory, apart from having constructed all this in the first place, lies in her art of narrative outwitting, her refusal of the humanistic novel, but also of the ostensible contingency of the *nouveau roman*, showing that even in a plotless world there is a plot. Not only is this not a humanist novel; its wit and metaphysical conceit make it decidedly fancy or extraordinary as a religious one. Of course in the end Lise may never outwit her author, whose omniscience is complete; but in larger fictions there are smaller, constructing the web of contradiction and variation on which narrative depends.

4 Perhaps it is clear from all this why Muriel Spark is a writer's writer, someone who in her manifest virtuosity, controlling skills and her capacity from all these activities to yield a contemporary and troubling metaphysic, commands the attention as few writers can. The brilliance, indeed, yields further secrets: establishing the power of plot, Spark shows that destiny, purpose and teleology do, for her, exist. The point is located near enough to the centre of her fiction-making process to be seen as evidence of her great aesthetic brilliance; but there is another seriousness here, and the true seeker is doubtless required to go further. Spark grants the practised reader of novels many remarkable fictional joys – as in *The Driver's Seat*, for example, when in a very inventive conceit a character who at the start seems the subordinate victim of writerly manipulation and omniscience becomes the consort of the writer herself, ironically free, doing willingly what lesser writers have to compel.

But the fable goes further. Not only is the creative energy dense, vigorous, and decidedly erotic, and the avid precision of rendering makes the fictional world a strong correlative of the real one, surreal, hyper-material, and absurd; but there is also a persistent assurance that all the follies and narratives of this world are threatened from the next, and this sense of the skull beneath the skin is very much to the point. Spark's aesthetics are aesthetic and modern, but also metaphysical and religious, and this raises the matter of the truth. She has explicitly rejected the arts of "sentiment and emotion": "In its place I advocate the arts of satire and of ridicule. And I see no other living art form for the future." She shares this view with many other contemporary writers, creating an art that is one of hard defamiliarisation. But there is still the matter of the Truth. "You know the old adage, Truth is stranger than fiction?" the central character of *Loitering With Intent* is asked. "I said yes," says the character, and so does Muriel Spark: one of the few truly fictionalist novelists to have an idea – itself strange, but also strangely secure – of the Truth in our truthless world.

THE NOVELIST AS IMPRESARIO
The fiction of John Fowles

"There is about the clothes, in the lavishly embroidered summer waistcoat, in the three rings on fingers, the panatella in its amber holder, the malachite-headed cane, a distinct touch of the flashy. He looks very much as if he had given up preaching and gone in for grand opera; and done much better at the latter than the former. There is, in short, more than a touch of the successful impresario about him."

John Fowles, *The French Lieutenant's Woman* (1969)

1 Foppish, Frenchified, flashy and "very minor", the lavish figure who inserts himself into the last chapter of *The French Lieutenant's Woman*, looking back at Dante Gabriel Rossetti's Chelsea house "as if it is some new theatre he has just bought and is pretty confident he can fill", and busily turning back fictional time on his watch, is one of the many disguises of the novelist John Fowles himself. He has been in this novel a good deal, and in a variety of disguises, as a Victorian narrator and a contemporary of Roland Barthes and Alain Robbe-Grillet, as a serious humanist concerned for his characters and a serious existentialist worried about them *en-soi*. Reading the book, we grow used to his voices, sometimes very sure and sometimes decidedly worried, here splendidly and chronologically nineteenth century, the master of an old art, and here disturbingly and a-chronologically twentieth century, worried about the Death of the Novel and the reader in the text. Most of these impersonations are decidedly serious and intellectual, but there has been the odd occasion when he has put on costume and sat inside the story, riding in a railway train, or imposing twentieth-century theories on nineteenth-century characters. But this final appearance, in the guise of the stout impresario, is one of the least creditable. For it is as the confidence man that he shows himself, and it seems a very irresponsible intrusion that he makes. The small mechanical task he performs – setting the clock back a little in order completely to transform the fortunes of and

futures of his two central characters, Charles Smithson and Sarah Woodruff, widely called "The French Lieutenant's Woman" – he appears to perform blandly, trivially and vainly, out of an arrogant power and while *en route* for fresher pastures. He is the novelist in one of his less likeable but perfectly proper guises, for in any strong fiction there is indeed a touch of the flashy, and filling theatres is one of the businesses of the confident novelist.

But perhaps it is fortunate that the writing appears, after this, to pass into more reliable hands, the hands of a novelist who has been seriously concerned about the Victorian problems of faith versus scientific scepticism, about being caught between two worlds, one dead and the other powerless to be born, about the statistics of prostitution, the impact of Charles Darwin, the implication of Karl Marx, the relation between the present, which in this book is past, and the future, which in this book is the present, and the relation between a much admired Victorian novel tradition and a twentieth-century situation which makes it virtually impossible to write within it. There is another John Fowles, sober, discursive, often sententious and decidedly omniscient, an author capable of narrating events as if he is reporting them, reflecting sturdily upon them, and taking very seriously indeed the destiny and fulfilment of his fictional characters and establishing with authority an ending which may not however *have* authority. For there was the impresario, and a few pages earlier a narrator just like this has given us an ending equally authoritative, told in much the same way and with many of the same words, but with a different result. He has also given us, for that matter, a third ending, two-thirds of the way to the story, but that ending, we and he are bound to agree, was far too conventional, too imprinted with the sentimental stuff of Victorian fiction, and we do right to eliminate it in order to permit deeper possibilities for the story, larger fulfilments for the characters, and in a sense vaster opportunities for history itself, insofar as novels are history, to spread and advance.

However, these two final endings, the ones at the end, or where the writing stops, are a little bit different. Each one of them is structured with full care out of an eventful and developing plot, a plot that has taken the two characters whose fortunes are here variously resolved very seriously. Both book's fulfil what might be called the argumentative level, or what used to be called the 'sentiments', and are fully invested with that mixture of Arnoldian humanism, Marxist history, fin-de-siecle self-awareness and existentialist authenticity that have had a good deal to do with the workings of the story as a whole. And the bifurcation of endings, the duplication of authority, has been undertaken not simply to show that endings are just endings, arbitrary breaks in the seamless web of life, or pure fictions flamboyantly conceived by flashy impresarios, or to lighten either the novel's responsibilities or the characters', by thrusting it all on the reader. We can, of course, 'make up our minds' which ending is right. We can accept that it might not even have been the novelist's idea to put them in like this, or in that order; a publisher might have helped. But the author is evidently not seeking to diminish but to increase his claim on the fiction, and endeavouring to grant a more than usual freedom to his characters, to dignify their act of choice. To any fiction a writer may come to any conclusion he pleases; and what he pleases is what we call the right ending. Here the book closes, and we are left with conclusions themselves duplicitous: the writer has the power to set his characters free, in a sense, by permitting them to choose as they best can and act as they wish to; he also has the power to make them victims of freedom, by withdrawing his own deciding authority and exposing them far more than if he had exercised it.

At the end of this novel, then, there is more at stake than what happens to Charles and Sarah, a topic I will come back to. There is the matter of the dominant persona of the novelist; nineteenth-century omniscient author, source of fact and authority, or the trickster and confidence artist; the humanist concerned in good faith about fate and freedom, and the manipulator; the plot-maker, or the plot-escaper? These are all guises of the novelist in the book, and they provide its surprising resolution, where the substantial action seems to end up in one world and the substantiating machinery, the technique, seems to end up in another. Which, then, is the real John Fowles? Readers may disagree, and in doing so come up with quite varied readings of the entire book. We might regard it as a brilliant novel of recuperation, displaying the availability of the Victorian tradition for the modern writer. It then becomes a very Whiggish sort of novel, constructed according to those modes of moral realism and ethical interpretation that belong to the nineteenth-century form, so that the novel extends the kind of moral insight and social awareness we gain from, say, George Eliot into a more modern form of perception, aided by increased historical knowledge and enlarged good feeling. It is a story of emancipation through history, where Victorian hypocrisy, prudishness, ignorance and sentimentality give way to modern truth and authenticity, good faith and freedom, and Sarah is set free from the imprisonment that, as a woman and a social alien, constrains her. Alternatively we might take it as a very modern novel, about two characters, and above all Sarah, discovering their very modern emancipation in a world that is framed, by a learned and well-read author with a great gift for pastiche and imitation, with the dress of Victorian experience and the background of Victorian society. Or, more obliquely, we might take it as a post-modern

meta-text, a commentary on writing itself, a work where the consciousness of the fictitious nature of all fictions is made clear, and the
characters, like those in Fowles's short story "The Enigma" (in *The
Ebony Tower*, 1974), become aware that they are in a story, and
attempt to seek their freedom from it.

These matters are important, because they bear on the whole
question of the relation of the contemporary British writer to the
tradition: to its usability, to its potential to perpetuate moral and social
truths we still see as relevant, to the way in which modern writing can
be informed or even testingly questioned by the substance and the
realism of Victorian fiction. For *The French Lieutenant's Woman* seems
to me one of the best books that have come out from Britain since the
war, and I think it very self-conscious. It appeared at an interesting
time, when many British writers were rethinking their relationship to
their tradition. It was produced by an author whose quest through the
novel has taken a dramatic and interestingly varied form, a self-
conscious writer who is to a considerable extent aware of the critical
fabric surrounding him, though in other ways very resistant to it. It
stands on the boundary that has caused perhaps most perplexity in
recent British fiction, that between the nineteenth-century realist and
the modern novel, and like a good deal of modern fiction it promotes
some bafflement by using elements that we are accustomed to
understanding and explaining with one form of poetics, but calling up
many elements from another. We are inclined to find our way through
the book as we might through some great realistic work, a novel of
liberal realism deeply attentive to character and social experience and
the way they feed each other. But we are also conscious of the
presence of a modern self-irony, a sort of patronage that goes out to
that sort of fiction and its limits. Like many modern novels it
summons up a sense of reality while forcing us to attend to the nature
and the falsehood of art. And like many modern novels, those of
Nabokov or Marquez, for example, it tends to touch on our critical
debates *about* the novel at their maximum point of tension and
uncertainty, the points where they explore realism and fictionalism,
discursive writing and enigmatic writing, reportage and fantasy.

2 The quest for John Fowles seems labyrinthine, like the quests of
the major characters in his novels, and, like them, they are best
followed through thinking about the practices and deceptions of art.
His work has become interesting to critics lately because of all this,
and because there has grown up a far better appreciation of modern
myth and fantasy and its significance in contemporary writing. The

appreciation has come slowly; it is worth noting that, like many British writers, he did not really gain a substantial reputation until his work was both commercially and critically successful in the United States. British reviewers and critics have a cautious way with their own finest authors, one reason why the literary account of postwar British fiction has been so thoughtless and so thin. Nonetheless Fowles has always won a certain attention, often of a mildly confused kind, for his commercial success has often seemed not the support of but the enemy of his critical reputation, and his decadent and erotic aspects have been thought to have – just like the old fob-watched impresario himself – a distinct touch of the flashy.

His first novel, *The Collector*, appeared in 1963, and it was seen, as British novels tend to be seen, as a novel of class relations: Clegg seems to have read himself into existence out of the lower-middle-class novels of the 1950s, and Miranda seems to arise from the middle-class fictions of the 1930s. Fowles said that in writing the book he decided to "write in terms of the strictest realism" for the surface feel of the book, going to Defoe and Jane Austen, Sartre and Camus. This is interesting, because the flavours of those writers are very different, and very different flavours come from the book, with its two narratives. But Fowles also said it was the "dramatic psychosexual implications of isolating extreme situations" that excited and interested him, and the novel, like all of Fowles's books, has a strong decadent dimension. Like much decadent literature it depends on the pursuit, down labyrinthine ways, of an obscure object of desire associated often with female sexuality and the strangeness of art itself. And like much decadent literature it transfigures the discursive or realistic way of writing into the symbolic and the enigmatic. Miranda is Clegg's obscure object of desire, the prefiguration of many of Fowles's subsequent heroines, and he wishes to pin her down and place her. Miranda in effect offers the revolt of art against naturalism: "When you draw something it lives and when you photograph it it dies," she says, and if indeed she dies the enigma associated with her persists, and certainly recurs persistently in everything that Fowles has written subsequently.

But it was really with his second book *The Magus* (1966) that Fowles established his flamboyant authority. It is a book that has persistently troubled him, and in 1977 he published a mildly revised version of it, as much to settle his own disappointments as to provide us not with one text but two in the manner of the endings of *The French Lieutenant's Woman*. It did not get a particularly good reception, though the sheer scale of the enterprise, its evident imaginative and intellectual aspiration, was unusual and obvious, and ought to have stood out in any intellectual climate attuned to such things. It ran to 617 pages, and amongst other things fairly clearly attempted a kind of history of consciousness in the West in our century, a rare enough enterprise, carried out with great wit, imagination and intellect. And, if *The French Lieutenant's Woman* was to be both a formal imitation of the Victorian novel *and* an elegant endeavour at assessing the historical and mental difference between such a story and a modern reader – involving the construction of the consciousness of the world of a hundred years ago and the consciousness of the world now, that consciousnessness underlying the whole society and producing a kind of cultural unity between the inner and the outer world – then *The Magus* was already and evidently an attempt to do something similar for the twentieth century. The conception of the book required several levels of awareness and perception, required social, emotional and psychological exploration, and it was clearly an enormously daring enterprise. It seems to me a central text in any quest for an understanding of Fowles, and I should like to look at it in some detail.

3 Fowles is sometimes described as an "existential" writer, and the word makes sense; a good deal of his fiction has been shaped by the preoccupations with authenticity and inauthenticity that have run through modern French literature. Existential flavours are strong in *The Collector*, and they play a very large part in *The Magus*, from the opening postwar atmosphere in London that Fowles elaborates for his story to the crises of good and bad faith that have occurred in wartime in the life of Conchis, the "magus" of the title. That said, Fowles uses his existentialism in curious ways, not so much to define the form of his fiction as its subject. His novels lack that precise clarity of language that Sartre summoned up as an aspect of the existential novel, the qualities he praised in Camus or some of his absurdist successors, for example. As Robert Scholes once said, his fiction is notably orgiastic, a refusal of that evocation of the inert and the banal that invests the concept of the real in the pages of the French *nouveau roman*. And if one theme of his fiction has been the pursuit of an authentic personal reality, then this has never been enough to prescribe the structure of his books. They are usually elaborately social and historical, and though in various ways he has given us pared down versions of what he is doing – in the epigrams of *The Aristos* (1965), or the parable of the writer and the muse in the brief conceit *Mantissa* (1982) – then these are small things, the writer at play, and the writer at work is a novelist of social breadth, historical attention, elaborate discursive detail. He puts right at the centre of his work a strong generative energy, a history-constructing curiosity, and what, until the word "story" weakened somewhat in credit, would have been called a gift for sheer storytelling. The aesthetic problem, the problem about the forms and powers of modern fictions, has everything to do with *The Magus*, but it is elucidated not so much in its form but in its theme. It is indeed a book *about* art, the sort of book a good novelist might write to explore, for himself and others, the possibilities open to fiction in a time when ideas of freedom, selfhood, and significant order are in considerable ferment, and we are oppressed by complex doubts about the tendency of modern history, the problems of modern psychic life and consciousness, and modern form. And these, we can say (though the reviewers at the time usually did not), are the inner themes of *The Magus*, making the book a form of technical self-questioning as well as of good strong storytelling. All this comes back in *The French Lieutenant's Woman*, but in a changed historical situation. In both books there is a male hero led, through his own feelings of inauthenticity and doubt and the power of a woman who is associated with special trans-historical properties, to a different view of consciousness, shaped certainly by the needs of self-realisation but also those of sound historical awareness. And in both of these books the capacity to learn through fictions is essential; in *The Magus* it is, of course, the central theme.

The Magus starts off in a familiar day-to-day reality; shifts to a universe of theatrical mysteries; returns us to the day-to-day world, conscious that the mysteries are in one sense a writer's or a magician's extravagant inventions but also a vision about contemporary history and individual needs and desires. Fowles does this by constructing round the first-person narrator Nicholas Urfe a vast and complicated psycho-drama, constructed (at, of course, great and improbable expense) for his own benefit. Just down from Oxford and living in London in the postwar existentialist-bohemian climate, Nicholas is an agnostic rationalist and hedonist who has no direction, poetic ambitions, and the strong period sense of "inauthenticity". He begins living with an Australian girl, Alison, and then gets a post as a British Council lecturer on a Greek island, Phraxos, and has philhellenist hopes of finding a fuller life. It becomes clear that Alison is in love with him, but Nicholas does not want the entanglement, and cannot adjust to it. He goes to Greece with a sense of victory over Alison, but once there feelings of isolation, despair, growing inauthenticity and an awareness of deathlike forces within him bring him to the edge of suicide. But, insufficiently "authentic" even for that, he resigns himself to a condition of *mauvaise foi*. So far this is a conventional existential tale. Now, though, another line of action starts, for Nicholas has found on the island a villa and meets its owner Conchis, a Prospero-like figure (*The Tempest* has played quite a part in contemporary British fiction) who has some influence over the school where he teaches, and is reputed to have collaborated with the Germans. Surrounded by magnificent *objets d'art*, erotic and obscene, he has a pleasure-seeking, privileged world-view which attracts Urfe, who begins spending most weekends at the villa; and finds himself surrounded by ever growing mysteries as the Magus exerts his powers.

The novel now shifts into a world of theatrical mysteries. Conchis first gives Urfe pamphlets on science and witchcraft; he tells stories about his own life during the twentieth century, which cross with two world wars and basic changes in life and thought. But suddenly in a strange theatre surrounding Nicholas, the events are enacted, at first at a distance, but then coming closer to him, engulfing him. A girl called Lily from Conchis's past, supposedly dead in the First World War, appears, and Nicholas, treating fantasy and strangeness realistically, gets the explanation: "Lily" is an actress named Julie. But this brings the masques into his own life, and the spectacle becomes a web which he tries to break by going to Athens and meeting Alison again, only to find he is really attracted to Lily-Julie, who, in her Edwardian decadent guise, lacks the sexual directness of the "androgynous twentieth-century mind". (A familiar decadent theme shows up here.) Back on the island, the mysteries take on more power and Nicholas sees them as a fable of the history and action of the godless twentieth-century mind. Conchis reaches the culmination of his own story, his enforced collaboration with the Germans during the war, when he is ordered by the Germans to kill three resistance fighters or he and eighty hostages will be shot. In a vision of freedom, a modern freedom "beyond mortality" but springing from "the very essence of things – that comprehended all, the freedom to do all, and stood against only one thing – the prohibition not to do all", Conchis refuses. This lesson in freedom as both transcendence and destruction seems to bring the end of the mysteries. Urfe claims Julie, who, he thinks, loves him, and the party seems to conclude.

But now the events all burst into Urfe's own world, as he is carried off to the Greek mainland as a prisoner, and undergoes a mock-trial at the hands of the masque-makers, who disclose themselves as social psychologists conducting an experiment on him. In a fine set-piece Urfe is taunted with all his psychic weaknesses, portrayed as a characteristic modern psychic type – auto-erotic, auto-psychotic, dependent on aggressive sexual relationships, pathological. In a parodic withdrawal-therapy Urfe is made to watch Lily in a pornographic film, then making love to a black in his presence, and he is then told, by Conchis, that he is one of the "elect", an initiate into the cruelty of freedom. But the godgame lingers on. Dismissed from his job, he finds Alison in Athens, to discover she is part of Conchis's web; and so, apparently, are most of his friends. No individual is safely in "reality", no past event is free from intrusion. He returns to Alison: is she inside or outside the plot? and has it been a plot against him, or for him? The final pages, even with Fowles's revision, remain somewhat ambiguous. Urfe does appear to have been saved, not damned, by his experiences, and the mysterious powers seem to be withdrawing from his life. But the mysteries remain mysteries, somewhere between a decadent trap and a psychic revelation.

4 *The Magus* is a mythic romance, a kind of fiction where the mysterious web of dangerous but instructive powers have always been central. Fowles himself draws out innumerable literary allusions to support the mode, making his magus Prospero, the magician and psychopomp, symbolist of the world of the unseen, agent of the supernatural, and maker of fictions that can be created and dissolved at will. But he is also of course the charlatan-impresario, and Fowles constructs him very ambiguously. An obvious comparison is with Iris Murdoch, several of whose early novels have magical figures or enchanters in them, suggesting aspects of Love, Power and Death that cannot be framed within the conventional liberal notions of reality, which presume new risks and new relationships that in the interests of apprehending truth and otherness must be explored. The problem with this sort of fiction is that it recognisably involves a good deal of fictional faking, and there is a danger in creating a sense of numinous mystery and insight for its own special sake, without granting any deliverance in "reality". But Fowles and Murdoch both endeavour to bring us back from the lost domain into some version of the real and the true, and in this sense they seem to carry a strong sense of debt to the realistic tradition of the novel. The role of cautious rationalist granted to Urfe is one that he shares with the reader; he is a natural violator of myths. This, of course, is an old procedure of gothic (the method of "The Fall of the House of Usher", for example) but Fowles roots it in the tonalities of the culture itself – in its distrust of myth, its sense of the firm validity of the familiar world, its doubt about metaphor and symbol, its suspicion of higher revelations. And in turn Conchis comprehends this, staying one jump ahead, unmasking the desire to unmask, and making his "godgame" not a timeless hermetic myth but a masque of contemporary history. His dark wisdoms – of serene endurance, and the archaic smile that can hold experience complete (Alison, the Fowles-

ian muse-woman, has it in the final scene) – is enacted within the terms of modern experience.

And, like many such contemporary fictions, *The Magus* is enfolded within the complex metaphor of theatricality. Our twentieth-century sense of lost authenticity has been much shaped by the Freudian view of the complex theatre of our unconscious, and by the thoughts of those modern sociologists and psychologists who have seen us as essentially role-players, the script of our existence written by forces we cannot control. As Erving Goffman says (in *The Presentation of the Self in Everyday Life*, 1959) the "dramaturgical analogy" has become a pervasive metaphor, touching not just on the question of whether the psycho-social theatre in which we lead our lives is substance or shadow, but whether the stage is one we can ever leave. The question parallels the problem of artistic construction, or authorship; may we create a sense of authentic reality in art, or must all art subsist eternally within the province of its fictionality? "Perhaps what he was doing sprang from some theory about the theatre – he had said it himself: *The masque is only a metaphor*," Urfe reflects when confronted by Conchis. "A strange and incomprehensible new philosophy? Metaphorism? Perhaps he saw himself as a philosopher of the impossible faculty of ambiguity, a sort of Empson of the event." Nicholas's uncertainty as he considers Conchis and his overwhelming "godgame" thus resembles our own as readers. As with Murdoch's psychopomp figures (Hugo Belfounder, Mischa Fox), the role of enchanter in fiction becomes strange and obscure. Conchis is transfigurative of both truth and falsehood, the voice of forces that lie beyond conventional social order and carry the potential of myth, yet cannot yield it as a total truth. He constructs with the magic of fiction and theatre a myth of modern historical and psychic consciousness, but the myth must be returned to the "real" world. This says something about fictions. They are not the real, and magicians who are also charlatans make them. The imagination has the power to design, but it depends on tricks and borrowed properties as well as the apparently unfictional structures of history and psychic understanding which give meaning to our sense of life.

So Conchis is not only the wise magician but also the sleight-of-hand artist, enabled by wealth and mysterious authority to dominate and control. The book's epigraph indicates this: the Magus is both mountebank and the magician who operates the cards of Tarot. This duplicity runs through the book, and troubles some readers of it. Does a trick which reveals so much remain only a trick? Fowles keeps the balance of suspense open. If Urfe's rational mind could undermind Conchis's game, he would be nothing but trickster, which is perhaps why it is necessary for him to have power within the world of

Urfe's reality as well as in the Greek theatre he constructs. If he were entirely the magician, his wisdom would have to be rare indeed, capable of providing an entire account of the meaning of the modern world. The ambiguity must stay, as it does in much modernist writing, where the symbol is both transcendentally lifted out of history and ambiguously returned to it. At the end of the novel, the watching eyes seem to be withdrawn, the theatre has gone, and Urfe feels the double anxiety of escape from "their" interest and a sense of empty exposure, he seems the man from Plato's cave in his modern variant. He has seen the real and been returned to a world of shadows which everyone else considers reality. But the problems are, as Plato said, the problems of art itself, the problem of how orders and symbols which transcend this life but implicitly order it can be mingled with the real. The real Magus of the novel is, of course, the novelist himself, who creates something that is only magic, but which is capable of acquiring the force of myth and incorporate some of the pressure and meaning of our history in the world. *The Magus* is thus a very self-conscious fiction, a book about itself which nonetheless seeks to be about more than a writer and his personal magic. And in this and other ways it resembles *The French Lieutenant's Woman*.

5 At first sight *The French Lieutenant's Woman* appears the far more conventional novel, a work that acknowledges and honours something that is very important in all our literary pasts, those funds that lie in the great repertoire of Victorian fiction and still exercise their power over the modern writer. Fowles is an avid reader of Victorian fiction, especially in its more minor examples, and his devotion resembles that of a good many of our of our contemporary novelists, like Angus Wilson or Margaret Drabble. Part of the splendour of Fowles's book lies in the fact that it is a work of great recuperation, a recuperation, in a way, not just of certain facets of the Victorian writers who lie behind us, but the very form or genre of Victorian novel, the underlying prototype. In this prototype, of which we can think of many strong examples, a young and intelligent middle-class man, with promising abilities and perhaps great expectations, finds the path of his life confused by conflicts of desire and respectability, personal wish and social duty. The path is an education in the disguises and conceal-ments of society, beyond which lies a dark underside, a troubling world of gothic and erotic disorders, of deepened sensibility. The choice often takes the form of a choice between two women and two forms of love, one of the two the fair domestic heroine who points to the world of sentiment and domesticity, the life of the middle ground, and the other the dark lady – she is very often a governess, that dangerous and socially displaced breed in the Victorian landscape, the bearer of radical and independent emotions and a strong erotic energy. Usually in the Victorian parable she is pursued but not finally married; the lesson of life learned, the hero returns to the fair lady to live not necessarily happily but sensibly and comfortably thereafter, acknowledging the claims of society and commerce. With small variations – both of the ladies are brown, and the darker one is not quite the outcast she at first seems – Fowles gives us this prototype, and even takes us through to the ending, with Charles having seven children and becoming a prosperous Victorian businessman.

This, however, will not do, for the modern reader and the modern writer; the historical imagination, conscious that that sentimental account is not even a true story of the Victorian period, cannot countenance it, and nor can the Charles Smithson Fowles has conceived, troubled by Darwin, living in the age of Karl Marx. The novel seems initially a story of Charles's difficult choice, between the sentimental Ernestina and the outcast Sarah, who stands on Jane Austen's cobb at Lyme Regis and walks the Undercliff, with its Darwinian fossils, and is generally held to be a treacherous whore, the French Lieutenant's woman. But of course it is the path of Sarah Charles must follow, and as he does so she becomes the outright heroine, and refuses in turn to remain in her Victorian fictional place, transgressing the novel's frame and carrying with her the intimations of a post-history, so that she can be read as an early twentieth-century new woman or a feminist precursor. Her position in the narrative begins to displace the familiarising, realistic voice of the story so far, for the manners of commonplace realism become more difficult. The world of reality becomes a world of historical forces and processes, the language a distant documentary, a form of historiography. The world of desires also needs its suitable locations, and Fowles finds them in the world of the pre-raphaelite artists, where evanescent and androgynous images and artistic enigmas have their place. Meanwhile the characters themselves have changed, acquiring stronger existentialist outlines, and "refusing" now to be social agents but demanding to be understood as independent free agents, as in a more modern kind of novel. As for the novelist, he is less the omniscient God than the modern trickster or impresario, his own skills and inventions acquiring an increasing importance.

From the moment the story turns along Sarah's way, Fowles seems not so much to be constructing as deconstructing the Victorian novel. But then he has confessed to this task all along, from the famous and intrusive Chapter 13 onward, where he acknowledges the difficulties of omniscience and freedom:

The novelist is still a god, since he creates (and not even the most aleatory *avant-garde* modern novel has managed to extirpate its author completely); what has changed is that we are no longer the gods of the Victorian image, omniscient and decreeing: but in the new theological image, with freedom our first principle, not authority.

Freedom, however, means a paradox. Fowles has said of the book that he was "trying to show an existentialist awareness before it was chronologically possible". For this he gives an interesting justification, that the powerful existentialist dilemmas of the fiction of Sartre and Camus actually lead us back by inversion toward the spirit of Victorian moral anxiety and sensitivity. Fowles, in Chapter 13, may acknowledge his contemporaneity with Robbe-Grillet and Roland Barthes, and indicate to us that he knows just what a novel "in the modern sense" is. But he has also told us that "I don't like artists who are high on craft and low on humanity," and he clearly means the novel to display a certain kind of existentialist humanism. It is the questioning of narrative over-determination in the ostensible interests of the character in the book that gives point to the divided ending. The ending is only relatively indeterminate, presenting a limited field of choice which is not resolved for the future; the characters are kept within the overall web of reality, and do not really break out of the main frame of the book. They have, in a sense, become more real for Fowles, and not less; this is, he says, why he feels the need to grant them a certain freedom. All freedom in fiction is of course a kind of deceit, since characters never live outside and beyond the pages on which their existence is imprinted; nonetheless the relations of writers to their inventions do construct forms of thought and creation which we can transfer back to our view of the world.

Thus Fowles is, in a sense, offering the claim that the writer can preserve his own creative options, and must not be driven by the sense of an ending to an ultimate resolution. Above all, though, what Fowles seems to preserve is Sarah's enigmatic qualities, her overall refusal to be understood. She stays in the mirrored world of decadence, an adversary of the entire discursive explanation, and preserves Fowles as himself an existentialist decadent, drawn by the enigmatic image that will not fully speak and will not let itself be entirely understood. At the end, Sarah stands for a mystery, the mystery of "the river of life, of mysterious laws and mysterious choice". The imagination itself seems to be granted greater power than the orders that narrative organisation requires, and with this enigma in Fowles we are very familiar. Indeed in the story "The Enigma" (in *The Ebony Tower*) a similar mystery is compounded.

Again there is an enigmatic counter-storyteller, Isobel, who says of John Marcus Fielding, MP, the strangely absconding subject of the tale: "There was an author in his life. In a way. Not a man. A system, a view of things? Something that had written him. Had made him just a character in a book." Fielding revolts against the social story that has been written for him, and made his life. Isobel preserves the mystery and she refuses a full interpretation of the revolt, protecting the enigma and transmitting it. And so does Sarah, who is not so much set free by the ending of the novel as preserved in her muse-like quality.

So *The Magus* and *The French Lieutenant's Woman* share, as we might expect, a good deal in common. They both depend upon a powerful and in many ways traditional narrative drive, the deployment both of the realistic and the mystery-making skills of the master storyteller. They are both concerned with the endeavour toward existential self-realisation in a world dense in its historical force and its social complexity, and to a large degree the characters live inside and within the decisive conditions of history. In both the heroes are led from the conventional and realistic world of consciousness into another world where enigma dominates, and something can be learned about the nature of stories, which are themselves forms of conditioning history. Or so, certainly, are conventional stories that follow the rules of genre and reach predictable outcomes. Neither book is a total rescinding of realism, and certainly not of literary humanism: realism is something Fowles is very good at, and humanism is something he believes in. They are a pressured reconstruction of the realism's ambiguities, a major exploration of the difficulties and the possibilities facing the modern novelist who is not prepared to dispense with the humanistic properties of fiction, and attempts their recuperation.

6 It is clear enough that Fowles is a sophisticated novelist, a novelist of Nathalie Sarraute's "era of suspicion", and a very interesting case of such a writer in a British tradition which has not greatly favoured this line of artistic exploration. Yet the question remains, is he a novelist "in the modern sense", the sense of his experimental contemporaries? Perhaps there is a kind of answer to his portrait, in "The Ebony Tower", of the artist Breasley, who chooses to express his innovation in a certain way, by writing an art of the present that incorporates much of the past: "behind the modernity of so many of the surface elements there stood both a homage and a kind of thumbed nose to a very old tradition." We can see how the phrase suits Fowles himself. He has – like other British novelists, including Iris Murdoch, to whom it seems very logical to compare him – pursued a contemporary magic in the mysteries of a modern art pressed by history and the lineage of our twentieth-century thought beyond the limits of Victorian fiction. He has, however, by no means repudiated those elements in art that belong with the heritage of realism and the idea of character. Where the traditional novel is a form entrapped in history, held by its notions of omniscience and evolutionary sequence into a certain controlling idea of story, Fowles will seek to break the frame, admitting into it an idea of modern consciousness and its entitlement to freedom. And where the discursive and familiarising mode of that fiction opposes the erotic, the decadent and the enigmatic, he will open the doorway out into that displaced kingdom. Where fiction can be tempted toward too sturdy an idea of the real and the true, he will insist on faking and feigning, magic and trickery. His typical novels have been bridging exercises, a set of strange artistic marriages conducted by a brilliant performer. I consider him one of our great writers, both because of his in many ways traditional virtuosity and his willingness to see there is a new encounter to be made between the conditions and options of modern existence and the form of art. The modern novelist can be both the god of freedom and the tricky impresario, and Fowles, aided by his enigmatic muses, has found extraordinary ways to be both.

PART FOUR

Celebrating the Occasion

ADAPTING AND BEING ADAPTABLE
The novel and television

1   The British television system, Dennis Potter once said, is the least worst television system in the world; and there is a lot of good as well as a good deal of bad to be said about it. Constantly dragged toward popularity and marketability, it has frequently resisted, and its role as a cultural institution as well as a medium of information and entertainment has largely survived through various kinds of pressure and vicissitude. It has maintained some place as an artistic medium; and one of the glittering prizes of the system has been its work with the original single play and the classic adaptation. Single plays are a difficult item to maintain in television's endless seriality, and over recent years the achievement has sadly diminished, though not gone altogether. In the area of the serious serial the more recent record of achievement has been stronger – so strong indeed that some of the central artistic triumphs of television lie here, in series like *Tinker, Tailor, Soldier, Spy*, *Bleak House*, *Brideshead Revisited* and *The Jewel in the Crown*. The BBC made the first two of these, and Granada the latter, showing that the achievement is not solely confined to the non-commercial arm of television. On the other hand, the massive costs of such series, the dependence that high costs bring on foreign sales and co-production funding, and a growing sense of demoralisation in some parts of the industry, make many of us wonder if this phase is not more or less over.

But for an important period British television drama was, in its way, a writer's theatre, developing a stable of very notable playwrights, some drawn from the stage and others emerging within the medium itself, some outstanding directors, a remarkable *corps de théâtre*, and a striking body of talented production people who have learned how to work to the highest standards, to develop their own narrative rules and adapt the changing technologies of an ever changing medium. It also developed some parallel shortcomings: a tendency to have a clichéd and simplified notion of what makes a good television play or series, an inclination toward fad and fashion, one that has oscillated rapidly between strongly naturalistic ideas and a taste for highly mannered and often pretentious art-objects, and an instinct to think nostalgia a safe common ground for engaging and saleable drama. It has been a highly concentrated medium, requiring a high professionalism and therefore often depending on too limited a range of talents and subjects. Uneasy complicities have long existed in television, between a driving originality and a very limited view of what makes for good television, good ratings, good family viewing. Like any generic medium, conventions grow and become habitual, change is slow, and innovation difficult. Out of it all comes a little that is good, a fair amount that is bad, and a general level of technical competence so impressive that it is often quite hard to tell the difference.

Most writers in Britain sooner or later engage in one way or another with the medium, not necessarily because they belong to some longstanding stable of conventional television playwrights, but because their work is adapted, they are asked to write for it occasionally, or they are drawn to seek it because in the right circumstances writing for television can be intensely creative and demanding. Such is the institutional nature of the television industry, so apparently complex its technologies and presentational conventions, that most are likely to do this in some state of nervousness, if not terror. If one is a dramatist, the step may not seem great. If one is a poet or a novelist, used to writing in private circumstances and then seeing what one has written printed, given an editorial change or two, more or less as written and so transferred with reasonable directness to the reader, it can seem very large indeed. The novel is a social form, and has its conventions, its genres, its narrative rules, and its public functions. It can be written essentially for the market, and even be specifically devised for it in some elaborate collaboration between the author, the publisher, and the publicity machine. But often writing fiction still retains its old-fashioned form as a species of individualism, functioning for its writer as a very personal mode of creative, linguistic and cultural exploration and discovery; the book you make is, despite all the theories that tell us otherwise, largely *your* book. Television drama is ostensibly made from the same materials – stories and plots, language and image, narrative orders and complications, beginnings and middles and ends – but it is made in quite different ways to a quite different end. In every sense the writer in television must adapt and be adaptable.

2 Over recent years my own encounters with television have been interesting, infuriating, exciting, troubled, and at times outrageous. I have written original plays for television, some with pleasing results and others with results not so pleasing, and I have indeed adapted and been adaptable. I have adapted several works for television, including a fine short story by John Fowles, "The Enigma", made as a television play, and two of Tom Sharpe's wonderfully farcical novels, *Blott on the Landscape* and *Porterhouse Blue*, made as television series; I have been adapted myself, my novel *The History Man* being turned by Christopher Hampton into a four-part television series; I have also simultaneously adapted and been adaptable, so to speak, by writing my novel *Rates of Exchange* as a five-part television series, only to have it cancelled for financial reasons after rehearsals and just before the first day of principal photography. All this has given me reason to reflect a good deal on the nature of the relationship between the novelist and the television institution, and the novel and television as a dramatic medium. I have found myself deeply engaged and deeply enraged, professionally excited and professionally infuriated. I have come to respect the potential of the medium as a form of expression, to admire the brilliance and technical skill of many of the people who work in it, to value the artistic education it has given me, and to distrust much of the machinery of administration and decision making, to tire of the conflict between original ideas and base limitations – in short to feel that sense that good things could be much better, which many would say is a definition of human life itself.

I have also come to appreciate the fundamental difference that exists between the world of writing fiction and the world of writing for television: the one private, closeted, and measured almost entirely against one's personal standards of form and integrity, the other public, hyper-active, institutional, social, and drawing its standards largely from rule and custom. Hence the novelist, or the novel, is not simply moving from one part of the literary world into another that is similar. It is moving from relative independence to institutional complexity, from one view of the purpose and function of writing to quite another, from a personal system of discourse to a very public and shared one. It is also moving from a world of modest outlays to one of high capital expenditure. When I write a novel it costs me time, paper, secretarial machinery, and not much more. When I write a television series I activate the lives of perhaps a hundred other people and a capital expenditure of perhaps two million pounds, enough to build a good part of a new university, if that were the sort of thing that the age desired. A novelist constitutes his or her words in an imaginary location, the realm of words, constructing a false universe which then transfers itself with reasonable directness to the imagination of a reader who performs a substantial part of the task (the newest criticism would say all of it). The writer of a television play writes a set of instructions or a complex advisory manual for a network of human activity, and nothing is actual until it has been processed, rehearsed, made, edited and shown. Behind it is a vast institutional world of ringing telephones, lifts, studio facilities, production managers, location finders, crews, designers, executives and programme planners.

And only if the words one's typewriter has typed are activated does anything happen; then everything does. Directors say goodbye to their spouses and children and block out many months in their diaries. Actors commit themselves to roles that will keep them standing on cold street corners, huddled in bleak church halls, and in distant hotels on location for extended periods. Planes will be charted, lines of huge vans will move across the country, caterers will fry steaks by the thousand, lions and giraffes and ambulances and even whole towns will be hired. Streets in cities will be blocked off and temporarily reconstructed. Small villages will be built from plasterboard. A great mobile party of talented persons will live together, feeding in skills and artistries, until, at last, what started as ciphers on paper become images on film, the object reverts to being an object, the people go, the edit is done, and so on one brief night the imaginary act will be given public transmission, some but not enough of us will see it, and then the flickering serial of television will move on to something else. And as for the novelist, he will probably return to the novel, to the Gutenberg world of writing and print, and to that extraordinary imaginative form where creation and invention can occur without any of this trouble, where at best the result will be decidedly better, but hardly known, hardly seen, hardly imagined, hardly remembered, because after all if it has not been on television it has not been fully published at all.

3 We could then conclude that so great is this difference, so large this gap, that the intercourse that has grown between the novel – especially the serious novel – and television does not have great profit. This is a view that can be and has been put in various ways. One is that a good novel is quite simply irreduceable; it exists already, as the right words in the right order, its aesthetic existence complete, and it can only be corrupted by being transliterated or translated into

another medium. Another adds to this that, if that other medium is television, it must necessarily trivialise the result in any case, because of the nature of the compact between television and its audience, and because the original work will have to be brought within the compass of conventionalising narrative and cultural conventions. Another is that the television version of a book becomes a dangerous substitute for it, often causing it subsequently to be read through the interpretative lens of the television series. "Adaptation is a process of reducing a pre-existent piece of writing to a series of functions: characters, locations, costumes, actions and strings of narrative events," explains one commentator, John Ellis, adding that the expectation that adaptations will be "faithful" is inevitably false: "The adaptation trades on the memory of the novel, a memory that can derive from actual reading, or, as is more likely with a classic of literature, a generally circulated cultural memory." "The driving tension of the novel is the relationship between the materials of the story (plot, character, setting, theme, and so forth) and the narration of it in language; between the teller and the tale, in other words," says another, James Monaco. "The driving tension of film, on the other hand, is between the materials of the story and the objective nature of the image." And it is awarenesses of this kind which led to Jonathan Miller's famous pronouncement that the better the book the worse the television series, or that only less than good books make good television.

If my views on that are somewhat different, they are partly so because my sense of the nature of literary fictions may also be somewhat different. Fictions may possess a powerful distinctiveness and originality, but they are also part of a shared community of story; they are, as we like to say now, "intertextual". Narratives are based on a sceptical rewriting of prior narratives, and if they have an intrinsic untranslatability they are also open to re-use. The habit of transfer and translation of story from one medium to another and one language to another is part of the essential history of forms. Theatre, opera and ballet have long depended on the principle, and it is one way of explaining the emergence of the novel itself as a genre, since it began as a parodic rewriting of romance. Writing is essentially based on rewriting, on allusiveness, on intertextuality, on reinterpretation; at best we may take recreation as a high form of criticism. It can also, of course, be a low form of it, and the question of whether the process is necessarily trivialising, because of the cultural expectations of those who develop the adaptation or the needs of the audience for which it is made, is more complicated. Television has at least the potential to function as an original and innovative adapting medium, and at its best it has been so. There is no guarantee it will remain so, some evidence that it is ceasing to be so, as costs rise and the audience to be gratified is redefined. But, as I have said, a high standard of expectation has been set within British television, and the problem is to sustain and extend it. A serious book can be given a serious adaptation, a significant and powerful equivalent, faithful to its spirit but transferred to a new discourse. And this, finely done, can be an important achievement.

4 But let us look at the difficulties. A few years ago I approached the BBC to make an adaptation of John Fowles's story "The Enigma", from *The Ebony Tower*, which had long interested me. It is, in its way, a story in a familiar genre, the detective story; it is also about fiction's deceit. A member of parliament disappears mysteriously, perhaps to defect to Russia, to escape with the profits of business corruption, perhaps because of some sexual scandal. Fowles tells the tale in the familiar manner, but then dissolves it, in a double way. "Nothing is real. All is fiction," says Isobel Dodgson, one of Fowles's truth-bearing heroines; she also says "Then if our story disobeys the unreal literary rules, that might mean it's actually truer to life." If Fowles, like many another modern writer, is parodying the conventional literary types, it is not simply in the interests of a pure fictionality, and indeed "The Enigma" contains a keen quarrel with the "social" author, convention itself, "a system, a view of things", which limits our existential self-awareness and discovery.

All this seems to me an essential mark of the seriousness of Fowles's literary enquiry, and indeed it is because I think that enquiry serious that I wished to perform the act of translation that a television adaptation is. I had written on Fowles, and naturally had a very "literary" reading of this story about Fowles's recurrent assumption that we are all in flight from "reality", and fictionalise our pasts and our lives. The "enigma" of the story was not just that of the strange disappearance of the Member of Parliament, John Marcus Fielding, and the lack of an explanation for it. The tale was about the enigmatic labyrinth of story itself, about the infinite recession of mystery and the way art seeks to pursue it, about the way the awareness of social enigma leads us into a need for fictions that are hidden like art but become a larger reality. John Marcus Fielding has been a social "character"; he has felt the need to become a self-realising person, energised in some way to this by a very female mystery, the mystery of Isobel herself.

But if these were my thoughts about the story, they were not quite of the kind that would convince the makers of television programmes that it was worth detaining their viewers for ninety minutes in order to watch a detective story that turned out not to be one, but proved a self-questioning parody or a self-conscious fiction. Moreover what was parodied was another prose form, the detective story, and though there was indeed a detective film its conventions were refined and rather different from those on which Fowles had depended. And there were other problems. Fowles's story, of about fifty pages, is told in a distinctive way, the first part largely through narrative, with no line of dialogue until the fifteenth page, and the second largely through dialogue, much of it Isobel's analytical interpretation of events that have already happened but whose meaning has not been fathomed. Much of the story works through its tone, which is semi-parodic, and its outcome is, as I have suggested, a reflection on literary plot and form as well as on the limitations of social and political life. In short the story was bound by many of the conventions and possibilities of prose, but these did not match the conventions and expectations of television, with its dependence on images rather than words, or indeed of drama, with its dependence on conflict rather than exposition.

The task therefore involved many transmutations; many dramatic interventions toward the beginning, and many concentrations toward the end. In the notes that passed between myself and the prospective director, Rob Knights, I said: "A film treatment requires some significant recasting. The idiom of the detective film is needed to provide the 'apparent' direction of the story. Three visual emblems of the 'enigma' itself need concentrating: Isobel herself, the sexual lure and the meaning-bearer in the story; the British Museum, with its world of the already written; and the lake at Tetbury, where, in Isobel's version, Fielding has drowned himself, though we should keep open the alternative implication that he has gone to Isobel's flat, just as the Special Branch man Jennings, who repeats many of his experiences, does at the end of the story."

Not surprisingly, and typically enough for television, the script went through three distinct versions, sometimes structuring the material chronologically, sometimes upsetting it, and so on, in an attempt to bring out all the significant elements of the story and its interpretation that had worked so well in one medium, and reproduce them in the visual and the dramatic grammar of another. Over the course of this enterprise I came to admire the enigmatic delicacy with which John Fowles suffered the process of adaptation. We met on occasion, and he offered a number of telling if gnomic comments, at the same time conducting a policy of only modest intrusion, a small education in the way a writer might behave towards his rewriter, once he had accepted the enterprise was worth undertaking at all. Indeed the whole process of relating fidelity to difference was an education in itself, as, by careful reading and rereading, we tried to get further into the original and at the same time carry this over into a medium that narrates through image, location and the power of the acting performance, which must always be fully motivated and carry the weight of felt life. The result, I believe, was a fair but forceful remaking that did address the aesthetic and intellectual texture of the original, which in a sense was not entirely an original, being something of a parody or pastiche itself. And indeed the self-awareness of the original story, its capacity to question itself and the nature of fiction, was precisely what made it worth telling again, as was, of course, John Fowles's *The French Lieutenant's Woman* in the Harold Pinter/Karol Reiz film version, where some of the same problems were faced, though answered rather differently.

5   Certainly it stood me in good stead when, around the same time, another project arose, the notion of making a television series of my novel *The History Man*. This proved to be a momentous event for me, and one that still has radiations and implications I am uncertain about. The novel was a hard abrasive satire, and also a very literary book with a dominant ironic tone and no sympathetic central character, even those characters who appear to be sympathetic, like the Scottish lecturer Annie Callendar, proving to be weak and deceitful supports when they are confronted by Howard Kirk, the "history man" himself. This indeed posed a problem when the notion of a series was first discussed, since it is conventional television lore that a series depends on an identifiable and sympathetic central character. The project was saved from an unusual source. Someone pointed to *Dallas* and gave Howard Kirk the name of "the thinking man's J.R.", and the venture survived.

All this made the project a difficult one, and, feeling protective about the texture and tone of the book, I finally decided, after an initial period of temptation, that I would not adapt the book myself. The book had had a difficult gestation, had come from an uneasy and pessimistic change in my own values and attitudes to fiction, and had taken nearly ten years to write as my initial excitement about the liberationist spirit of the 1960s moved toward a darkened unease. I was not inclined to resummon the experience, especially as I was now writing a new novel. But the matter was happily resolved one bleak evening on my university carpark, when Christopher Hampton, come to lecture, expressed interest in undertaking the obviously difficult task of reconstructing a decidedly literary book for television. Not

only did I admire his work as a playwright; I felt it had some real
kinship with the themes of my own work and my formal preoccupations, and the solution – a version that might lie somewhere between
my work and his – seemed ideal.

So Christopher Hampton was commissioned to write the script,
which he did, I believe, with great virtuosity. We met from time to
time at this stage, and I made a small number of suggestions with
what I hoped was an enigmatic Fowlesianism. From the start it was
clear that some fundamental changes would have to be made, if only
to fit the format of fifty-minute television episodes, which must have
their own inner structure. It was finally decided that the narrative
should fall into four days in 1972; I had myself favoured five, to bring
into the story the back history of the central couple, the Kirks. The
novel was written very much as a novel, and like "The Enigma" was
concerned with the form itself – an essential theme was the relation
between plotlessness and plotting, between what is random and
accidental and what is shaped and inevitable, between the ordinary
diary of ordinary days and the wonder days Howard Kirk wants to
create to replace dull time with visionary history. I had told it mainly
in the present tense, unusual in English fiction, to emphasise
Howard's sense of historical immediacy, an important bookish device
meaningless for television, which is in a sense always narrated in the
present tense (indeed its scripts are conventionally written in that
tense).

I had also shifted into the past tense for part of the story, that of
the early Kirk marriage, an important alternative view of things which
emphasised the role of the hidden central character and victim of the
story, Howard's wife Barbara, and a part of the story that was more or
less totally dropped from the television version. This meant that
Hampton had to invent, as he did, some strong new scenes to
represent Barbara's situation in the present of the story, all set in the
late months of 1972, the fading moments of the 1960s. This gave the
story narrative clarity but also a kind of accelerated hyper-activity,
making Howard seem even more of a prodigious Don Giovanni. But
the larger problem was to sustain the tone of ironic detachment which
is natural to fiction but not to television; it is hard to have an ironic
camera. This posed problems of direction for the director, again Rob
Knights, and meant that much depended on the playing and performance. But Hampton sharpened the plot and its ironic contrasts,
extended the detail of Barbara's present-day life, and developed the
complexity of Howard's complex plotting. I greatly admired his final
script, and Rob Knight's work on the casting. In all modesty I
disappeared to China, so missing, to my lasting regret, the chance to
play the very small part of Malcolm Bradbury, who appears briefly in

the script and helplessly attempts to halt the inevitable triumph of Howard. So my next view of the project was to see the finished version, minus a final edit or two, just before the viewers did.

My first feelings were of terror as I saw the scale of the changes that had taken place, gradually turning to admiration and excitement. The work had been transformed by the extraordinary performance of Anthony Sher as Howard Kirk. He bore no resemblance physically to the character I had imagined, though so powerful was the interpretation that he has become the Howard of my imagination, more or less effacing the original creative image I drew on to write the book. Enacted, he had become a figure of dark contemporary unease as he attempted to provoke, prod and vitalise at any cost everyone and everything around him in his dead autumn of 1972. The year 1972 (which, as I said in the book's preface, "bears no resemblance to the real 1972, which was a fiction anyway"), which when the book appeared in 1975 still seemed, in effect, contemporary, had undergone similar transmutation, being lovingly recreated by that designer expertise which is one of the triumphs of television, and makes it an art of curious and powerful nostalgias, dissolving, I felt, some of the satire and irony.

The whole story had, as it had to, moved out of the controlled, private, strangely personal spaces of a literary text into a massive enterprise of teamworked reconstruction, a powerful ghost from the recent past. Above all, an imaginary story had become literal. A novel is a text, its words are figures, and it says as much as and no more than it wants to say. What is not said is meant to be unsaid, concealments are as important as revelations. In television or film the unspecific becomes specified, located; the university ceases to be an imagined and becomes a real place, Howard's over-detailed kitchen becomes an actual kitchen. Characters take on fleshiness, sometimes a great deal of it. Howard's radical politics of sexuality may lead him in the book into many bedrooms, but the sexual scenes are all ironic rather than erotic, the dialogue of the mind being juxtaposed against the activities of the body. But, as John Cleland points out, in matters of the flesh words and pictures are not the same, and when naked lovemaking bodies appear in image, attention somehow focuses on the image and not on the ironic dialogue, however fine-honed.

As I was to discover when the series was shown and caused much reaction, there were other problems to do with the word being made flesh, fixed in a visual version. The tone diminishes, and the supposed "subject" of the book becomes its centre. The History Man is a dark comedy or satire, but it is not simply a satire on radicalism, sociology or new universities. If asked to explain its satirical theme, I would say, I suppose, that it was directed at modern behaviourism, determinism and instrumentalism. I wanted to display in Howard Kirk the modern man of plots, something of a radical opportunist, living somewhere between the world of radical belief and that of fashion, intellectually enraged by modern liberal inertia and believing in some promise of future betterment, but not likely to make things any better. He believes in behavioural politics, but his transforming history is largely radical chic, history and style being a trendy, sexy, marketable badge in the secular modern dance of self-promoting personality. Howard lives by the journalism of the years, and you might find him anywhere, as architect or Member of Parliament, television personality or priest. Sociology can be his guiding way of thinking; a new university, born of the Sixties dream of new beginnings, a natural habitat, though a concrete high rise and the architectural behaviourism of the times would have suited him just as well. Recreated in Anthony Sher's powerful and commanding performance, a charismatic figure bursting into life as a committed radical and teacher, Howard Kirk is indeed a paradox and in his way a parody, a modern hypocrite. His paradoxes turn to a pain suffered by others, especially Barbara, his wife. He is the spirit of radicalism in 1972, its master and its victim, and he is partly the spirit of the new university – which was an attempt to create a serious intellectual community from the resources of humanism but also those trends in thought and social theory which dominated the time when such institutions were founded, which the series could well seem to challenge. But thus Howard could become a figure in a new demonology, a despised figure; and so to some viewers he did. The phrase "history man" acquired a general meaning, and Howard came to seem more contemptible than the script or the brilliant performance suggested. And the new university came to seem a bleaker and less humane place than I know it to be.

Here too there were sharp lessons to learn. A television adaptation is not simply the transformation of a story from one medium to another, but a move from a world where a story told with all the indeterminacies of prose is carried into a larger one where cultural images trade in a different way. The first audience for a book like *The History Man* is somewhere between five and ten thousand people, many of them graduates. The audience for a television series is five to ten million, reading the mythology in a different way. It so happened that the appearance of *The History Man* on television at the end of the 1970s coincided with, perhaps even fed, the cultural change in British life that broke the liberal consensus of the postwar period and pointed the way toward what was called "the new realism". I have never much liked realism, preferring to acknowledge fictions as fictions, and as far as the troubled fate of humanism is concerned there is little to chose between the radical behaviourism of the 1960s ("a little Freud, a little

Marx, a little history") and the economic determinism of the 1980s. One might even say we are freer than we think, and more entitled to call ourselves persons than we like to claim. Between the public fate of our collective myths and fictions and the individual scepticism of novels there is an anxious gap. The process worried me, but also reassured me. For it seemed to me that those who had made the series had indeed made a deeply troubling and abrasive adaptation, and had not lost the edgy nature of the book. Television can too easily confirm expectations, reinforce cliché, and what should worry us are the sentimental and nostalgic myths that television in its brilliance of production can often lure us into, and programme makers often prefer. The television *History Man* was not that, and I have come more and more to value it, while feeling the more committed to the form of the novel itself – not a pre-technological hangover, but a form of wonderful plurality and ambiguity.

THE TELLING LIFE
Thoughts on literary biography

" . . . whatever the reasons for his reversal of good intentions, his monstrous metamorphosis, his ill-timed, misleading revelations, of one thing I am certain. I should not care to be in his skin, and the devil knows I am not ecstatically happy in my own. And, when his passion of remembrance is spent, I have no doubt he will wish devoutly he could cast off his sins and needle-pricking skin, like a strip-teasing snake in fright, and change it for another unrecognizable one . . . . "
Caitlin Thomas on Dylan Thomas's biographer John Malcolm Brinnin

1 When some of my colleagues at the University of East Anglia resolved to hold a conference on modern biography, I was, I confess, very taken by the notion – and largely because, in the academic world in which I spend at least a part of my being, the idea of biography, especially literary biography, is something of a challenge, even a provocation. Literary study today is not really to do with writers but writing, not with authors but texts, not with penny lives but conceptual theories. This may seem strange to those who live in what they like to call the "real world", where, of course, writers' lives are frequently found more interesting than their works, literary biographies are staples of the book market, and any revealing record of the psychology, associations, scandalous behaviour and stylish deviance of an author can vastly outsell any actual book by the writer in question. We live, in short, in two worlds, and this is a fascinating state of affairs, well worth a conference or two.

There can be no doubt that this is an era of the Great Literary Life, and the publishers' lists are crowded with them. The record of the histories and quirks, the habits and mannerisms, the travels and marriages of our great authors is an active area of preoccupation, and some of our most talented and readable books are accounts not so much of writers' works (that is educational, and expensive) but of their existences. Thus the vogue for contemporary biography, lives of the newly dead or the still just living, writers whom we can probe not just through documentary record but through friends and witnesses, always ready to give the game away, and on occasion the cooperation of the biographied author him or herself. Of such books we have many excellent examples: Humphrey Carpenter on W.H. Auden, Peter Ackroyd on T.S. Eliot, Deidre Bair on Samuel Beckett, Carlos Baker on Ernest Hemingway, Arthur Mizener on Scott Fitzgerald, Douglas Day on Malcolm Lowry, James Atlas on Delmore Schwartz, Richard Ellmann on James Joyce, and more. The writers are often spectacular in their living, but not always; frequently it is as if their works have left an obscurity that only an account of their existence can penetrate. Beyond them, of course, are many other fine modern biographies of writers of the past, where the records are more remote but the methods are contemporary and recreate the subjects as figures for the present: Leon Edel on Henry James, George Painter on Marcel Proust, Gordon Haight on George Eliot, Edgar Johnson on Dickens, Maynard Mack on Pope, and so on. The lives keep coming, the task is worthy, and the accounts not only transform our sense of literary history but of the significance of authorship and the creative process.

Indeed we regard biography as an essential means by which writers become known to us. The genre thrives, the skills are substantial, the record enlarges, the subjects multiply. It no longer seems to matter whether the subject is major or minor, or their lives of flamboyant if not scandalous adventure or of tedious respectability. It is all a contribution to the fullness of the record, the fascination of the creative, and in the great archive of modern culture, extraordinary in its accumulation and stockpiling of record, the potential remains vast. Libraries purchase papers by the ton, and augmenting records beg for recorders. With seven tons of Upton Sinclair papers in the Lilly Library of Indiana University, a foot-high pile of drafts of *Tender Is the Night* at Princeton, a vast papermine of contemporary writing and writing paper at the University of Texas, and with research grants still not too hard to come by, the task has a promising future. And, with the stockpile of biographical weaponry augmented by psycho-analytical awareness and modern scepticism, the biographer's own dignity has grown greatly. We live in an age when no stone seems left unturned, no oral source remains mute, no postcard in the dead letter office remains dead. We live, too, in an age of thoroughness, when there are studies so substantial that they outweigh, in bulk and in cost, the entire published work of the subject, an age of detail so well consumed that – as with Josepeh Blotner's two-volume life of Faulkner – it seems hard to believe that a single individual could have been busy enough to live a life that could fill so many pages and still write great novels as well.

And yet at the same time we live also in another age, an age not of the celebrated literary personality but an age of the Death of the Author. It is one of the triumphs of modern thought to have proved that none of us actually exists, or at least that our existences can be "demystified" (one of those strange words that means exactly its opposite). Concepts of literary creativity, of genius, of an original individual who is the onlie begetter and valid first cause of a literary text, have been stripped from us. We have high literary theorists who propose the tactical elimination of the whole concept of a single, secureable, person-like source of writing, who consider that literature is an imaginary institution, that our writerly canon is a suspect fiction, that writers do not write but get written, and that it is not authors who construct books but readers, who can only misread them. The most we can have is not biography but anti-biography.

The French deconstructionist philosopher Jacques Derrida has, in a recent work *Signeponge/Signsponge*, offered an example. Studying the French writer Francis Ponge, Derrida deconstructs the "heresy of the proper name", noting that the name clearly contains the word "sponge", and that this word is a guiding metaphor for the work rather than an authenticating signature. Thus "Francis Ponge" is an attempt to construct a proper noun from the mechanism of the poetry that the author has written, or rather has written him. This must be a clear challenge to the biographer, who clearly colludes in that heresy of the proper name. No longer should we assume that literary art is created by authors born in the conventional way, grown up in family circumstances, authors who have imprinted words on papers, had them published, and communicated them clearly to readers in a friendly intimacy. "Linguistically, the author is never more than the instance writing, just as *I* is nothing other than the instance saying *I*," Roland Barthes explains in his famous essay "The Death of the Author" (1968). Just as there is no author in the text, there is no self-sufficient and authentic ego who can be said to have authored anything; the Death of the Author is part of the larger Death of the Subject, and presumably it is the Death of Biography.

Thus we indeed live in two ages at once: the age of the author hyped and promoted, studied and celebrated; the age of the author denied and eliminated, desubjected and airbrushed from writing with an efficiency the envy of any totalitarian regime keen to remove past discredited leaders from history. The situation appears peculiar. In the commonsense world, authors commonsensically exist, in inordinate numbers. We may not think of them as highly as pop-stars or politicians, nor reward them with honours as we do our civil servants. But they have visibility, a certain fame; they are *there*. We can see them, touch them if we are lucky, have them put their ostensible signatures to their ostensible books in our ostensible bookshops. They gesture at us from TV screens, punditing on warfare, peace, diet, sexuality, and sometimes even their own work. They have lives and wives, lovers and mistresses. From time to time they go to France, or jail, or win prizes or sell their film rights or become publicity advisers to political parties. Some engage us with major moral and ethical issues, some satisfy our yearning for form and beauty. All they say and do suggests that it is they – not writing in general – who write, derive their images and themes from their own experience, base characters on their once intimate friends, and so on. They will tell you, if asked, just how they write: with pen, secretary, or word processor. They have friends who will report on them, reporters who will befriend them, and the record of their lives is to be found in church records, passport office, and police files.

This cannot be denied: but in the refracting mirror of modern culture it can certainly be questioned. How then does this double vision of the writer – all too there, and not there at all – come about? A simple but not complete answer is that it comes from the difference, or *différance*, between the public view of authors, and the academic one. In the commonsense world, authors have common-sense existences, and the reader takes the name on the spine of a book as a real sign, the name of a true person – true in a special way, of course, capable of bearing wisdom, genius, moral insight, the qualities both of the magus and the celebrity. Like most people in the public eye the name is an image, a mystery, and becomes the stuff of news, illusion, gossip, scandal and vicarious public involvement. Biography itself may be one more form of that news and gossip and vicarious engagement, though often it is also an analysis of it. This suggests that biography is in a sense itself a popular form, and indeed its history long predates "serious" literary study, certainly going back to Johnson's *Lives of the Poets* or Boswell's *Life of Johnson*. To this day, especially in Britain, many of our best biographers are not academics, but free-lance writers, like Michael Holroyd, Peter Ackroyd, Hilary Spurling, Humphrey Carpenter, Ann Thwaite, Victoria Glendinning and many more. Their work maintains the highest standards of scholarship, the exactitude of good research, the powers of strong and vivid narrative. But it is not usually invested with the more advanced critical argument, and indeed it often stands as a kind of adversary or query to it.

In the academy, on the other hand, there is a theoretical suspicion of biography, even though it is equally true that many of our finest biographers *are* academics. Fighting its battle with old-fashioned literary history, the New Criticism of the 1940s and 1950s questioned biography's dominance, and insisted on the centrality of the literary *text*. As René Wellek and Austen Warren argued in their famous and influential *Theory of Literature* (1949), biography could often *aid* literary history and scholarship, but, "Whatever the importance of biography in these respects . . ., it seems dangerous to ascribe to it any real critical importance. No biographical evidence can change or influence critical evaluation." But this was only a modest dismissal, in the interests of rightly reading the text; now there are no right readings, and no place for biographical scholarship either, scepticism having gone deeper. To understand this, we need to remember the changing nature of the academic institution, and the rising role of literary theory. With the postwar expansion of high education and the growth of a critical salariat, we have seen a great professionalisation of literary study, a growing church which has produced an ever more complex theory, and been riven, as growing churches are, by schism and scepticism. Some fifteen years ago I myself edited a book called *Contemporary Criticism*, an attempt to bring seriousness to the field. It has just been replaced by a new book, *Criticism and Critical Theory*, its editor rightly pointing out that the period between the volumes has been one of massive change. It is a change of spirit as well as method. I edited my own book in the ecumenical spirit of T.S. Eliot's view of criticism as "the common pursuit of true judgement". In contemporary literary study, a world of semiotics, structuralism, hegemonies, hermeneutics and hermetics, of late Marxism and feminist deconstruction, there is little that is common, no such concept as truth, and nothing to be said for judgement.

There is no doubt that biography has been challenged, but it has not gone altogether. This was brought home to me when a few years ago I was invited, as writer and critic, to a university in northern Australia where, under tropical heat, many of these theories had reached a state of exotic enrichment. The department I went to was severe, specialist, and not even called a department, while the phrase "English literature" was no longer used, both concepts having been deconstructed. The faculty, many imported from British and American institutions in the 1960s and 1970s, had rooted and grown large, and taught their students, most of them in thongs and shorts, fresh from the sheep stations, a sturdy training in structuralism and semiotics, hegemonic paradigms and late Althusserian revisionisms, and set them essays on the difference between early and late Foucault, a term they indeed found frequent use for. Yet, wandering under the kookaburras one day, I found a major institution of literary biography, waiting, like some alternative government, for the regime to topple. Here people who wrote "lives" talked to people who wanted to learn how to write "lives", and discussed strange matters: how to assess evidence, construct narrative, explore creative psychology. Biography was not dead; it was alive and well and living in another building.

From this we may draw several conclusions. One is that the modern academy is divided – between scholars and critics, canonisers and decanonisers, students of writers and students of writings. That is partly true, but only partly; for strange tentacular relations do in fact exist between modern literary theory and modern literary biography, or at least some part of it. If there is estrangement there is also an intimacy. For biography itself has entered the Era of Suspicion, and indeed has been there for some time, certainly since Lytton Strachey. Once biography's task seemed clear, and its methods obvious. The biographer celebrated the achievement, the fame, the genius of the literary individual, and was the guardian of accuracy and decorum. Respect and discretion were desirable job qualifications, as they were indeed for the biographied. But the age of genius and exemplary lives has gone; we no longer acknowledge the virtuously successful individual; biography itself has grown far more sceptical, less sure what constitutes a character, the surface of a life, genius or virtue. And in this, of course, it bears a resemblance to what has happened in all writing, which is what biography is. For it is not only critics, but writers too, who have insisted on the gap between the writer and the text, or between, as T.S. Eliot put it, the mind which suffers and the mind which creates. Writing, too, has lost a clear concept of character or the narrative wholeness of a life, the certainty of the word or the relation of the signifier to the signified. Historians question the principles and truth of historical writing, sharing with novelists a sense of the ambiguous line between fact and fiction. Poets have come to question the sacralisation of the word. And the biographer, yet another writer, has felt the same anxieties.

Biography is inclined toward the plot of a life, toward structure and assertion. "The life of Ivy Compton-Burnett falls into two parts, sharply divided by the First World War," declares the first sentence of Hilary Spurling's fine life of Compton-Burnett. The plot works, neatly dividing her book into two separate volumes, and also affording a sound account of the way Compton-Burnett's early life and society acquires its ritualised character in her later writing. Yet we can fairly ask, how and why did it fall, and who pushed it? Indeed by mischievous chance another author wrote a simultaneous biography, interviewing much the same people, but finding only one life and one volume. Biographies are plots of a life, nor the life itself. And literary biographies are indeed the plots of the lives of those who are themselves plotters, and likely to leave on biography the trace of their own complex plottings. There are those who plot to elude biography altogether, as Eliot and Auden did, refusing the idea of an official life

as they might well have refused an official portrait. Both fell posthumously to the biographers in the end, but left them with obscure and difficult quests. Modern writers have frequently found the need to claim the space between life and art, through masks and personae, strange labyrinths of obscurity and escape, not simply from publicity but from fixity itself. So it has been with B. Traven and J.D. Salinger, Thomas Pynchon and Vladimir Nabokov. These are writers who present themselves in the world as familiar, domesticated, recognisable wholes, but many more who do not, like Samuel Beckett, that great writer of the characterlessness of modern character, who permitted a biography to exist, as long as he in effect was not in it.

The strange and hungry desire of the modern biographer for the biographee has not then always been reciprocated, and for good reasons. Fiction can suggest to us why; William Golding's splendid novel *The Paper Men* shows the strange and terrible symbiosis between the writer seeking to hold his disreputable and scattered soul together against the depredations of the life-writer, hungry for his academic promotion. Writers know their existence is somehow counterfeit, and they need their elusiveness; the notion of the author as fake and forgery runs deeply through modern writing. John Fowles, in *The French Lieutenant's Woman*, impersonates himself in the text several times, but in many guises: as social historian and reporter, as modern literary theorist, in the end as flashy impresario and imposter. The modern Death of the Author is not solely a fiction of the critics; the modern author has frequently and elusively conspired with it, disappearing ahead of the critic like the rabbit in Alice down into the labyrinth of writing, with all its holes and trapdoors, its refracting and contradictory mirror images. It would seem, then, that for the modern literary biographer who is responsive to art and its nature there is only one way to go. And that, too, is into the labyrinth, where there is not one image but many, not one name but several, and where biography itself becomes part of contemporary writerly anxiety.

PERSONS OF LETTERS

In a recent collection of his splendid essays, *A Man of Letters*, V.S. Pritchett chooses to describe himself as coming at "the tail-end of a long and once esteemed tradition in English and American writing", the tradition of the Man of Letters himself. The Man of Letters, Pritchett explains, does not have a captive audience, and puts his wares into a declining market of periodicals and magazines. He is rarely an academic, though he owes a great debt to scholars, and, earning a living from the writing he does, he has a strong attachment to the common reader. His criticism often diminishes to mere reviewing, because of diminishing space for the literary essay; but he is less a critic than an imaginative explorer. "We do not lay down the law, but we do make a stand for the reflective values of a humane culture . . . . We ourselves have written novels, short stories, biographies, works of travel. Some of us are poets. And we know that literature is rooted in the daily life of any society but it also springs out of literature itself." Pritchett's own essays then show us the rewards; they are extensive, considered, thoughtful pieces, clearly and subtly expressed, granting to writing and to past writers a human dignity that makes them virtually coeval with the author who writes about them. He loves writers, their obligations, their absurdities, their reltionships, their madnesses. He ranges massively, from the classic to the minor, the British to the Europeans and the Russians, on whom he is especially brilliant. The writers themselves lead us to the issues they raise; there is little theory but a general air of loving wisdom, and everywhere Pritchett seems to be displaying not only his own fine scholarship and breadth of thoughtful reading but his respect for the tradition of writing in which his own arguments and sensibility belong.

He also writes on the dying fall, the fading gasp of the Man – or perhaps nowadays we had better say Person – of Letters. This elegiac note has been widely expressed in our times, and with reason. In a fascinating book on the subject, *The Rise and Fall of the Man of Letters*

(1969), John Gross gives us a very clear idea as to why. The Person of Letters rose in the nineteenth century, when literary discussion moved to the centre of social affairs and touched on the most central mattes of politics and public feeling. Criticism became a matter of general debate, and the great magazines and reviews saw themselves as representing a current of serious thought in which issues of literary moment meshed with what Arnold called "the best that is known and thought in the world". But the centrality of literary discussion began to die with the breakup of the Victorian consensus. With the weakening of the moral debate, the subdividing of culture, the rise of the avant garde, and the academic professionalisation of critical activity, the Person of Letters did not disappear but certainly diminished, winning small space on the reviewing pages and in the occasional long article. Thus Evelyn Waugh described his own father, a publisher, editor, and essayist, as one of the breed, "a category, like the maiden aunt's, that is now almost extinct".

And indeed ours is not an age of Persons of Letters. We have few flamboyant reviewers, not even those of the Arnold Bennett or the Cyril Connolly kind, who shape the fate of a book and guide the choice of cultural direction. Few of our writers are powers in the public or political realm, exercising influence and magic over our leaders or our community at large. Somehow the trace of the Person of Letters stays on in our culture, and despite the splendid innovations of modernism, the triumphs of the twentieth-century avant garde, the rise of critical pedagogy and the strongly theoretical basis of modern literary studies, a few of the breed do still hold a significant if persistently threatened place in our cultural affairs. But with the fading of the type there goes a weakening of public literary debate, the lack of a general stir of criticism, and perhaps even a decline in the capacity to construct the public role of the writer for ourselves. Our best reviews keep us abreast of radical new theories, but they do not reinforce judgement, nor do they seem to provide a strong stimulus to creative activity. As for the Person of Letters, he or she often seems incorrigibly middlebrow, the writer attempting to straddle some impossible gap. The best modern examples of the Person of Letters are often those writers we feel most equivocal about, the ones we would place as less than great.

Reading two literary lives – Susan Cooper's *J.B. Priestley: Portrait of an Author* and Malcolm Foster's *Joyce Cary: A Biography* – of two authors active in the interwar years who represent not its experimental and political flamboyance but its more conventional mainstream, authors who, in Stephen Spender's useful distinction, belong in the spirit not of the "moderns" but of the "contemporaries", I have found it interesting to see the way in which they each characterise, in very different ways, both the possibilities and the difficulties of the Person of Letters. If neither strikes us as a writer of the very greatest class, both surely must strike us as important. Both were curious about the spirit of modern experiment, and drew in some ways upon it; both do not quite belong with it. Both were writers of enormous intelligence without being "intellectuals", and both had a somewhat quarrelling relation with the academy and with the academic practice of criticism. One was capaciously public, the other intensely private; one intervened in political life and matters of history, the other, while having played a part in these, turned to the imaginative reserves of art in order, as it were, to escape from the mundane, the practical and the political.

Priestley, of course, was the public man, the writer as cultural politician. Indeed during the later 1960s the British electorate had a good deal of commerce with a major public personality not unlike his. In fact, since Susan Cooper's book is, sensibly, not so much a work of literary criticism as a study of a personality, it is hardly surprising that from time to time our readerly attention slips, and that this rounded visage with its stuck-in pipe, these northern intonations and com-monsense mannerisms, this spirit of Bradford practicality lit with an instinct for idealism, this bulldogged honest Englishness mixed with radical social conscience, should seem like a portrait not of an important British writer but a former Labour Prime Minister, Harold Wilson. Perhaps the problem of the book is that, if this *were* a portrait of a political figure, we would need an interpretation of the political energy behind the tone, the nature of its public appeal, the reason why this cultural mode has an electoral drawing power. About a writer we think differently, possibly rather more benevolently. But the comparison is not inappropriate, for the fact is that while Priestley was a man of conscience and integral and deeply felt values, he was and knew himself to be a British cultural artefact, as self-made as they come. He summoned his readers to values he felt he and they possessed in common, travelled the land and landscape to summon up his identification with it and its people, and when crisis came and war began Priestley had an extraordinary success in conveying to the common people the nature of the common cause. It was this same central way of thinking and writing that made Priestley into the best-selling author he was – a writer with an identifiable seriousness and also a certain kind of facility, of innovative powers but also solid and habitual literary manners, indeed, it might be said, one of the most English of our modern English writers in an era when our best arts were both experimental and internationalist.

So in his way Priestley seems a rare kind of author for the age of modernism, one who managed to be popular without disgrace, and

serious without separatism. Like one or two figures who have
followed him – Richard Hoggart and Raymond Williams are examples – he possessed the power not only to analyse the salient and
central powers and directions of the culture but to possess and
embody them. But the more salient comparison is with certain
novelists of the past, above all Dickens and the English humorists. It
was a comparison Priestley himself was very conscious of, and it
helped sustain him in his middlebrow and public role; it also clearly
separated him from those writers who nowadays do strike us as our
most serious, our most intense, our most discovering, and who have
taken far more oblique postures and extreme formal decisions and
apparently drawn little of their funding from the broader social life.
This in turn has meant that professional literary criticism had little to
say about Priestley, and apparently had small regard for his kind of
achievement. Certainly in his often bitter later years, Priestley
believed this, and considered that the tradition in which he worked
was being intellectually undermined. During the 1950s, when there
was a revival in the fortunes of the novel of Arnold Bennett and H.G.
Wells, Priestley too stimulated a certain amount of critical interest,
and he obviously lies in a related tradition and carries on with some of
their themes and resources. I suppose we should call him a later
naturalist, and naturalism is often set against modernism. Arnold
Bennett famously said when he saw the Post-Impressionist Exhibition
in London in 1910 that had he been younger he would probably have
felt the need to begin over again; but in those classic quarrels between
Wells and Henry James, or Bennett and Virginia Woolf, we see now a
decisive moment in modern literary history where the modern novel
divides – and in dividing seems to maroon the Wellses and Bennetts
somewhere in the past of the form. The impact of modernist
sensibility and its insistence on formal making has thus been of
devastating importance in the fate of the modern novel.

Priestley was perfectly conscious of all this. "Where I differ from
most of them [the advanced 'modernists']," he commented in a 1931
preface to a reissue of his first two novels, "is in my conviction that
the novel demands some sort of objective narrative. I still believe that
a novelist should tell a story, and if possible a fairly shapely one, no
matter how strong his subjective interests may be. Indeed, I consider
this problem – that of combining a reasonably clear-cut narrative, in
which may be found definite characters and scenes, with these
subjective interests, this flickering drama of the mind or soul – easily
the most difficult problem a modern novelist is called upon to solve.
You may dodge it, of course, by simplifying or eliminating your
subjective stuff, and thus bringing out a plain tale. You can also dodge
it by giving subjectivity its head and wrecking the form of the novel

..." As this says, he was concerned with "the most difficult problem", as so many twentieth-century writers have been. We could say that he simplifies the issues of it, but it is clear that he found his answer somewhere in the region where we find the Person of Letters. The answer he offered was like that of Wells and Bennett; it was to devise a notion of writing as a form of practical professionalism, and Susan Cooper's book perhaps wisely does not set out to make strong critical claims for any one single work of Priestley's – his books do not offer a great deal to modern critical practice – but to display the enormous range of his activities and talents, the spread of his work, from novel to drama, general essay to criticism to autobiography; she also establishes the enormous cultural respect its honest Englishness provoked. She also justly notes that it is wrong to see Priestley solely as the naturalistic recorder of common life, and indeed argues that his gifts as a social critic and interpreter were in fact linked to a speculative philosophy.

But this simply poses the problems a little more sharply. Priestley's theory of culture, his notion of community, and so on, are of strong importance and continuing interest. More difficult is his notion of "time", an issue where his thinking might seem to point him toward the complexities of Pirandello and the narrative indirections of modern fiction, toward that "flickering drama of the mind or soul" of which he comments in the passage I have quoted. Priestley does offer us his cerebrations on this topic, most famously in the "time-plays", where he shows how his notions owe much to Ouspensky and Dunne. Yet when we consider the complex time-experiments of some of our greatest writers, from Pirandello to Proust or Faulkner, we realise that Priestley is not thinking in anything like the same way. Priestley does not dismember the traditional sequences of causality and chronicity in favour of a more subjective vision. He holds to the naturalistic rules, the laws of cause and effect, and then jolts them for dramatic impact. The moments of "timeless joy" he seeks to summon are cultural artefacts, usually moments of connection between an individual and the family or community. They bear on the same cultural critique as the rest of his writings, showing that Priestley can inject some of the principles of modern stage-craft into the well-made play. They do not carry the weight of a radical new vision of form, and they function essentially as device. They are part of Priestley's strong acquisitive intelligence, his sense of the assimilative power of fiction.

To go back to Priestley's plays and some of his novels – the early ones in particular, and *The Good Companions* above all – is to find a writer of high powers. But in the end Susan Cooper is right to suggest that Priestley is not best judged on the strength of any single work, but rather on the sum of an oeuvre and the achievement of a tone – a way of speaking and feeling, an engaged interest in society and a manner of address to it. In all this he explored and exploited the ways in which the workable and sociable spirit of prose can acquire a sense of common realism and a feel of visionary integrity. A very intelligent and well-educated man, Priestley sustained a tradition many of his contemporaries thought was no longer viable, but which he found still alive. Yet, interestingly, it was George Orwell, who shared a good deal with him, who was to hand on most of the realism that came back to British fiction in the postwar years. Priestley by then had won his fame, established his popularity, and extended his influence, becoming the exemplary English voice of British resilience in wartime and what followed. He probed the postwar problems of Americanisation, witnessed to the new mood of social reform, wrote widely and powerfully. But he cannot, in a literary sense, be called an influence or a guide, except to that fundamental sense of professionalism which is, below or beyond all aesthetic debate, one of the key principles of writing.

By contrast, Joyce Cary must be seen as a writer who took the other path, toward the fulfilment of an aesthetic desire and the highest possible valuation of the creative imagination, that power that divides the individual from his fellows and the artist from society. The result was the paradox that Walter Allen once noted in *Tradition and Dream* (1964), that few novelists have invested as much in the power of creativity, and yet though his own work can surge with its vitality – most notably in his portrayal and exploration of his most famous character, Gulley Jimson – it is often flat and notoriously uneven. His career in the Nigerian political service separated him from British literary and cultural life, and gave him both an extraordinary subject – the Africa of *Aissa Saved* (1932) and *Mister Johnson* (1939), as well as other books; indeed to the treatment of Africa in British fiction he was a very striking and original contributor – and a sense of independence from the literary manners of many of his contemporaries. The belief in creative originality invests his greatest portraits, which are either of artists like Jimson or female images of creative fertility like that of Sara Monday. At the same time Cary had an elaborate social story to tell, one of a history of visionary radicalism which represented a necessary underside to conventional British life. All this seemed to place him toward the sidelines of British culture, as Priestley's way of writing placed him near the centre. Cary wrote prolifically from his twenties onward, but did not publish a novel until 1932, when he was forty-four; his best books, the Gulley Jimson sequence, appeared in wartime, and not until after it did he attain anything like a broad critical or general reputation. By this time his work, though lively, was growing more political and religious in preoccupation. There were essays, poetry and political studies, and a mass of unfinished writings some part of which has been put into print since his death in 1957.

By this time his public had grown, and the critics had at last become interested in him and were beginning to see the importance of his work. That interest has somewhat slackened since – a pity, though it is not hard to understand why. His novels do vary much in quality, and their sheer prolixity of method makes a very protean impression. They can be read in the light both of a liberal theme, that of the need to reform convention with feeling, and in the light of an exotic romanticism. They have often quite strong experimental and modernist constituents – the multi-narrations of the Gulley Jimson sequence, or the striking present-tense method of *Mister Johnson* – but also a traditionalism of subject and of narrative discursiveness which makes them seem less than radical. This was what Frederick J. Karl, in his useful study of the postwar British novel, argued; out to prove the traditionalism of British fiction, he presented him as one of a number of British writers who employed stylistic and verbal manners of a complex modern kind but which never fully permeate down into the vision. Though vision and individuality was his theme, his books seemed to some to lack vital struggle, to lie dormant. Some of this is true, and Cary is a heavy writer at times. But kinder things can also be said: that his best novels – the two remarkable trilogies, the Gulley Jimson sequence, *Herself Surprised* (1941), *To Be a Pilgrim* (1942) and *The Horse's Mouth* (1944); and the Chester Nimmo sequence, *Prisoner of Grace* (1952), *Except the Lord* (1953) and *Not Honour More* (1955) – show a very striking disposition of material, in which psychological, artistic, social, political and moral life are densely interwoven, that Cary is capable of strong comic effects, and that his powerful if often highly romanticised treatment of the creative passions is not only driven by a fertile energy but is always handled with generosity of range and a large sense of history.

Along with some of the African novels the Gulley Jimson sequence is the work of Cary's likely to go on being remembered, and in its various narratives we find the presiding contract of his work: that between the moral intelligence and the creative passion. As he explained in his *Writers at Work* interview: "Roughly for me, the principal fact of life is the free mind. For good and evil, man is a free creative spirit. This produces the very queer world we live in, a world in continuous creation and therefore continuous change and insecurity." The history of the moral intelligence reaches back into religious and social history; the notion of creativity is associated with a kind of intellectual liberalism but also a Blakean venereality, an artistic romanticism. Malcolm Foster's book interprets this as a kind of contradiction within Cary himself, a decent and concerned man with a radical and anarchistic artistic impulse, in whom the liberal and historical awareness is in a kind of warfare with a romantic passion – a man whose letters and papers reveal little but a public face, as if the creativity were a lonely function, locked within. For this there is, of course, a potent tradition; we indeed think of Blake, or Lawrence, where the visionary impulse is of a piece with a kind of auto-didacticism. Like them, Cary is inclined to amass ideas, to accumulate thought, and convert thought to passion. The artist thus stands outside culture in a kind of roguery, making his urgent and transient things. This is the spirit of Gulley Jimson, an artist dependent on serving wholly his inner vision, and willing to commit any kind of rascality to sustain it. Gulley's work has nothing to do with fashion and only a certain amount to do with thought. It comes from the driving spirit within ("The everlasting creation of delight. The joy that is always new and fresh because it was created. The revelation ever renewed, in every fall," cries Gulley in one of his paeans of sexually stimulated creative pleasure). And art, like prayer, is joy; Gulley's comic ragings are an abundant expression of thought made over into feeling, and feeling into the visionary glow that provokes the raging battles of creation.

Against this, there is a vision of society and a strong sense of social history, a history of the nonconformist and the displaced, that perhaps in part reflects Cary's Irish rentier background and a career that largely separated him from the conventional literary world. The "Joyce" of his first name was taken from his mother's family, and he felt it established a link with James Joyce, a writer of whom he shows a strong awareness, not least in the presentation of Gulley's flow of consciousness. Yet nearly all his writing was done at a long distance from the capitals of modernism and under pressures quite different from those of much modern literature. Foster's book offers a portrait of a writer of conventional middle-class decencies and duties who possessed a strong artistic urge that came largely from isolation and lack of literary and cultural contact. After an education at Clifton School and Oxford, Cary did study art for a time in Paris and Edinburgh; but a taste for adventure took over, and he went to the Balkan War in 1912, where he fought with the Montenegrans and conducted himself with heroism. Thereafter he joined the Nigerian Political Service for a long spell between 1913 and 1920, fighting again during the Great War and being wounded. He then returned to work as a magistrate and political officer in the remoter Nigerian districts. His work was isolated and demanding, and he did it well; yet, in the most unlikely circumstances, he also became passionately committed to the idea of becoming a writer. There was an element of practical expediency in this; he wanted to leave the colonial service and return home to a wife and children from whom he had been too long separated. But he wrote prodigiously, under the most improbable conditions, on his various Nigerian stations, and wildly and variously, as if engaged on some quest to bring himself together both imaginatively and intellectually. These years generated more than a dozen well-worked novels, none of them entirely completed. They served at various levels; it was finally by selling some potboiling stories to the *Saturday Evening Post* that he gained the independence he wanted, returned home in 1920 to England and Parks Road, Oxford, and began the task of trying to live by writing.

Cary thus seemed the man of action and affairs who had found his path to mental and social independence through the ways of the imagination. But even now literary success did not come readily, nor did the writing flow easily. Indeed it was not until 1932 that he finally completed and got into print a novel he had been working on for many years, the fine African story *Aissa Saved*. Three more novels with African themes appeared during the 1930s. He had begun them stimulated by his own experiences and perceptions in Nigeria, and remote from the European sources of modern writing. And though they are indeed touched with modernist influences as well as a sense of the tradition they are marked by something of that sense of lonely and private creativity that Gulley Jimson carries: the conviction of the imagination as a radical freedom of spirit. Yet, as he told one of his best critics, Mark Shorer, we do not create alone, but in a world, which limits our materials, and so the freedom of the imagination – the freedom his books struggle to celebrate – is in the end a comedy of our human limitation. He drew on what he had known in his life, a strong sense of culture as control and containment, but also as a necessary power for community and convention. His was, as Lionel Trilling has put it, a liberal imagination, one which sees both the yes and the no of culture, and sees that art comes from an opposing self, a romantic adversity, which nonetheless needs the carapace of social existence to survive. It was appropriate that the Gulley Jimson novels were followed by the Chester Nimmo books, which deal with political life. In sum, Cary seems to write about two contradictory impulses of the self, one that points into culture and the other that points out of it. And his own work oscillates with the contradiction, making him a writer hard to grasp as a unity. The contrast between the public and political man and the private imagination lasted to the end, and as a result Cary to this day remains a writer who does not seem quite a full citizen of the world of letters, solid and substantial as his achievement is. Part of Oxford, he was never quite part of its intellectual community, a writer well-read but perhaps not well-learned in a conventional literary sense. Nor was he quite part of the literary community either, his late start in fiction and his continuing financial uncertainties always shadowing his life. To the end he remained something of the loner, his work liked but never quite clearly identified as strong, his reputation fluctuating, as indeed it still does now.

So we might say that Cary is the opposite of Priestley's kind of writer – not the cultural mediator, the public voice, the inhabitant of the middle ground, but the public and conventional man driven toward the impassioned and romantic energies of art, which represent a kind of anarchic freedom which can invest the commonplace with revelation. As it happens, it appears that neither kind of writer – the public voice of culture, the voice that seeks to find the imaginative power beyond culture, while not denying its necessity and power – quite suits us today. Our theories of art have quietly changed, and our expectation of writers seems different. For Priestley and Cary were in their different ways traditionalists, one reaching back into common life, the other into a tradition of nonconformist feeling, which time seems to have distanced for us. The usable past seems to feed us with little in the way of a sense of culture or a sense of the dionysian energy of art. And the writer who seeks to inhabit the middle spaces of culture has a harder time of it now, one reason surely why we do not so easily produce the Person of Letters in our midst. Our writing tends to come from harsher experience and a far less communal sense of language. Both Priestley and Cary call up traditions and visions in art which we have grown less and less inclined to use, and for the moment neither of them has a particularly strong literary reputation. No doubt when we begin to resurrect the complex cultural history of our century and look back through the ways in which we have produced our modern versions of the artist, we will find that they both have a lasting interest. In Priestley we will find the energised record of a loving feeling for culture; in Cary we will find the energy that belongs with art as inner fertility. I hope we will value them both, but if we will value Priestley for his power of felt record it is, I suspect, in Cary that we will find the fuller satisfaction; for his books, if not quite great, still hold the pleasure that his urgent, lonely and half-hidden passion for art has left imprinted on them.

WILLIAM TREVOR'S DUBLINERS

When Henry Fielding was hunting for a neo-classical definition of the new form that we have come to call the novel, he called it "the comic epic in prose", and so emphasised an aspect of fiction that has stayed strong in the British tradition ever since. The comic has been an energising power in our novel to a degree unusual in most other countries and cultures. And now, when it has grown fashionable to suggest that British fiction has lost its capacity to possess a style or present to us a common literary language, then we might note that it is that comic mode that still seems to give us our common ground. Many of our best writers practise in the comic way – Angus Wilson and Muriel Spark, Anthony Burgess and Kingsley Amis, William Boyd and Clive Sinclair. They may not be close kin, but all in their different ways have the capacity to write with a distinctive mannerism, and create a world in which realism and fantasy interlock through the power of comic means. For comedy in the novel means not simply the ability to write humorously, but a way of seeing human experience and its fictional presentation in a certain light. It means not just a gift for tone and effect, but a language of fictional placement, a tactical mixture of sympathy and distance. And it seems significant that a good many of our comic writers seem to owe much to Evelyn Waugh, and above all to his way of suggesting that we live our lives in a world of desperation and loss where society functions as an elaborate power without a definite meaning, and we conduct in our lives a sad human performance ever stirred by intimations of something better. The human figure of comedy is normally non-heroic, the world contingent, the appropriate fictional tone is pathos, but the effect is one that bears the power of laughter.

With a good body of novels and a brilliant repertoire of short stories behind him, William Trevor has earned a high place in this – for want of a better word – tradition. Like the best comic writers, he had managed to establish not only a gift for greatly amusing us but of creating a world of striking consistency and temper. His persistently wry observation is of a world of insufficiencies, lost hopes, social displacements, erratic or mistaken pilgrimages, the wasting parts of life. And *Mrs Eckdorf in O'Neill's Hotel* (1969) offers some glimpses as to why, and indeed even begins moving toward the intimations of a religious novel, a tale of small epiphanies, without entirely completing itself as such. It is set in Dublin, the home of epiphanies, and mostly in a once impressive but now rundown family hotel still presided over by the remote Mrs Sinnott, deaf and dumb, charitable and forgiving, the focus of an ideal family that is ideal no longer, a figure of saintly values in a world from which most trace of virtue has departed. Her son gambles, her daughter and her son's wife have left the hotel for petty bourgeois existence elsewhere, and her three orphan protégés serve as hotel porter, pimp and whore. Now it is her ninety-second birthday, and they all come together again. But into the occasion there comes an intruder – Mrs Ivy Eckdorf, born in Maida Vale, now living in Munich, and twice divorced. She is a photographer who has sensed a "tragedy" in O'Neill's Hotel, and wants to make it into a coffee-table photographic montage: "I photograph human stories of quality," she says.

Trevor's cast gives him all the opportunities for the comic evocation and improvisation that he does so well. For the wheel of human misunderstanding turns, and the obsessions and routines by which each one of his characters lives comes into focus. Morissey, the pimp, yearns for friendship, and is aghast when his tactics, which turn on a walletful of photographs of his stable of whores, fail to win him comrades. O'Shea the porter, yearning for the hotel to recover its great days again, jostles absurdly against the self-satisfaction of Eugene Sinnott, who has become content to live in a world of dreams that offer up racing tips. But the basic comic collision is that between the rundown petty bourgeois world of the hotel and the camp, cosmopolitan world of Mrs Eckdorf, the worldly image-maker. Having scented a newsworthy tragedy, she now scents, in the virtuous form of old Mrs Sinnott, a newsworthy saint. Having come first for reportage, she now seeks atonement and redemption. Indeed Mrs Eckdorf is having a breakdown, and the book ends on her psychic collapse, as instead of photographing the strange sad world outside she finds it incorporated within herself. As Father Hennessey comes to observe, all this has an ironic religious implication. But, being a very elegant and well-made fable, it also has a literary one. Mrs Eckdorf has come to O'Neill's Hotel to find realism but has found a pathos and extremity she did not expect, and found it outside and within. And this seems very much the experience of the narrative and the novelist himself, finding pathos and comedy lying strangely in wait in the world of reportage. Like Mrs Eckdorf, the novelist cannot simply remain abstracted before absurdity and pathos, but must enter into a compact of sympathy, itself absurd and possibly destructive. Like many books these days, *Mrs Eckdorf* is a cunning commentary on itself, a reading of its own delicate, admirable comic realism.

CAMPUS FICTIONS

In the early 1950s, a very innocent young man, I went off to a small redbrick university called University College, Leicester, today a big redbrick university called the University of Leicester. I was the first of my family to aspire to such educational heights, and when I disembarked at the college gates, opposite the cemetery, and confronted the converted lunatic asylum in which the emergent university was then housed, I had little idea of expectation of the strange world I was entering, and little confidence in my right to be there. Even so, I had had some glimpses of what to expect, and these came from what can be called university novels. Even at that date it was something of a sub-genre in British fiction, having emerged in bursts at various points in modern literary history, usually at times of strong generational consciousness when the experience of sensitive young men – it was, then, mostly young men who went to university – was of moment. It was this kind of university novel (as opposed to the other kind, where the university is backdrop either for murder or romance) that I had read. And it was from such books – Forster's *The Longest Journey*, Waugh's *Brideshead Revisited* – that I knew what to expect: rooms shared with a son of the aristocracy, hours spent writing poems that had better be modern, or else, late night philosophical conversation, mostly about G.E. Moore's *Principia Ethica*, conducted over a mixture of claret and cocoa, and so on. I knew that a university was an ideal place for a young writer, being invisibly connected with Bloomsbury and Montparnasse, and magazines and small presses. All this knowledge did not, it has to be admitted, serve me in good stead.

But then, like so many of us, I had not yet grasped the spaces that exist between fictions and fact, image and reality, nor how the territory taken by fiction becomes mythicised, timeless, and both truer and less true than – but never as true as – the real thing. Moreover I had not quite understood how times change, and places differ. The novels of the pre-war period I had read – Beerbohm and Forster, Huxley and Waugh – were both temporally and geographically remote from me; even Philip Larkin's *Jill*, much closer to my experience, was not it exactly, since this was not Oxford nor was meant to be. Indeed very little had been written about the kind of university I was going to, the provincial redbricks being largely off the literary map. In the fiction of H.G. Wells and C.P. Snow, one could half-glimpse a university life distant from Oxbridge, and different from it in social character – a world of urbanised, techno-scientific, populist and hardworking New Men. In the work of D.H. Lawrence, there were glimpses of a life at University College, Nottingham, forty years earlier, that came closer to my case. But none matched or meshed with the post-Butler experience of provincial redbrick life at the beginning of the 1950s; and I inevitably found myself beginning to write my own novel, a book about the relation between the disinterested liberal values by which I had been drawn and the environment of ordinariness in which they were actually lived. In turn, however, these books became, even as I wrote them, fictions, and now they have passed into their own mythological hinterland, not unlike that in which those previous novels lay for me.

Today, it seems, there is an acknowledged genre of the university novel, and I am assumed to have contributed to it. In some ways the term annoys; whether Joseph Conrad relished being called an author of "sea-stories" I cannot recall, but few of us who are not instinctively popular or market writers like to have our novels labelled by their settings. At the same time there clearly is an institution which is known by that label, just as a university is known as a university. Indeed in Howard Jacobson's book *Coming From Behind*, about which much more in a moment, the institution is given the name of "Bradbury Lodge", and many novels nowadays seem to be set there; this suggests there is a genre of a kind. And one must acknowledge it to be true that, in the social rather than aesthetic history of fiction, British and American, there are a good number of novels, in some ways consecutive and interactive, which have taken the university or campus as a significant setting, and read the world of student, academic or general intellectual experience as an emblematic place in culture. If there is a tradition, it goes well back, certainly to the middle of the nineteenth century, when the sentimental academic *bildungs-roman* told tales of moral, social and religious education in the world of Oxbridge. And from such romantic tales to the sharper wit of *Zuleika Dobson*, from the story of Rickie Elliott's philosophical education in G.E. Moore's Cambridge to that of Charles Ryder's social and religious education in the already fading romance of Oxford, the university landscape was most usually seen as a warm, enlightened setting for young emotion, so that such stories became part of the accumulated charm of the institutions and the universities in which they were so pleasantly set. Even *Jude the Obscure* celebrates, if from outside, the mystery of ancient Oxford, and many of these novels depended on a common social knowingness, bore the romance of the powerful social institution which one whole part of the culture, the dominant part, knew in common. Indeed it was the capacity for nostalgia in such materials that made the television version of *Brideshead Revisited* the success it was, even for those who knew no more of Oxford than its lasting and deeply printed image.

This, one might say, is the university novel, and we might then need another term – say the campus novel – to serve to account for the kind of novel that appeared after the war, around the time I began writing myself, and was much less concerned with nostalgia or social recollection, more with intellectual and social change. Perhaps Larkin's *Jill* belongs in the category, and the novels of Wells and Snow are important antecedents to it. While I was a student and writing my own novel, Kingsley Amis's *Lucky Jim* came out, and though it does not now carry so strongly its air of social defiance the book's way of contradicting attitudes toward art and intellect, culture and education still holds its power. Jim Dixon's university hardly invites nostalgia, and its relations with the commonplace provincial community round about are critical enough to give the book the morality of a realistic commonsense. It was certainly outrageous enough at the time to stir Someset Maugham to violent denunciation of heroes like Jim Dixon and John Wain's Charles Lumley (in *Hurry On Down*):

> They do not go to the university to acquire culture but to get a job, and when they have got one, scamp it. They have no manners, and are woefully unable to deal with any social predicament. Their idea of a celebration is to go to a public house and drink six beers. They are mean, malicious and envious . . . .

Certainly a number of the university novels that came out in Britain during the 1950s were voicing a cultural and social change not just in university life but in the novel itself. And probably one reason why the form became noticeable and was thought important was that it carried a spirit of social and intellectual dissent both from the older forms of scholarship and scholarly life and the spirit in arts and academe that was called Bloomsbury. Hence perhaps the intimacy between some of these new novelists and writers like William Cooper and C.P. Snow, though in Snow's Cambridge novels of much this time – *The Light and the Dark* (1947), *The Masters* (1951) and *The Affair* (1960) – his narrative has taken a step onward from the provincial university college and moved into a world of scientific research set in and flavoured by ripe Cambridge glow, power and Leoville Poyferré being dispensed in roughly equal measures. The New Men have become the Old Masters.

These days when provincialism and realism looked like cultural renewal and the redbrick setting could acquire a critical, even Leavisite, glow were certainly the stuff of my own endeavour, in *Eating People Is Wrong*, to capture the world I had entered, one that hardly shone with the glow of cosmopolitanism or aestheticism, but with critical puritanism. Begun in the early 1950s, it was not to appear until the end of them, and it became, through its many revisions, a try at reading an entire decade in which critical energy had directed itself less through politics than morals, less through aesthetics than practical literary criticism, and when the role of the writer, the intellectual and the academic had greatly changed. If books form a genre by being intertextually related to other books and narratives, mine was certainly generic in that sense. As George Watson has said in some illuminating if testy comments on the whole matter ("Fictions of Academe", *Encounter*, November 1978, pp. 42–6), the rise of the university novel over this decade was undoubtedly because universities were becoming important in the lives of many more people, and were playing a large part in the social changes taking place and the general formation of culture. But this was also a period when the values of liberalism, humanism and intellectual criticism were being reasserted in the wake of a terrible war and a new era of intellectual self-doubt. Hence the genre appropriately had its match in the United States, where the theme of the "new liberalism" sounded through fiction. The intellectual and moral crisis of liberalism and progressivism thus sounds firmly through the two great American examples from the time, Mary McCarthy's *Groves of Academe* (1952), a very sharp novel about a progressive institution exploited by a member of faculty who protects his tenure by pretending to be a communist, and Randall Jarrell's *Pictures from an Institution* (1954),which adds a new level of irony by in fact being a comment on Mary McCarthy writing her book. Thus is genre born. Both are indeed the sharpest of satires, on the innocence of the new liberalism, and they explore amongst other things the relation between the writer or general intellectual and the intellectual institution which now served as a new artistic milieu in the age of a fading avant garde and an incorporated intelligentsia, the campus itself. Perhaps the book that lies behind them both, and many another campus novel, is Nathaniel Hawthorne's *The Blithedale Romance*, the tale of a visit to a pastoral utopia, Brook Farm, where good Transcendental men and women are summoned to work, think and be good, and crisis ensues. McCarthy and Jarrell both deal with the snake in Eden ("In fact, it must be confessed that, both in this world and the next, the wicked are always a source of considerable embarrassment," reads the epigraph from Rousseau to McCarthy's earlier novel *A Source of Embarrassment*), the gap between idealism and naked self-interest, liberal hope and actual practice. My own *Stepping Westward*, about a British writer on an American campus, was indeed a comment on the matter, a story of one form of liberalism encountering another.

Perhaps all this suggests, as I hope it does, that the university novel was made of a good deal more than selecting a convenient academic setting and then writing a *roman à clef* which would allow alumnae in their later years to lift the book and remember dear old Professor X, and how it was all like that. If my own books dealt, as they did, several times with the university theme, and if by this time I had become an academic myself and hence a university novelist in another sense, it was largely because I saw the university not as an innocent pastoral space but also a battleground of major ideas and ideologies which were shaping our times. It was a space in which people did discuss ideas, theoretical and aesthetic, contemplated literary and cultural theory, and experienced and responded to the large intellectual and social changes that have shaped our late twentieth-century world.

Indeed the change in ideas and ideology was a matter of much concern to me when I came to write *The History Man*, hardly a *roman à clef* or an account of life on any specific university campus, but an imaginary place for testing out the challenges to humanism that became so powerful a part of the intellectual life of the 1960s. Howard Kirk, the radical as opportunist, the reader of history as the urgent now, is desperately trying to keep the embers of apocalypse aflame, one kind of history man. But the novelist is another, trying to imagine and realise the appropriate forms, structures and languages that will bring the world into fiction in a contemporary way. The book, I suppose, reflects a challenge to the idea of the university as much as to the university novel, but its ironies seem clear; and today they would need to be directed at a new conservatism as indifferent to humanistic values as was one segment of the radicalism of the late 1960s. In short, for me the university is the landscape of humanism, a troubled modern territory at the centre of our difficulties, and that is largely why I have kept on writing about it.

It cannot be for much longer, though, for today the university novel is indeed a genre, a species so familiar now as to have grown elaborately self-allusive. The logical next step was clear, and Howard Jacobson is to be congratulated on and celebrated for having taken it. His *Coming from Behind* (1983) is a Polytechnic novel, which is not only the university novel so to speak one step down, or across, but also one step further on. I wish him well in the disputes he will doubtless suffer about whether he has got it right, whether his theme or tone is elitist (of course it is), and whether his saddened landscape of faculty ex-Lawrentians and struggling female students striving to get away from the nappies is an accurate one – whether, in short, the fiction is true. The jacket information dangerously suggests the author has had familiarity with this world and taught in it, and the author's biography implies analogues between him and the book's anti-hero, Sefton Goldberg; but the matter is irrelevant. It is more than and less than the truth, I have no doubt; for it is a fiction, and a very self-aware one. It is, like most of the genre, a comic novel, bitterly intelligent, about a thirty-five-year-old failure who is richly envious of the success of anyone else he knows, or does not. He is Jewish, with a father expert in conjuring who magics a card from F.R. Leavis's ear, and an agoraphobic mother who wishes not only not to be seen but not to be heard. He teaches at Wrottesley Poly, somewhere in the debased and deteriorating Midlands, where the nights sound with barbaric yawps that are not Whitman's. His Jewishness is largely expressed as a passion for indoors and sex, which he contrasts endlessly with the gentile passion for nature and sport. He teaches, with some passion, English Literature, though it is in process of being converted to something called Twentieth Century Studies, and moved over to the premises of the football club, with which the Poly shares a problem of falling attendances. Goldberg has taught at various institutions in what appears to be a descending series, and the nagging desire to succeed, publish, and step upwards again, and to Cambridge, dominates his days.

But literature and culture belong in other hands, mostly despicable; it is not surprising that he rakes through history for people who were failures. The underlying rage is large; badgewearers, homosexuals, post-structuralists, experimental women novelists dressed as parachutists, all appear to offend him, as does the salty goodnaturedness of the Midlands working classes. He is the victim whose essential purpose is survival, and his life is a critical battle with all: the novelist Cora Peck, who is undergoing some complex hormonal battle within, his teaching colleague Nick Lee who manages to send telegrams from Montevideo while succeeding in getting a pile of marked essays onto his desk every day, and the dons of Holy Cross College in Cambridge, where he hopes to become Disraeli Fellow. It is in every way a literary text, a crossover of the British academic novel and the Jewish novel, where characters retire to Bradbury Lodge and there is a constant bellow of Roth. Generic repetition with variation has always, as we academics say, been part of the evolution of the novel, and the species has for some time been evolving in the spirit of sceptical and reflexive self-enquiry. As David Lodge says in his turn, it is a small world, but one that travels into the larger cosmopolis of modern life, and it is certainly not free of its intellectual and cultural contradictions, nor of its pains, its pressures, and its economic anxieties. It is, of course, also and ideally, a world of the mind, and engaged in the lasting enquiries of the mind. But then so, I believe, is a novel. As for myself, I set my own last book not in a university but in an imaginary Eastern European country, where the contradictory images of the two great contrasting ideologies of our age, the two largest and most controlling fictions, might cross. As some critics noted, the imaginary country was not entirely unlike a university – just as a university is not entirely unlike an imaginary country, where some very important and troubling contemporary events, events that could shape and change us all, are even now happening.

BUSY BURGESS

Anthony Burgess is a writer of prodigious range and exhilarating versatility, and a prolific producer not only of novels and critical studies and reviews by the cartload, but also of musical works of, you might say, an ever-extending scale. Somewhere along the line, we may feel, his work greatly changed. His early novels from the 1950s suggested that he might be a performer in the habitual field of social comedy, and his early Malayan novels are, if now reread, delightful but curiously modest objects, held in by the graces and formal constraints, though relaxed by the comedy, of the fiction of the season. In *A Clockwork Orange* (1962) he gave us what is surely his best formal book, a work tightly held in by its mood and tone, though given a special creative energy by its linguistic inventiveness. There was always, perhaps, a hint that Burgess maintained a quarrelsome relation with the British literary scene, with its containments and conventions, its well-regulated forms and languages, its general air of good behaviour, which as Molly Keane has suggested is often the case in which we set our bad behaviour. There was always a prodigious delight in language and languages, in the widening of the human dictionary, and the great and guiding love of Joyce, a Joyce who set a standard not for modernist exactitudes but who was the patron saint of play, punning and pastiche. And there was always the hint that writing possessed for him the quality of a demonic passion, that it poured out like some unremitting source of energy, going here and there, demanding not shape and design but an offered occasion. By the 1960s a kind of release seemed to have come, as if the library of the world had to be recreated again, as if the writerly energy had become unstoppable. And so it has gone on. The bibliography could run to volumes, the variety of forms shows up not just from book to book but inside each book, and in an age of stylistic multiplicity Burgess seems to be that multiplicity, the fund of production grown so complex that he has been known to review himself in an understandable accident. When the record is done, he will probably turn out to be Iris Murdoch as well.

Burgess is one of our most likeable writers, and one who is well entitled by now to claim all the freedoms of pastiche and prolixity he likes to claim. The Enderby books are perhaps a special clue to him, a sequence of tales about a poet-lecher much tormented by sex, death and literary misfortune, where the surrogate role of the author figure seems more nakedly used than usual. These playful literary romps are normally founded on what nowadays is called an intertextual relation with previous literary works, with Burgess parodying his reading not only in other writers but reconstructing and recalling work of his own. Thus *The Clockword Testament, or Enderby's End*, not only allows him to reconsider the critics in print and life who raged at his finest novel, but allowed him to bring Enderby to his end in a death of complicated sexual torment. Typically in Burgess, ends, though they matter much, simply breed new beginnings, text being about life but staying text. In due time there came *Enderby's Dark Lady or No End to Enderby*, which resurrected the hero, took him off to an American campus, had him write the book to a musical of Shakespeare's life, gave him a real dark lady, as well as the chance to do lyrics, and permitted several crucial textual interpretations and interpolations to be introduced, the whole thing being done in a modern ragbaggy way of writing that shows the author as literary clown. And that Burgess is; what is striking is that the literary clown can also deliver, through methods not dissimilar, works of a striking substance.

An interesting case is the later Burgess novel *Earthly Powers* (1980) – big book Burgess at his most expansive and ambitious, and it brings out both the prolixity and the underlying creative force. Not surprisingly it teased the critics, and enraged some of them, being what it is, a cross between an Enderby romp and a novel of managed concern with major issues of morality, evil and violence, the issues that gave their force to *A Clockwork Orange*. It is the narrative of Kenneth M. Toomey, a very famous homosexual, lapsed Catholic English writer of middlebrow persuasion who, at the age of eighty, sets down the events of his sexual, religious and literary life across the spread of our violent, morally horrific and sexually neurotic century. Toomey acknowledges himself as in all things something of a compromiser, and a mildly evasive, sentimental writer whose books would, "from the technical angle, have seemed unremarkable when Arnold Bennett was a boy". But Burgess has devised his role to cross with the lives of many of the major literary figures of the century: Havelock Ellis and Norman Douglas, Ezra Pound and Aldous Huxley, Ernest Hemingway and Rudyard Kipling, James Joyce, Gertrude Stein and Alice B. Toklas all make brief appearances. Often their roles seem curiously statutory (Hemingway shadow-boxes and Pound says "Make it new"), but it is that encompassing grasp, that fullness and often learnedness of reference, that readerly and writerly largeness, that Burgessian grandeur that brings off most of this side of the book. Toomey may be a machine to work a fiction, but he crosses with the best and most revealing literary-historical locations – expatriate Paris and also the exotic Orient in the 1920s, Hollywood and also Hitler's Germany in the 1930s, and the Euro-American literary and media circuits of the 1950s and the 1960s. This is the amusing face of the book, played somewhere between pastiche and parody. It's comic and sometimes overdone, somewhat too ready to suggest that modernism was a fashionable idiocy, the bulk of modern writers pederasts, and literary creation always something hastily fitted in between endless sexual encounters – a truth, in my own experience, only very partially true. But it constructs a writerly history of writing that gives the pastiching freedom of fiction which nowadays Burgess regularly likes to claim, and there is much more than this to the novel, which is laying groundwork for a deeper purpose.

Toomey's personal struggles start in the pederastic Celtic twilight – he is youthfully initiated into homosexuality in a Dublin hotel on what has to be the first Bloomsday, in 1904 – but they develop to cross with the violence and sexual extremism of suicidal Paris, homicidal Nazi Germany, disordered modern America, disordered black Africa. And early on in the book he becomes embroiled with the Italian family Campanati, from Gorgonzola, the seat of the cheese, so to speak. He comes to know the priest of the family, Carlo Campanati, who is evidently *papabili* and indeed at last ascends to the Supreme Office, after various interventions from fate or the Divine Will. Fictional popes may be a well-used literary device from the decadence, which is where Toomey undoubtedly belongs, but Carlo is indeed the triumphant characterisation of this novel – an extraordinary figure of ecumenical leanings, superb digestion, divine fortune at the card-table. It is his belief that man is sinless, and evil exterior to us. He is a great performer of exorcisms, and at one point achieves the miraculous – indeed it is the recording of this that is the proferred occasion for Toomey's narrative. He is a deft negotiator of the modern historical world of pain, violence and holocaust – an adversary of Mussolini, a partisan smuggling Jews out of Italy to freedom. Through his story, and Toomey's own, we are taken through the world of modern evil, from solitary agonies and deaths to the collective genocides of the German concentration camps, and from the perverse gay ghettos of California to the new religious settlements where murderous gurus mount guards at the gates to keep the faithless firmly out and the faithful firmly in. The world of the book reaches from Kipling to Goebbels, Gertrude Stein to Himmler, and the loose autobiographical web that holds it together becomes a strange fable exploring the relation of literature to faith and history.

If later Burgess has an open and sometimes slapdash way of writing, it is because he writes still with a patent fertility of ideas and inventions. And the book, on one level amusing for its international historical record, its ranging scenario of settings and moods, turns into a good deal more. For Burgess is not only a buoyant and comically inventive writer, a great player with texts, but an urgent one. And the subject here reveals its largeness, its concern with the deepest of all paradoxes: the relationship between the local acts of good and evil we perform, and the larger plot of the world, which we call history. Like his own Enderby, or like his Toomey, Burgess is not all gold, and he says so. But he is fecund, pained, intelligent, and morally honest, and we must be very grateful for him.

Earthly Powers, for all its pastiche, is clearly intended as a serious modern novel. In this it compares interestingly with its successor, *The End of the World News* (1982), which is, we are advised, an "entertainment". It takes its punning title from the close-down announcements of the BBC Overseas news service, much listened to by expatriates like Burgess, who lives in Monaco. Or we may hope he does, for the book is presented as the posthumous papers of the author – who was, we are told, stirred to write it by seeing a photograph of President and Mrs Carter in the White House, watching three television channels simultaneously. The same dead author also believed that the three most important events of modern history were Freud's discovery of the subconscious, Trotsky's doctrine of world socialism, and the invention of the space rocket. These are the subjects of his three tales, happily put into some sort of order by a certain scholarly John B. Wilson, who reassures us in another way – for informed rumour tells us that Wilson is none other than the real name of the pseudonymous Anthony Burgess. And in fact the tales all mesh nicely, each being apocalyptic, about the ending of one world or another. In *Earthly Powers*, Burgess offered a tale that manages to be an intercontinental record of modern history, a massive literary memoir, a religious fable about the papacy, and a moral fable of our insufficiency in defining the powers of good and evil. In effect only apocalypse itself was missing; now *The End of the World News* collectively provides it.

Thus the story of Freud tells of the progressive advancement of his theories, his struggles with Viennese anti-semitism, with cancer of the jaw, and with the heresies of supporters like Jung and Otto Rank, reaching its apocalypse with Freud's expulsion from Austria by the Nazis. Burgess tells us all this in the form of a dramatised historical narrative, good on political events, rather weaker on evoking the significance of the subconscious for our modern awareness, and inclined to popular dramatic cliché. The Trotsky tale is about Trotsky's visit to New York in 1917, when he encounters the alluring New World just as revolution breaks out in Russia. Here the form is that of the Broadway musical, with much bouncy lyric-writing that somewhat mutes the sense of historical urgency. The spaceship story is a tale of a planet that comes from elsewhere and collides with our own as the century ends; as the sea-quakes rage and the cities tumble, fifty people go aboard an American spaceship to take a remnant of mankind into space. Now the method is SF, a genre Burgess clearly has a taste for, and does well. Like most SF, it is a parody of other SF, but it opens up to other Burgess territory, the world of the moral fable. *The End of the World News* is a book of pleasurable fertility, a virtuoso enterprise in switching styles and registers and modes of storytelling. The seriousness returns, as the spaceship leaves, and Burgess asks what we should save from the detritus of modern history. The answers are predictable, if one has been reading Burgess for long: a fragment of faith, a passion for gambling, some science and technology, some remnants of art. But above all, if the race is to continue, what it will need is a storyteller or two. It is not hard to believe that what Burgess would indeed take out into space is more, and more, and more stories.

CROSSING THE LINES

One of the more exciting literary events of recent years has been the re-emergence amongst us of William Golding, one of our greatest postwar novelists, and one of those authors to whom we can point as a protector and extender of the novel as a moral form. This, doubtless, was the recognition granted to him when he won the Nobel Prize for Literature, an honour not frequently granted these days to British writers. There was no doubt with his debut in 1954 with the wonderfully powerful *Lord of the Flies*, which turned the stuff of the classic boy's book into a profound moral fable, that Golding was a major modern writer, and through the 1950s and 1960s he sustained his achievement and deepened his methods with a sequence of classic novels – *The Inheritors* (1955), *Pincher Martin* (1956), *The Spire* (1967), and others. As Frank Kermode said in an essay of the time, the view that Golding was the most important practising British novelist was "almost a commonplace". Yet, as he also noted, there was something troubled about the reputation; his books had in them something obdurate – a brooding timelessness, an isolation from intellectual fashion, even a bare simplicity of mind – that made them seem strangely angular to their time. His themes were of religious force, his manner was close to allegory, and his mode of metaphysical romance was not the general way of an age more inclined toward realism. His vision was dark and troubling, a challenge to the liberal or progressive spirit which the age after the holocaust was ready to test, but perhaps not to the salutary degree Golding proposed. *Lord of the Flies* – much the same can be said for most of the other novels – is founded on a sense of civilisation as a moral and religious paradox, and Golding's universe is one where the stuff of the world is laid over primitivism, where only by knowing our primitive roots will we know what to expect or not expect of our "civilised" state.

Golding's books were much studied and much read, though their manner was bleak and their world strange. Today, when the presumption that the novel is eminently a social and realistic genre has somewhat diminished, we might suppose that the feeling of Golding's distance from contemporary fiction has itself begun to fade. But it is not simply that Golding's novels pass beyond the familiar bounds of social and moral interpretation; they go further, to question our very idea of the human being, as, Kermode suggests, he contemplates modern sentient man through the eyes of his predecessor, the Neanderthal. Some of them refer to historical occasions, but the conventional idea of history as a narrative of progress is one they explicitly challenge, often concentrating on moments when the articulation of social functions, or the emergence of man as a language-speaking or ritual-making animal, occur.

The three stories of *The Scorpion God* (1971) thus turn on the encounter between various orders of primitivising society. In the title story, set in an ancient Nile kingdom, the lord who contains the rise of the river and holds up the sky is translated into a motionless Now, entombed. His successors refuse the role custom prescribes for them, sacrificing the coherence of the kingdom to the old lord's fool – The Liar – who tells them theirs is one of many kingdoms in a wide and plural world. Self rises against society, and brings silence. "Clonk Clonk" is about a tribe where identity is partial and protean, about a pre-verbal world called up in the epigraph: "Song before speech/ Verse before prose/Flute before blowpipe/Lyre before bow." If the figures of Golding's world frequently are found struggling into identity, discourse, and form, so are his stories. His work seeks the mythic or theological archetypes behind the historical process, and for this reason he has been interpreted, by some of his best critics, as an exponent of a very modern form of fabulation. But this is not exactly an identification Golding has sought, and he has claimed his work as mythic in rather a different sense. "I do feel fable as being an invented thing out on the surface," he once observed, "whereas myth is something that comes out of the roots of things in the ancient sense of being the key to existence, the whole meaning of life, and experience as a whole." It is certainly that aspect of his work which has given it its air of timelessness, deceptive simplicity, or allegorical clarity. Yet that is not quite all, for the complex nature of language and the paradoxical nature of creative energy have also concerned him greatly. Indeed this is the theme of *The Spire*, a book of troubled paradoxes about creative energy which, in retrospect, is not only one of his best novels but seems to set down one of his essential concerns.

There was, however, a period in which retrospect came to seem the only way we *could* see his work. For after the 1960s a general silence fell, as if the ebullient imagination and rhetorical energy that had driven his first group of books into being had somehow tired for a while. Happily, after a long silence, he brought out in 1979 *Darkness*

Visible, and then in 1980 *Rites of Passage*, which understandably won the Booker Prize for Fiction. This was a novel that proved the old hand had lost none of its cunning, the religious and moral analyst none of his intensity and subtlety, exact, tight, and drawing its strength from a newly measured understatement, a dense style, a careful and inch-by-inch unravelling of the story by a technical master. About the posture of religion in the secular and debased history of the world, the book is set on an old ship of the line, newly converted for general use, and travelling, with a new crew and a mixed group of passengers, across the Equator on the long sea-voyage from Britain to Australia. The time is just after the Napoleonic Wars, when the structure of hierarchy and the confidence of religion are both shaken, and when eighteenth-century attitudes toward rank and order are turning toward nineteenth-century romantic views of liberalism and cultivated feeling. The record is set down by one Edmund Talbot, a socially and morally naive young man of high rank and considerable blindness, though with some modest qualities of charity; he reports on the voyage to his wealthy patron and godfather. His report becomes, as he says, a kind of sea-story, an old kind of tale, but one "with never a tempest, no shipwreck, no sinking, no rescue at sea, no sight or sound of an enemy, no thundering broadsides, heroism, prizes, gallant defences or heroic attacks!"

What happens in the novel is a birth, a copulation, and, above all, a death: a complex intersection of events surrounding the crossing of the line, when Talbot himself boards and discards a mistress, when all those conventional blasphemous romps and feastings of misrule, the triumph of the carnivalesque, occur; and when, as a result of what happens on the vessel, which is commanded by an anti-clerical captain, an innocent weak clergyman, the Reverend Colley, withdraws to his hutch-like cabin, and there withers and dies. His death has something to do with the drunkenness and impropriety, the crossing of many lines other than that of the Equator, but it comes above all because Colley, who has been ignored by the enlightened new passengers and despised by the captain, who has been seeking out the common sailors and been hunting the divine in secular things, is drawn by the sturdy foretop-man, Billy Rogers, into the ultimate indiscretion. There is a direct literary allusion here, and you can take the book as Golding's variant commentary on Melville's famous tale, *Billy Budd, Foretopman*, another narrative fable where life on shipboard turns into microcosm of life and metaphor for a great historical transformation, as the old age of reason gives way to the new age of war and power and industrialism, where innocence and sin are tested in new ways, and the large questions of order and hierarchy, liberty and freedom, are played out in a fabulous world. But where Melville creates a myth of innocence paradoxically salvaged, a hope that is set against the historical fall, Golding insists on the darkness visible in his tale.

What is clear is that the sense of mythic energy is as strong as it ever was in Golding's work, and the structure of the book is one of struggle between religious and secular authority, hierarchy and ignorance, social blindness and the human need to cross the line and break the law. Something in us persistently qualifies virtue, renders it paradoxical, and Colley's confusion of the pastoral and the pederastic is a form of the muddled principle of human energy we found in *The Spire*. It reminds us that Golding is a novelist of the post-Freudian world. Golding divides the story between two narratives, Talbot's and the short record by Colley, and the two tales, double versions of single situations, each man blind to the real nature and motives of the other, are brilliantly set into textual conflict. Here is the hardest crossing of the line of all, the passage from one vision of life to another. But in the end it is Talbot who finds the lesson, loses his innocence, and enters a mystery only a writer as dense as Golding could offer us. Forced to unravel Colley's story, Talbot unravels himself, finding a strange alter ego in the clergyman whose tired death he has indifferently witnessed. Golding's tale of moral ambiguity and human contradiction turns in the end into a literary interlocking, a result of some moment, for it points the way to Golding's next book, *The Paper Men* (1984), an unexpectedly playful novel, and not quite what we have been used to expect from this novelist of psychic torment, damnation, extremity, and rooted myth.

The Paper Men is a short book and a comic one, its theme sounding rather more like one from Beckett or Spark than from the author of *Lord of the Flies*. Its central character and raging narrator is Wilf Barclay, an elderly, drunken, deeply self-engrossed and very famous writer, who has a complex domestic life and a taste for global travel and flight. After a late night encounter over his dustbin, when a suspected badger turns out to be a human predator, he discovers that, as one paper man, he is being pursued by another, Rick L. Tucker, a hairy and opportunistic American assistant professor whose career and future depend on his becoming Barclay's biographer. "Biography first convinces of us the fleeing of the Biographied," Emily Dickinson once remarked, and Rick Tucker is no conventional believer in that Death of the Author Roland Barthes has announced (the author's hand is cut off from any voice, borne by a pure gesture of inscription, and traces a field without origin, or no origin other than language itself, Barthes tells us in his essay), though Barclay, it seems, is. Certainly the persecuting power of the biographer and the elusive flight of the biographied has rarely been written up so terribly in fiction, as Barclay tries to shake off the modern biographer who would fix and write him, seeking to hold onto the sum of his own complex soul. Meanwhile Tucker, like an avengeful alter ego, another paper man, pursues his quarry through the world's hotels, haunting Barclay with camera and tape-recorder, searching through the detritus of his literary life, both human and textual, and even offering him his wife in exchange for the one crucial piece of paper that would confer on him the ultimate status of the "official" biographer.

The terrible Tucker is indeed an alter ego, for Barclay is one of Golding's heroes in torment, a cosmic sufferer whose intolerance is a casing over his deep sense of sin and his profound fear of mortality. But he is also a comic sufferer, who expects his personal nemesis to come in the form of farce, as it does, and at the hands of Tucker himself, the love-hate relationship going to the mortal limit. The fixed life is the tombstone of literature; the very meaning of writing is the elusiveness of the literary personality and the ambiguous sources of creation. Biographer and biographied confront each other, in violence and in changing postures of domination and submission, over the paper object that each of them feels entitled to possess: the "reality" of Rick Barclay's life. "I shall give you a full and free account of my life without concealment and you can write what you like about that," says Barclay, hoping to turn the tables. "But you will also give a clear account of the time you offered me Mary Lou and of the time you offered Halliday Mary Lou and had the offer accepted. In fact the biography will be a duet, Rick. We'll show the world what we are – paper men, you can call us." The duet deepens, and the relationship becomes mysteriously ever more necessary, so that Barclay is compelled to turn the chase around and pursue the recorder who has been seeking him. Barclay is forced onto paper, to tell his own life story, the story we read, the story that comes to a sudden arrest . . . .

The Paper Men is a brilliant *jeu d'esprit*, sometimes slipping here and there into an over-ripe inexactness of prose, the risk that with Golding we have always had to take, and one of the features of his work that has troubled many of his critics. But the theme and its reversals are brilliant, and managed with much wit and wisdom; the old cunning is more cunning than ever. John Fowles's deliberately small book *Mantissa* asserts the right of the writer to display the inner mechanisms of his own creation and the paradoxes that abound in the paper world. *The Paper Men* is a book of the same kind of self-consciousness, a playful thing, an elaborate literary comedy that in an age of anxious biographers and elusive and counterfeiting authors acquires not only a high level of literary self-knowledge but a metaphysical resonance that sustains its suspense through to the end.

UNLIMITED DREAMS

In her fine book on *Fantasy: The Literature of Subversion* (1981), Rosemary Jackson draws together some important ideas about the nature of modern fantasy and the role it has played in the best literature of our time. No longer concerned to reach the otherness of the sacred, it focuses, she says, "upon the unknown within the present, discovering emptiness inside an apparently full reality. Absence itself is foregrounded, placed at the semantic centre of the text." The world, waiting for a revelation that never takes place, becomes filled with a myth of endlessly unsatisfied desire, filled with waiting and impossible expectation. As Cortazar says, "nothing is missing, not even, and especially, nothingness, the true solidifier of the scene." Waste, disorder and the landscape of modern materialism often provide the setting. This kind of novel is international in our modern literature, its most forceful examples frequently being European, American or Latin American. By contrast the British tradition has tended to regard the fantastic as something of an eccentricity or indulgence, though of it there are of course many significant examples.

Rosemary Jackson's book is probably itself a sign of the increased interest in the fantastic, and of its sub-department, the gothic, that has itself had an effect on some of the most interesting British writers. And one of these is J.G. Ballard, whose fiction has played fascinatingly in the space between imaginary invention and well-specified modern reality. His book *Empire of the Sun* was a splendid novel made on factual foundations, the story of a young boy caught in a Japanese prison-camp during the Second World War and witnessing from that place some of the major events of our history: the fall of Shanghai, the dropping of the atomic bomb, the coming of an uncertain peace, the realisation of modern anarchy and his own solitude within it. Like Kurt Vonnegut's *Slaughterhouse–5*, which plays in the space between a personal memoir of horror in the firebombing of Dresden and the displacements and alternative fictions belonging to his own imaginary planet of Tralfamadore, Ballard seems here to go back toward the sources that fed his own science fiction. Today Ballard, who has many titles now behind him, looks more and more like a leading figure in a rich and developing tendency.

Ballard, for his early work, was normally classed as a science fiction writer, a genre that has of course been well-cultivated in Britain but largely regarded as a form of genre-writing for the market. Interesting exceptions have made us more alert to it, and several of our notable writers, like Kingsley Amis, have written fascinatingly inside its generally well-established and playful conventions. Ballard himself hardly looks comfortable in the pocket, again like a good number of his best contemporaries, and like many excellent moderns from Calvino to Pynchon he seems best thought of as a writer of what Rosemary Jackson calls "modern fantasy". He is an author of great inventive powers and a strong explorer of the displacements caused to modern consciousness by the blank ecology of stark architecture, bare high-rises, dead motorways, featureless technology. Like Calvino, he has a remarkable gift for filling the empty, deprived spaces of modern life with the invisible cities and the wonder-worlds of the imagination.

The Unlimited Dream Company (1979) is a fine example of this side of Ballard at his best, a remarkable and indeed visionary piece of imagining which takes us strangely out of the emptied and blanked-out world of the real into fantasy's secondary cosmos, here, as often, a super-abundant universe of dream and desire. It is a flight from the world as it is, and images of flight dominate the book. Blake – a young man who has failed at being a medical student, a Jesuit novice, and a pornographic novelist – grows obsessed with the idea of flying. He manages to take a job at London Airport, steals a light aircraft, and crashes it into the Thames at Shepperton. It is an ideally luminous landscape for Ballard, who lives that way; a landscape webbed by water, locked in by a motorway, heavy with suburban mores, and housing a major film studio. Miraculously and mysteriously, Blake survives his crash, and steps out of the water into a world like a modern surrealist painting, populated by strangely posed figures – a doctor/mistress, a mother/madwoman, a father/priest – who both preside over his rebirth from death and water, and struggle for possession of him. When he tries to leave Shepperton the town holds him in, and the citizens seem already to be expecting him, as a messiah or a magus.

Blake has been through the metamorphosis of fantasy, and finds he has the powers they expect of him. The crashed plane shimmers in the water with a dead man, perhaps himself, in it; and meanwhile for the citizens of Shepperton Blake performs strange wonders, spilling abundance and sexual energy and drawing them from a world of work into one of polymorphous perversity, a world of "unlimited dreams". Blake is evidently no accidental name; he opens the doors of alternative perception and performs the apocalyptic marriages of heaven and hell. Ballard, as if enraged by the material universe, invents a world of exotic abundances for him to perform in, calling in the classic motifs of fantasy, the fracturings and subversions of conventional law that open our universe to dream and potential. Dreaming of birds, animals and fishes, Blake becomes them, a free wanderer through air, earth and water. When he spills semen exotic trees and flowers grow, and wild animals and birds join him. So do the children, the old, the mothers, and all he can incorporate into his own body or project into flight. It is a dreamy pastoral, a fertile contradiction of the world of cement and iron in which he has set other novels.

Like other writers who have explored such terrain – from D.M. Thomas to John Hawkes – Ballard seems to make of the world of fantasy a safe house, a protected space, a lush place of imagining fed by creative joy and innocence. It is one of Ballard's warmest displays, but what it shows is his prolix invention and his great power of myth. The mood is dense, deep and erotic, and for Ballard a strangely affirmative one. For once, what has been called fantasy's "subtle invitation to transgression" works for freedom and the good. Dream is both powerful and dangerous space in fiction, but in much newer writing it has become a field of creative release and new energy. In British fiction, as in D.M. Thomas's work for example, it has opened a sense of the power of the driving unconscious in creativity which has put a new pressure on form, a pressure, of course, that Thomas is poet and maker enough to answer. And so too is Ballard, who also shows himself a very important fantasist for our times, capable of opening up our instinct, never wasted, for realism and scepticism into something more.

THE WHITE MOUNTAIN

D.M. Thomas's *The White Hotel* was one of the great literary successes of 1981, though like so many British novels it made its mark first in the United States and then acquired a later reputation in its country of origin. This perhaps reflects the book's unexpected qualities; its profoundly European sense and its evident Russian influences, its concern with Freud and the unconscious, its extraordinary range of registers and styles, the repertoire of a novelist who is essentially a poet. The book earned much regard, and came close to winning the Booker Prize; it also caused some offence, especially among feminist critics, who distrusted its erotic intensity, its claims to depict female sexuality and especially female sexual fantasy, and above all the violence of its ending, the bayonet rape of the central character at Babi Yar. This won it something of a reputation for sensationalism, much exaggerated, for it is throughout a work of profound critical intelligence and thoughtful construction, and its intensity is guided by a powerful awareness of Freud and Freudianism and an analytical address to the relation between psycho-analysis and the crises of modern history and historicism. It seemed clear that in Thomas we had found a writer of European intensity who had taken themes and found narrative powers unusual in British fiction, whose psychological awareness and historical anxiety went along with technical brilliance, evident in the mixture of prose and poetry, realism and fantasy, eroticism and analysis, that he displayed in an extraordinary and finely constructed book.

The technical virtuosity, the erotic intensity, the troubled consciousness, and the search for a pastoral beyond the world of history have come back again in the sequence of "improvisational" novels that Thomas has been writing since, starting with *Ararat* (1983), and continuing with *Swallow* (1984) and *Phoenix* (1986). The sequence is a self-confessed homage to the great Russian master of prose and poetry, Alexander Pushkin, and a central point of reference is a poetic tale of Pushkin's *Egyptian Nights*, which was left unfinished at his death. It is not hard to see its appeal for Thomas, for it is about a writer and an *improvisatore*; it exploits, as Thomas does, both prose and poetry, and it stops short just before an erotic climax, as, in the *improvisatore*'s inner tale, Cleopatra is about to offer to three lovers a night of love which will be followed by a morning execution they not surprisingly hope to escape. In *Ararat*, Thomas brilliantly completes the inner poem, and he completes in two different forms the outer story. But he enfolds this in a web of new stories, set in the hard and difficult Cold War world we live in now, a world of dissidents and massacres, broken allegiance and old faiths. *Ararat* starts with the narrative of a contemporary Russian poet who finds that a night of love with a blind admirer has not satisfied him, and so he begins to improvise for her a story about three writers who set out to improvise three stories – stories which must mesh, and contain within them the story of Pushkin, and Pushkin's story. His modern writers come from the age of dissidence, *samizdat*, exit visas, and move from Russian provincial life and literary culture to that of New York and, in the later books in the sequence, yet further afield. But the quest of all three in the first of these novels is toward Ararat, the great magic mountain of Armenia, where the pastoral space of the imagination, beyond love and death, eros and thanatos, opens again, just as it did at the end of *The White Hotel*.

Freed to the incidental and the contingent by the improvisatorial method, which permits the new sequence to move toward ever larger complication, as frame-tales become framed inside yet newer frame-tales and images generate new tales and possibilities, Thomas has made the novel into a narrative form that can claim all the freedoms of poetry, using both the formal devices conventional to prose and verse and the play and openness of oral narrative to become, himself, an extraordinary contemporary taleteller. *The White Hotel* was a work of insistent virtuosity, its exotic opening poem showing his power of generative imagery and his free and fertile creativity, and passages like the casebook account of Freud's treatment of Lisa showing his great powers of pastiche. By definition, the new sequence, with its improvisatory principles and its multiplicity of stories, is framed far more loosely and less exactly than was *The White Hotel*, and it is inevitable that it lacks the concentrated focus, the psychological universality, and the profound historical intensity of the earlier book, with its dark implication that Freud's premonitions were not readings of the traumas of the past but those of the historical future.

So the sequence makes a different claim, offering itself as an articulation of the poetic and the creative impulse in all its versatility and freedom, and in all its power to challenge and distil the contemporary historical world. Thomas's earlier erotic vigour is there, perhaps at times to excess. Yet we may fairly read it not simply as a stimulant to the reader but as a firm assertion of the sexual and erotic foundations that underlie narrative and myth, dream and fantasy, and bring the poetic impulse into being. Like his poetry, Thomas's fiction is charged with a sense of the complexity of every act of the imagination, aware of the strange springs of the creative, derived as they are from the half-conscious promptings of the imagination which the arts of improvisation romantically call forth from us to the processes of high formal control, which in his artistic management Thomas also displays. He *is* a romantic, but one who knows the modern way we view language and its delays, deferrals and its *jouissance*. He is also a very contemporary writer, with a deep historical sense and a strong feeling for the pain of modern political and social experience, for the crimes of the conscience of the age. Perhaps only a poet would see the novel as open to such a range of languages, forms and registers, or see it as a form so concerned to enact the spirit of its own creativity. "The mysterious way in which a word, an image, a dream, a story, calls up another, connected yet independent, is one of the main themes of *Swallow*," he explains. The "mysterious ways" allow him to display his skills as a translator, an imitator, a pastiche maker, a writer alert to the habits and forms of writing; they also feed an enormous fluency of creation, a free motion from prose to poetry, from the figures of life to the figures of art. Thomas's is an unusual order of imagination, rare in Britain, Russianised, dense, an imagination that possesses the powers both of pastiche and genuine innovation. His new sequence offers excitements of a different kind from *The White Hotel*, but confirms his creative fluency and force – indeed his status as one of our best contemporary writers.

SINCLAIR'S SPECTRUM

In these dark times of recession and unemployment, nuclear proliferation and nuclear cloud, new fundamentalism and breakfast television, there is much reason for despair and very little for cheer. But for those of us of literary devotion there is much delight to be had from that revival of serious fiction that – tentatively, perhaps, but undoubtedly – has taken place in British fiction over the last ten years or so. Fed perhaps by such strange stimuli as the Booker Prize, influenced by the widening map of the novel that has changed and varied its forms and manners and made it a much more multi-cultural species, the revival has suggested the coming into being of a significant new generation of novelists and short-story writers, some of them by now quite well-established, and others still in the process of shaping and directing their careers. It has also been shaped by changes in book-publishing, book-selling, and book-buying. It is still all early enough to be examined and reflected on with some caution, and there is no doubt that the difficulties of the literary book in Britain remain considerable indeed. In the usual way the new tendencies remain exposed to the pressures of hype and fashion, but beyond that one can see or sense a transformation in the nature of fiction itself. Indeed one could fairly say that not since the early 1950s has the fictional scene in Britain looked so interesting, so inventive, even so internationally significant. After a long period in which the British novel acquired the reputation of being traditionalist, unexperimental, and unaware of major developments taking place elsewhere, we can see a new spirit of engagement with the excitement and variety of this most open and plural of literary forms.

Even so, well into the 1970s a general pessimism persisted. A gloomy survey in the last issue of Ian Hamilton's *The New Review* showed that a sense of the limitations of the British novel prevailed even among novelists themselves. And when, just after this, Bill Buford began his magazine *Granta*, here too the misty mood prevailed. The third issue of this journal was indeed devoted to the theme of "The End of the English Novel", and reported that publishers were defecting from the publication of serious fiction, that most writers were clustering in the safe, middlebrow, middle ground of the novel, while recognition of quality was grudging and scarce. The book trade was reshaping, and clever publishers' editors were devising new types of book-resembling objects which sold for reasons scarcely to do with the interest or rigour of their contents. Declining book purchasing by individuals and institutions encouraged the fear for the literary book, and some publishers seemed to be trimming their fiction lists down to vanishing point. Yet for some reason – a number have been advanced, from the rise of the literary prize to a recession in theatre and television drama, which had long been attracting many of the best British writers – the novel began to display a striking range of new talents. They were not a tendency or a movement, and not even exactly a generation, the spirit spreading from well-established writers to newer ones. But there was a break with the late colonial mood, the celebration of provincialism, the domestic spirit that had been a mark of much British fiction previously – a willingness to move toward fantasy and the grotesque, to question realism, to challenge the conventions of the British novel as many had known and regarded it. The newer writers were as likely to acknowledge the influence of Marquez, Calvino or Kundera as they were the "great tradition", and a fair number of them – like Salman Rushdie, Kazuo Ishiguro, Timothy Mo, or Clive Sinclair – explored multi-ethnic origins. Both the sources and the structural form of the novel became open again to questioning, and the result was a new ebullience and energy that for ten years or more has made British fiction into a matter of international attention.

The examples are several, but Clive Sinclair is one of very great interest, because he has been one of the most curious and playful of our recent younger writers. He made his debut very early, with a striking, very clever first novel called *Bibliosexuality*, which appeared in 1973, and, like so many first novels, gained almost no attention, though the novel had the additional handicap of being almost *too* clever, again like many first novels. The condition to which the title alludes is that of a disorder of the senses in which an unnatural relation with a book is desired and sometimes obtained. And his own book is an elaborate game about bibliophiles and bibliotecs, all greatly concerned with the delights of stories, the erotic magic of fictionality, and the analogy – greatly pursued these days by the structuralists and the deconstructionists – between the pleasures of sex and the pleasures of the text. The notion that there is, in some decadent equation, a parallel between the grammar of narrative and the structure of desire, and vice versa, is not new, but it has certainly engaged us anew in modern literary thinking – and Sinclair, like a number of the young writers, has been alert to a good deal of contemporary critical theory, even footnoting it in his novel. *Bibliosexuality* suggests to us that it is only through indirection laid over direction, only through the extension of anticipation and the deferral of satiety, only through angled moves leading to an oblique outcome, that either sex or text acquire anything like a complete complexity or pleasure. Indeed it is only on the page that sex approaches anything like full potential; art, though useless, is not as useless as life. The book plays therefore with its orders and completions; the author glowers at us off the dustjacket, photographed with a naked girl lying in the background, and with a sullen gleam in his eye. He types away at, of course, a book.

Sinclair's first novel then seemed to come from the dark, seamy Soho of the mind where so much literature comes from – on the edge of the erotic, in a half-world of decadence, where mind and body, text and reader, lock in troubled relations of engagement and displacement. The result was a gothic fantasy in which Poe and Bram Stoker, Borges and Nabokov, had clearly had a hand, and all these dependences and allusions are discussed in the text, and laid out sturdily in the notes and bibliography at the end. Rewriting, parody, or, as we say now, intertextuality are the essential service functions, letting the novel operate in a Nabokovian space between the real and the fictive, the imaginary and the referential, the text and the reader. What goes wrong with the book is that it is a little bit too much of a single extended verbal pun, and the sparring game it plays with Nabokov and other European and American authors that Sinclair had profoundly digested in some ways exposed the twenty-five-year-old author to harsh comparisons. But here was a writer who had penetrated the reflexive issues of modern fiction almost to the point of exhaustion, and there could be little doubt about the excitements of his talent. Unhappily the book came out at a time when the reflexive energies that were shaping fiction in other countries, and which of course have sturdy roots in the British novel tradition, had not acquired much prestige with British readers, who always have to be wooed away from an unregenerate realism, and the novel sank quietly back into its own world of literary transience. Sinclair himself has been uneasy about reissuing the book, though it is a striking declaration for the start of a now vigorously developing career, and it may have led to an unease about the problems of the novel form which has driven him, like a number of other young writers, into a central devotion to the form of the short story.

Certainly during the 1970s Sinclair concentrated on this form, collecting thirteen of them together in *Hearts of Gold* (1979), a striking volume that was as exciting as Ian McEwan's appearance with *First Love, Last Rites*. Like McEwan's, Sinclair's narrators in most of these tales are perverse and in some ways highly literary figures, constructs of writing – the Jewish private eye Joshua Smolinsky owes much to an elegant generic cross-over whereby the American detective story is crossed with the Jewish-American novel, and there are vampires and classic schlemiels, various kinds of sexual fantasists, and indeed a Jewish giraffe. All are seedy exploiters of their own intelligence, experts in the arts of playing victim, and Sinclair confers on each one his own art of manipulating the habits and manners of storytelling. They belong in a world where our heads think, but we vote with our loins, and mind contends with body in an endless dialogue – so the professor of philosophy in the typically titled "Titillatio" struggles, in the act itself, between Spinoza and spermatozoa, Kant and cunt. A pathos of outflanked or exhausted desire haunts everything, and fuctions almost to the point of providing a morality. Though many readers are outraged by Sinclair's willingness to outrage, these are moral stories. But above all they are indeed stories, asserted as such, presented with a high stylistic guile which is part of the pleasure as we engage with image generating the new level of image, metaphor becoming realism becoming metaphor.

Indeed Sinclair is that fairly rare thing in contemporary British fiction – if that is indeed where we can rightly put him – a novelist and storyteller completely immersed in matters of style and discourse, and yet also concerned with major issues, above all with history as our modern pain. If the themes of the earlier book – the fictionality of fictions, the joys of parody, the arts of titillation – are here again, the novelist is more assertively the Jew in the age of Zionism, guilty, corrupt, and hungry for absolution. The stories range in settings from Israel to the United States, where Sinclair spent some time, and from Paris to Transylvania. He also, in the best story, comes to contemporary Czechoslovakia, in a tale about a rogue narrator who, like all good fictionalists, is out to win permanence out of transience, simply by struggling to get himself snapped by the camera of a Western visitor. Thus Sinclair has been one of the few British-Jewish writers to explore – as have Jewish-American novelists like Bernard Malamud and Philip Roth – the ambiguous interface between life and art, between the self-serving lie and the potential for truth, between corruption and confession. The stories, often interlinked, multiply these games to the point of anxiety. The first in the book is "Uncle Vlad", and makes its nod to gothic Transylvania and Vlad the Impaler, but to the other Vlad too, Vlad. Nabokov. It is a meal of fine sensations served from the decadent table, elegantly hung in the space between free fantasy and parody, sensation and pure artifice.

The second, on the other hand, defers in a quite different direction. "Call me Schlemiel," it begins, in a double nod to Melville and Jewish fiction. "You will after you read this." And the story, "The Promised Land", narrates the hero's desire to implant his seed in contemporary Israel by bedding a Jewish girl, only to suffer the schlemiel's persistent fate of being constantly interrupted in his intentions by misfortune or the working of the universe. In the end it is only by an act of violence that Israel will take him, a theme that returns in the dark fantasies of Sinclair's second novel, *Blood Libels* (1985), where the birth of the narrator and of the modern state of Israel mesh, each written into the other.

Indeed it is partly through the process of narrative assimilation, of multiple fictional lineages being placed one over the other, that we get Sinclair's literary tone and also the anxiety that underlies the tone. His stories are remarkably funny, often highly erotic – the narrator of "Among School Children" has the Nabokovian taste for nymphets, those butterflies of sex, and the psychiatrist narrator of "Le Docteur Enchaîné" finds himself a pimp and pandar of the sex he seeks to interpret. Stylistically playful, the stories are at the same time stylistically serious, and an energetic assimilation of several literary traditions as well as of the major paradoxes of literary presentation – if you can imagine a Borgesian Joseph Heller or a Nabokovian Isaac Bashevis Singer, you start to reach into Sinclair's very distinctive tone. The peculiar temper of his imagination – exotic and erotic, ravaged and rabbinical, troubled and guilty, slavering and parodic – seems firmly set in this collection, beginning a good many new themes that in turn feed the next book of stories, *Bedbugs* (1982). Indeed in Sinclair's fiction burial is never forever, and the second collection of stories thus brings back Smolinsky in two more of his famous perverse cases, while the all-Jewish Wingate Football Team not only reappears here but gets a fuller history in *Blood Libels* too.

But Sinclair's intentions in *Bedbugs* are more complication than reprise. In one story here, "Genesis", carefully *not* set as the first tale in the sequence, an angel returns to earth and is held there with lead-weighted Chinese shoes ("Never stray far from the Oriental quarter if you want your shoes to fit"). He impregnates an earth woman of characteristically randy appetites who wants his child, but finds that direct connection is not possible, for it would lead to the woman's being fried to a crisp. Instead the angel, gazing on another woman he can see undressing through a window, discharges the semen from his anti-gravitational penis into an empty artichoke tin. The tin is labelled "Hearts of Gold" – and, so, of course, is Sinclair's previous story collection. The whole fable perfectly suits the metaphorical complex and the parodic energy that creates this whole webbed world of Sinclair's fiction. Indirect connections, constant displacements, metaphorical disjunctions that lead toward the mysterious process of generation and creation, are the strange, Chagall-like energetic stuff of Sinclair's world. The lawless laws of fantasy that have been claimed by Jewish fiction and folktale before have all been summoned here. Identities fade or fail. Time bends and twists. The living are not distinct from the dead, or the angels or dybbuks from the living. Language plays with itself, sometimes to amuse and sometimes to engage the author who must use it for his instrument. "Somewhere Over the Rainbow", a story set in Oz, California, tells us: "this is no comedy of manners; it is a story of masks and of hidden meaning, and of all possible masks language is the greatest."

Sinclair's stories, then, are comedies of creation itself, in all its ambiguities, especially those emerging from that word's own double meaning. In "Tzimtzum" we are reminded of some of the guiding Jewish folklore on the matter. "Tzimtzum" is, or so it is said, "the cabbalistic doctrine which explains creativity as a synthesis of good and evil". And such ambiguities, such odd metaphysical couples, abound in Sinclair's work, as if engaged in competing acts of creation, in turn creating more mysterious bites and rapes, dominations and victimhoods. Sinclair has perhaps a male, sometimes even a consciously slavering, view of eroticism. But marriage, childbirth, womanhood and feminism have now come into the landscape, and the landscape itself has enlarged further, taking its field of fantasy all the way from a Singer-like Polish ghetto to the Nathanael West-like world of southern California, the land of newer fantasies and extremities, "psychedelically baptised" by the spirit of secular Western desire and the candyfloss baroque of Oz and Disneyland. We are taken through some of the rites of passage that lead from the one to the other. The Polish Jewish boy wants his promised land in America, and finds it, debased and abbreviated, in a Californian whore called Erika. In turn, the Westernised, secular Jew wants Florianska Street, the faded old photograph of the old ghetto that is somehow the past and the irrecoverable strange reality behind his corrupted modern imagination.

Sinclair's two books of short stories pull together, while having their own themes and their processes of evolution and development. They make a comic, complex composition, an enlarging web of metaphors founded on the fertile imagery of birth and creation. The world is fantastic, gothic, extreme; rape, violence, pornography become forms both of release and extreme disquiet. In one piece, the private eye Smolinsky is found telling a dark tale of pornography and feminist rage to an interlocutor, none other than Sir Isaiah Berlin, who, confronted with the problem of where to find its ethical meaning, wisely stays silent. Art and ethics maintain throughout an anxious and troubled relationship, but that is the law of "tzimtzum". Jewish guilt constantly drives toward Jewish revenge, and victimisation breeds violence. Sinclair acknowledges the imagination as a mischief, erotically energised, and so opening alike to the creative and the corrupt. Desire, freed, takes on strange forms; the relational guru readily turns into the National Front candidate. Even the place of satisfaction, the bed, breeds bedbugs. It is a difficult world, where the artist has many impersonations to perform, themselves as ambiguous as the creativity of which he hopes to have possession. He is rainbow artist and course tutor, private eye and cuckold, father/progenitor and adulterer, and always there is something seedy about the powers he possesses, a sense of sham in the soul. Creation is thus the stuff of troubled desire; the writer writes and is written on; language is an imperfect instrument, a hungry pen or penis led to strange destinations. In the story "Genesis", we are told that God invented gravity to sustain the myth of the fall, but the penis still seeks to defeat it. These are the themes that, to extreme effect, Sinclair comes back to in *Blood Libels*, which uses the concentrated metaphorical manner of the short story to produce a result far more complex than *Bibliosexuality*, and which returns us to the fearful effects of literature as lie. Sinclair is a novelist who carries with him all the troubles of creation, a writer who bears like some great comic pain both the invigorations and corruptions of a contemporary literary imagination.

RUSHDIE'S EMPIRE

With the publication of Salman Rushdie's *Midnight's Children* in 1981, it was, I think, clear that a rare thing had happened, and that we had quite suddenly seen the emergence of a major new writer. The book received the 1981 Booker Prize for Fiction, and it so fell out that I was chairman of the judges that year – one, it seemed to me, of remarkable fictional publication, with outstanding novels by, among others, Muriel Spark, Doris Lessing, Ian McEwan, George Steiner and D.M. Thomas, whose *The White Hotel* was a close contender for the Prize. It was a year that said much for the strength of current fiction, and the experience of reading the books of the year, and Rushdie's and Thomas's in particular, convinced me that there was now in the English-language novel out of Britain and the Commonwealth a new movement or tendency in fiction, successor to the spirit of social and moral realism that had dominated British fiction for the previous twenty years. Both were books that acknowledged a large history for the novel, one that for Thomas incorporated the achievements of Russian and continental fiction and the intellectual pressure of Freud and Marx, and for Rushdie went back to Sterne and Rabelais but also drew upon the Latin American tradition of magical realism and the novel of Grass and Calvino. Both could be fairly called postmodern novels, returning to the exploration of those major issues of form and history, of humanistic crisis and pressure on consciousness that had created the great works of modernism early in the century. Both possessed a freedom of form, a fertile creativity, that related the spacious world of consciousness and the unconscious to the oppressive conditions of modern politics and totalitarian history. With backward reflection I can see how directly both these works satisfied my sense of what makes for a remarkable novel – aesthetic freedom and originality, an historical relevance and awareness, a deep psychological sympathy, a governing intelligence in the writer, along with that capacity to break out of the straitjacket of genre and conventionalised narrative that has limited so much modern British writing.

This sense of an extraordinary creative fertility, an enormous spanning of styles and languages, registers and forms, suggested that at last the kind of freedom claimed for a modern fiction by the great successors of modernism – Borges and Nabokov, the American postmoderns and the Latin American magical realists – had found their equivalent in "British" fiction. Yet in a sense the term "British" was an irrelevance. Rushdie's book familiarised itself to the British audience by being about India (it was said at the time that *all* books that won the Booker Prize were about India); yet it disputed that imperial and post-imperial tradition into which it seemed to fall, centering its story on the moment of Indian independence and the new imagination that it summoned, and expanding the English language in which it was written with the narrative freedoms afforded by the myths, the folklore, and the storytelling rituals of the Indian narrative tradition. It was a fiction marvellously and perfectly familiar with the modern and postmodern experiment of the novel, a book self-conscious about its *being* a novel, a work of an author exploring the role of author and storyteller with the absolute narrative command of a master. It was a work of modern symbolism, balancing the individual lives and stories of the characters with the largest of historical moments, so that its symbols become profound constructional devices. Like Marquez's fiction, or Grass's, its ebullient creative energy was driven by an intense, outraged view of modern history, from which it sought no aesthetic release or escape.

It turned on an elegant conceit – that on the midnight of Indian independence the children born on the hour were all endowed with special, supernatural powers. Saleem, the book's narrator, is one of these, and he follows the story of the waning and castration of those powers through to the present. The divisions and ruptures of modern historical existence are incorporated into the text itself, opening it to fracture and fragment, to small units of seeing, shards of metaphor, "pickles", as our narrator has it. A basic image is of a female body seen by a doctor through a holed sheet, held up by two attendants to protect the patient's modesty. The body so seen is loved, the lady is married, and duly grows fat and gross. The narrator is the son of this marriage, and in time he himself fragments, splits under pressure, cracks physically into two, along with the text he writes. He is the victim of history, and the direction of history is itself a source of narrative rage, directed in particular toward Mrs Gandhi, who is blamed for the failure of the midnight's children, the fading of the magical powers. Yet the powers, we may say, persist, in the magical imagination that drives forward the book and makes it one of the finest of recent novels.

Rushdie had published one novel before this, *Grimus*, but not one that gave promise of this kind of talent or this scale of literary intention. He was to follow *Midnight's Children* with another book, *Shame* (1983), which clearly confirmed and elaborated his talents. *Midnight's Children* was and was not about India; *Shame* is and is not about Pakistan, that invented and in a sense imaginary country, "a failure of the dreaming mind", planted down onto the map like a writer's plot, though one that then led off in all directions, toward dream but also horror, toward innocence but also toward guilt and crime and punishment and the distortion of fantasy into evil. As in *Midnight's Children*, Rushdie acknowledges that the troubled new history of his sub-continent calls insistently for realism, yet at the same time outrages it. An infinitely loquacious and subtle narrator acknowledges that a realistic novel of Pakistan might be written ("Just think what else I might have to put in"), and he offers us historical details for one, which prove quite as fantastic as the fabulous tale he tells. So modern history puts poets to shame: "Realism can break a writer's heart." And he is no realist ("Like all migrants, I am a fantasist") but is "only telling a sort of modern fairy-tale, so that's all right; nobody need get upset . . .". Thus the fertile, free abundance Rushdie had offered us in *Midnight's Children* is renewed under a variant contract; and the novel is an extraordinary sequence of inventions in oblique order, spun by an inexhaustible storyteller who loves folklore and the chatter of narrative discourse, who has a kitbag of old tales from the *Rubaiyat* to the *Arabian Nights*, the *Kalevala* to *The Trial*, and who freely invents and gladly transforms and decorates. Yet he is also bound to history – able to change its cast, and at times even vary its process, but not, though he would like to, its essential direction and its destructive spirit.

So our narrator introduces us not to another fragmented Saleem but to the fragmentary tale of Omar Khayyam Shakil, born not of one mother but three, the product of one actual pregnancy and two sympathetic ones, and nourished by six lactating breasts. Omar is a fat man outside history, a "sidelined hero" and migrant witness to the terrible story that follows. This should be, we are advised, a love-story – but few love-stories have been told so indirectly, or brought to so grim an outcome. For the object of Omar's desire is Sufiya Zinobia, who proves brain-damaged, and is also the bearer of that most troubled and sometimes violent of human passions, the sense of shame, which releases itself as a beast. And shame and shameless-ness, "the axis upon which we turn", "the roots of violence", are the guiding motifs of this elaborate book, a fairy story about the founding of a new state according to religious and militaristic ideals. It must be said that this abstractified metaphor does not yield up the extraordin-ary metaphorical concentration that gave such grandeur to *Midnight's*

Children, but it certainly sustains the extraordinary mood and the fantastic and urgent tone that has come to seem the mark of Rushdie's work. Again the revealed and the unrevealed, the recession of the erotic into the distorted, the open violence of public life played against the blushing, damaged physiology of the individual self, create a world where emotion is in history, constructs it, and is defeated by it. *Shame* is made out of all the buoyancy of modern storytelling, a storytelling free to use the literary past and the folkloric tradition and merge them into a form of high fictional self-awareness. It is also made out of the bitterness of the modern novelist who knows he lives in a world of political hatreds, riven identities, mad mullahs, raging fanaticisms, of those who rule with a God of some sort at one shoulder and a violent vision of statecraft at the other. Like Marquez and Kundera, with whom he is imaginatively and historically contemporary, in a world of troubled and raging powers that insist on controlling the laws of reality, Rushdie seems to tell us with what measure of fantasy the novel of modern history must be written, if we are to comprehend it, penetrate it, stand free of it, save it.

THE FLOATING WORLD

Kazuo Ishiguro is one of a number of young writers whom we choose to call British but who, writing in Britain and in English, belong to a culture that feels vastly wider than the one we usually think of as ours. The British novel of the 1950s made much of its provincialism, its return to the resources of the immediate and the culturally familiar; it was as if the imperial world that had once fed the British novel was no longer there except for materials of anxious elegy, the elegy that comes through so forcefully and testingly in the novels of Paul Scott or J.G. Farrell, but seems to say that a manner and a scale of writing is itself coming to an end, leaving us short of capacious themes for the present and the future. There is perhaps little wonder that the most exciting of the newer novelists are those who, breaking with the nostalgic mode and the backward glance at the old tradition of British fiction, seem somehow to merge its resources with those from narrative sources and styles drawn from far elsewhere. The excitement of African, Australian and Canadian fiction owes much to this, but it is there too in writers who have settled in Britain, write to the British audience, and indeed interlock with certain aspects of the British tradition.

Kazuo Ishiguro was born in Japan, but has lived in Britain since childhood, and writes in English, now his native language. The subject of his work is the world from which he is displaced, the life of modern Japan in the period since the dropping of the atomic bombs on Hiroshima and Nagasaki and then the Japanese defeat and the American occupation. His first novel, *A Pale View of Hills* (1982), mingled the refined and aesthetic technical manner of Japanese fiction with a dark subject, life in postwar Nagasaki after the city was shattered, along with the old ways of life that had been led there, by the atomic attack. Like much Japanese fiction, the novel appears to resist all the simple conventions of realism while creating the circumstantial laws and powers of historical experience, functioning with an extraordinary reticence. Since the Japanese novel was not entirely bred in the bone for Ishiguro, its recreation, its construction as a potential English language form, is a considered aesthetic endeavour. Anthony Thwaite compared it to Soseki, and yet noted that it seemed somehow less derived than constructed, a wholly successful book in its own right. Ishiguro sees through the eyes of a central woman figure, Etsuko, who is living alone in England but is suddenly forced into reminiscence less about her own life than those of other women she had known in postwar Nagasaki. Her own reticence and self-masking is both a characterisation and a function of Ishiguro's distinctive prose, creating a fictional world where ostensibly real events are filtered into delicate intuitions and function like metaphors.

Ishiguro's brilliant second novel, *An Artist of the Floating World* (1986), is an even finer book in the same mode – a work of extraordinary precision and nuance that makes it clear he is an outstanding talent. It is a portrait of Ono, a famous Japanese painter whose career has developed in the years just before and then during the war. In his early years he had grown from being an apprentice painter into an "artist of the floating world" – the night-time world of pleasure, entertainment and momentary impressions, a fundamental Japanese painterly subject – and then into an artist of the New Japan, taking on social and political issues in the time of revived imperialism and militarism. But as the narrator of the book the story he has to tell is of the postwar world. He gives us a sequence of scenes, ostensibly small and incidental, from the period between 1948 and 1950, and only gradually do we realise that he is a person of enormous political ambiguity. Through the marriage prospects and difficulties of his daughters and his former pupils, who are caught between respect for the patriarch and master and the new era of American domination and democracy, we see the life of a nation in fundamental change. Etsuko had said: "I never thought war could change things so much," and that same change for a people itself divided by a historical pride and sense of the customary and a feeling of the pressure toward a new life links this book to its predecessor.

What sharpens it is Ishiguro's enormous and articulate artistic sense. The novel, again, is a work of fine shadings, a novel of concealments in which the hidden secrecies of a cunningly constructed narrative merge with the practised concealments of a mannered and civil culture. By choosing to present the story as Ono's own narration, Ishiguro sets the narrative in a world of high stylisation and complex aesthetic awareness. The result is a world that is topographically designed and abstractified, so that every instant of the verbal composition feels like a certain kind of Japanese art. Ishiguro hence forces us to read exactly, aesthetically, as few modern British writers do. The story hides behind itself, forcing the reader persistently to unlock it, since the strange distances of politeness, respect, deference and reserve that dominate Japanese social and expressive practice allow little to be said but much to be implied. Ono apparently commands universal respect – the respect of his daughters, relatives, acquaintances, former pupils. His fame is unmistakable and is respected; but it is also deeply tainted. In a culture deferential to teachers and authorities, he cannot be shown as wrong, but he can never be accepted as right. Like some devastating irony, concealment dominates every scene and every relationship, functioning both as courtesy and as hypocrisy.

So, once more, Ishiguro constitutes a world made out of a fundamental historical change and the pressure of an historical necessity, changing and transforming the lives of individuals who seem never directly to acknowledge or assert their awareness of the alteration that is taking place in their lives. And above all it is before Ono himself – the notable figure to whom, out of respect, nothing may be clearly revealed – that history must be represented as the obscure thing it is. His daughters ceaselessly attempt to guide his behaviour and shape his ways, but always by indirection. He in his turn seeks the clues that will let him understand what is being hidden from him, circling around the smallest signals of life to find the right significance and the necessary direction – only to learn that, once he has come to confess his own doubts about what he has achieved, that very confession is a cultural embarrassment.

This is indeed an extraordinary novel, never dramatic and never direct, played by the complex rules of deference and shame, nuance and indirection. It is a cunning reflection itself on the role of art in the political world, and in this sense is deeply aware of itself and its implications. It suggests that art is the story of a floating world, a world of hidden significances, and that to attempt to coerce it is itself a loss of strength and power. Yet it is a story, too, about the urgency of history and the way this laid itself with inordinate power across the lives of the Japanese in the crucial years with which so much of Ishiguro's work deals. It plays, therefore, on the complex interaction of tradition and originality, of form and history, matters on which Ono as artist has reflected much, just as he reflects on the changing landscape and cityscape around him, where the old pleasure districts give way to a new world of concrete, the old floating world turns into a world of new office blocks and new materialism, the Japan of baseball and Americanisation. We can read this as a work of odd mannerism, a stylised piece of Japonaiserie. But it is much more, a novel about the universal postwar crisis to which much of our best fiction has persistently returned, a crisis where old lives change terribly, the old ways fade, and the reflective mind – as Ono's is, and Etsuko's too – struggles with new forms of power and history. In *An Artist of the Floating World* Ishiguro confirms all the promise of his first novel and his few short stories. Indeed this is one of the best and most finely finished novels I have read for some long time.

BOOKERING AND BEING BOOKERED

Over the last years the Booker Prize for Fiction has gradually and with no shortage of controversy established itself as one of the world's major literary prizes, comparable with the French Prix Goncourt, and rather more generously endowed. It has become a key event in the British literary calendar, shaping the publishing year, the willingness of publishers to print serious fiction, and generating its own hopes and disappointments, its gambling and its gossip. Probably few writers in its territory – it is described as for "any full length novel, written in English by a citizen of the British Commonwealth, the Republic of Ireland, Pakistan, Bangladesh and South Africa . . . , a unified and substantial work" – would not regard it as a mark of quality and reputation were they to win it, and most readers over the widest range of reading regard it as the mark of a major book. As a key literary award, it reflects much of the best and some of the difficulties of the British literary scene. It can transform a reputation, establish a major new author, bring exceptional sales and rewards to an increasing degree (Anita Brookner's *Hotel du Lac* went to a 70,000 hardback sale after winning rather controversially in 1984). Fame is fame, whether the choice of the judges has been good or bad, and whether the definition of the novel worthy of winning the prize is that set by notions of the highest literary measurement or the desire to satisfy the public with a good read. Since this prize and other similar ones were established there has been, Martyn Goff has said, "an upsurge in the sales of serious books to a remarkable degree", and an intensified debate about the value and interest of good fiction in Britain. And the British novel has again risen remarkably in regard in the international scene, with newer writers attracting worldwide interest.

But all prizes are surrounded with controversy, and the Booker has not been spared. The Prix Goncourt has often been found too intimate with a few major publishers, the American National Book Award with the business of hype and promotion. The British prizes, the Booker and the Whitbread in particular, have generally sustained a spirit of independence from publishers and the pressures of the book trade, though not from gossip, fashion and commonplace and conventional judgement. "Far too good to be a candidate for the Booker," wrote Anthony Burgess of John Fowles's excellent novel *A Maggot*; in any case, Fowles, like several other leading writers, did not enter the lottery. There are writers who refuse because they distrust the entire process, challenging the view that the novel can be judged by anything so resembling a contest or a horserace, others who prefer to see such honours go to the new and the under-recognised. There is similar uncertainty among those who are asked to judge such prizes, and an inevitable difficulty in acquiring judges of the highest standard when the physical task of judgement – over a hundred books to be read over a summer – is so daunting. The historical record of the prize is interesting if uneven; many minor books have won, sometimes because of a dull publishing year, but often there have been outstanding choices. Some of our finest well-known writers – Iris Murdoch and William Golding – have won; others – Muriel Spark, Doris Lessing, Anthony Burgess – never have. Major books that might have missed full notice – J.G. Farrell's *The Siege of Krishnapur*, Paul Scott's *Staying On*, John Berger's *G.* – have been brought firmly before us by the prize; other prizes like the Whitbread have a more notable record of success with important young writers, like Angela Carter, Graham Swift and Peter Ackroyd.

Somewhere between a public outrage and a chance for the fate and future of the novel to be seriously debated, the Booker has both strengthened the claim of serious fiction in Britain and subjected it to harder and harsher market forces. In 1981 I was chairman of the judges, and I can only report my experience as gratifying and reassuring. It was a year of strong publication in the novel, and a sturdy and demanding panel of judges determined to maintain the aim of the prize as it was expressed to us by its management committee, that it be for a novel that would still be read in twenty years' time. The reading, though massive, was carefully done, and the judging sessions were like a good seminar in contemporary fiction. Two years later, I was a shortlisted author myself. For judge or judged, the drama ends uncomfortably, if effectively, in public, under television lights and the gaze of the cameras. The result of the final deliberations, held immediately before, is given; the winner is announced and the losers who are also in a sense winners (to be shortlisted also greatly assists literary sales) hide their disappointment. There are also, happily, many judges of judges, many apprisers of the prizes; the sales of the winner soar, the debate on the decision begins, and the question of how well the British or the English-language novel is doing rages again. And since my own speech on the night chose to deal with some of the issues surrounding the prize, as well as the state of fiction as we entered the 1980s, it seems worth reprinting it in abbreviated form here.

The story is told of the Russian party member who was advised that Stalin had died, and was asked if he was going to the funeral. "No, it is not necessary, I believe you," he said. Rumours of mortality, as Mark Twain suggested, do need checking carefully, and this is certainly true in the field of the novel. The Death of the Novel has been alive through all my lifetime, and goes back to the era of modernism. This compounds a mystery, since everywhere one goes there are people writing novels, the coffee tables groan with them, while the shelves of the bookstores seem short of nothing fictional except works of my own. The season has been lively, and you do not look as if you are here to attend a funeral – rather, perhaps, an annual report on the condition of a patient who for most of this century has been said not to be feeling well. For suspicion that something has gone from the novel, that historical surgery has removed some vital organ, is commonplace. There is gloom about fiction, in the market place and the academy, where the notion that the state of the novel is not up to the state of the world is widespread. We are often told that we do not live in one of the great ages of fiction – not in a great age of public realism, like the era of Dickens or Balzac, nor yet in a great age of experimental fictional innovation, like that of Joyce and Proust, but in a silver age. So should we not, looking around at that obscure, massive entity the Present State of Fiction, feel a little despair?

There are good reasons to do so. The publishing economics of fiction are in many ways disheartening; the best-seller syndrome distorts and narrows the market; our writers, when consulted, profess to be disappointed, harrowed and worn. Yet internationally this is a major age of fiction, the age of Grass and Handke, Beckett and Borges, Calvino and Marquez, Bellow and Roth and Pynchon, and it will, I think, be looked on as one of excitement, advance and innovation. It is true these writers question the habits of the traditional novel, and sometimes propose the total exhaustion of story. Some indeed profess what seems like a kind of despair, a fear for the novel, challenging its realism, its humanism, its optimism and its power to create a major myth or narrative. But to do this they write novels, or something closely resembling them. Indeed they do what major novelists have always done, which is to challenge, re-examine and extend their form in the light of the experience and the dominant ideas, the ideologies and the anxieties, of their own times, hoping to extend the distinctive knowledge that may be carried by the novel itself. There is an international energy in the novel, and this applies even in the English novel, or rather the wider map we are concerned with, the novel of Britain, Eire, the Commonwealth. The postwar British novel has not always had the best of presses, and critical attention has tended to move away from it and toward fiction elsewhere, on the assumption that it is there the real energy lies. There is a widespread rumour that the novel is alive and well but living in New York. Meanwhile British fiction seems to chatter on in a familiar way, Hampstead talking to Hampstead, Islington and Camden Town. This is a common view, which, as an English novelist, I naturally deplore; but it is real. A recent issue of *Granta* surveyed the scene and made the often justifiable complaints – lack of serious aesthetic debate surrounding the form, conservatism among publishers, superficiality and brevity in reviewing, the failure of British readers to respond to the new.

Yet a time when the novel can display talents like those of Angus Wilson, William Golding, Iris Murdoch, Muriel Spark, Anthony Burgess, Doris Lessing and John Fowles seems a notable time. Moreover I think for some years now there has been every sign that the narrowing realism that tempted British fiction into provincialism and conventionality has been for a long time lifting. What then of the newer generation, whose work forms a large part of that submitted for the prize? I have spent this summer in the unusual task of reading, re-reading and often re-re-reading some eighty novels of this year, books offered for or called for the prize – more books than anyone not on a desert island has ever read, re-read and then re-re-read, it has come to seem. Then I have discussed, re-discussed and re-rediscussed them with my fellow judges, Hermione Lee, Joan Bakewell, Brian Aldiss and Samuel Hynes. What did we find? First, quite a number of well-written bad books, works elegantly done in stock conventions and genres, graceful but modest. Then many fine books from well-established writers which were enjoyed by all but did not create an exceptional excitement. And then some twenty-five or so which did much more, showing great invention and range, and leaving an impression of strong energies driving the best of current British fiction. Possibly ours has been a lucky year, but the fruit has been heavy on the bough. Over the last ten years or so we have seen the emergence of a number of important new writers who have shifted the novel sharply away from older conventions, towards largeness, moral strangeness, fantasy and grotesquerie. The experimental sense has sharpened, and the year has seen some remarkable self-questioning novels like Maggie Gee's *Dying, In Other Words* and Gabriel Josipovici's *The Air We Breathe*, both from an important small press, Harvester; Alistair Gray's *Lanark*, from

Canongate; Graham Swift's *Shuttlecock*, Martin Amis's *Other People*, Peter Carey's *Bliss*, and William Boyd's *A Good Man in Africa*. There was major work in fantasy and science-fiction – Christopher Priest's psycho-fantasy *The Affirmation*, J.G. Ballard's *Hello America* and Michael Moorcock's remarkably researched *Byzantium Endures*. There was Nicholas Mosley's *Serpent*, part of an experimental sequence, and George Steiner's extraordinary, disturbing, uncategorisable short novel *The Portage to San Cristobal of A.H.*. There were other books, closer to realism, that struck us as of great power: Nadine Gordimer's *July's People*, Brian Moore's *The Temptation of Eileen Hughes*, and then Verity Bargate's *Tit for Tat*, A.N. Wilson's *Who Killed Oswald Fish?*, and John Banville's historical novel *Kepler*.

Such books made us feel we were striving for judgement in an exceptional year, and we finally came down to a list of seven, all I believe novels of very high merit and originality, some from our leading writers, some from much newer names. Muriel Spark is one of our greatest novelists of fiction's deviousness; and the deviousness of fiction, the cunning ways the writer loiters in life with suspicious intent, generates the tight wicked economy of *Loitering With Intent*. Doris Lessing's *The Golden Notebook* is one of the finest of contemporary enquiries into the novel; she has now entered on an experiment in science fiction or science fantasy of enormous courage and great analytical distance, and *The Sirian Experiments*, the third in the sequence, is a crucial hinge of it. Ian McEwan is a writer of the modern grotesque, and *The Comfort of Strangers* is an exactingly written exploration, both formally neat and terrifyingly imagined, of the mirrorings, transfigurations and violations of our modern sexual roles and identities. Two more books used established conventions in order to question and transform them. Molly Keane's *Good Behaviour* speaks of convention in its title, and then, with remarkable ironic mastery, topples its own polite world and shows how conventional politeness overlays the most appalling behaviour. Molly Keane is an older writer who has reverted to her original name to write in a new way; Ann Schlee *is* a new writer, at least in adult fiction. *Rhine Journey* is set in the mould of the novel of Victorian pastiche, exploiting the sentimental tour story of the mid-nineteenth century to intrude onto it the emotional and political crises of the world just after the revolutionary season of 1848.

But two novels in particular break through the frontiers of fiction in quite exceptional ways, generating the same excitement as did reading *The French Lieutenant's Woman* in the 1960s. The revolution brought about by Freud in our acknowledgement of the world of the unconscious and of the fantastic is amazingly exploited by D.M. Thomas in *The White Hotel*, a work of extraordinary formal complexity, told in a range of languages – those of reportage and those of poetry, those of historical realism and those of psychological fantasy. It marvellously fractures the familiar world in order to reach the universe of the subconscious, the strange language of desire and hysteria, the world of love and death. But the book returns its fantasy back into a history that itself seems a condition of modern collective fantasy, in all its power and horror, and the book reaches a bleak conclusion at Babi Yar. Some critics have too easily read it as a simple erotic fantasy; it seems to me a critically intelligent book with an extraordinary complex form.

The other book which competed with Thomas's in the final discussions was Salman Rushdie's *Midnight's Children*, a work of experimental fertility, absolute comic joy and dark political rage, and another novel where the historical world commands human lives yet can only be grasped through the metaphorical and fantastic imagination. This makes it a work of imaginative fertility in a modern mode of symbolism as well as political courage, a tale of the largest intentions, dealing with the emergence into independence of India and Pakistan and the magical powers this historical change hoped to summon. Behind it is a fictional lineage – of *Tristram Shandy*, *The Tin Drum*, *One Hundred Years of Solitude* and perhaps Thomas Pynchon's *V.*. But its fertility is its own, and gives it the looseness, prolixity and free storytelling of massive invention, along with a metaphorical and symbolic code that does not use formal arts to escape the historical world, but to explore it in the largest way.

The sense that this was an exceptionally good crop might heighten the sense of injustice this year, but it reinforces one's belief in the present strength of serious fiction. The Booker Prize is, as we understand it, intended to display a contemporary classic that will still be read and valued in twenty years' time, if we survive, and if the idea of the classic does. In all such prizes commerce cannot be absent, money might at times be mentioned, judges will prove fallible, compromises will occur, and judgements will prove contentious. But this is a prize for serious fiction, a term difficult enough to cope with. As for what it means, I can only express my own view, as a critic, solemn in criticism's cause, as well as a writer, deeply committed to an idea or ideal of the novel form. The sources and uses of writing are many, from commerce to entertainment, fashionable exploration and excitement to enduring experience. The novel is a capacious yet often very conventional form, and it is all too easy to become an able contributor to an elegant convention, an artificer of repetitions. The serious novel is not always obviously jagged and experimental, though often it is, but it is certainly the work of a writer who is pressing at the edge of the genre, taking it as a form of enquiry, into the grammars and orders, the means and structures, by which we build up sufficient fictions of the world. The novel is a major mode of enquiry, as serious as science, as thoughtful as philosophy, but always conscious of its fictionality.

Serious fiction in this sense of a discovering form does not always do well in Britain these days, though there have been great seasons of it in the past. I hope the Booker, as our leading fiction prize, will affirm the novel in this way, and the critical standards used to judge the prizewinner be those of a seriousness commensurate with the seriousness of the novel-form itself. I believe that is the spirit in which we have chosen this year's winner, Salman Rushdie's *Midnight's Children*, a work of great aesthetic and political importance, a powerfully original novel, and one that reinforces the feeling of hope for the present and future of the English-language novel which this year's reading has brought home to us.